*incog*negro

a memoir

incog
negro

of exile & apartheid

Frank B. Wilderson, III

South End Press | Cambridge, MA | Read. Write. Revolt.

Published by South End Press
7 Brookline Street, Suite 1, Cambridge, Massachusetts 02139
www.southendpress.org

page design and production by Jocelyn Burrell/South End Press collective
cover photo provided courtesy of author

Library of Congress Cataloging-in-Publication Data
Wilderson, Frank B.
Incognegro : a memoir of exile and apartheid / Frank B. Wilderson, III.—1st ed.
    p. cm.
ISBN 978-0-89608-783-5
1. Wilderson, Frank B. 2. African Americans—Biography. 3. United States—Social
conditions—1960–1980. 4. United States—Social conditions—1980– 5. African
Americans—Race identity. 6. Civil rights—United States—History—20th century.
7. African Americans—South Africa—Biography. 8. African National Congress—
Biography. 9. South Africa—Social conditions—1961– 10. Anti-apartheid movements—
South Africa—History. I. Title.
E185.97.W6128A3 2008
305.896'073—dc22
                                    2008019051

Printed by union labor on acid-free, recycled paper in Canada.

13 12 11 10 09 08   1 2 3 4 5

for

Rebaabetswe Wilderson
Nehanda Abiodun
Jalil Muntaqim

and in loving memory of

Merle Africa
Safiya Bukhari-Alston
Bushy Kelebonye

It seemed to me that Christopher's options and possibilities could change only when the actual framework changed: and the metamorphosis of the framework into which we had been born would almost certainly be so violent as to blow Christopher, and me, and all of us, away.

—JAMES BALDWIN
Tell Me How Long the Train's Been Gone

one

ABROAD

nothing of my mother's voice
in the clicks of these women sotho or zulu
now smug and thankful for wounds
sutured by the sea
i answer the rasping of a coloured widow
who enters
behind her asthma and
buys my bread with stories of the sea
and its hunger

1

"Mr. Wilderson?" It is impossible to place the accent amid the newsroom clatter behind his voice. Not Afrikaans, but not completely English. At least not the pristine English one hears in the suburbs of Sandton, Parktown, or Rosebank. Those dulcet shopping mall voices made all the more tranquil by the resonance of Muzak, the purr of Mercedes, and the stabilizing presence of the army in the townships just over the hill. Still, I am put off by his voice and by the questioning tone with which he has answered the telephone. I am, after all, returning his call. A pause. "Mr. Frank Wilderson?"

"Yes," I say, anxiously, but not irritably. "I'm returning your call."

"Of course, thank you so much." He pauses again. "My name is Stefaans Brümmer. But then you know that. I'm an investigative reporter for the *Mail & Guardian.* You probably know that too."

I try to calm my breathing. "I've seen your by-line."

I am suddenly aware of Khanya sitting in the next room, no more than twenty feet away. She is watching me—or trying not to watch me—from the parlor that combines with the dining room. We have been married exactly five years. For all I know today could be our anniversary. Maybe this is why she called this morning, suggesting we end our separation. Perhaps she thinks that I, for once, remembered the date and that is why

I suggested we dine at the Carlton Hotel. But if we were married five years ago today, why didn't she say something at dinner? She's testing me. That's the only explanation. I have a sinking feeling that if it is our anniversary and if she does believe I remembered, then this call from this man will not only cause me to fail the test but it will confirm the truth of her most biting criticism. "You love anarchy," she had said when we separated, "more than you'll ever love me."

The scent of heat on damp wool wafts from the parlor as her fleece, draped on the chair beside her, dries in front of the gas fire. I hear the Orrs' polite conversation trying to draw her attention away from me. Their failure is clear, a fertile void where Khanya's voice should be. I do not look at her.

We are still wet from having queued in the rain for a kombi on Bree Street. Earlier this evening, or perhaps the day before as it has rained all week, lightning hobbled one of the pillars of our would-be taxi shelter; a shelter that would have otherwise kept the heads, though perhaps not the shoulders, of six or seven adults dry. We will all have to stoop beneath its sagging roof if we want to stay dry, I thought, as Khanya and I dashed through the taxi rank. Instead, through the silent consent of African *ubuntu*, the adults relinquished the crippled shelter to several children who shared it with an old woman.

From lampposts some of us tore down cardboard posters that read The '94 Elections Brought Democracy to the Nation, The '95 Elections Will Bring Democracy to Your Community. Others tore down posters of Nelson Mandela with his eyes commanding us to VOTE ANC! We held them above our heads for respite from the lashing rain. But the soggy cardboard umbrellas upon which Mandela's face was painted soon surrendered and water ran mercilessly down our arms and legs.

I had tried to keep my spirits high by marveling at the play of lamp light on Khanya's high cheekbones and dimples, at how happy she was that we were reunited, and wondering, shamefully, how anyone could be happy to be reunited with me. It wasn't long before my thoughts wandered to our dissolving metaphor of protection—the new state president-cum-umbrella—and I found myself rehashing questions that seemed to be erupting across the country whenever and wherever Black people gathered to contemplate the future: Will the ANC improve the economic position of the poor or simply enlarge the middle class? Does Mandela's consolidation of power in the wake of Chris Hani's death portend personal rule from the top? Will we become a one-party state, like the US where the one party is capital?

But as alarming as these questions are, I know (as I hold my breath and wait for Stefaans Brümmer to link me to what only Stimela Mosando and his people should know about) that such questions are not the elemental source of the pit in my stomach. Which is not to say they are false or a ruse of concerns hiding a true anxiety. They are neither false nor a ruse. I do dread the New World Order. The "New" South Africa. The flag-and-anthem cardboard cutout of a country that we are fast becoming. But what I fear even more is the recurrence of an image I thought I had left in that country which, for lack of a more ambiguous word, I once called "home": my black face in the mirror.

—ɯ—

My voice drops when I say "by-line," in an effort—I can only surmise—to draw less attention to myself. It has, of course, the opposite effect. Mr. and Mrs. Orr and Khanya lock in on me like radar. The more they try to go on with their conversation and pay me no mind, the more attention they pay.

"Is this a good time to talk?" Brümmer asks. Before I can answer he says, "Look I'm working under a deadline. The paper goes to bed tonight and I'd really like your side of the story."

"How did you get this number?"

"I did some research and found that you had had an ANC attorney for the Vista—" He stops short of calling my dismissal from Vista University in Soweto an "affair." He wants to be tactful. He wants to get a story. "Someone at Shell House…" Shell House was a tall office building in downtown Jo'burg that the oil company with the same moniker had given to the ANC in the hopes, we were all assured, of getting nothing in return. "Someone at Shell House told me Christopher Orr was your attorney. I called him and found that he was your landlord too. Look, I'm sorry about your dismissal. The new South Africa seems slow in coming."

"Yes," I agree, "slow in coming," acutely aware that he and I might agree only on the pace and not the destination, for he is certainly no communist. I have been standing the whole time. Now, I sit down on the small awkward chair the Orrs keep beside the wrist-and-elbow sized table upon which the telephone rests. "Is this about the university?" I ask, my eyes darting over to the parlor. Khanya and the Orrs have brought their conversation to a halt. They are looking at me looking at them.

"I'm afraid not." His voice betrays a tone that I have come to fear and dislike during the last five years of my life in Johannesburg. It is a tone of apology laced with accusation. A tone that White English-speaking South Africans are noted for. Unlike the Boers, they do not possess the iron-willed conviction that god has ordained them to rule South Africa, but nor are they willing to subordinate themselves to the ethical, much less political, authority of Black people. The Boer bloodhound has been good to them. His bark and bite have protected them from the uneven and unmanageable proliferation of Black rage, for they were disinclined to bark and bite themselves. No, the intonation of English voices is more difficult to assess. One must listen more carefully (What does this White man want of me? or What does he plan to do to me?), for their voices walk a line between subdued irritation and hazy patronization—and don't telegraph their intent.

I brace myself.

"One moment," he says, and slowly the din and bustle of the newsroom falls into emptiness behind his closing door.

I rack my brain across five years of political activity, some aboveground, some underground, some legal, some not, most in a hazy zone that will always elude clarity. What could be more damning than the storm around my dismissal at Vista and my solidarity with the South African Student Congress when we took the campus by force and held it for nearly a year?

The kombis for Black people don't take you door to door like the metered taxicabs that were, until two years ago, reserved for White people. But nor are they nearly as expensive. So, Khanya and I had been dropped off several blocks from the Orrs' house. Mr. and Mrs. Orr, an English-speaking couple with affinities to the Freedom Charter but whose politics beyond that I did not know and did not ask, had spotted us as we hurried down their driveway to the carriage house in back which I now rented from them. Mrs. Orr dashed out of the house holding the *Mail & Guardian* over her head as an umbrella. In her hand she held a message. She said Khanya could dry off by the gas fire in the parlor while I used the telephone in the next room. On the back of an old shopping list she had written all that she'd been told: Stefaans Brümmer, *Mail & Guardian*, then the number, and *Please call, urgent.* The word *urgent* had been scratched out and the word *important* written there instead. No doubt, Brümmer did not want Mrs. Orr to alarm me and risk my not returning his call; or worse, prompt me to skip the country.

"No," Stefaans Brümmer repeats when he has closed the door and secured his privacy, "it's not the student/worker occupation of Vista University. Well, in a way it is and in a way it isn't."

"Then what," I hiss. I don't know what embarrasses me more about my sudden outburst, the fact that it was made to an otherwise sympathetic reporter who is only doing his job (and unlike our treatment in the mainstream press, his reporting on the Vista takeover did in fact cast us more as communards than as a blight upon civic stability), or the fact that Khanya and the Orrs overheard it and took note.

"It's about what the National Intelligence Agency is calling..." Another pause. "Your 'subversive activities.'" This is it, I think. But I don't say a word. The first one to speak, someone wise and now forgotten once told me, loses. But what has Stefaans Brümmer got to lose? Somebody tell me that. "Joe Nhlanhla," he continues, "the new NIA chief, thinks you're a threat to national security." He waits for a response. I am looking at my wife. She is looking at me. What can I say to make her turn away? Then he drops the other shoe. "So does Nelson Mandela." And he lets this sink in before adding, gratuitously, "The new state president."

I can hear myself breathing. I am sure I can be heard breathing for a hundred miles. "Would you care to comment?" I almost laugh out loud at the irony of his canned question but there is a word blocking any such outburst: prison. I try to remember where I keep my passport. Is it in the carriage house out back or is it among the things at our house—at Khanya's house—on the other side of town? I wonder if I have enough money to make it to the border of Swaziland and whether or not they will let me cross.

"Mr. Wilderson, I said Nelson Mandela thinks you're a—"

"Yes...I heard you."

—◊—

Sometimes, as I close my eyes to look at the sun or simply at the bulb in the lamp of my study, I see roses exploding one after another on my eyelids' inner canvas. But if I hold them closed too long, the roses melt with the bursts that bore them and I see flowers of a different kind, that bed of shy carnations and pungent chrysanthemums upon which professor Mureinik died. I see where his crumpled body has been removed. All that remains, besides the spectacles flung into the flowers on impact, are indentations of soil as though a two-toed ungulate tantrumed about in one place. I see empty bottles of prescription pills in Etienne Mureinik's suite on the 23rd floor and the "important documents" soon after impounded by the authorities. From this rich and subtle world the professor prepares to descend. Now rising, now airborne, now falling...a life opens...it opens...it is breaking...

I once asked Stimela Mosando point blank if I—if we—had killed professor Etienne Mureinik. Stimela was a thin Motswana man of medium height and sparkling eyes. His lean physique made it hard for me to think of him as a man who'd been trained in hand-to-hand combat in Libya, and who had used that training to take down Red Beard, a strapping Afrikaner from Special Branch, in thirty seconds flat. He looked more like a swimmer than a guerilla, much less an Umkhonto we Sizwe commander. And because he did not wear horn-rimmed spectacles like his younger cousin Jabu, or sit for hours pensively contemplating indecipherable mathematical equations (my jaundiced image of an engineer), I often forgot that he had also been trained in some obscure discipline that combined telecommunications with electrical engineering when MK sent him to the Soviet Union. He looked like an ordinary guy from the township. In response to my question he threw his head back and laughed in a way that soft-spoken Motswana men were not, supposedly, known for.

I'd been told that such raucous outbursts were what one could and should expect from Zulus but not from Motswanas. When Khanya and I were still engaged—it was either two days after Christmas in 1989, or two days after New Year's in 1990, though the holiday now fails memory—we drove from Pretoria to Botswana on a whim. I recall clearly that it was during the time when I still had a pocketful of US dollars (dollars that, in those last years of apartheid, I often tried to buy our way out of our black skins by buying our way into restaurants or lodgings beneath signs that read Not Multiracial or Right of Refusal Reserved). She wanted to show me how her people, the Motswana, lived when they were not under the boot of apartheid. I had been reluctant to go, for no good reason, or none that I can recall. But her older sister, who was under house arrest at the time for having traveled to Zimbabwe to see her boyfriend, a militant in the Pan Africanist Congress, and thus could go nowhere, said, "Go, go, you must go to Botswana. When you cross the border you will smell the freedom!"

At the customs house, a small, hot pavilion in the middle of a desert road, two Botswanan guards had just shared a joke at which one of them was still laughing with the sprawling abandon of Stimela's laugh when I asked him if we had killed Mureinik. A woman who was old enough to be Khanya's mother but only old enough to be my older sister had the misfortune of having to stand at the counter and wait for the two customs officers to finish savoring their private joke, to wait for the one who could not stop laughing to dry his eyes and peruse her documents. When she turned from the window her face registered every emotion from exasperation to disgust. She spoke under her breath in Setswana to Khanya who, because she was facing the customs officers and had yet to have her documents approved, remained as placid and as non-responsive as possible. When we were cleared and had stepped over the line into Botswana, when we could finally smell the freedom, I asked Khanya to translate what the woman had said. "She said: 'The way they laugh you'd think they were Zulus. I can't believe I'm coming home.'" The woman would have been equally dismayed had she heard Stimela's laugh: not like a soft gust of wind and sand on a gentle desert night, the quiet, unassuming laugh, no doubt, of the man whom she had probably married and raised a family with, but a laugh like a Zulu.

"You're greedy," Stimela said. "A greedy capitalist. You want a little something for yourself; something that you can take back to America. But I'll tell you this," he added, "Etienne Mureinik killed Chris Hani."

The only thing that startled me more than Stimela's accusation that professor Mureinik murdered Chris Hani was my transparency, my neediness. It embarrassed me, for I did want something for myself, something to authenticate my involvement with him, and with his cousin Jabu, my ex-student Trevor, with Precious, and with Oupa (yes, even with Oupa). Something tangible, a representation from what Precious had called the three theaters: propaganda, psychological warfare, and operations: the shrunken head of a White man to hang from my belt. A little something for myself. Precious had demarcated and named three theaters not because they could be marked, named, and separated but because she knew that that was what I needed. They were all like that; even Jabu who gave me what I needed not by fabricating an answer but by asking me another question, thereby soothing my anxiety with the sound of my own voice. Their answers to my questions were cushions of stability, what I needed to go on fighting, that would be pulled from under me just when I'd settled on a clear, coherent, and respectable narrative of who we were and what we were about.

I recall a meeting where Trevor Garden, the lone White person in Stimela's network (or the only one I knew, for I never knew the true extent of Stimela's network), argued passionately with a former treason trial defendant, an MK commander who, after several years on death row, had narrowly escaped the gallows through some sort of last minute stay of execution or deal that was brokered between highly placed notables. "We're freedom fighters," the middle-aged Xhosa man insisted, pounding the table with his fist, "and the world should think of us not as terrorists but as freedom fighters." "No," said Trevor, "we're terrorists. It's not a term I'm ashamed of, for the simple reason that I don't give a damn what the world thinks. I don't even care what my parents think or don't think—they're White. That's what we mean when we say 'the world.' To the world I'm a terrorist—an albino terrorist, as Frank likes to call me," he smiled and cocked his head at me, "but to Soweto we're something else, and that's what matters."

Just seven months after Chris Hani's assassination, in December 1993, Nelson Mandela (or Madiba as he was known affectionately) gave the order for Umkhonto we Sizwe (MK) to be disbanded. It was an order only two people could have given without being crucified. One was Madiba. The other was Jesus Christ. It shocked and demoralized Black South Africa. It shocked and demoralized Soweto, the township that was the heart and soul of the struggle, where twelve-year-old Hector Pieterson, the most famous among the casualties of the Children's Revolution of 1976, was killed—Soweto, the hub of the underground railroad through which thousands of youth had left South Africa and joined the ANC in exile. But for some reason, on the day it happened people in Soweto disavowed their feelings, and the day became one of rejoicing.

F. W. de Klerk had not as yet handed over the government and English capital was still as entrenched as ever. Chris Hani would have battled Madiba at the assembly of the National Executive Committee of the ANC, an assembly to which Hani had been elected with a 100 percent vote count of 2,000 delegates to Madiba's 1,995 votes, or 99.75 percent; which is to say that in all likelihood the room would have been split and Nelson Mandela's order would not have carried—leaving MK intact.

Thousands of people were in attendance, as though every African from the sixteen townships surrounding Jo'burg had come to see a secret army unveiled and retired. Next to January, December is the hottest month of the year. There was no overhang to shield us from the relentless sun as we sat in the stands of Soweto's Orlando Stadium. One by one the names of MK operatives boomed over the loudspeaker, and we would observe the figure of a man—and sometimes, though rarely, a woman—dressed in crisp green combat fatigues take the stage, approach Mandela, stand at attention, and stomp their boots in place as the swift blade of their hand sliced the air in salute. As Mandela and the insurgent stood face to face an MK commander at the podium continued to read: his or her field of operation, the pedigree of their training, and a short narrative of their most daring mission. Comrade so-n-so stole into South Africa from the camps in the Frontline States by wading across the Limpopo River with her gym shoes tied around her neck, then, making her way to Venda, she rendezvoused with her contacts, and proceeded to bomb the such-n-such installation of...and the name of a municipality would be drowned out by the cheers. Comrade so-n-so was captured by state security forces in the outback of the Karoo, where he was severely beaten and tied to the top of a Land Rover like a felled springbok, but en route he freed himself, yes, comrades, the comrade is no springbok, he's an MK soldier! Please, comrades, quiet, comrades, there's more, yes, there's more. He untied himself and kicked in the windows of that Land Rover, and those Boers, yes, comrades what do you think he did to those Boers, he moered them, yes, he moered the two Boers inside, thus securing his freedom, and then he went on to accomplish the mission he'd been sent to carry out! Then Mandela pinned a medal on the comrade and shook the hand of the man or embraced the woman and the crowd went wild with ecstasy and toyi toyied in the bleachers, shaking the whole stadium to its foundation.

The disbanding of MK was one of the biggest public relations bonanzas of all time, for I have no doubt whatsoever that every Black person in the stadium (and here I include myself for there were moments when I could not contain my joy and I, too, stood and toyi toyied) felt as though something of true value was finally being given to us, when in point of fact, one of the only true things we had ever possessed, a People's Army, was being taken away.

I was seated between Trevor Garden and Stimela Mosando. To Stimela's right sat Joy, whose surname I could never remember, and who was not—to my knowledge—an operative, but Stimela's fiancée. And next to Joy sat Jabu Mosando. On that sweltering December day in 1993, Stimela and Joy were in their late twenties or early thirties. Jabu and Trevor were still university students in their early twenties. And I was a lecturer pushing forty. Jabu had dreadlocks down to the nape of his neck and wore the horn-rimmed glasses that I always thought were out of place for someone majoring in sociology; they belonged on his older cousin. Trevor was the only White person in our section of the stadium, though not the only one in the stadium. Some were ANC members and supporters, some were police, and some were both. But Trevor was never mistaken for a cop for the simple reason that he did not carry himself like one. Oupa and Precious were not with us. But this wasn't unusual. Neither one of them had a formal connection with the University of Witwatersrand where I, so the cover-line went, met Jabu and Trevor while teaching there. I rarely met Precious out in the open; Oupa thought so little of me that he wouldn't consent to waste a moment with me in the open, or in the safe house, unless Stimela had ordered him to. Throughout the entire ceremony neither Oupa nor Precious took to the stage to be decorated by Madiba. Nor did Jabu, Trevor, or Stimela. As Mandela pinned the medal to the soldier who let the Boers know he was no springbok to be tied to the top of a Land Rover, I stood and toyi toyied and cheered. When I sat down, Stimela, who had neither risen nor cheered, looked at me sternly.

"That comrade is now useless as an operative. He's been exposed. That medal is a shackle. He's rendered himself inoperative and given his consent to the end of armed struggle—not to the temporary suspension, which is all this was supposed to be, but to the end. That's nothing to cheer about."

"But you're already exposed," Joy told him. "The bombing last April exposed you."

She had brought his uniform in a brown shopping bag, in case she could persuade him to change his mind. Throughout the ceremony she had chosen moments, discreet and understated moments, in which to gently press the bag to his leg and ask him to go down beneath the bleachers and change so that he might take his rightful place on that stage with Madiba and get the medals that were due him, get the cheers and adulation that were due him, let the air resound with the scripture of blows he struck against this racist state. "Yes," he told her, for though he was no supplicant for recognition, he was a man with needs, and what he needed now, what she knew he needed now, was for someone to speak his name and mark his moment in history before history came to an end. "Yes," he said again, "I want to go up there." He nodded toward his cousin Jabu and toward Trevor, two of the earliest members of his network. "I want them to go up there as well, they deserve it as much as anybody. But not like this, Joy, this isn't recognition. You don't disband an army," he said, now resting his arms on his legs and lowering his head to his clasped hands as though in prayer. "You don't disband an army."

As the ceremony ended, Jabu stood quietly and let his body be pulled into the sea of bodies that flowed out to the aisles and down the stairs. Stimela, Joy, Trevor, and I remained seated. The revolutionary music still blared over the loudspeakers, and now and then cries of *Amandla!* shot up to the blistering sun from the stands still vibrating from the toyi toy-ing youth who did not want to leave. Without turning his head to look at Trevor and me, Stimela whispered, "Now," and we stood and let ourselves be jostled and pushed and swept from the stadium into the street.

"How many are with us now?" I asked Trevor as we minnowed our way through the crowds leaving the stadium.

Either he pretended not to hear or he was doing what he always did when he found himself on open ground: scouring the environs, listen-ing for a sound that wasn't right even in the din of a crowd, watching out for the same face twice.

"What?" he said. Then it registered. "Do you know why Stimela never issued a firearm to you, why you've always had to borrow mine or Jabu's?"

I knew I'd like the answer even less than I liked the question.

"Because you seemed to need it," he said. "It would have been a crutch, not a weapon. The fetish that says 'I'm a guerilla.'"

"I was just curious."

He declined to even dignify this with a laugh.

"You once said there were five thousand, maybe more, MK insurgents who were willing to back Chris Hani when the time came, ready to see the revolution through. It's only natural that I'd ask how many there are now—after today."

"After today? Okay, after today there are fifteen hundred. How does that sound?"

"Sounds okay."

"Or maybe five hundred."

"But you just said—"

"Fifty. Make that five. Why do you need a head count? What will the number do for you? Will it stiffen your resolve; take the place of a gun? A long time ago Stimela told me: 'You're White, which makes you more needy than most. Stop needing what you need.'"

—⁂—

But even when I left South Africa three years later, when I said goodbye to Trevor, Stimela, and the others and returned "home" in 1996, it was still an open question: had I learned to stop needing what I needed— notwithstanding the fact that I, unlike Trevor, was Black? And Stimela's laughter, what that woman at the Botswanan border would have surely called a Zulu laugh, let me know that I had not asked about professor Mureinik out of curiosity but out of my need for a narrative, for a causal link between his death and our actions under cover of night. It was as though a place in the narrative of Etienne Mureinik's death was the missing page in a narrative of my life. Something I'd been cheated out of and needed desperately to regain.

The press had cheated me. Even the foreign press which often took a more critical view of White South Africans than, for example, Johannesburg's *Star* or *Citizen*. But even the obituary in London's *Independent* had tended miserly to my needs, imploring me to weed through the minutiae of what I already knew: Etienne Mureinik "was 42 when he fell," a verb tactfully spaced between jumped and was pushed, "from the 23rd story of a hotel in Braamfontein, Johannesburg, not far from the university, on Wednesday 10 July." It told me that he joined the faculty of law at the University of the Witwatersrand, or Wits, as we called it, in 1977, rising through the ranks—junior lecturer, lecturer, senior lecturer—becoming a professor at the age of 32, dean of faculty, and advisor to the Democratic Party at the age of 37. All this and more was in the files we kept on him and his twelve collaborators. There was nothing there that fed my need, least of all the fact that his death was "a watershed event for the mainly English-speaking White liberal establishment in South Africa, suggesting severe strains in its relation with the aspiring Black middle class." This to me, though true, was a red herring, for the fire and brimstone antagonism between these two groups was, at some level, a simple disagreement over which color capitalist should accumulate the spoils.

I could have added Mureinik's favorite word to his obituary: calibrate. A word he chewed and moved around his inner cheeks like cud when he lectured. A word that seemed to steady his nerves as, year after year, he looked out across the lecture hall and witnessed how it seemed to blacken exponentially. He was wrong, of course. There was no exponential increase in Black students, no mass invasion of that Harvard of the south. Khanya, my wife...my ex-wife, could attest to that. She was one of his law students. One Black face in that delirious sea of Black faces. In point of fact, no more than two in ten students at Wits were African—in a country where 8 in 10 people are African. But Mureinik's mind had inverted the world and "calibrate" was a word that cured his motion sickness, restored his equilibrium, and kept him from falling overboard into that ocean of hatred that the Afrikaner, not the English, were known for. It also saved him from the tsunami, the rising clamor for socialism and what he once described as "naked, uncritical racial solidarity" among Black militants, a solidarity that could "destroy all hope" of equal accountability in a post-apartheid South Africa—should that day arrive.

If memory serves me right, it was a year after the call from Stefaans Brümmer and a month or two after the death of Etienne Mureinik when his name came up unexpectedly. I had moved back in with Khanya after a long separation. She was trying to put the war—against apartheid, against Mandela's people in the ANC, against the English architects of liberal hegemony—behind us. My confrontation with Mandela in March of 1994, when he told me in no uncertain terms that "we" in the ANC, are not going take power and seize control of the institutions that White people have spent decades, centuries, building—that too, Khanya thought, was well behind us.

If I had been honest with her I would have told her that we never singled out Mureinik as a target. He was too equivocal. Too torn between his need for African acquiescence and his need for African approval. But I didn't tell her because she didn't ask. And she didn't ask because, perhaps, she didn't know what or how to ask. But she knew how to look at me that day Ntombi spoke his name.

I could feel her gaze that day, like I'd felt it before, on the night Stefaans Brümmer called. Ntombi, Gladys, and Naledi (three young women with whom she had shared digs at law school) came to our house for tea. Ntombi and Naledi kissed Khanya and lovingly put money in her hand before coming through to the living room where I was waiting with Gladys. It was a custom among young African women who were gainfully employed to give a gift of money to their friends who were not so gainfully employed. Khanya didn't out me in front of them, which is to say, when the name Mureinik came up, she didn't ask if there was a trail of bread crumbs from Stimela's safe house in Hillbrow to the bell calling out the 23rd floor in the lift of the Parktonian Hotel, bread crumbs sprinkled along the carpet-hushed hallway leading to the room and around the luxurious suite with its sheets of Egyptian cotton that no one in their right mind would have ever abandoned for the vertigo of the balcony, for the cold steel of the rail, for the garden grounds rushing up to meet him.

"Remember how he balanced his spectacles on that long pointed nose?" Ntombi said as she lowered her glasses down to the bridge of her nose and scrunched her face.

Gladys and Naledi laughed heartily, egging Ntombi on, but Khanya and I were silent, neither of us wanting to prolong the topic. I cleared the spent tea bags from a saucer on the coffee table and asked Khanya if I should fetch fresh ones and hot water from the kitchen. "If you like," she said, flatly.

Ntombi and Naledi were dressed for success, smart business suits and leather briefcases, the way two beautiful high-powered lawyers would be expected to dress, two women who'd landed good jobs in the White world right out of law school. Khanya was, by the standards of all the men who, I used to note jealously, hung around their law school digs when I first met them, just as pretty as Ntombi—though none of those young men thought she could hold a candle to Naledi whose eyes were large and whose complexion was as light as a Coloured person's which apparently was all that beauty required. Khanya had chosen to focus her legal training on community advocacy and the NGO world. She dressed in jeans and casual wear much of the time, so as not to diminish people in the township among whom she moved. Gladys's attire was much the same as Khanya's. This had less to do with her post-law school pursuits (which for the life of me I can't recall) and more to do with the fact that she had dated the same man for fifteen years, since the day she turned fifteen, which accounted for the fact that her demeanor always eclipsed her attire and her demeanor was decidedly settled.

When I returned from the kitchen, Ntombi was in full swing, lighting up the room with her Etienne Mureinik impersonations.

"Do calibrate!" said Gladys.

Ntombi rose to her feet like an Oxford don. She unruffled her imaginary robes. She cleared her throat. "Calibrate," she said looking down at them through her glasses.

"Voetsek, professor Pinch-face!" Naledi interrupted. "What has calibrate to do with anything?"

"Without this word," Ntombi admonished Naledi, with a posh English tone, "the African will not be able to govern properly. Is the African ready to govern, ladies and gentlemen? That is the question. Or will he be hobbled in his attempts to take his place—his rightful place, of course—beside us in a free, democratic, and civil society?"

"I want you to take your place in my pot of English stew," Naledi said.

"My dear girl, my dear, dear girl," Ntombi lorded over her, "shut—up!" She went on: "The law, ladies and gentlemen, the law. Jurisprudential reason. This is all we have at our disposal; all that can calibrate, yes, calibrate, the tension between this rising tide of Black economic, political, and social expectations that we are experiencing at the end of apartheid—legitimate expectations, make no mistake; apartheid is a blight upon civilization, unworthy of a European lineage—but only jurisprudential reason can calibrate the gap!...the tension between these rising expectations and our need for social stability free of both tyranny and anarchy."

"Please, me baas," Naledi implored, "I am a very hungry African and would very much like you for my English stew."

Ntombi waved her off.

"Let the fall, last Christmas, of the Soviet Union be a lesson to those of you in this lecture hall who still dream of socialism. I am well aware that some of you are members of the South African Students Congress and other such radical groups."

"No SASCO here, me bass, just cannibals."

"And I am well aware of your plans to push beyond the dismantling of apartheid for a socialist state and that your demand for the transformation of this university is merely a red herring—the first step in a takeover."

"Stew, baba, me just wants stew!"

"But where there is totalitarianism, there is no jurisprudential reason. And where there is no reason, there is no calibration. Now, for next time, I want you all to meditate on 'calibrate.' You must each write an essay on the social, political, and above all jurisprudential implications of this word."

Ntombi sat down and drank the fresh cup of tea I'd poured her as Gladys and Naledi gave her a round of applause. "Shame," she said, ruefully.

"What's a shame?" Khanya asked.

"The way he died. Professor Brassy told the papers that 'irrational attacks' had taken their toll, that the world 'just overwhelmed him.'"

"Irrational attacks have been levied at me all of my life and no one checked to see if I was overwhelmed," Naledi rejoined.

"What irrational attacks?" Ntombi asked.

"Apartheid." It was enough to silence us all. Then Naledi continued. "I left work early when I heard the news."

"To mourn?" Gladys asked, in all sincerity.

"To celebrate," Naledi corrected.

"You're lying," said Gladys.

"I'm not lying."

"Where?"

"On the Concourse."

Gladys gasped. "You drove all the way from your law practice, to the university, to demonstrate and cheer with those...those militants? What if you were caught on television?"

Naledi shrugged her shoulders.

"You're not a student anymore," Gladys said to her as though she were her mother.

"I may not be a student anymore but I'm still a militant."

"Is that the way a grown woman acts?" Gladys insisted.

"We can't all be as grown as you, Gladys," observed Naledi. And then to all of us, because we all looked a little surprised, "Yes, I toyi toyied and cheered and sang right there on the Wits Concourse, with all those faculty and staff watching us, with their mouths hanging open, shaking their heads. 'Disgusting. Heathen. African.' To which our bodies said: True. True. True."

"Didn't you feel strange or embarrassed?" Khanya asked.

"I never felt better. 'Kill the farmer! Kill the Boer!' That's what I learned in his lectures."

"Hey, wena!" Ntombi cut in. "He wasn't a Boer, he was a Brit."

"They're all Boers," Naledi said without flinching. "There's nothing to calibrate."

—⁂—

Had Etienne Mureinik been dead the night Stefaans Brümmer called, my panic would have been more tangible and focused. In lieu of myriad

offenses, my mind would have been able to concentrate itself on one accusation, the death of a White man, the only death worthy of expiation.
Instead, my mind ran over a range of other episodes that no less vio-
lated the suspension of armed struggle Mandela had imposed. Brümmer
himself seemed none too sure of what he was looking for. He knew that
under Mandela's National Unity government, the National Intelligence
Agency included MK operatives as well as agents from the secret world
of the former apartheid state; together they were working to ferret out
what they termed "extremists" on the Left as well as the Right, and I was
the subject of such an investigation. That much he had tricked the chief
of the NIA, Joe Nhlanhla, into revealing before he called me.

Brümmer needs me to help him fill in the rest. I am loath to oblige.

The war is over, Frank, we can live like normal people now.

Khanya hadn't said it just like that. But she had said it in her own way.
Earlier this evening, when we dined at the Carlton Hotel, she might not
have believed it herself. She had wanted to believe it. But how can she believe it if I won't believe it with her? I didn't tell her, 'Yes, the war is over,'
but nor did I say the other thing.

*For Christ's-sakes, Khanya, stop staring at me! Even the Orrs are being po-
lite, chatting to themselves, pretending not to hear. She's worried. She's afraid.
She thought tonight would be different. She'd spend the night here and then,
maybe, over time, with some effort, some healing, some words of reconciliation
on my part, some words of forgiveness on hers, maybe I'd come back home. Perhaps we'd be normal again. Were we ever normal?*

Yes…it's true. I called her this morning. Or did she call me? No matter.
We spoke on the telephone for the first time in weeks. That's what counts.
We each said, "I love you." She didn't say, The war is over. I didn't say, It's
just begun. We were trying not to argue. We met for drinks, expensive
drinks, in the lobby of the Carlton Hotel and said, What the hell, if we're
going to spend this much money we may as well go into the restaurant
and have a nice meal. All through dinner there hung suspended between
us the unvoiced question: are we going back to our separate homes or is
tonight the night we start all over again? When the coffee arrived, she
reached across the table and held my hand.

"Okay, I'll settle the question."

"What question?"

"The one we've been avoiding. I'll come back to your place. We'll talk about the rest in the morning."

And we laughed and shook free of our nerves. We drank our coffee and had the waiter place two sweet, syrupy *koeksisters* in an elegant little box tied with a gold lace ribbon. We walked out into the rain, dodging the watery pellets as best we could, holding fast to the stone façades of Jo'burg's skyscrapers until we reached the taxi rank on Bree Street.

There, we held each other beneath Mandela's modest cardboard shield. We kissed. The war is over. The war has just begun. It hardly mattered. Not as long as we were silent. We dashed down the Orrs' drive with no more than a hot shower, a dry towel, a glass of wine, and a warm inviting bed on our minds. But Mrs. Orr intercepted us with a message from Stefaans Brümmer. Brümmer with his questions. Brümmer with his reminders. Brümmer with his perfect end to a perfect evening.

How did I get here? What possessed me to emigrate from de facto apartheid in the US to official apartheid in a country I hardly knew?

I watch her watching me as Brümmer delineates my status, an enemy of the state, an enemy of the "New" South Africa. The "New" South Africa that I fought for and am still fighting for now, I want to say, to Brümmer and Khanya and the Orrs. And to myself.

I traveled to South Africa twice before I finally "emigrated," if that's the right word. Once in July and August of 1989, on a research trip funded by the Jerome Foundation on a grant for emerging artists. I was supposed to spend two months here, gather enough data to complete a novel, and get out. Get into apartheid South Africa and then get out. That was the deal. Plain and simple. But on the second day of my first sojourn, I met Khanya. Two weeks later we were engaged.

Then there were the two months after the Jerome Foundation trip, December/January 1990/1991. I was in love then, yes, that's it. I came back to South Africa because I was in love. Though I said I came back to complete my research. Each time I departed I returned. The third time, later in 1991, I thought it would be like the other times, nothing as short as two months, perhaps, but nothing as long as five years. But one by one, five years approached, arrived, and departed.

—∞—

As I recall (and Khanya, no doubt, recalls it differently) the "plan" was for Khanya to come to New York while I finished my masters at Columbia. We'd go to Europe or South America and she would go to film school where the education was good and cheap and I would teach and write.

That was July of 1990, when the violence in South Africa that, unbeknownst to us, was to characterize the political climate of the next five years (by 1992 the massacres perpetrated by the Inkatha Freedom Party (IFP) and de Klerk's security forces brought the death toll to upwards of 300 deaths per month) was in its terrifying infancy. An estimated 100,000 impimpis were being transported from KwaZulu and Natal into the sixteen townships that surrounded Johannesburg. De Klerk, who had only been in office a year, had just lifted the ban against the ANC and the Communist Party and had released Mandela from prison. But part of the deal was that the ANC guerillas of Umkhonto we Sizwe and their fellow travelers would not be allowed to return to South Africa and would not be freed from prison until most of the ANC moderates had had a chance to return and fill the void with the common sense of bourgeois accommodation. The devil is always in the details. Mandela had agreed to this. Somewhere in the desert of the Karoo there may even be a time capsule chockful of documents, which someone will dig up in two or three hundred years and find that Mandela had not simply agreed to this, but had proposed it. Into this "compromise" de Klerk facilitated the "immigration" of Gatsha Buthelezi's fifth column from Natal into the Transvaal.

As a cool winter night in July settled over Johannesburg's bracelet of Black townships, Inkatha's impimpis tore through the thin wooden doors of old brick and corrugated tin homes, shattered kerosene lamps on kitchen floors, and watched ribbons of flame unfold to the beds of old people whose throats they had slit; as children cried wildly for someone to rescue them; as men who could run, ran, leaving their families behind; as women too young to die from one simple hack of the panga were raped and then killed; as the large yellow casspirs, de Klerk's armored personnel carriers, waited impatiently for their passengers to return. It was midnight in the townships. It was midday in Manhattan. The pasta was being served al dente at sidewalk cafés in Little Italy; the pigeons vied for a spot on the outstretched arms of the birdman in Washington Square Park; near Times Square, the cabbies were singing with their horns; and we were being wed at Tammany Hall.

We'd had an agreement, she and I. As ironclad as our marriage vows, to hear me tell it. A loose ensemble of suggestions, whenever her story got there first. Rio or Amsterdam, that was deal. By July of 1991 we'd be up on a hill overlooking Ipanema or down in a houseboat on a Dutch canal. She'd be in film school. I would teach and write. Soon we'd send for Rebaabetswe, my stepdaughter who'd turned three that May before we were married. We'd be free. Free of South Africa. Free of America. Black and free.

But one morning in February she woke up and said she was leaving.

"I'm going back to South Africa," she said.

My feelings whiplashed between confusion, sadness, and a biting sense of betrayal.

"Why?" I said.

"She told me she thought I was British on the phone. She said she had no idea I was Black."

"Just like that?"

"Not just like that. I could have handled it if she said it just like that. She was about to say 'Black' then she caught herself. That made it even worse. Why can't they come clean in your country?"

"It's not my country—why do you always call it my country?"

"They're in need of a certain—oh, I can't remember the word she used—a certain image for their point of sales people. I've got two years of law school and she's telling me that! She said she would have saved us both the trouble had she realized on the phone."

"We could sue."

"Sure, with all the money from your student loans."

"It's a racist country. To the core. I told you before you came."

"You're supposed to have laws."

"Why are we arguing about this? I'm on your side. Besides I told you before you came."

"You already said that."

"I'm sorry."

"Why should I stay here?"

"Khanya, we agreed."

"We discussed. We didn't agree. Trade one South Africa for another? Does that make sense to you?"

"I graduate in May, we'll leave then, okay?"

She was already dressed. "Trade one Boer for another?"

"Why don't we take a shower together?" *Wrong thing to say.*

She put on her shoes, and then looked outside to see that a fresh film of snow had fallen in the night. "Besides, my family's there." She rummaged in the closet for her boots. "Maybe family doesn't mean the same thing to all of you—"

"Who's 'all of you'?"

"I'm an African. For me, family is everything."

I sat up in bed but I may as well have been standing on my hind legs. "Why don't you just say what you mean?"

"I've seen the way you treat your parents."

"Then you must have also seen the way they treat me."

"Doesn't matter."

"Doesn't matter?"

"Our duty is to them, not vice versa. I thought things would be different here and then she said that to me. That White haus frau, said that to me."

"What are we talking about?"

"I'm leaving. I'm going back. I hope you can come when you're finished with school."

"You thought things would be different here? I told you they wouldn't be."

"You don't know what I thought."

"You don't need a law degree to know that African immigrant is an oxymoron, a contradiction in terms. All it takes is a little common sense."

She stopped at the foot of the bed and looked at me. "I used to think that you were only occasionally impolite—I was wrong."

"A land of opportunity. A step up in the world. You were so inebriated with your arrival that you thought you'd pass through customs and be changed forever."

"Don't lecture me, I'm not one of your students."

"A vertical leap from kaffir to immigrant, when all you made was a lateral move from kaffir to nigger. That's what's eating you. You'd rather leave than be mistaken for one of us. Well, I've got news for you."

"When I want news I'll read the *New York Times*," she said, leaving me in the bedroom.

I threw my robe on and followed her to the door. "That woman at. Macy's—"

"I'm going to the travel agency."

"—the Human Resources minion who snubbed you—"

"Goodbye, Frank." She disentangled the menagerie of chains and locks and left.

I leaned over the banister as she twirled down the stairs. "An eight-year-old child could have done what she did without wasting time. Without shuffling papers. Just by pointing a finger and saying, 'Look, mommy, a Negro.'" I ran back into the living room and struggled mightily to lift the ice-sealed window. She scurried down the sidewalk and stopped at the light on 168th street. At last the ice cracked and the window jerked open.

"Hey!" I yelled, "October's not that far off, you can still be an immigrant for Halloween!"

The engines of morning delivery trucks were clearing their throats in the streets below, the cold grates of the bodegas were screeching open, and a barge horn blared as it pulled itself across the water from the Bronx to the Washington Bridge. She hadn't heard a word.

—*∞*—

"He may as well be a White man." That's what her father said when she returned to South Africa. She'd gone home to Mmabatho in the "homeland" of Bophuthatswana for the weekend. She'd talked primarily about her returning to law school, hoping this would soften him up, show her reinsertion back into his fold, that she might broach the more difficult subject, the subject of her desire to marry me, without revealing the even more difficult truth, that we were already married in New York.

He grunted as he folded his Sunday paper, which was not the same as saying "No, you can't marry him," but could not be precisely translated as "Yes, Frank's a really wonderful guy, I'd have wished no one else for you." He stood up and looked around for something. What? He didn't smoke a pipe. There was nothing he wanted to see on television. It was too early for a drink.

"He'll pay the *lobola*," she said, plaintively, hoping against hope that at least my willingness to pay the bride price would also soften him up. This "willingness" on my part was, in point of fact, a fabrication on her part. She might say "we agreed" that I'd pay the lobola, but I would say, "we *discussed*" it. Whose story crossed the finish line first hardly mattered to Mr. Phenyo. He folded the newspaper and went out into the yard.

The hot desert sun of Bophuthatswana baked his cheerless attempts at gardening or maintaining a lawn. It made him sad just to look at it. He used to raise cattle. Not here but where cattle could be grazed and watered. He used to plant crops. Not here but where crops could drink their fill and flourish. The good land had been taken by the Boers and he and his people had been sent here; here, where the earth's skin wrinkled before its time; here for "their own good." She came up beside him and tried to get his attention while he watered what for lack of a better word he called his lawn. She wanted to say, you're just making mud. But he might turn on her and tell her that he had eyes, didn't he, that he could see that he was just making mud, couldn't he, that if he wanted to make mud what business was it of hers?

"Did you hear me, papa, I said he'll pay the lobola?"

"He doesn't put milk in his coffee," he said, more to the mud than to her, "or sugar. He's not an African, he's a White man."

In May of 1991, I graduated from Columbia University. I bought a one-way ticket on South African Airways, an apartheid-era airline as inviting as disinfectant.

I followed her to South Africa as blindly as she had followed me to New York. I went without the fat foundation bankroll of my first trip. I was going to have to live on rands, not dollars. The only American currency I had was five hundred dollars and a letter of recommendation from professor Edward Said. I was counting on the money to tide us over until the letter could land me a job. I had lied to get back into South Africa; just as I had lied in 1989 to make possible my first trip there.

My visa application had been denied in 1988. Someone in the embassy in Washington found it highly inconceivable that a Black American would want to vacation in Johannesburg, the industrial hub of South Africa, in July, the dead of winter. On top of that, Jesse Jackson and several Black politicos, clergymen, and academics had submitted their applications at the same time I sent mine. So I waited another year, then bit the bullet and shelled out a significant amount of money to hire a Washington based "visa consultant." The day he got my passport and application was the day he called me.

"Mr. Wilderson, I've got your passport in hand and I'm looking at your photograph. Mr. Wilderson, you're Black, sir."

"Last time I checked."

There was an uneasy silence. Then he said, "And you want to go to South Africa?"

"That's correct."

"Well, sir, we're a visa consultancy. We don't guarantee that our clients will get a visa. Have you applied for a visa from them before?"

"Last year. June of 1988."

"What reasons did they give for denying you?"

"They didn't give any reason."

"Are you sure?"

"Of course, I'm sure," I said, though I might have been lying. I don't remember.

"Mr. Wilderson, now I don't know if you've read anything about South Africa—"

"I studied Southern African politics in college." *Wrong thing to say.*

"Did you, whereabouts?"

"Dartmouth College."

"You're a Dartmouth man! My uncle was a Dartmouth man." *Right thing to say!* "You must have been one of the first—well, it's just that there weren't any Blacks in my uncle's time. Okay, well fair enough. But I must tell you that from all indications South Africa could declare another state of emergency any day now. Are you sure you wouldn't rather have a visa for Zimbabwe, they've been inde—"

"I need a visa for South Africa."

"Certainly, sir. Now, Mr. Wilderson, I'll say one more thing and then we'll get down to brass tacks. You do realize that accommodations are still not what they call "multiracial"? That would mean you would have to stay—"

"I'll work it out when I get there."

"Of course, there is the Honorary White status which many Black American businessmen are accorded when they travel. And they stay right downtown with that status, at the Carlton Hotel. Are you a businessman, Mr. Wilderson?"

"No."

"Well, fine, fine, that's alright. So...let's get right down to brass tacks. What are you?"

"What am I?"

"Your occupation."

"I'm a guard."

"A security guard," he said with a little too much enthusiasm.

"No, I'm a guard at the Walker Art Center in Minneapolis."

"I don't think I understand, sir."

"I rotate through the galleries and tell children not to touch the paintings."

"I see," he said with all the air escaping, "and before that?"

"I worked for various brokerage firms."

"As a guard?"

"As a stockbroker."

"I beg your pardon?"

"I was a stockbroker with Merrill Lynch, Oppenheimer, E. F. Hutton, and Drexel, Burnham, Lambert from 1981 to 1988."

"And you left that to walk around art galleries monitoring children?"

"It isn't as simple as that."

"It never is."

"Look, are they going to want to know all of that?"

"Mr. Wilderson, I have to ask this because it has been asked in the past: are you an artist?"

"No, I neither paint nor sculpt. I like modern art and the job is easy and lets me—" I almost said "write." I was shocked at myself but I almost said it. "Let's me have free time to figure a few things out in my life. See I'm coming out of difficult divorce." This was a lie, because I wasn't married to the woman I'd broken up with, but it put him back into a world he could understand.

"I understand, Mr. Wilderson, I do understand. Had a bit of a spat like that myself. Now, Mr. Wilderson, I'm going to cut right to the chase. You have to be truthful with me and I have to be truthful with the South African embassy. If I lie to them, if I lie to them just one time, when I come back with my next client they are not only not going to let me jump the queue but they will show me the door. They will know me to be less than an honest man and that will be bad for business. I'm an honest man, Mr. Wilderson and I believe that you're an honest man so I'm going to go over the more pertinent questions, boxes you've already checked but we just need to...well, you know."

"Shoot."

"Are you a journalist?"

"No."

"Are you an artist?"

"No."

"Are you a writer?"

"No."

"Have you ever published an article in a journal or a newspaper?"

"Didn't you just ask me that?"

"Not, really, sir. Some people don't claim writing as an occupation, but they've published before."

"No."

"Alright, sir. And the purpose of your visit?"

"Tourism." *I hear the repression is divine this time of year.*

"Now, sir, that answer's going to raise a few eyebrows."

"Okay, then check something else."

"It's not a matter of checking something else, Mr. Wilderson, it's a matter of the truth."

"Then check tourism."

"Mr. Wilderson, they're going to ask questions, such as how well I know you."

"I went to Dartmouth with your uncle."

"Those are not the facts, Mr. Wilderson."

"Can't we be a little creative?"

"Creative is the one thing we can't be. You and I, with our democracy and our freedom of association, our freedom of ideas—what we might think of as creative the people in the South African embassy think of as, well...They're not very creative at the embassy. The fact of the matter is I really don't know you that well. And I have yet to work for a Black American trying to get a tourist visa to visit Johannesburg (which is not exactly a tourist destination) in July, the middle of winter. My credibility, you might say, is inextricably bound to yours."

"Fine, tell them the truth. I'm a poor museum guard who wants to take a vacation abroad. So I'm going to a typically non-vacation spot in the middle of winter because it'll be summer here—and too hot for me—and because off-season and off the beaten-track is all I can afford."

He accepted this. He said he'd call me back in a week. Somehow he got the visa. In July of 1989, as P. W. Botha imposed his state of emergency, I bought a ticket on South African Airlines and flew into South Africa for the first time in my life.

I was terrified on that first trip into South Africa. I could not believe I was actually going. *Into South Africa.* Thirty thousand feet in the air, the insanity of what I was doing seized me. *Here I am, a Black American choosing to go into South Africa when every African with two rands to rub together is trying to get out. This is crazy.*

The buzz of Afrikaans coils through the cabin like bees. I understand not a word of it. The stewardess demurs to take my drink order. For the third time I tell her I don't speak Afrikaans. Now I must have the courage to ask these two men beside me (speaking perhaps of cattle ranching, or me, they must be speaking of me in their bastardized Dutch, waving their bratwurst hands in the tiny air) to rise so that I can pee or flush myself into the sky.

We break through the underbelly of clouds. Rain glistens on the windows. Here and there on the ground below, clusters of suburban light are broken by patches of blackness. I tell myself to get a grip; that those black lightless spaces are just fields where jack rabbits run and where the genius of developers waits. Tomorrow I will learn that those tracts barren of light were not fields at all, but townships like Thokoza and shantytowns like Phola Park; "locations" the Africans call them, where people live without electricity.

What possessed me to make this journey? I wonder why, when speaking of Europe, people speak of going *to:* "I'm going *to* France", "I'm going *to* Spain." And why, for a handful of other countries, people speak of *going into?* "We're going *into* Bosnia." "She got *into* Albania." "I'm *going into* South Africa." I look down upon the rising runway. Nothing reveals the truth of this country to be any different than others. What did I expect—the tarmac to be lit with luminous skulls?

Into South Africa…with no more companion than this diary with its empty pages waiting for my words and these black hands "stained" with the ink of fear. Are you out of your mind? They will kill *you. They kill hundreds like you every year. I've got to go back. This is mad.*

We bump and stutter and skid across the tarmac. In the driving rain we taxi to a halt. I have only one wish, to be airborne again.

I cleared customs without incident. I called Montshiwa Moroke, my contact. A journalist with Pan Africanist Congress affinities and one of three or four Black men who wrote for the Johannesburg *Star*, I'd met him in Minneapolis in 1987. He invited me to South Africa. No, he said I must come; that as a writer—a Black writer—it was my duty to see for myself, to bear witness to apartheid. He had promised me a bed at his house in Soweto.

Inside the airport, I called him. But he wasn't home. What complicated matters was the fact that I did not speak any Sotho languages nor could I make his mother understand my—to her ears—tortured and foreign English. She kept telling me that Montshiwa had gone to Zimbabwe. And I kept trying to explain to her that I was a friend who'd been promised a place to stay, that I was Black and alone and terrified with no one to turn to and nowhere else to go. She would tell me Montshiwa's in Zimbabwe and then she'd hang up. And I would call her back and desperately try to get more information out of her and she would repeat, Montshiwa's in Zimbabwe...and hang up. And I would call back and she would hang up. Finally, I ran out of change.

The last plane was towed into the hanger for cleaning or repairs. All the arrivals had arrived. All the departures had departed. I turned from the wall of windows and, for the first time in an hour I noticed the Black people in the airport. None of them were at eye level. Under the currency exchange window, women wearing *doeks* scrubbed the floor on their hands and knees. Atop tall ladders, I could see the ashen ankles of men, sockless in worn shoes as they polished lamp shades in silence. Soon, I thought, I will have to venture into this night and find a place to stay. *Why didn't I get Honorary White status from that visa consultant? Didn't want that in my historical record, that's why. To hell with the historical record. What am I going to do? A few years ago, they automatically stamped it in the passport. He said something about it being in the bar code of the strip the customs agent taped on the passport. Could I take this to a hotel and get in?*

It was late. I decided not to risk it. Instead I locked myself in a stall in the bathroom and removed my shirt. Strapped around my torso was a secret money belt. But more than money was in the belt. Into it I had folded photocopies of my favorite pages of Frantz Fanon's writings, along with three pages from the tour guidebook *Africa on a Shoestring.* Oddly enough, both books were banned in South Africa. The former because its subtitle read "The Handbook for the Black Revolution in Africa," and the latter because the authors had made the kind of disparaging remarks about apartheid which all the other guidebooks had shied away from. I sat on the throne and read. It said that there was a part of Johannesburg called Hillbrow-Berea which was "slowly" becoming "multiracial." The book described it as the Times Square of Johannesburg. This did little to excite me; I'd always avoided Times Square when I went to New York. But the allusion was certainly a drawing card for someone other than me. I wrote the telephone number of a bed and breakfast place on my hand. I started to leave the bathroom. At the door I panicked. I went back inside and spent a good ten minutes washing all the ink off my hand. *Memorize it man, don't let 'em catch you with anything written.* Still, I wasn't sure. I went to the coffee shop, ostensibly for change, but in reality I wanted to kill time and keep time from killing me.

An hour in the airport coffee shop nursing the same cup of tea with Black waiters and cleaners too cautious to speak to me; with the only conversation being that of errant barking from German shepherds as they pass each other, up and down the empty corridors under the silent leashes of soldiers. The coffee shop closed, so I bought a paper dated July 24, 1989 — yesterday's news. I read the headlines. A renewed State of Emergency is being imposed. Three bombs have gone off in the last three days. Two in Jo'burg central, allegedly placed by Umkhonto we Sizwe. One placed by Whites, demolishing a township clinic in retaliation.

If there'd been a plane to Burma Shave, I'd have taken it just to leave. I was thirty-three years old. Too old to think that I could live forever; too young to have accomplished anything so worthy in life as to face death with equanimity and resolve. I was scared and alone. I went back to the telephone and let the last coins fall.

The woman on the other end spoke English with a thick German accent. At least she can understand me, I thought. "Come along my American friend," she said. I was so elated that I put the phone down, picked up my backpack, and ran to the exit to catch one of the last shuttles into the city. It wasn't until I was comfortably seated on the soft felt cushions, and my eyes began to close from the fatigue and fear of the journey and the calm reassurance of finally having a place to stay, that it occurred to me that I had neglected to ask if the Sommer House was "multiracial." I sat up with a terrified start. I was set to jump off and call her back. *No, fool, don't do that. Then what should I do?* The bus careened out of the airport and onto the highway, answering the question for me.

A young African woman came from the back of the bus and sat down next to me. I hadn't seen any Black people get on the bus, only the last dregs of late arrivals—all of whom were White. She asked if I was an American. I said I was. She told me she was completing a BA in Biology at the University of Bophuthatswana. *Ha! You take me for a fool? You're no student. You're with Special Branch. They sent you. This is a trap. A set-up. Name and passport ID number, that's all you're getting, sister.* She asked why I had come to vacation in South Africa in the middle of winter. *I knew it, I fucking knew it. Stay calm, breathe, just breathe, don't say anything that would incriminate you.* My heart was pounding so hard I thought she could hear it. I felt a panic attack coming on, like the early stages of angina. I did my best to keep my voice low and my answers vague. Finally, she asked if I was married. *What kind of question is that for a cop to ask?* No, I told her. Do you have a girlfriend, she said. *This is getting strange.* I told her that I didn't have a girlfriend. Then who takes care of you? *Who takes care of me; is this some kind of newfangled lie detector test?* I don't understand, I told her, no one takes care of me. Why don't you have a girlfriend? We broke up almost two years ago, I said. And you've been alone since then? Hardly, there are hundreds of women in my life: Ann Petry, Toni Morrison, Assata Shakur, Toni Cade Bambara. Womanizer! she said with disgust. I thought Black American men were different—but you're just like a South African man; no wonder your woman left you. What do you need four women for? Those are just the ones whose names I can remember, I smiled. She turned away from me and sucked her teeth. I'm joking, okay? They're not women, well, they're women but I've only met one of them, Toni Cade Bambara. A womanizer *and* a liar, she said. Look they're novelists, writers. I spent time with them in the Minneapolis Public Library. I read their books, okay? This made her laugh and it also seemed to relieve her. But then she said, you read books and you don't have a girlfriend? I wake up, I write, I go to the gallery—I'm a guard there, when my shift's up I go to the public library. Why? she asked. Because I can't check books out of the university library—I'm not a student. No, I mean why do you go to the library after work, why not go out with friends, you won't meet a woman at the library. I'm not trying to meet a woman, I'm trying to become the smartest person I know. You're worse than a South African man, she said. *Well, no one asked you to sit down.* There were moments of uncomfortable silence in which I thought that I should have been relieved to finally realize that she was not there to arrest me for visa fraud or for carrying contraband (Fanon's writings and *Africa on a Shoestring*).

The bus arrived at the rotunda on the White-entrance side of the Noord Street Station in the center of Johannesburg. She told me her name was Grace and that she'd gone to the airport to see a friend of hers off to London. The young man had said he was going to study, which is how he was granted permission to leave but, she told me, he just couldn't take it anymore and he was really going into exile. Why anyone Black would want to come to this country, she said, when all we dream about is leaving, that's a mystery to me—you're a mystery to me. I'm no mystery, I said, I'm a writer. I write fiction and poetry. I've won $13,000 in literary awards this year and I'm traveling. This, well, this is a research trip for a novel that I'm writing. What's it about? she asked. Well, I'm...I'm not exactly sure. How does one do research for a novel, she said, is it like research in the lab? Well, no...not exactly. Then what? I...I don't really know. You need someone to take care of you, she nodded, where are you staying? At a bed and breakfast place in Berea. They're not multiracial in Hillbrow or Berea, she warned. Oh, yes, yes they are, it's all in one of my books, my travel book. This place is multiracial, I assured her. I really don't think so; you must come to my aunt's house with me. She works in Auckland Park, but she lives in the Meadowlands, in Soweto. She'll put you up; you must stay with us, in the location. Thank you, but I'm already booked. Give me the telephone number of the inn, she said. I gave her the number. She walked toward the other side of Noord Street station, the Black side, to sit in a Black people's kombi and wait for it to fill to the brim with passengers for the Meadowlands.

As I approached the metered taxis a White woman who was ten to fifteen years older than Grace, a woman in her late thirties, apprehended me. "Did I hear you say you're from the States?" *Okay, here it is, yep, this woman, yep, she's the agent. Now, think, what did she hear, where was she sitting—behind you, in front of you, on the side. Okay, what if Grace was the decoy...or the set up...or the finger man...and this woman—yep, here it comes—she's the real cop. Don't answer any questions, just say, I want to call the American embassy.*

"I'm a...I'm...yes, from the States."

"Splendid, I love people from America. And you're going to Hillbrow, I heard you tell that African girl you're going to Hillbrow."

"That 'girl' has a BA in Biology."

"Yes, the Africans are cleverer than they've ever been—but are they ready to help us govern, that's the question."

"I'm not going to Hillbrow. I'm going to Berea."

"Hillbrow-Berea. It's all the same. Hillbrow's where the fun happens, the naughty, naughty fun. If you know what I mean. Berea is where one sleeps it off. C'mon we'll share a cab. I live in Berea. I'll show you the sights."

"I'm tired."

She leaned in: "You'll need me to help you get a taxi."

"I can manage."

"We're going to the same area and there's the cost—we could split it. It's late, you might need my help in getting—"

"Fine." *I get the point. No, Frank, don't. She must be with the police. What can you get for a visa violation? There's a state of emergency on. You could get whatever they give you, that's what you could get. Please, somebody let me go home.* Surprisingly, one of the taxis in the queue had a Black driver; the rest were White and Indian. He was the only one who didn't turn away or roll up his window when we approached the queue.

She jabbered all the way from Noord Street Station to the neon lights of Hillbrow. And when we got to Hillbrow she turned into a tour guide. Those are the news kiosks for immigrants and others wanting newspapers from around the world; see how the cafés in Hillbrow serve coffee on the sidewalk—we're just like Europe here; and look, look up there, that's our Strydom Tower, it's our Seattle Space Needle, only no one can go up in it now, it's been closed for I don't know how long—bombs, you've heard of bombs, the Black communists—I'm not saying that all of our Blacks are communists—but those Umkhonto we Sizwe people, Mandela's people, they come from Russia with their bombs, it's a bother, such a bother, they've forced us to close the Strydom Tower. I want you to know that things are changing; we've eleven years to the new millennium, things may very well change by then. Look at all the lights, look at all the people, by the year 2000 this whole area will be multiracial. That's what my astrologer says. Do you have an astrologer? I understand that in the States you can pick up the phone and call them toll free, is that true? This whole area is soon going to be multi-racial. Things are changing. But can our South African Blacks handle the responsibility? What if we do let them come to the city, then what, chaos, communism, anarchy? That's the question on our minds. Can our Blacks learn to behave like the Blacks in America and Britain? Is it time? Are they ready?

The African cab driver was silent throughout all of this. We left Hillbrow's main drag, Pretoria Street, and entered a quiet tree-lined street of well polished apartment buildings. We were in Berea. He stopped at a posh complex and got out of the car to help her with her bags.

"She didn't tip me," he said, when he got back in the car. He put the car in gear and pulled away. "The nice madam didn't tip me."

When we got to the inn, he looked in the rearview mirror and said, "Hey, boss, you know where you're going?"

No, I thought, I have no idea where I'm going.

"Yes," I said, "this looks like the place. Say, I don't have rands. Don't know what I was thinking. I didn't change enough before they closed at the airport." *What was I thinking; that I didn't need rands because in reality I was going to be on the next flight home?* "Let me go inside, register, and get the concierge or someone to make change for me then I'll pay you. How does that sound—or would you like US dollars?"

"Concierge?" he said, quizzically, as though I'd told him I was going inside to get change from the penguin.

I rang the bell. The door opened. A White woman ("large" in White vernacular; "healthy" in Black vernacular) peered out and looked on either side of me. She seemed puzzled. Now, she looked at me and said, "Yes?"

"I'm Frank Wilderson. Frank B. Wilderson, the third." It was happening so fast, but one thought, one absurd thought flashed into my mind and then quickly out again—*she thinks I'm the cab driver*—due to its presumed absurdity. She hadn't said anything. She was still recovering her own wits. "I'm here for a room."

"We're not multiracial."

"I called you." I felt a forecast of tears in my cracking voice. *Don't cry, you bastard, you better not cry!* "You promised. I mean, you booked me in. I called you less than an hour ago."

"You didn't call *me*. You might have called someone else." She had a thick German accent that, for some reason that I can only think has to do with all the World War II movies I watched growing up, infuriated and frustrated me more.

"Now look," *you fucking Nazi*, "I called you from the airport."

"I've had one call all night and that was from an American."

"I *am* the American!" I tore my shirt open, which terrified her and would have sent her into shock had she not seen the pouch and the passport that I snatched from it. She looked at my photograph. She flipped through the pages upon pages of all the places I'd been in the world—first with surprise, then with envy, finally with irritation. She thrust it back at me.

"We're not multiracial."

All this time, she'd been blocking the entrance with her imposing frame. I dropped my backpack at her feet and turned toward the street. *Where am I going to go? What am I going to do?* I thought I was going to break down and cry. At the end of the walk, the taxi was idling. The driver's eyes met mine. He wanted to help, but he knew better than to get out of the cab. I walked over to him. I asked him what I owed him. He told me. If I pay you in dollars, but pay you double the amount, will that be okay? You don't have to do that, *baba.* Are you going to be alright? Yeah, I lied. I'm from Chicago, I lied again. *What could being from Minneapolis possibly mean in a fight?* That heifer best raise up, and quick! I told him, making extra damn sure that my voice didn't travel up the walk, 'cause I'm three seconds and counting off her ass. To which he repeated, Are you sure you'll be alright? I nodded, and kept nodding as he drove away. I turned back up the walk. She was still there, barring the door, my backpack at her feet.

"Now, look lady, a deal is a deal, okay?" I picked up my backpack. "I don't want to call the police."

This made the folds of fat in her arms shake with laughter. I pushed past her as she laughed.

"We—are—not—multiracial."

"The guidebook says you are."

"The guidebook is wrong."

I looked around for the register. The foyer and front area was void of a front desk, just a hard floor and a wide opening onto a living room, a narrow passage under the stairs, and another passage that led to the kitchen. *Eureka! There's the book on that little side table next to the stairs.* I rushed over to it and signed my name.

"Okay, lady, now my name's in the register. So you've got to be fair about it. We could call the police right now and they'd see that I'm registered."

"Use the phone in the hall and then you can wait for them outside."

"Damn it, I don't have any place to go!" *If you cry, I'll kill you.*

"We're not multiracial."

She called softly up the stairs and her two sons (Bruno and Gestapo—okay, so I don't remember their Christian names) appeared. As they came down the stairs I sized myself up, 5'10," 189 pounds. But my musculature had diminished since I stopped being a stockbroker and began working at the Walker Art Center. I no longer lived in a nice apartment by Lake Calhoun, but rented a room in a boarding house, a room just big enough for my books, my typewriter, and me. I hadn't had the money to continue my gym membership—so I wasn't lifting weights. And I hadn't studied martial arts for almost ten years, which was about the last time I'd been in a fight. They reached the bottom and moved on me like zombies. Well, not exactly. The older one, Gestapo, was clearly in charge. With a flick of his wrist he motioned for his younger, slighter, blonder, brother to pick up my backpack. It was then that I noticed his little brother's eyes: they held even less resolve than mine. The older one, who must have been twenty-five, looked like he played rugby. This was just a scrimmage for him. He'd do what needed doing and clean me off his cleats with the mud. He slammed his palm into my chest.

"Alright, now!" I said, "Don't make me go off in here." He pushed me again. "Back the fuck up," I said, but it was I who was backing up. He kept pushing me toward the door. "I said don't touch me!" His little brother, who'd been walking behind him, was now beside him, holding my backpack in what I remember to be his right hand. I stepped to the side and punched the younger brother as hard as I could. He groaned and fell back. I fell upon him and kept swinging. There was nothing especially strategic in this move, for it left my entire backside exposed to Gestapo who had no more scruples about attacking me from behind than I did about attacking the least likely suspect. I was all over Bruno, and Gestapo was all over me. We fell into the table and something, maybe the register, perhaps a few knickknacks fell to the floor. I was trying to stay on my feet and trying to absorb the punishment I was taking from Gestapo and beat Bruno at the same time, but Bruno was fighting back and Gestapo was fighting me in the back. I grabbed the younger brother for not all the punches I threw were connecting, and we went down, with Gestapo straddling us from above. Somewhere from across a long distant border I could hear a voice, yelling, screaming, ordering us to stop. Bruno stopped. Gestapo stopped. I stopped.

"He can stay," she said. "We've got Germans from Siemens Corporation up above. Better he stays than we wake them." She ordered me to pay some outlandish amount. Right there on the spot. I said I only had dollars. All the better she said. Her sons backed away, but loitered by the banister. The ruckus had pushed us to the other end of the large foyer, all the way to the opening to the kitchen. I didn't want to wipe my mouth, but it was stinging. *Don't let them see that you're hurt. And don't you cry. I'll kill you if you cry.* My ribs ached. I was drenched in sweat and I was dirty from rolling on the floor. My backpack was on the floor over by the staircase, where the storm troopers stood. I retrieved it and faced them again. I wasn't squaring off with them, I just had to get past them to go up to my room.

"Not upstairs," she said.

"The rooms are upstairs," I insisted.

"I've got Germans, from Siemens Corporation. I'll not have you up there with them."

"That's where people stay and that's where I'm staying." Her sons barred my way.

"You can take this," she held the wad of bills I'd given her, "and let my sons throw you out. Or you can follow me and let me show you your room."

I followed her through the kitchen and out the back door. "You've got to be kidding," I said. "This is such a fucking cliché." She paid me no mind. "Where are we going?" Still she was silent. She seemed to know her way around the yard, even in the dark. She led me along a row of doors in a concrete structure that looked like a cross between a jail and a stable. She opened one of the doors with a key. She threw the switch. The floor was concrete. The bed had a thin sheet and blanket that looked, and ultimately felt, like horsehair. Later that night I would discover that the bed was 5'9" long as I found myself continually drawing my knees in an inch to keep my feet from falling off. It was wide enough for one person and had a pancake mattress over a mesh of springs. There was a sink, but no mirror. Where do I shower, I asked. She motioned outside with her head. Where do I find the toilet? She made the same motion. It's cold in here. She pointed to a space heater the size of squirrel. I saw that there was a good three inches between the bottom of the door and the concrete floor. I'll catch my death of cold in here, I said. She shrugged her shoulders. She said I could take breakfast in the kitchen but not in the dining room. She told me no visitors and no Africans—as though the two were somehow irreconcilable. She placed the key on the chair. She left.

I could not stop my body from shaking as I sat on the bed. I was convulsing as the terror and loneliness welled inside me. I threw myself on the bed and buried my face in the pillow and cried like I'd never cried before.

After a while the crying stopped. I went over to the sink and washed my face. I looked at my watch. It was almost midnight. *They're lucky that shit ended when it did. I was about to serve those two muthafuckas. Don't get me started. I will HURT somebody up in here! Talk about judgment at Nuremberg. Better thank your Nazi-ass mama she called it off when she did.* I lay back down on the bed and began crying all over again. *You should get some sleep. I can sleep when I'm dead. I'm here to research a novel. I'm a BLACK MAN, okay? Can you get that through your fucking head? Can't nothing faze you, alright. Not two punk ass muthafuckas like that. Hell, no. Hell—fucking—no! They almost got served...I swear to god! Shit, I don't know karate, but I do know ca-razy. I will act a fool up in here, okay? Don't get me started.* I drew my sleeve across my snotty nose. *How the hell does one research a novel? What the hell am I going to tell the Jerome Foundation? I don't know where I'm at or what I'm doing. It's cold as hell. You need something to eat. Like where, it's almost midnight. Why did Montshiwa leave me hanging? Get the street map, man. Get your jacket. Let's go. Let's walk. Let's hat the fuck up.*

For a good thirty minutes I walked in one direction, downhill; downhill from Hillbrow-Berea. I found myself on what I would learn was the underside of downtown Jo'burg. I passed by a mosque. To my surprise, many people were in the streets. Africans, Coloureds, and Indians; very few Whites. *So this area must be 'multiracial.'* But where were they going and where had they come from and what were they doing out so late? I dared not stop someone and ask them. *But that's what a researcher does, fool; he talks to people.* But I'd forgotten what I was supposed to be researching or what my book was to be about. I minnowed past the people on my way to god knows where, and wave upon wave, they swept over me on their way to the very same place.

I was standing on a corner gaping vaguely at the sights, listening to the sounds without knowing what I was hearing, crossing the street without waiting for the light, when a car ran over my foot. A tiny Japanese car, but a car nonetheless, and there were people in it. It cut so close to me that had I been one inch further into the street it would have dismembered my knee. I screamed in agony. As the wheel spun up my arch and over my toes I was so close to the passenger I could kiss him or reach out to hold him. I took his face into my pain.

Groaning, I sat on the curb clutching my sides. It did not occur to me to draw my leg back on the curb, lest another car come along and amputate it. I was in such a state of shock that I could not take my shoe off and look at the damage. *He was laughing at me. That face in the car was laughing at me.* No one paid me much mind. I took my shoe off. They were hiking boots with reinforced toes and a hard exterior. That's the only thing that saved me. Nothing broken, I told myself. (Years later, I was to learn that bones had indeed been fractured.) I pulled myself up a light pole. I braced myself against the pole and put pressure on it. The pain was still there, but it was bearable. I tried to stand on my own. Yes, I could do that. I walked. Yes, I could walk. And then, a sharp pain shot up my right side to my hip and I had to brace myself against a lamppost again. I was next to a *Bimbos* fast-food joint. *What a name. Why not just call it Burger King?* I went inside and, finding they did not cater to vegetarians, ordered a hamburger with everything on it. Nothing before and nothing since has ever tasted better to me than that food drenched in trans fats.

This was no window-order Burger King. They had table service with waiters, Black. They had cleaners, Black. They had a kitchen crew, Black.

And they had a manager, White. I looked up to get the waiter's attention, only to find that he was standing at the counter with the cleaners
and the kitchen crew. They were all staring at me. They were all smiling
at me. I looked down and took another bite. As I chewed I looked only
at my plate. A few minutes later I looked up and they were still there.
Staring. Smiling. *What's up with this?* I smiled back and motioned for the
waiter to come over.

"Hi, um, I'd like the bill please. I think I should pay."

"Yes, master," he smiled.

"I beg your pardon."

"You want to pay, master, is that it?"

I leaned closer to him. He leaned closer to me. "I don't think you
should call me 'master.'"

"Yes, master, I'll tell the master you want to pay."

"No, I'm serious, that master thing, man, that's not cool. That's some
old plantation shit—well…anyway, look why don't I just pay you and you
bring me change for the tip."

"No, master," he lurched back.

"No?"

"Don't give me the money; I'll call the master for the money,
master."

"Ain't you the waiter?"

"One moment, master." He started to leave, then he turned back and
said, "May I ask master a question?"

"Man, look, cut that master shi—look, ask me, man, but don't call me
master."

"Are you from America or Great Britain, ma—"

"America."

"Heyta!" He clapped his hands and bounced back over to the lunch
counter. "Heyta, *m'china!*" I heard him shout to one of the kitchen crew,
"I told you m'china, the gent's from America! Great Britain—*voetsek,*
man! That's a *real* Black American in my section."

A short, obsequious White man with mean eyes came over to my table
and took my money. He told me he ran an international restaurant and he

was always pleased to see foreigners. I almost said, So, you are multiracial. But my foot was hurting and I needed to leave. I told him to bring me some change for the tip. Tip? he said, as though he'd never heard the word before. Yeah, tip, for the waiter. Ohhh, he said, you can give it to me; I'll see that he gets it. No, I'll give it to him. He looked over at the counter of onlookers. They don't handle money, he confided, I must handle money. Forget it, I said. I decided to stay until this little man went in the back again and then pay the waiter myself. I began to read the newspaper. There was no activity too minuscule—whether sipping my water, or turning a page of the newspaper—for the attention of my onlookers. I felt like an anthropology specimen.

Two young White women came over from a nearby table and (after they were seated) asked if they could join me. At first the Black men around the counter were startled, but after a moment it seemed to all make sense to them and they nodded and whispered approvingly to each other, and gave me even more of the total attention they'd been giving me all along. Great, I thought, just great.

"Are you from America?" the older and more vivacious of the two asked me.

"No, I'm from Transylvania, I just say I'm from America because I don't like to brag."

It took them a moment, but they got it, and they laughed. "Oh, you're very funny. Are you always this funny?"

"Always."

"May I see your palm?" said the one who appeared to be several years older.

She drew her index finger back and forth across my palm and I felt myself becoming aroused. "You have a long lifeline," she said. "And you've come from far away."

"New York. What are you a palm reader?"

"You are fiercely independent."

I repossessed my wrist and told them I needed to go. They told me that they had chosen me. That there were things they wanted to discuss with me. I was attracted to and aroused by the woman who'd held my hand and besides, where else did I have to go, back to Gestapo headquarters?

"So, where we going for this interview?"

"Our apartment."

"Your crib, eh."

"We don't own a crib, why would you want one, do you have a child?"

"No, it's...look, what kind of questions? I mean what's this all about?"

"We're with the Church of Scientology."

"L. Ron Hubbard!" I leapt to my feet.

"You know him?"

"Of course he knows him," said the younger and taciturn woman, "he's from the States."

"I'm not interested."

"Why not? Have you been to any of his meetings?"

"Look, a car ran over my foot and I've got to go."

"A car ran over your foot? We must bring you to a doctor."

"No!... I mean, I don't want a doctor. Not in this country."

"We have good doctors here."

I made a beeline for the door. I don't remember if I tipped the waiter or not. I stumbled back into the night. I walked: walking into the pain of my foot; walking through the pain of my foot. I walked for two hours at least, across the southern edge of downtown Jo'burg, up the western avenues, north then east along Jan Smuts Avenue until I'd come full circle back to Eva Braun's bunker; back to my new "home."

—∿—

I woke up around noon. The shower was outside, with a three-quarters wooden door across it. The warm water did not go the distance. The haus frau let me have some cold cereal as long as I ate it in the kitchen. There was a young Coloured boy, perhaps he was sixteen or seventeen, in the kitchen. I learned he was staying in the stall (or room) next to mine. He was from Swaziland and had actually come to South Africa for a "better" high school education. A private school, he said, for Indians and Coloureds. She got on well with him; they spoke to each other in Afrikaans. He was too obsequious for me.

She told me there had been a call for me. That's impossible, I thought, I don't know anyone here — not anyone who has this number. An African, she said, an African girl. I'll not have any Africans in my house. You'll be out without a refund. More puzzled than angry, I went to the hallway and dialed the number. It was Grace from the night before; Grace from the bus to town.

Grace told me to meet her in Hillbrow if I wanted to see a very nice part of Johannesburg. *Why not, it beats the Church of Scientology.*

I walked the five or six blocks through Berea to Hillbrow. I was famished. The milk and cereal had not exactly hit the spot. I sat down at a sidewalk café and felt a sense of hope, even joy, rise up from deep within me when the young White woman waiting on me did *not* say that they were not multiracial or that I was too late for toast and eggs. While my breakfast was being prepared I walked across the street to a news kiosk and bought the *Mail & Guardian,* the Johannesburg *Star,* and the *International Herald Tribune.* I crossed the street and took my seat by the sidewalk. It was a lovely day. *Everything's gonna be all right today. I can feel it.* Though it was winter I basked in the warm noon sun, sipping coffee, reading my papers, while awaiting my food in the sweet spot of the day.

Then the sirens came. Loud swirling sounds lancing the air, approaching from all directions. I began to sweat. I grew panicky. But the young waitress was beside me with my food. Stay seated, she whispered, and be calm. She placed her hand on my shoulder. Pretend nothing's happening, she said, eat your food. Relax.

Blue squad cars and yellow casspirs pulled up to the curb no more than ten feet away from my table. The same such vehicles had stopped at the opposite end of the block. White and Black policemen scurried out of their bellies like roaches. They swooped down on Black and Coloured men who, as far as I could tell, were simply walking or idling on either side of the street. Some slipped through the dragnet. Others were thrown up against the nearest wall, frisked, relieved of their identity documents. Some were detained. Some were released. Many were herded into the casspirs. It was like a dream that I was in but was not part of. Everything was so real and so close. Yet everything was so unreal, so cinematic, and so far away. I was a spectator and they, the police and their detainees, were simply figures on the screen. There seemed to be no plan or pattern to the whole affair. And it was over as quickly as it had begun.

"It's a good thing you were seated," she said, "they won't arrest you when you're seated and having breakfast. It's a state of emergency, you know. Lucky for you, you were seated. You should wait until all the fuss is over before you leave. Would you like more coffee?"

"Coffee? Yes...please."

"Are you an American?"

"Yes," I said, hopelessly, "I'm an American."

"I would love to visit America one day."

"I know."

"How did you know!" she said elatedly.

"I just knew."

Grace and Emily were two Motswana sisters ten years younger than me. The home they took me to was in Auckland Park, a suburb on Jo'burg's western perimeter, just west of Braamfontein where the University of the Witwatersrand is located. The kombi let us off at a regular stop and we walked several blocks to our destination. Grace asked me if I had ever seen houses like these. I said yes, adding they were modest compared to the homes in Kenwood where I grew up. The two sisters took this not as a form of boasting but as an out and out lie.

When we came to the house, I saw two White women wave from the bay window of the living room and I started up the long walk toward the front door. "Where are you going?" Grace cried. Her sister clenched a fist full of sweater along my spine and pulled me back. There'd been no time to argue with them, and besides, I didn't know what to say. But by the time we reached the back of the house I was livid.

The two women from the living room materialized at the kitchen door. Emily was quiet and Grace was a bit too deferential for my tastes as she chatted with the woman whose house it was. It was as though I was witnessing my mother or my father in Louisiana, ten or fifteen years before my birth. On our journey, Grace and Emily had been having the most animated and uninhibited conversation; suddenly, having reached our destination, they had taken on new, unrehearsed but uniformly subordinate, demeanors.

From a small hut at the end of the backyard an old woman emerged. She stared at me blankly until Emily began to speak to her in Setswana. Several years later I was to learn what was said: I was, she said, a Black American whom her sister Grace had met at the airport last night while seeing a friend off to study in London. Emily told her that it was my first time in South Africa and I was so nervous that I was prone to telling lies, such as I lived in a triple-story mansion in America. The old woman had told her niece that I looked a little stupid. Was I dull in the head or just using my mouth to catch flies? Emily assured her aunt that I would be alright after a few days, and that I was intending to marry Grace and take her to America. At this the old woman smiled at me and continued smiling for the better part of the visit. At the time, all of this was lost on me for Emily did not, of course, translate this for the benefit of Samantha, the woman whose house this was, nor for me.

Samantha and her friend Margaret placed three stools in the middle of the sun-tortured driveway and beckoned us to sit. This pushed the mercury of my anger even higher. Then they gave Grace, Emily, and me each a glass of translucent tap water while the two of them sat shaded beneath the awning of the back door and drank ice-cold Cokes. Samantha had bought a whole new wardrobe, for tomorrow she was leaving "this wretched place" and immigrating to Houston, Texas, where her husband had been accepted into medical school. Grace and Emily were there to pick through her old clothes. After a while my silence became an item of concern and Samantha, in lieu of speaking directly to me, chided Grace for being too rude to introduce her "new beau." Say what! I thought.

I offered my hand to them, coolly. She asked me to say something, anything, just say something again. I did. And now she chided Grace more vigorously than before, this time for not informing her that I was an American. Offering me Coke and ice and trying to tug the tap water from my hand, she apologized to me with more contrition than a lapsed Catholic. "We're drinking tap water," I said holding the glass firmly. This, my first gesture of political solidarity on South African soil, was lost on just about everyone including—especially—the African women. Neither Grace nor Emily nor their aunt seemed to appreciate my refusal of Coca-Cola when one was on offer.

Margaret stared at me with the glow of someone meeting Denzel Washington for the first time, while Samantha hollered at the top of her lungs for her husband and Margaret's husband to "Come, now! Now! I say, come meet our American friend!" The joy of Grace and Emily's aunt, having registered Samantha's, swelled to cosmic proportions.

Two men appeared at the kitchen window. They looked out and saw three stools, three tap waters, and three bloody kaffirs. They gave their wives that *you-two-been-drinking?* look and disappeared.

"Men are so ignorant," Margaret said.

Samantha riddled me with hundreds of questions about the States. Never in my life have I been as monosyllabic as I was with her. Grace and Emily gave me the evil eye. The evil eye, I thought, now there's something that didn't get lost in the Middle Passage. *They want me to stop acting a fool; to stop before Samantha and Margaret catch on that I'm not shy but arrogant.* I was all set to refuse the sisters' evil eye and Samantha's questions when I was seized by a most delicious idea.

When I was eleven, I stole my mother's copy of Truman Capote's *In Cold Blood* from her library. For four nights I read it under the covers with a flashlight. Each night I wet the bed. The book was so terrifying I vowed to give up reading completely, lest I find myself forced to leave the light on at night for the next twenty-five years. The vow lasted only a month, books were my life; but the images of what happened in that Kansas farmhouse never left my mind. *If it worked for me, it should work for Samantha.*

"Where did you say you were moving to, Dallas?"

"No, I said Houston. Houston, Texas. My husband's going to study there."

"You mean at the university?"

"Yes, you know it?"

"Well, not exactly...but...never mind."

"What is it?"

"I shouldn't alarm you. After all I'm from Minneapolis. It might not even be true."

"What might not be true?"

"Listen, Sam, may I call you Sam? Sam, look, forget it. Really. When you get there you should check with the local police, let them tell you. On second thought, they can't be trusted."

"You mean they're like our police?" Margaret asked.

"Can't be trusted how?" Samantha said, growing frustrated.

"They just want your money," I said, "that's all. Foreign trade. They're on the mayor's payroll. What can you expect? On top of that they want to hide their incompetence. After two years, you'd think they'd have caught the bastard. But noooo. My guess is, you and your husband ask them and they'll stonewall you. We call it covering your ass where I come from. Plain and simple, covering your ass. The cops won't say a word."

"A word about what?"

I lowered my eyes. I looked at my hands. I thought any minute I'd guffaw and blow it, but I held my nerve. I made Samantha promise me that if I told her she wouldn't hold the telling of this information against me; that it would be unethical on her part to want to kill the messenger. She agreed before I finished asking her. Very well, I said, I'll tell you. And with that I launched into the most stimulating recapitulation of *In Cold Blood* imaginable. I tailored the narrative to fit the needs of her imagination. For example, the killers were not operating in the 1950s but in 1989, not in Kansas but in Houston, and not only had they *not* been apprehended and executed but they were very much at large, due to a royal *kaak up* by the Houston police. Then, pushing the whole thing further over the top than I'd ever intended, I told them that the m.o.— *modus operandi*—of these serial killers showed a jingoistic, even rabid, predilection for foreigners. That's why so many of the murders had occurred in the vicinity of the university's International House.

"And that's why the damn cops can cover the whole thing up. If they were killing Americans you would have heard about it on the news. I'm sorry to be the one to tell you. Maybe you should change your accent on the plane, or try not to speak to anyone until you get the lay of the land. Or just stay inside."

When we left, Margaret, who heretofore had been green with envy over Samantha's ticket to paradise, was emboldened enough to actually console Samantha and promise to come and visit and check in on her (here the sincerity in her voice trailed off).

Grace and Emily were pensive riding back in the kombi. It never occurred to me that that they actually believed that whopper.

Then Emily said, "Shame, what if we never see Samantha again?"

I thought they would appreciate the joke but when I told them it was all an elaborate form of retaliation they soured on me. I told them that Black folks in America pull that kind of shit on White folks all the time.

"It takes different forms, I'll admit. Break the Xerox machine, steal some supplies, give 'em southbound directions on a one-way street going north. But we manage to get our licks in."

You have too little *ubuntu*, they told me.

"And you have too much," I replied.

"All this because they made you go to the back and drink tap water?"

"Because she's who she is, where she is, when she is."

"I suppose you visit Boers all the time where you come from," Emily said.

"Whenever I feel like it."

"Don't you remember, Emily," Grace said, "his father's house is larger than a Boer's."

"How could I forget?" And they laughed.

The other passengers in the kombi had taken little notice of our conversation. But when Emily said, "I suppose you walk right up to a Boer's front door, ring the bell, go into the living room, and start drinking tea?" I felt everyone's eyes on me. I could see the driver looking at me in his rearview mirror.

"He even sleeps in the White woman's bed if he wants to." Now one of the passengers chuckled. In the rearview mirror the eyes of the driver were also laughing.

"Damn skippy, I do. I do or else."

"Or else what?"

"Or else I blow the muthafucka up!"

Someone in the kombi let out a soft cry. People muttered to each other. The driver's eyes flashed in the mirror. He screeched over to the curb. "Hey, m'china, out!" He came around to the side. He slid the door open and gesticulated wildly. "Out! Out of my taxi. I'm a businessman, you hear me? I'm no Umkhonto! I'm no Inkhata! I'm no *tsotsi!* Nothing like that, m'china. I'm a businessman. Out, *m'china!*" I'd completely forgotten that in the past week three bombs had gone off in Jo'burg and the surrounding area. Under the circumstances, my rhetorical flourish was not appreciated as a rhetorical flourish. He'd hear no explanations. He told the two sisters they could ride on without me and, for a moment, they seemed to consider it.

The three of us left his taxi and walked two miles to Newtown where a flea market was in full bloom outside the famous Market Theatre. Indian cloth vendors had come from as nearby as Mayfair, that part of Jo'burg where they'd been allowed to live under the Group Areas Act. There were tables of woven baskets from the "homeland" of Venda. Shona craftsmen had brought their soft stone sculptures from as far away as Harare.

As Grace, Emily, and I descended down the slope into the market, I noticed four beautiful young women moving from table to table together. One of them wore a bright yellow dress and a maroon sweater draped around her shoulders. I found myself drifting ahead of Grace and Emily. I was headed straight for her. Her cheekbones were high and when she smiled she dimpled. I was excited by the way she held the soft stone sculptures in her knowing hands and wanted those hands to hold me that same way; how she laughed and shook her head at the artist whose opening bid must have been too high for her.

Tell her you're an American. They all seem to like that. Then what? Then feign vulnerability. Remember, Grace said I needed someone to take care of me. Maybe she wants to take care of me. Something simple like, hey, baby, can you help me with the metric system, or the exchange rate, or help me bargain for this piece of art work that I'm planning to buy for your foxy self. Yeah, that oughta get it. Well...don't say, "baby" and not "foxy" she might not dig that. Anyway, can you help me... that I'm lost and alone persona. Right. Okay. Show time!

As I drew within ten feet of her she turned and smiled at me. *Well, goddamn, I ain't said word one and she's already hot for me. Shit, I'm the MAC in macaroni.* Then she waved. *We ain't even gonna need a rap. Don't wave back, just smile, that's right play it cool.* Then she began to walk toward me. As we met I managed to get the first croak, though not necessarily the first syllable, out of the word "so" which was to be coupled with the query "what's happening"—but she walked right past me.

I turned to find her kissing first Grace and then Emily. Her three friends followed her and greeted Grace and Emily similarly. Now, I found myself on the periphery of six Motswana women speaking gaily to each other in their language, aware only vaguely of my presence if aware of my presence at all. I cleared my throat, prompting Grace to tell me how sorry she was for ignoring me, but she hadn't seen these women in ages. They'd all been at university together in the "homeland" of Bophuthatswana. But these four had come to Jo'burg to study law and that was the last she'd seen of them. This is Ntombi. This is Gladys. This is Naledi. And this is Khanya.

"Khanya," I said, stepping forward, "what a lovely name," and taking her hand. "My name is Frank. Like, I'm from New York," Grace and Emily shot me a look, "by way of Minneapolis."

I was suddenly aware of my foot and its searing pain.

CIVIL RIGHTS

Mother never spoke of slavery
she was born and raised in a debutante ball
but when they killed King she wrote every blue
hair blonde eye a letter

like any spring of no reply winter
was late in leaving and we were her
only postage
my sister and I walking end to end

through the seep of slush and the push
of wind
no one dabbed a crystalled eye for
she would have no crying

MINNEAPOLIS: 1964

When I was eight my mother embarrassed me by coaxing my father from the religious depths of a bag of potato chips and a cold-stunted tumbler of whiskey—the Body of Christ, the Blood of Christ, existential morsels savored each night at High Mass, the Johnny Carson Show. She called him to the kitchen for what had become a weekly ritual since the day we broke the housing barrier in the all White enclave of Kenwood.

"Frank, come into the kitchen!"

A rabbit's foot thumped against my lung as I sat on a stool before her and imagined my father in the living room groaning on bended knee like a bishop breaking genuflection. Shortly after the sandpaper growl of his slippers on linoleum, he appeared, tall, gaunt, bleary-eyed and whiskered beneath the kitchen's white trumpets of neon.

"It's time to cut the boy's hair. You should have done it hours ago. He's reciting "Gunga Din" tomorrow in the talent show, or have you forgotten?" She looked at his eyes. He turned away. If not for the exigencies of keeping me still on the stool, holding me down as the hum of clippers dive-bombed for me like a river of bees, she would have added, "And don't ask for my liver when liquor pickles yours." Instead she reminded him of more pressing matters. "We don't need these people to think we're raising a long-haired militant."

My father was quiet during these proceedings unless I squirmed or cried out. Then he'd whack me several times across my thigh with the comb and whack me again if I whimpered. How could he hear Johnny Carson in the living room if I was crying? The razor dragged swiftly and painfully over my scalp like the blade, now the back of a shovel digging through gravel. By the end, I was tired and in tears.

"Now don't we look like the moon?" mom laughed. "Needs a touch of shine." She rubbed baby oil all over my scalp, forehead and face, stood back and winced, put her hand to her forehead like a visor, "Oh no! The glare is too much for me. Off to bed before you blind me."

Teary-eyed and vengeful I climbed the back stairs on my way to bed. The front stairs, soft and bouncy with two layers of wine-and-revolver red carpet and the balustrade of mahogany gleaming obsidian over white hand-carved balusters, were not to be used by my two younger sisters and I, just as the "antique" chairs in the living room were not for us to sit on. The front part of the house, kept spotless, was for company whenever company came or for show during the long dry seasons when they didn't come or to remind us that indeed they were coming; that "company," our buzz-word for White people, had, at that very moment, packed their bags and taken the high road to hobnob with mom and dad.

"Remember your lines?" she asked marching halfway up the stairs behind me, "Or should we go over them one more time?"

Her words barely registered. I was a million miles away at a gun store, fondling a pistol, counting the bullets I would pump into her chest.

"I know you hear me talkin' to you, boy." Her New Orleans drawl was upon me, a bad sign indeed, a portent of the yardstick, the strap, the shoe, the hand, or whatever's handy, prophecy on the wings of dialect. One day I'm riding into town with my posse, mother, gonna deputize all my friends, gonna hang you from the highest tree. Then it struck me that I had no friends. The whole school, every student save my sister Fawn and I, was White. They could hardly be called my friends. By third grade, the year in which they shook themselves of the notion that my black skin was a new form of leprosy, they'd begun to warm to me the way one warms to furry, but caged, zoo creatures. Not with the most elastic stretch of the imagination could I call them friends. My posse vaporized on the high chaparral.

"I said ah know you hear me talkin' to you!"

"No, I don't need to recite the poem again," I sniffled.

"No, who?"

"No, mom."

It is a curious twist in the Black male psyche, or the way this gender is socialized, that I did not have nearly as much rage toward my father as I did toward my mother in those early days of traveling incognegro. Even now it's hard for me to unravel skein upon skein of memory and understand why. All I can do is take the plunge and write it all down. Mom was a rage-junkie. Dad was a somnambulant dragon who could slash and quarter me with his tail as his eyes rolled the sea of a drunken stupor. I never knew what infraction, however small, would incur his fire-breathing wrath. Sometimes a smart remark would send me hurtling before him down the basement stairs to a whipping in the woodshed; sometimes it would conjure no more than a sullen look. Unlike mom, who criticized every third move I ever made and thus unfurled the text of what was and was not permissible: daily, hourly, minute-ly: So it came as no surprise when, three years later at the age of ten, she slapped me then flogged my head and shoulders. In response to one of her tedious monologues on how hard she worked to put clothes on my back and food on the table, I had looked up from my scrumptious bowl of Cheerios, bored and disinterested, and replied, "What can I say, Ida-Lorraine, that's your job."

On the morning of the talent show, I was nauseous. Each spoonful of oatmeal had a life of its own, wanting to come up. For a kid who normally yakked to the point of driving people from a room, I was remarkably quiet. At eight, memorizing "Gunga Din" was not my idea of a good time. The thought of reciting it to the whole school was even less appealing.

Two years back, in 1962, the people of Kenwood had humiliated mom and dad: five hundred households, not families, but households, in the posh enclave on the hill overlooking downtown Minneapolis, had signed a petition to keep us out. The man who owned the house was selling it for the going rate of thirty-five thousand dollars. The problem was simple, he'd love to sell it to us—he was moving to Seattle—but "you do realize, don't you, that I'll have a black mark against me forever, that I can never come back to Kenwood, they'll turn a cold shoulder to me. You do realize that don't you? However, if you can get a loan we'll see what we can do."

In the end, we moved into the white stucco mansion on the hill, not with a bank loan, but with every cent of our insurance policy. My father cashed it in and made a heretofore unheard of down payment of fifty percent. For the other half, he and the owner came to terms on a note. How long did we go without insurance? The rest of first grade? Part of second grade—third grade? I don't know. But I need no help recalling the symptoms of being uninsured in a place where you're not wanted. Dad sunk deeper into drink. Mom blitzkrieged antique shops, buying Greco-Latin statues; a small fountain (boy on a dolphin: dolphin spitting water); and antique furniture that she drew tape across, arm-to-arm, in case one of us kids wasn't wrapped too tight and got a notion that the living room was a place for us to sit down in. The walls were re-papered with eighteenth-century landscapes replete with the landed gentry striking poses like bargains. She was waiting for the day when the neighbors would finally creep through our front door to see what they could see. She set up this grand display of culture with the cheery enthusiasm of Charlie the Tuna; at all costs she would prove Starkist wrong with her desperate rebuttal to the tag line, "Sorry Charlie, Starkist doesn't want tuna with good taste, Starkist wants tuna that tastes good." And I was scalped on a weekly basis and made to memorize long classic poems, the longer the better, and to recite them at the end of each month when all I really wanted was to eat tutti-frutti ice cream, sing a Chubby Checkers song, and do the Twist.

It was then, somewhere between January of '63 and the late autumn of Jack Kennedy's death that same year, that my parents decided that to keep the teachers from treating me the way my classmates treated me (the girls wouldn't touch me, the boys called me "nigger" and gave me "snuggies"—two boys hold you down while one boy pulls the back of your drawers high up your back, thus crushing your testicles against your pelvis, while still another boy mashes your face into the snow) was to insure that I was more verbal than anyone else. Verbal people, they surmised, are intelligent people; and intelligent people are well liked. It was B. F. Skinner's S-R psychology taken to a whole new level. "Verbal" was the stimulus, "well-liked" was the response. Needless to say they were both clinical psychologists.

"The oatmeal makes me sick," I told her.

"Same oatmeal you had yesterday." She pushed the bowl back in front of me.

"Mom, do I have to? I feel sick."

"It's thirty below outside. Oatmeal sticks to your ribs."

Dad stopped on his way out the door. "If you're sick, go to sickbay," he bellowed, "Don't droop in front of everyone at the kitchen table."

"Can't go to sickbay today," mom said, "he's reciting Gunga Din in the talent show." Then she looked at my bald head and laughed, "My, my, the moon in the morning."

C'mon posse! Ride into town. Dig in those spurs. We got us a live one here.

Four hours later, on knees of rubber, I took the stage. The hush in the auditorium made me seasick. My head was empty. I forgot why I was up there. The lights, a sharp stab of glare, dug into my eyes. I started to leave when I caught another glare, the glare of mom's eyes from the back of the auditorium. It jogged my memory.

"My name is Frank B. Wilderson, the third. I'm in third grade, Miss Johnson's class, PT [portable classroom] number two. I'm going to recite 'Gunga Din,' by Kipling." Again, mom's sharp swift glare. I corrected myself. "By Rudyard Kipling. A turn of the...turn of the..." I forgot; and then remembered. "A turn of the century British writer."

> You may talk o' gin and beer
> When you're quartered safe out 'ere,
> An' you're sent to penny-fights an' Aldershot it;
> But when it comes to slaughter

You will do your work on water,

An' you'll lick the bloomin' boots of 'im that's got it.

Now in Injia's sunny clime,

Where I used to spend my time

A-servin' of 'Er Majesty the Queen,

Of all them blackfaced crew

I was dumbstruck; blank again. I had said, "Of all them blackfaced crew" at least three times. I caught mom's eyes. She shifted nervously in her chair, and looked around to see who, if anyone, was looking at her. We were both naked. The murmuring in the auditorium brought me back. I remembered the next line and clothed us. I pushed on.

Of all them blackfaced crew

The finest man I knew

Was our regimental bhisti, Gunga Din.

He was "Din! Din! Din!

You limpin' lump o' brick-dust, Gunga Din!

Hi! slippery hitherao!

Water, get it! Panee lao!

You squidgy-nosed old idol, Gunga Din.

…

'E would dot an' carry one

Till the longest day was done;

An' 'e didn't seem to know the use o' fear.

If we charged or broke or cut,

You could bet your bloomin' nut,

'E'd be waitin' fifty paces right flank rear.

The recitation went well from that point on, although I spoke a little too swiftly, if memory serves me well. But it may have been because each pause caused the din of silence to roar in my ears and I had to avoid the silent spaces at all costs. Then another line seized me by the throat.

An' for all 'is dirty 'ide
'E was white, clear white, inside

Again, I stopped. I'd done my best, there was no way I could remember the ending. All it took was one half-step toward stage left for me to visualize the beating I would get for giving up. My posse rode into town with the poem's ending in their saddlebags.

An' for all 'is dirty 'ide
'E was white, clear white, inside
When 'e went to tend the wounded under fire...
...
Din! Din! Din!
You Lazarushian-leather Gunga Din!
Though I've belted you and flayed you,
By the livin' Gawd that made you,
You're a better man than I am, Gunga Din!

The applause was deafening. I had no idea for whom. When I reached the back of the room, not so much as a hug, nor the promise of a tutti-frutti ice cream cone.

"That was good," she said, "but why did you stop so many times?"

—⁓—

After a snowstorm, if there is no wind, the drifts peak high as ocean breakers. And when the shovels are laid to rest, white walls of snow, tall as a twelve-year-old, line the sidewalks. If you're seven or eight, there's no seeing over them. Only your memory can guide you through the white labyrinth to school. More often than not I was late. Being late through the labyrinth meant staying after and writing on the blackboard "I will not be late for school" over and over and over again. Sometimes, I had the option of writing one long paragraph beginning with "The most important thing I learned today was..." But I had no way of knowing what the most important thing was and because I was Roman Catholic and did not want to lie—not because lying was disdainful to me, but because the confessional smelled of dust and decay—I chose line after line of *I will not be late.*

I used to watch my parents to the near exclusion of all others, as though if I ever stopped watching them they would disappear. I watched them so intensely that I could even see them when they were not there. As though I was a movie camera, I followed my mother down the hall to her room to the books she had put aside after her master's to raise her children; I followed my father into the very seminar rooms at the university where he taught. My imagination was so accurate I could sit in my room and see my father miles away in his classroom. A tall black frame lecturing twenty fair-haired corn-fed kids. Only a few are truly attentive, the rest are in disbelief of his presence—it hadn't said "Negro" in the course catalogue. Whoever heard of a Black psychologist?

He is dressed in dark English tweeds which would make him a caricature of an Eastern seaboard professor if not for his piercing eyes, made all the more dramatic by a cleft where his nose meets his forehead, and a beard; in fact, his face has all the strength and sorrow of Frederick Douglas, but his voice has none of the resolve. He is explaining competing theories of child development using Jung's epistemological break with Freud as an example. He struggles to remain dignified, to keep those elements of his Louisiana tone from invading his diction. This will be on the exam, he tells them. They are not taking notes. Who does this nigger think he is? In the deafening silence the hiss of steam from the radiator precipitates a whistle on a train he wishes he could board to leave this wretched place. Outside the classroom's large window snow falls thickly, like the wings of moths. Class ends. He leaves before they do; though not in a huff and certainly not in a hurry; he is simply the first one out the door. He sifts through the crowds of students pouring out from the classrooms. Now, up the stairs. Now, down a deserted hallway. He struggles with the lock to the door of his office. Once inside he lifts the shade rather than turn on the desk lamp which leaves the room swathed in the dim winter light of late afternoon. On his desk is the

Minneapolis Tribune. Half the front page is taken up with a photograph of US destroyers on their way to blockade the island of Cuba. The paper is two years old. He has no idea why he's kept it so long. He covers the page with his briefcase from which he draws a bottle of Jack Daniel's. He wipes the inside of his coffee mug with his index finger and pours himself a stiff one. His hand is less than steady. He sips, sighs deeply, and relaxes. The pained look is gone from his face. He moves to the window to look at the drifts that line the university's sidewalks and windowsills like a child who is seeing snow for the first time.

At home, the boy who thinks he's a camera is sitting at his desk in a large furnished bedroom with a globe and small record player. The bookshelf next to his desk is lined with Dickens, Stevenson, Poe, Brontë, and Verne. The room is as dark as his father's office, but the study lamp is on over the book he is reading. Someone is playing a muffled, unrecognizable piano concerto somewhere in the house. Like his father he goes to the window to look at the snow that has collected in drifts. From his window he sees the mansions of Kenwood. The architecture is eclectic: here Victorian, there old Tudor, at the end of the road a sprawling single-story house which bears the signature of Franklin Lloyd Wright. The street is lined with elm trees, tall and gray; long swaths of snow cling to their leafless branches like cotton wool on the limbs of skeletons. From either side of the street the trees reach out and touch each other, their branches meeting above the road. A Rolls Royce pulls into the winding drive of the Franklin Lloyd Wright dwelling and a chauffeur helps a slim-silver haired woman out of the backseat. As he hoists himself upon the sill to get a better look, the boy lets the book drop from his hand. He stares at the woman for several seconds, but his gaze is broken by a sudden increase in the sound of the piano. His mother enters on the peculiar F sharps and B flats of a Béla Bartók composition.

Ida-Lorraine Wilderson is a New Orleans Creole (at least her husband once said so) with pointed features and "manageable" hair. Her only regret is that she was only able to pass her physical traits on to her daughter and not to her son as well. The boy is as dark as his father and has lips that seem to get fuller as he gets older and a nose which she hopes will not have what she calls the drunken thickness of Indians, the nose of her husband's grandmother who was a Native American. For these reasons the boy is in his room memorizing Edgar Allen Poe and the girl is downstairs practicing Bartók.

"I haven't heard you in quite a while."

"No one else at school has to memorize poems. They do the Twist."

"They'll grow up casual, with no sense of mission. They can afford to."

"What's a mission?"

"What stanza are you on?"

She won't leave until he's back at his desk.

> I was a child and she was a child,
> In this kingdom by the sea;

The sound of his recitation and the faint sharps and flats of her daughter practicing the piano below follow her as she mounts the creaking wooden stairs of a shoulder-width stairway to the attic.

> But we loved with a love that was more than love—
> I and my Annabel Lee;

She enters her husband's study in the attic. On one side of the desk is a photo of her in cap and gown, on the other side is the cap and gown photo of her husband. He is smiling without inhibition, so broadly that she hardly recognizes him. She picks it up and tries to remember, but the time of his happiness is as elusive as what she came here in search of. She decides to give up, when she has a notion. She pulls the large swivel chair from beneath the desk and discovers an empty bottle of Jack Daniel's on the seat.

As she walks down the narrow attic stairs, bending her head to keep from grazing the ceiling, the music and the poem grow louder. She emerges in the kitchen where her mother-in-law sits at the kitchen table reading the newspaper. She walks to the counter and pours herself a cup of coffee, barely glancing at her mother-in-law.

"Can't you speak?" asks her mother-in-law.

"Can't you?"

The music from the living room has stopped but neither woman seems to have noticed.

"If my son were here you wouldn't disrespect me."

"I'm a proxy for you both."

"Don't use that high tone talk with me, gal. Say what you mean."

"Your son gives me...lessons, when it's you he really wants to school. He married me because he couldn't marry you. Is that too high tone for you?"

They turn to find the little girl, standing in the doorway.

Dr. Wilderson drives slowly over the snow-dusted avenues of Kenwood. His car is a shiny black Dodge with fins protruding from the back like the Batmobile of his son's comic books. He takes note of the Rolls Royce parked majestically in front of the low, long house on Mount Curve. Two men on the radio are discussing the legacy of the president who was laid to rest a year ago, the missile crisis on the island of Cuba, and the weekend Marilyn Monroe may or may not have spent at the White House. Then one of them says, "We've got our own missile crisis right here in town." He explains how a family of Negroes has block-busted the historic Kenwood neighborhood. A plot, he wonders, to bring down property values? His co-host asks if Communists have put the Negro family up to this.

I see my father. I see his hand squeezing the life out of the steering wheel. I see his fingers snap the dial of the radio. I hear the silence of the car and the tires gnashing slush.

In the antechamber he stamps his feet and removes his galoshes. He enters another door and finds himself in a huge front hall beneath the hand-carved balustrade of the front stairs and a chandelier on the ceiling two stories above. He opens a slice of the wall beneath the stairs—a hidden closet—hangs up his overcoat and scarf. He moves into the living room. His daughter is placing sheet music inside the piano seat. She closes the lid of the piano.

"I practiced for an hour, daddy."

He nods.

"Mommy talked mean to grandma. Are you going to spank her?"

He doesn't answer.

"Well," she insists, "are you?"

He shoves open the door to the kitchen as though it were a hobo pressing him for small change. He enters the kitchen. Ravished by the sudden glare of neon, he squints. A floor of yellow linoleum, green Formica countertops, a table and cabinets whose plywood constitution is veiled by the dark veneer of lacquer. Despite the fact that he and his wife had chosen everything themselves and with great elation at the thought of finally having the money to remodel, top to bottom, like any other family in Kenwood, despite all this the kitchen has the feel of back issues of *Better Homes & Gardens* strewn by wind and rain, resettled in this damp remodeling. The oven door is open. His mother sits before it with her back to the table and the newspaper's retrospective on the anniversary of the President's death: the open air motorcade trying to make its getaway and Jackie Kennedy, too late to shield his body with hers.

"Mothadear, why are you sitting in front of the oven?"

"Ask Mz. Lemonade. If she don't kill me she'll condescend me to death."

"Mothadear."

She musters a tear that will not fall; leans closer to the oven and holds her hands to it as though warming them at a campfire. He notices all the dials are turned off. He dabs her eye with his handkerchief. He picks up the newspaper and scans the headlines and the photographs.

"Why can't you move back home?" she says.

"A Negro psychologist...Louisiana, Mothadear?"

"You'd be the first. Your father was the first in Lutcher with his own truck, the first to start an NAACP chapter, the first with his own store, the first to show race movies, Lord, how I loved the Oscar Micheaux films, the gangster pics, the cowboy movies."

"It's not the same thing, Mothadear."

"It's Mz. Lemonade, putting ideas in your head."

There's no graceful way to leave the kitchen without making her feel that he's leaving because of her. "I wish you'd call her by her name."

"Humph. Next thing I know you'll be cussing me out, too."

"She swore at you?"

"It's my fault. That's what they all said in Lutcher. Your complexion was my fault. She blames me for everything, just like they did."

"What did she say?"

"I should talk as foul as her? I don't think so. We didn't cuss in my house. That's something new. We didn't show grown folks disrespect. Treats me like the furniture."

He takes the back stairs two at a time. The thud of his wing tips echo on the wooden stairs meant for the quiet climb and descent of servants.

In the master bedroom, Ida-Lorraine paces anxiously about. The room is enormous with a concave window overlooking the street, the glass-walled belly of a rampart running top to bottom along the house's front façade. Dusk is dying. Across the street, snowflakes fall through a cone of soft lamp light. She is dressed in tight patio pants and a sleeveless blouse that Sarah Vaughan and Doris Day have made chic and accept-able for housewives.

Her husband moves hurriedly down the hall but stops at the boy's bedroom. Edgar Allen Poe is turned down on its spine at the foot of his bed. Clad to his elbows in his mother's gloves the little boy waves his toy sword in the air and paces up and down inspecting the regiment before it marches off to defend the Raj. In this dusk darkened room, with the only gleam being that of the desk lamp and the glistening snow collect-ing on the windowsill like silt, the splendor of his possessions, his wall of adventure books and poetry, his clipper trunk of toys, his posters from the 1920s advertising ocean voyages, he seems less the child of middle-class professionals than a young inmate at Mettray Penal Colony seized by the splendor of his delusions.

"What on earth are you doing?"

Spinning around at the sound of his father's voice the boy says nothing.

"Answer me."

"I was almost finished memorizing 'Annabel Lee' so I just wanted a small break so that—"

"In women's gloves?"

"They're from mommy's closet."

"I know where they come from. Why are they climbing up your wrists?"

"The Brigadiers wore them when they went to defend the Raj."

"Not women's gloves, they didn't."

"I'm playing pretend."

"Where's your mother?" He knows perfectly well where she is. But he wishes he didn't know—he looks at the boy with eyes that are pleading, imploring, the boy to save him from himself.

In the master bedroom the last pale light comes through the window and mixes with the light of Ida-Lorraine's tall reading lamp whose pole and curvature resemble the streetlight below. To calm herself she reads quietly aloud from Edward Albee's *A Delicate Balance*. "And here comes Julia home from the war, two Purple Hearts." It only heightens her anxiety as she waits. Why, she wonders as she reads, do White people turn slender frustrations into burly ordeals? They haven't lived. She puts the book down and walks around straightening items in an effort to steady her hands.

He enters the bedroom and lays out Mothadear's accusations. They argue, shouting at each other from opposite sides of the room. They both are hoping a third party will intervene and rescue them; or a natural disaster will erupt outside the window and give them a common cause.

"You swore if I came to this tundra I could finish my doctorate," she says. "'You'll play your part beside me in JFK's New Frontier.' Little did I know you swore the same thing to Mothadear."

In the kitchen, grandmother Wilderson looks up at the ceiling to the sound of scuffling and the thud of bodies. She wrings her hands and draws the little girl to her bosom. Enfolds her like a swan with her duckling and rocks back and forth in her chair.

In his bedroom the boy slices the air with his sword like a madman.

In the master bedroom the spine of *A Delicate Balance* lays broken on the window seat and the rest of the books from the curved bay window-sill lay strewn on the floor beneath it. The sound of heavy breathing and grunts comes from the bathroom off the master bedroom. The faucet is running; there are drops of blood on the tap. A bar of soap, broken into small chunks, lodged in the drain, causes the soapy water to back up—and there is a toothbrush floating in the murky dregs.

Ida-Lorraine is breathing ferociously, gasping for air, coughing. "You gonna rip my blouse!"

On their dresser outside the bathroom is a photograph of the two of them one June-orange afternoon in a cottage for "Colored Newlyweds" on the Mississippi River, circa 1955. Her blouse is tied at the waist. He is barefoot, the cuffs of his pants rolled up his shins Huck Finn–style. The newlyweds are clowning for the camera. To complete the parody, she has tied a handkerchief above her brow Aunt Jemima–style, while he holds a fishing pole in one hand and a string of catfish in the other. Had the picture been taken later in the day, the sun setting behind them and the oceanic reach of the Mississippi River would have thrown them both into silhouette and cast their smiling faces into shadow. She bolts from the bathroom, crashing into the dresser.

"Blouse be the least of your worries, you don't get back in here and wash that filthy mouth out with soap." He is coming out of the bathroom into the bedroom, with the soap in his hand. "Swear in my house!"

She gropes along the bookshelf tumbling everything in its wake. She licks the sliver of blood from her lip and paces the bombed out room in a swift but careful pavane with her husband who is looking for the right moment to lunge. She is the flag. He is the bull.

Downstairs, in the kitchen, grandmother opens her arms and re-leases her little duckling. Neither one of them can concentrate on the story she is telling or keep their eyes from roaming the ceiling.

"Child, we were glorious beyond glorious!"

"This glorious?" The girl extends her arms so far in either direction the strain can be seen on her face.

"No, baby," grandmother Wilderson extends her own arms to let the child bear witness to an even wider reach, "this glorious!" And together they sit, the grandmother with her arms stretched out as far as they will reach, her granddaughter nestled against her with the back of her head resting on her bosom.

"This glorious!" they laugh, together.

Then, a thud. A bump. And the muffled sound of voices above them.

"I'm going to see," says the girl.

"It's grown folks' business. Stay here."

"Mommy says we weren't glorious—just slaves."

Kneeling on the floor, his arms and face slumped on the bed beside the sword, the boy is sobbing. He wipes his tears and snot on the bedspread and rises to the window where his miniature collection of the British army lines the sill. Into a new formation of attack he begins to place them, but he is distracted by the view from his window. The parade of elm trees is gray and leafless. The bark is sheathed with snow. From either side of the street their skeletal fingers stretch up and across; they almost meet over the street in a stark, tangled canopy. This is James Avenue. Upper James to those who need to, or are fond of, calling it. For though these houses boast only fifteen to twenty rooms, at the end of Upper James (one half block away) is Mount Curve where the mansions earn their names. And it is this noble proximity of unearned wealth that makes the difference for those who need the difference. On the corner of Mount Curve, the boy spies what cannot be seen through the lush foliage of summer and fall: the bronze dome of the east wing of a long one-story house where Mrs. Proudwell waits in the drive for her chauffeur to open the door of her Rolls Royce. The Rolls Royce floats slowly over the circular drive. It turns onto Upper James. The spiky-fingered elms reflect on the polished hood as the car glides to a stop in front of the Wilderson home.

Frank and Ida-Lorraine are entangled on the seat beside the curved bay window; pulling at each other too furiously to see the car that stops just below their window. He pulls her to the bathroom where the faucet runs and the toothbrush swirls in the gurgle of soapy water. Again, she yanks free of him. Again their dance begins: Ida-Lorraine, moving like prey with her back against the wall; Frank, inching forward for the lunge. "Words? Words?!" she says moving about the room, never turning her back to him, pretending not to be afraid. "You would beat me for words?" Frank lunges at his wife, catching only her shoulder.

In the snowy street in front of their house, Mrs. Proudwell's elegant black boots step from the car and light upon the snow. She waves away her chauffeur's hand, a ritual of elderly assertion she performs whenever she thinks someone can see her.

On the first landing of the front stairs, Frank and Ida-Lorraine press against each other like lovers. With his left hand he grips her collarbone and holds her, pinning her to the wall. With his right hand he is squeezing her jaw.

"Wash this mouth out with soap. Not to my mother you don't." He pants and thrusts. She writhes in his grip and struggles to pull his hand away from her face. Tears roll down her cheeks into his hands.

Now she wrenches his hand away and slips, grinds, maneuvers out from under the press of his pelvis. She begins to walk down the stairs (taking advantage of the interlude in which his hand rests on his knee as he tries to catch his breath) massaging the palm print from her face with one hand, holding the other aloft like a tired and inexperienced boxer. "You'd sleep with her if she'd bear you a child." He grabs her and raises his hand. The doorbell rings and...

...for some strange reason...

...he hears it.

The doorbell rings again.

They are there, now. The little girl. The little boy. Professor Wilderson and Ida-Lorraine. There, at the bottom of the stairs, just this side of the door. They wait like fugitives trying to decide what to do. Dr. Wilderson cuts them all a straighten-up-and-fly-right look. He opens the huge plate glass door. They shiver from the rush of cold air as though being washed by the build up of water between the first and second hatches of a submarine. He steps into the antechamber.

It is Mrs. Proudwell, the doe-eyed widow whom the boy often spies from his bedroom window. There, just there, beyond the outer door. Her breath is steaming the glass from behind her veil. Dr. Wilderson turns to his family once again. This time his eyes harbor a plea for help that they have never seen before. They are thrown off balance by it. The walls start to sway and their heads begin to swoon. He turns the lock on the last hatch to the sea.

With voices joyous as the Vienna Boys' Choir, Dr. Wilderson, the girl, and the boy sing out: "Welcome, how good of you to come!" as though they have been practicing for years. Ida-Lorraine leans against the wall and looks up in disgust.

Mrs. Proudwell is upon them. Something, she thinks, has happened here.

—⁓—

Sometimes I wish that doorbell had not rung. I tell myself my life would have been different had Mrs. Proudwell not come that day. It's as foolish a thought as it is selfish. For the doorbell was what saved my mother. And it's a foolish thought in as much as I summon it, if only in my mind, to explain, or explain away, my love for Alice as being inextricably bound to my childhood fascination with Mrs. Proudwell. Never mind all the bread crumbs missing along the path from here to there. It gets me through the day. That's what one does when one is possessed by what can't be named—one finds a way to get through the day. Alice would say there was nothing of Mrs. Proudwell in her. No painted face in a vain effort to hide her wrinkles. No pompous sipping of tea. No chauffeur to guide her from her Rolls, because she hadn't a Rolls but a twelve-year-old Honda with a stick shift and she drives it herself, thank you. And all I'd be able to offer in response would be the press of my images, my associations, as elusive as snakes of vapor. I used to dream that, had that doorbell not rung, my family could have been saved, hunkered down with our house as our bunker, safe in our sanctuary, safe from Mrs. Proudwell and her two hundred million relations, White Americans, rich and poor and in-between, scattered all across the land, protected from the thing we needed protection from the most, the future.

Alice would chafe at the thought of being called a relation (rich or poor or in-between) of Mrs. Proudwell. Why, she would have asked, sardonically, because I'm in my sixties and she was in her sixties? Because I'm White and she was White? And we would both wait anxiously for my answer, knowing that more than a night of sex, or not, hung in the balance. I would know the answer that would settle her mind—a simple "no" followed by a small list of all the things which made Alice special: her fine poetry, her history of left-wing causes, her travels to the third world, our long literary nights together—just as she would know the answer that would settle mine—a simple "yes" followed by, You're all alike, there's nothing to calibrate.

I'd been back from South Africa for less than a year when Alice introduced me to Virginia, her daughter. A poet mother and her Buddhist daughter. They taught at a sleepy, northern California college seven miles south of Santa Cruz. Alice: English, for twenty-five years. Virginia: Dance, for nineteen years. They were devotees of the Dalai Lama, organic gardening, public nudity, and unconditional sanctuary for stray cats—Crown Princesses of the New Age Dispensation. There were, however, important differences between them. Alice had survived the Depression in the dust bowls of Montana and Wyoming and rubbed shoulders with Black militants in Oakland and San Francisco. She'd even taken one as a lover when her husband wasn't looking. But her daughter, Virginia, had no such bracelet of charms and credentials. She was a product of ballet lessons in Mill Valley in Marin County, a bedroom suburb of San Francisco in the '60s. An artsy-craftsy-tennis-and-yacht-club-swimming-pool hideaway, sheltered by ninety-eight parents' groups, thirty-nine women's clubs, one-hundred five church groups, thirty musical organizations, and two-hundred-sixteen sports clubs.

It was the spring of 1997. There was still some time before the Cabrillo College Dance Recital was to begin. Virginia was standing in the middle of the auditorium speaking to one of her colleagues from the dance department when Alice and I entered the auditorium arm in arm laughing, having just shared a private joke. Something terrifying was triggered in

Virginia's eyes as she watched me down the aisle. Or maybe something clicked inside her as she looked at her mother with me.

Her colleague drifted off to find a seat. Virginia came over to us, sat down, and launched into a strange soliloquy. In her manner of speaking there was something anxious and clipped; a certain shortness of breath. An apparently oblivious Alice seemed excited, almost thrilled to be introducing me to Virginia. Perhaps if I had spoken, I too might have sounded just like Virginia. Her conversation was completely associational; it had no through line, as though she was talking to hold at bay some other form of engagement. The only topic she held onto long enough for me to gain a conceptual toehold was her anger at the invasion of hip-hop and jazz dance in her department. Her specific animus toward Lisa, the lone Black woman in the dance department—Virginia's subordinate, the actual "culprit" in question—was omitted. In fact, Lisa was not mentioned by name by either her or Alice; and I could not have mentioned it for I did not yet know her name. As a result, one could not be faulted for getting the impression that a whole tribe of Black dancers had descended on Santa Cruz, with no other intention than running amuck in Virginia's department. To hear her tell it, these Black dance forms were poised to engulf the entire curriculum; she probably meant "cannibalize" but wanted to spare me the pain of knowing that she was opposed to our dancing as well as our fine culinary traditions. I smiled. I nodded. I listened the way one listens when traveling incognegro. I was careful not to frown, lest she think I disapproved of what she was saying. I was careful not to show too many teeth, lest she think I wanted to eat her.

As far as I could gather, she feared "the students"—she didn't say the White students but there were only three or four Black students in the whole department—would become so captivated by hip-hop and jazz dance that they would never take another ballet or modern dance class again. So enthralled was I by the breathtaking spirit of Virginia's thrusts and parries that I became anxious and fearful. As her words spiraled and expanded I envisioned an army of large barefoot Black women descending upon the flaxen maidens of the dance department, chasing

Virginia with spears and incomprehensible oaths across campus, throwing her headfirst into a pot of boiling water, stirring vigorously, seasoning excessively, and chanting ugga-bugga, ugga-bugga all night long. It was frightful.

The house lights dimmed. Virginia left us and went to her seat. But in the void of her sudden departure I grew increasingly frustrated, sensing that two melodies had expressed themselves in our brief, but heady composition. The first tune was that well-known hit called "Negrophobia": a neurotic little ditty the orchestra plays when confronted with the energetic and incomprehensible movement of Black bodies. It was a song I'd heard one version or another of since the day Mrs. Proudwell arrived.

As the curtains parted, something else nagged at me. Virginia's defensive soliloquy on the plague potential of Black dance had a specific and empirical genealogy. The sight of me or, to be more precise, her sighting of me (look a Negro) or the sight of Alice arm in arm with me (look a Negro in bed with my mother), had triggered her torrent of discordant and associational speech. I embodied Virginia's common anxiety about a common, well-known contagion. (As the Klan used to say, "Everyone in America's got nigger on the brain.") I suddenly realized that I had been caught off guard by this. In my mind, I had not entered the auditorium as a contagion, but as Frank, Alice's newfound love. Virginia and I had no history—we were meeting for the first time. Yes, I was that naïve. But we did share a history. She was speaking our history. But I didn't want to hear it.

These thoughts rushed in and out again between Virginia's departure and the dimming house lights. I didn't want to know what I knew I knew. But as the first dancers came on stage my emotional state shifted from confusion and despair to hatred and anger, directed not as one might think, at Virginia, but at Alice. I was no longer sitting beside Alice in the auditorium; I was sitting beside her in the car, driving down the Pacific Coast Highway. We are being pulled over. The music began and the dancers, slowly, languidly, began to move. I tried to keep my mind on what my eyes were seeing, White women gliding abstractly to and fro. But it was no use. Instead of the smell of old fabric in the seats where I sat, I was thinking of the air that tasted of salt on that oceanside highway; and I heard not the music being played for young dancers but the sound of suicide being practiced on rocks by the waves.

You like being on the road with her, don't you?

Yes. It's one of the few things I really enjoy.

But you particularly like it at night.

Yes, at night.

Why at night?

The dark car is our cocoon. There's no Black, there's no White. It's just the two of us.

Really?

Really.

But here in the college auditorium, you feel as though you hate her?

It just came over me—like a wave.

You'd like to be back in the car, driving along the coast?

Yes.

Who's driving?

We trade off.

Who was driving that night?

What night?

That night.

I don't remember.

Let's talk about your other trips. What do you like about them?

The world is small. Like a cowbird on a fencepost, the world vanishes in the rearview mirror.

How can you see a cowbird on a fencepost at night?

I can touch the back of her neck in the darkness.

Strangle her?

Caress her, damn it! I love her!

We don't have to do this, you know. We can watch the dance recital.

I run my fingers through her hair.

Hmm.

What's that supposed to mean?

Just hmm. So you're driving along on one of your trips. There's no Black, no White. The lid is sealed on that can of worms. Just Frank. Just Alice. The wind. The waves. The moon. Do you ever stop to urinate?

Don't be stupid.

The Highway Patrol, they're okay with you strangling a White woman while she's trying to drive? You sure there's not a law against that?

I'd like to watch the recital.

You've never been stopped?

Never.

Never?

Well…once.

Oh… And?

And nothing.

You'd rather not talk about the incident.

It wasn't an incident.

Fine. It wasn't an incident.

He asked her for her license and registration. No big deal.

So, she was driving.

Is that relevant?

Is it?

Yes, she was driving.

Why did he stop you…her.

A tail light or something. I don't remember.

How did the cop and Alice get on?

Like a house on fire.

How did you feel?

He didn't see me at first, he came up on the driver's side and didn't lean too far in. They just chatted.

They chatted?

Yeah.

Alice and the cop? Was he her nephew?

Kiss my ass.

Well?

I said, kiss my ass.

When's the last time you turned a traffic stop into a social call?

I want to watch the recital.

What did you feel?

I didn't feel anything.

But the lining of your cocoon was torn.

It happened so fast.

Then he sent you on your way?

Sort of…

"Sort of" isn't standard police procedure.

He shined his light on her hand as she reached over to the glove compartment.
The light lit upon my feet.

You mean your shoes.

My feet.

You mean your socks.

My feet.

Your ashy, blue on the top, pink and splayed on the bottom—?

Feet.

Hardly incognegro of you.

I guess not.

Wait. What's the connection between the glove compartment and your feet?

My feet were on the dashboard.

You just as loose and breezy as your White woman, ain't you?

Then he shined the light in my face.

Back up. Why were your feet on the dashboard?

We were in our cocoon. I was reciting poetry as she was driving.

Got it.

We were happy.

Got it.

We were together.

Got it.

I was—

Reciting poetry with your big King Kong feet spread out on the dashboard—
got it. So, he shined the light on your feet and then he looked at her and said, "Gee,
lady, where'd you get that Negro foot ornament? I'd like one for my dashboard."

He shined the light in my face. Then he looked at her and he said—

"Haven't I seen those feet on a Wanted Poster?"

—"Ma'am, are you alright?" And she said, "Yes, officer, I'm alright."

And?

And nothing. We continued on our trip.

How did you feel?

We dodged a bullet, okay?

"We" dodged a bullet?

There was this silence between us.

You didn't go on reciting poetry.

She said something like, what a sweet cherub face he had, how he was just a young boy; something like that.

How did you feel?

She was nervous. She was trying to diffuse the situation.

What situation, the cop was gone? Are you "the situation"?

We needed to break the silence…break the ice between us…I don't know.

So, your cocoon was all frozen?

I don't wanna think about this anymore.

What did you say to her?

Nothing. Not right then.

What were you thinking?

I was thinking: How could she speak so endearingly of that…that fucking pig!

Because of what he did to you?

Because he's a pig! Not a cherub.

How did you feel?

Horrible…Horrible!

Because she liked his face?

Because she was predisposed to like his face.

Which says something about her predisposition to you.

Don't put words in my mouth.

Surely things change when you get to the motel; when you're no longer on the road; in the room when it's just Frank, just Alice. No Black, no White. Just the two of you in the room.

Yes, things do change.

Your cocoon returns.

It's better in the room. She registers and I unload.

Really?

Yeah, division of labor and all that. That way we get a good room if they've got a good room.

Hmm.

We don't have to worry that they gave us a shitty room because of me, or because of her and me.

Hmm.

We get what everyone else gets.

Hmm.

No sense provoking the management in these tiny out of the way places.

So, those places are not cocoons, I take it—not like the car?

In the room we can close the curtains and be alone together. It's groovy again.

Who closes the curtains?

I do.

You're worried that she'll start running around buck naked in front of the open windows.

Look, we're there, okay. It's fine. We turn off the cell phones. No one has our number. No one knows where we are. We can hold each other. We can read novels. We can recite poetry. We can listen to music. Or just talk about tomorrow's drive. I love her in those rented rooms.

That's the only place you can love her—those rented rooms and the car.

I wouldn't go that far.

Are there televisions in those rooms?

Of course.

Do you ever watch them?

Of course.

What do you watch?

Whatever's on.

Two intellectuals like yourselves and you watch 'whatever's on'?

Reruns. You know, vintage stuff.

Vintage what?

Cop shows…mainly.

Hmm.

The house lights came on. It was intermission. Alice asked me what I thought of the performance thus far. I managed something between a word and a grunt. Truth is, I couldn't recall any of the performance, and the dancers had all floated before me without registering. I was seething, but I could not articulate my anger. I wanted to get out. I wanted to stay. Ma'am, are you alright? The nerve of that pig. If he had had any sense of history, or just a fart's whiff of reality, he would have seen me with her and asked me if I was alright. I see you're traveling with this White woman, sir, are you going to need any assistance? Instead, something warm and filial had passed between them; a private and quotidian consensus, like the one arrived at by her and her daughter as the specter of Black dancers cast menacing shadows on the wall. They were all family: the dancer, the poet, the cop. Where do I fit in?

The question was untenable. It oozed into our arguments without ever being spoken. And its answer, its eternal and uncompromising answer made me hiss with scorn whenever she and I argued.

"I can't bear the contempt in your voice," she had said.

To which I rejoined: "You people always hone in on the form of what's said."

"I am not 'you people.'"

"You should thank your stars for our contempt. Virginia should say, 'I had lunch with Lisa and I got off with contempt. Whew! But come to think of it, she did stab at that chicken rather pensively. I guess she was hungry.'"

"I am not 'you people.' Your attempt at inversion is racist and juvenile."

"'And mom, did I tell you I was served by a Black waiter? Chicken salad on croissant, but no strychnine. A side order of contempt, but they always serve that. Boy, was I lucky, mom.'"

"Are you finished?"

"That's what you people should say."

"I'm a woman and my name is Alice."

"You're a White woman who likes to run around the house and the yard flaunting her nude body for whoever passes by."

"I've heard enough."

"You're what makes things sell. White Alice. That's your name. And your racist daughter with her Tibetan pretensions; guess what her name is—"

"Get out."

"White Virginia. And your—"

"Get out!"

"—blonde-haired, blue-eyed, wonder-boy grandson: Orgeen, Borgeen, Schmorgeen—however you say that phony Tibetan name. Three guesses what his name is? And don't say 'Jesus.' That's not the answer."

"If you hate me," she said looking me in the eye, "why do you fuck me?"

I looked at her and thought how much I had miscalculated. She had brought me face to face with the question I was most terrified of. But I wasn't about to break down and become vulnerable. I pressed on, hoping against hope that she had not seen the flicker of doubt and dread in my eyes.

"On second thought, why not call him Jesus? Virginia could increase the congregation tenfold."

"It's a Buddhist retreat, not a church," she said. "You don't know the first thing about what goes on up a there. It's a very spiritual place."

"Okay, Spiritual Schmorgeen—not Jesus. There. Satisfied? His father is a burnt out acid-head from Santa Monica and his mother's a burnt out yoga-head from Mill Valley. And he's Little Baby Schmorgeen."

"Why don't you stop tormenting yourself and get a Black woman?"

"How much of Schmorgeen's Similac comes from the CIA?"

"You'll sit by the fire long winter nights and confess your sins to her."

"The Dalai Lama is on the CIA payroll."

"Weave your soliloquies into an epic: my lost years with an old White woman by the sea."

"But you already knew about his CIA connection, didn't you?"

"You'll tell your story a little differently each night. No, that's not your style, you loathe mendacity, or do you? You'll serialize it rather than fabricate it. Hold her in suspense, make her feel more appreciated each night until she forgives you."

"But Virginia hasn't read the exposé on the Dalai Lama and the CIA. She's allergic to books."

"You'll both live happily ever after."

"Whatever."

"I hate you."

"Good," I said. "Now we're getting somewhere."

—m—

If you hate me why do you fuck me? When I was a boy in Kenwood it never occurred to me that I would one day be thrown by a question as burnished and pristine as this. It caught me by surprise, so consumed was I by the other question, *Where did I fit in?* The question that Alice would never think to launch across the bow. It was mine and mine alone. It had resounded inside of me long before I lived and worked in Santa Cruz. Since the day my parents pulled and scratched and cursed and tumbled down the stairs to meet Mrs. Proudwell. I'd thought South Africa held the answer, but that was not the case. As far as I'm concerned, Khanya's father had said, he's a White man. If only that were true. Then I wouldn't be with a White woman, I would be with Alice, and *being*, whether hers or mine, would not be in question. Whatever our fights would be about we would know, without even having to know, what they were not about— they would not be about my Black death and her White life. They would be about "issues."

When I was a boy in Kenwood, I wanted to live on the ocean floor. That, I might have intuited, would keep the question *Where do I fit in?* high above me. On the ocean floor that question, as well as its probing cousin *If you hate me why do you fuck me?*–which I had no idea at the tender age of eight had already taken the high road to meet me—would drown if it tried to track me down. I read Jules Verne's *20,000 Leagues Under the Sea* over and over again in hopes that Captain Nemo would come for me and take me to a world where I could replenish myself on fish and flora while living beyond the reach of dry land. But now I had lived five years in South Africa and was back in Kenwood again—Santa Cruz, California, a Kenwood by the sea. I'd come full circle and gone nowhere. I'd become my father, bracing myself in the presence of Mrs. Proudwell's precious body, taking great care not to touch her skirt as I cleaned the tea she spilled on herself and the sofa, taking care with my words, even when enraged, just as he had always taken care with his. Waiting for Alice to make the first move in my heart, the way my father had waited for Mrs. Proudwell to make the first move in his house. Watching her as she watched us. I see Mrs. Proudwell standing there as if unsure whether or not she should enter. Catching sight of our faces in the foyer, she quickly became aware of her advantage. Something, she thought as she stood in the cold space between the outer door and the inner door, has happened here. Oh, Mrs. Proudwell, if you only knew.

—ɯ—

She eyes us like General Patton inspecting the troops. With her icy palm on my sister's cheek, she quips, "Be a dear and show George, my driver, to the kitchen." Dr. Wilderson closes the outer door behind George, who stomps the snow from his feet. My sister looks questioningly at mom, who turns to dad, who initiates a chain of nods back to my sister, which Mrs. Proudwell pretends not to see. Yes, she thinks, something has happened here.

Mrs. Proudwell shivers dramatically. "Be a dear, Dr. Wilderson, close the foyer door." She smiles at me. "And will you help me with my coat?"

The boy steps forward. "I will, miss."

"And you are?"

"Frank B. Wilderson, the third, miss. I know 'Gunga Din,' by heart!"

"How charming." She tugs at her long black gloves and places them on top of her ermine, draped across the boy's arms. Now turning to Ida-Lorraine, "You're to be commended. A girl as poised as any girl in finishing school and a boy who knows Kipling." Now even Ida-Lorraine is beaming. Suddenly guests in their own home, my parents follow Mrs. Proudwell to the living room. "Two Negro children," she says over her shoulder, "who don't smell like Negro children." Ida-Lorraine is too stunned to respond.

"And this room," she arranges herself on the sofa under a Grecian fresco. "Wait until I tell them about this room, an impetuous but beguiling juxtaposition of Restoration and Louis the Fourteenth. We all work with what we have." Speaking as though to herself she says, "It's odd... your children standing there. They remind me of something. Little Kennedys. Yes, little Kennedys. If not for the fact that—"

"They're Negroes," offers Ida-Lorraine. Dr. Wilderson blanches.

I remember Mrs. Proudwell having stayed for hours, though I was told it was less than thirty minutes. Perhaps it seemed like such a long visit because the time of our isolation had been so long. She told us that the death of John F. Kennedy had compelled her to take a good hard look at things.

"I told the Kenwood Committee 'This has to stop. This isn't Selma or Little Rock. Just because they're Negroes doesn't mean they're not our kind of people.'" She sipped her tea and waited for our response, but my father could think of none, and my mother hadn't quite recovered from my father's attack on the stairs. We are together, the four of us, the Wildersons, together in our antique living room for the first time in the nearly two years that we have lived in Kenwood, yet we can think of nothing to say. Mrs. Proudwell does not like the silence.

"My late husband was a star gazer," she says. "He had an observatory built in our roof, though Mr. Lloyd Wright said alterations and annexations were forbidden. That bronzed dome, you've seen it?" She pauses but we are still too ungrounded to respond. She fidgets. She has no cookie or cake to eat, nothing to alternate or vary the single motion of lifting her cup to her lips. Parched options in a room full of Negroes.

"Last night I saw Orion," says Mrs. Proudwell, "through my late husband's telescope."

I remember how I tried to change the subject; for reasons that are still unknown to me. I told her about Gunga Din and my plans to defend the Raj. My sister Fawn was quiet, taking in every twitch of every eye, every facial movement of every adult.

"Kipling," Mrs. Proudwell repeats, "well, yes, but I was speaking of Orion. A nocturnal spectacle for my optimism on the night Kennedy was inaugurated; and now, the vision of my pessimism on these cold nights of missiles and civil defense. How many missiles did Brinkley say, thirty?"

Mother corrects her: "Thirty-two."

Dad leans forward: "No, honey, Mrs. Proudwell is right. Brinkley said thirty. He was counting right off the U-2 photographs."

Mrs. Proudwell nods. "Thirty—pointing at us. White and Negro. Gentile and Jew. We could have all been blown to smithereens. Then they killed him. We hardly had time to catch our breath after the Missile Crisis and he was gone. Shot by some silly little communist. He didn't even have the good fortune to die for civil rights." She took a deep breath, let it out, and looked directly at mom. "You might say that's why I'm here."

"To die for civil rights?" mom said. "All the way down the block in your limousine, to die for civil rights. You must be exhausted. Did the Kenwood Committee send you off with provisions, or did you hunt wild game along the way?"

"Sarcasm is the last refuge of wit, my dear. But I'm not surprised you're bitter. Your first few months here have been…inconvenient."

"Years. Two 'inconvenient' years."

Then Fawn said, "Mommy never lets us sit in this room or in these chairs. We have to sit in the kitchen."

Mrs. Proudwell was incredulous. "I don't believe you, child."

"It's true," Fawn insisted. "These chairs are for when our good White people come. Only they don't come. Mommy says—"

"Fawn," mom said.

"You're our first good White person to come."

"Fawn."

"The bad ones don't come either."

"Fawn!"

"Now we get to sit here. Can we bounce on them?" she deliberately asked dad and not mom.

But dad was lost in his stoic anxiety. He had not recovered from battering his wife; from his mother's bottomless demands; from his son's practiced erudition and effeminate gestures; from the cold drive home and the radio talk show hosts chatting about him and his family as if they'd invaded from Mars; nor from his students who had stared at him as if they, too, were sure he'd come from Mars. Could she bounce on the chairs? She could piss in them for all he cared. He wished Kennedy had unleashed something fierce on Castro and Khrushchev, who in turn would have surely blown the living room off the map and stopped the aching in his brain. He asked himself why this woman had chosen this day of all days to decide that they were well-deodorized enough to visit? Behind him was the certainty of Southern isolation, ahead of him was a life too baffling to envision. Why couldn't time stand still?

Mom looked at me and said, "Take your sister outside to play."

"Don't wanna go outside, it's cold," answered Fawn before I could, looking again to dad.

My father tensed and I sat there realizing that until he corroborated mom's order, my mandate for its execution was at best uncertain; or, more precisely, given the presence of a good White person, Fawn could push the limits of non-compliance far beyond the line Khrushchev would ever think to push Kennedy. Mom and I hung there, suspended in mid-air. Mom and Fawn took two or three seconds to exchange the evil eye with one another and then Fawn looked at me with the corners of her mouth turned down and her come-on-boy-I-dare-you look.

Mrs. Proudwell said, "I'm sure your mother's concern is that the furniture is antique and needs to be preserved."

"I know it's antique," said Fawn, "that's how come she bought 'em at an antique store. I went with her."

"I'll bet you're mommy's little helper," said Mrs. Proudwell.

"Me and Mrs. Finkelstein."

"Sweetie," said Mrs. Proudwell carefully, "who's Mrs. Finkelstein?"

"She's mommy's Jew."

Mrs. Proudwell splotched her dress with tea. Dad and I nearly fell over each other handing her napkins. Dad was careful not to wipe the stain on her dress. No matter how good his children smelled.

Fawn sat aloof. "Whenever we go shopping for furniture, mommy always takes her special Jew: 'my special lipstick, my special pocketbook, and my—'"

"Boy, take her to the kitchen!" Mom commanded as though I, and not Fawn, had transgressed.

I lunged for Fawn but she slid off her chair with a juke-n'-shake like a halfback coming off the line of scrimmage.

"You don't rule me, boy," she said as I fell forward. My big head landed on the seat where she had once been. "You're not my daddy." Then she perched herself on the knee of the daddy I was not.

Neither dad, nor mom, nor Mrs. Proudwell knew how to salvage the conversation.

Finally, Mrs. Proudwell said, "You think my visit disingenuous, don't you, Ida-Lorraine? May I call you Ida?"

Mom said, "Ida-Lorraine will do."

"Perhaps we should change the subject," said Mrs. Proudwell, "talk about our hobbies. I've told you mine, astronomy. What is it that you do, Ida-Lorraine?"

"I'm an apprentice housewife."

"Ida-Lorraine," dad sighed, "please."

"I'm lonely. Is that a hobby? But I no longer pine for the how-dos and potluck dinners of New Orleans. Who could preserve New Orleans in this weather? But a simple hello. A bit of chitchat. Some pointers on the art of snow shoveling. I'd take those up as hobbies, were they on offer—but they're not. I look out the window and see a neighbor. I cover myself from head to toe: boots, scarf, muffler, and mittens. Maybe this will be the day they speak. I'm out the door with my pride tucked beneath the most cheerful of smiles and my arm makes a big Dixie wave, big enough, I hope, to bite back the snub. Which *always* comes. Lord knows we're all cast from Adam's rib. Lord knows," she now laughs out loud, "the snow that falls on their steps falls on mine."

"This *is* the day," said Mrs. Proudwell.

"But they turn and swim upstream."

"We can't dwell in the past."

"So, you came because Jack Kennedy died?" asked mom.

"Yes."

"You should have come when Medgar Evers died."

"You're not equating Medgar Evers with the president, are you?"

"Wouldn't dream of it."

"Then what are you saying?"

"That your visit is whimsical and arbitrary."

"You are the most articulate Negro woman I have ever met."

"Who doesn't smell like a Negro woman?"

"Give us a chance, Ida-Lorraine. It's going to be hard at first. There'll be mistakes on both sides. If I offended you, I'm sorry. Kenwood *is* Minneapolis. My house is one of only a handful that doesn't date back—"

"To slavery?"

Mrs. Proudwell leaned back, closed her eyes, and held her finger aloft: "To emancipation. Our mutual emancipation, won with the blood of Kenwood's sons. We've never had Negroes here before. Well once...at least we think so..." she trailed off and was quiet.

My parents were suddenly interested. Who were they? they wanted to know. What did they do for a living? mom asked. Mrs. Proudwell looked at her as though "do" and "living" required translation.

"We couldn't tell whether they really *were* Negroes. They might have been Syrian or Portuguese."

Mom tried a different tact. "Where were they from?"

All Mrs. Proudwell could offer was, "Someone said they were with the circus."

The circus. She may as well have said they were all born on a barge. Cargo of unknown origins and unknown destinations.

My mother asked no more questions. The call and response concerning the possibility of another Black family whose Kenwood arrival and departure predated ours was fraught with greater implications than I could comprehend at the time. For Mrs. Proudwell had said that a Negro family *might* have lived in Kenwood before 1962, *before* the arrival of the Wildersons. But she had also said—and herein lay the rub—that it was impossible to tell simply by looking at them whether or not they were Syrians, Portuguese, or Negroes. And no one in Kenwood ever went close enough to them to learn the truth.

My mother's disposition sank like an air mattress caught by a thistle. For Mrs. Proudwell's revelation could mean only one thing: that these Negroes, if indeed they were Negroes, had not only beaten my mother to the place that she had fought so hard to get to first, but that they were also lighter in complexion. Lighter than her. Lighter than her daughter, which she needed to believe was impossible if her daughter was to marry a decent man. Lighter than her husband, which restored her to the horns of an existential dilemma: in marrying him, had she traded "passing possibilities" for Black "industry" and "integrity" (to the degree that "industry" and "integrity" would ever rub shoulders with "black")? And they were lighter than her son, who was now at the age of eight, as black as space. He would have to be tutored and managed for another ten uncertain years before her question—*Will he grow up to be someone who imbibes her breeding or would he act his color?*—could be answered.

Mrs. Proudwell prattled on, oblivious to the fact that my mother was as unsteady and traumatized as her great-great-grandmother must have been when she stepped off the ship in New Orleans. Blinded by the sudden burst of sunlight, perhaps she too tried to silence her chains and steady her hand on the guardrail the way mom now steadied her hand on the antique chair, this unnamed woman, waiting to be branded and named, looking everywhere for a landmark that would tell her if not where she was at least who she would become. And there, at the other end of the dock, is my father. The long voyage has resigned him to his chains. He counted the days as best he could in the solid darkness of the hold. Now he knows there's no way back. Why, he wonders, didn't we throw ourselves overboard? He watches her. He holds his breath. He hopes their disembarking will pass without incident. With all his telepathic power he is telling his wife (if "wife" is what they will one day let him call her) to be calm, please, be calm. Don't bolt. Don't explode. Just let these Proudwells bring us ashore.

"Where," mom asked, "did they go?"

Mrs. Proudwell looked up. Puzzled. Intent. "Go?" she said slowly. "No one knows. That's funny.... Was it Fred and Minnie who said the Committee should pay them a visit and see if they really *were* Negroes? Or was it Fred and Minnie who said that they really *weren't* Negroes, so no visit was needed? You'd think I had Alzheimer's. At least I've got age as an excuse. Minnie's as bad as me and she's thirty years younger. Fred hardly minds. Why should he? Men go for her sort. You know the type," she whispered loudly to my mother, "lights down low, Frank Sinatra on the Hi-Fi, a tray of cocktails on the carpet; still seducing Fred after ten years of marriage. Shameless."

The seconds that went by with no word from my parents could only be measured in years. On their own accord, my legs had stopped swinging against the chair. It was then, in the stillbirth of dialogue that Mrs. Proudwell actually looked at us. And our poised devastation unnerved her.

"Well," she said, "whoever they were, they were nothing like you. The children may have swung in the air or juggled—who knows. But they didn't know Kipling or Béla Bartók. The wife did not have a master's. And the husband was no professor. That much we know."

She rose. My father followed her to the foyer and helped her with her coat. She turned to face us.

"They were probably renters. Whereas you have an equity stake in Kenwood."

It was then that my grandmother ventured from the kitchen. She unfastened her apron as she entered the foyer. Dad stood tall and proud as he held Fawn and me by the hand. I felt loved and reassured.

"Ida-Lorraine you *are* resourceful," Mrs. Proudwell beamed, as though mom, and not grandmother, had suddenly appeared. "In a few parsimonious months—and with no help from the Kenwood Committee—you've found a maid."

Grandmother was too shocked to speak. Instinctively, mom touched her elbow; steadied her. The conflict between them was now of another age. My father managed to remain standing but only by squeezing the life out of our tiny hands.

"Mrs. Proudwell this...this is my mother, Mrs. Valentine Wilderson."

Now he became aware of Fawn's prying at his grip. He released us.

"Oh," said Mrs. Proudwell, flush with embarrassment, "I see." Then, she looked at my father as though he had betrayed her. She punched her fingers into her gloves. George, her chauffeur, came through from the kitchen, not knowing nor seeming to care what had happened. She managed a charitable smile. "Then you're permanent too, *Mrs.* Wilderson," she said to grandmother, "welcome."

We watched them down the snowy stairs.

NOORD STREET

Between the ashes of apartheid
and what they say is coming
are the merchant stalls of Noord Street Station
where a woman sells bruised fruit.
Above the rock and tumble of trains her feet
hold down the earth,
her hands,
move over late mangos and pears turning each imperfection
inward against the eye. It is July in Johannesburg.
Winter, where from lampposts politicians await
wet oblivion of night. In the last seeds of daylight
I fill my bag with apple and guava, attempt
nonchalance at the track of stitching under her eye,
say "keep the change," as always.
                                        This is not my country.
For years I marked my calendar by two seasons: rain,
when jacaranda petals bleed their purple hue into the soil
and not rain, when awaiting this season of rain.
Now it's marked by days of abstinence from this face of scars,
a spectacle for my optimism,
for though I am aging, the face in my passport
still lays claim to me upon
demand and shares my unclipped skin.
As dusk and the first lampposts flicker and choke like promises,
I wonder which locomotive en route to which desert
turned its steel into her cheek, and say
how I loved the last fruit, spoiled on my kitchen table.

3

Hillbrow was lit up and alive, as candescent at night as the rest of Jo'burg was in daylight. The smell of chickens roasting on a spit enticed us from the café above. Disco music could be heard from across the street. A man sold an assortment of hunting and fighting knives from a card table on the sidewalk and handguns, with the serial numbers filed off, from his car parked nearby. Everyone seemed either terribly well-dressed in fashions that had not quite caught up with the 1980s (which would be over in just five months) or dressed terribly in the rags of any era. This was Hillbrow at night.

"Why are you limping?"

"I'm not limping."

"Of course you are."

"A car ran over my foot."

"When? Where?"

"Four days ago. The night I arrived. Downtown, I think."

"No wonder Grace said you walk like you're in a fog. You're in pain."

"I'm okay."

"Have you seen a doctor?"

"No."

"Why not?"

I took a moment to rest, to lean on the railing at the base of the stairs that led to the Café Zurich. We had walked almost twenty blocks from Khanya's dormitory in Braamfontein to Pretoria Street in Hill-brow. For two days the pain in my foot had subsided. But the long walk had brought it back with a vengeance. She'd been reluctant to go out with me. I thought perhaps she didn't like me. Or maybe she was put off by my need to say that I was from New York and not Minneapolis. Later, after we were married, she told me that she didn't want to seem as eager for the attentions of an American as other women. Unlike Grace and Emily, or Samantha and Martha, or that insufferable woman with whom I shared a taxi on my first night in Jo'burg, Khanya appeared neither awed by nor drawn to my American accoutrement.

"I'm afraid to go to a doctor here."

"A big New Yorker like you?"

"Okay, rub it in. I was trying to impress you. I figured if I said I was from Minneapolis that all the appeal would be lost."

"What appeal?"

"Ouch."

"I mean that seriously. What appeal? I'm not with you because of where you're from."

"I never claim Minneapolis."

"But it's your village."

"Black Americans don't have villages."

"What do you have?"

"Plantations."

"I never know when you're joking."

"We were picked up and dropped off. It was a scream."

"I'm sorry."

"It's no big deal."

"It must be hard having a slave past."

"I keep moving; so it doesn't get to me."

"Don't you want to settle down?"

"Nope."

"What about your children?"

"What children, I ain't got no children!"

"The ones you plan to have."

"Plan to have? Shoot. You seen this world? You have kids?"

"A daughter, she's two."

"Oh, well...that's nice."

"Her name is Reba."

"Oh...that's nice."

"She's at home, in Bophuthatswana with my parents."

"That's nice."

"Where were you born?"

"New Orleans, Louisiana. And it's not a village. Look, why don't we go up-stairs and eat."

"You should see a doctor about that foot."

"I'll see a village when I get...I mean." She laughed for the first time since we'd met. I didn't tell her that it wasn't a joke but a slip of the tongue.

At the top of the stairs she held back. I asked her what was wrong. What if they're not multiracial? she asked. I told her that I had eaten at a sidewalk café down the block just four days ago and that I was staying at a bed and breakfast inn in Berea less than a mile from here. I omitted the spectacle of the dragnet that was served up with my coffee and eggs; I omitted the brawl I'd nearly lost with Eva Braun's sons Bruno and Ge-stapo; and I didn't tell her how I'd cried on a cold bed in a cold room in the back of the inn until I had gathered the strength to take myself out again into the cold, uncompromising night. So driven was I by a need to impress her that I postured as though I could protect her from animus so fine and ubiquitous it filled the very air we breathed.

"Just walk in like you own the joint," I said. Still, she held back. I touched her gently at the elbow. "Okay," I said, "let's go somewhere else, it's our first date, it should be fun; it's your town, make a suggestion."

"It's not my town," she said, softly.

Several White couples trickled up the stairs, slipped past us in our anxious indecision, and crossed the threshold of the Café Zurich's glass façade. They took their seats in the dark interior of cushioned chairs and candlelight. The entire mise-en-scène gave the café the ambiance of a dinner theater; the landing where Khanya and I stood, paralyzed by uncertainty and dread, was the perfect spectacle for their optimism and amusement as they sipped their wine and savored their dessert. For whatever tragedy could befall them, they could thank god that they would never be cast in our roles. Unable to bear the prolonged humiliation of their gaze, I urged Khanya to go inside.

A stout little man wearing a maroon vest and pretentious cufflinks intercepted us as we entered. He spoke with an Eastern European accent, as did the garrulous onlookers at the bar. By November their numbers would double and they'd toast the fall of the Berlin Wall; two Christmases later, when the Soviet Union fell, they'd commandeer the entire café for a party that would last two days.

"I'm sorry," he said with a tone that was both obsequious and menacing, "but we're not multiracial. Not yet. Soon-soon. Okay? Soon-soon."

"We just want—"

"The management is to inform you that soon-soon, yes, but not-now."

"The law has changed!" I may have been lying but I didn't know it. I only knew that he probably didn't know either. Perhaps I could front him into submission and thereby save face in front of Khanya and the steady gaze of the patrons.

"Yes, the law, okay, maybe, but the management, not okay." He pointed our attention to the transom up above where it read: *Right of Refusal Reserved.*

"Okay, my friend," he said, with an unctuous, authoritative smile.

"Let's go, Frank."

"Our money's not good enough for you but theirs is, is that it!" I said pointing to the patrons who watched us.

"Frank, let's go," Khanya repeated

As we stepped back out onto the landing he followed us.

"Wait! My American friend! Sorry-sorry. Come back. Sit. No problem. Eat. Drink. Is she with you?"

"No," said Khanya, "she's not."

Walking down the hill on Twist Street I knew that our date was over. I let her steer us toward the Black people's kombis queuing to the west at the bottom of the hill. *Well, this should make the Guinness Record for the world's shortest date.* I saw a line of metered cabs a couple blocks in the opposite direction.

"Let's take a cab," I said, "rather than wait all night for a kombi to fill up."

As metered taxi drivers came into view, and as we came in view for them, I became horribly aware of what a bad idea this was. But we had too much forward motion. The first and second drivers shook their heads and rolled up their windows. Khanya was set to leave when I noticed the third driver was an Indian and, unlike the others, he was rolling his window down.

"This guy'll take us." I made a beeline for him and she was compelled to do the same.

He said, "I'm not going to Soweto! I'll tell you that right now."

"We're not going to Soweto," I said in a tone that wanted to be accommodating for him and indignant for Khanya. It fell into a pit between the two.

"Or Alexandra, either. I don't go to the locations."

"We're not going to the locations. We're here, in town. Braamfontein. Wits University."

Khanya was even more disgusted than before: "We're going to walk," she said and turned back up the hill. There was nothing to do but follow her.

My accent finally registered with the driver and he called after me: "Hey! You American? Okay, why not? Get in."

"Khanya," I whispered, "he'll take us."

"He'll take you." She continued up the hill.

"New York! Chicago? LA! You from LA?"

"Minneapolis," I muttered as I dragged my shame behind her. *It's not the end of the world but you can see it from there.*

After that night I thought that she wouldn't want to see me again. So, I was surprised when Eva Braun knocked on my door and said,

"An African girl wants you on the phone. Remember," she said following me to the phone, "this isn't a brothel. I've got Germans from Siemens staying here. I want no African girls here."

It was a *braai*. Khanya had called to invite me to a good old fashion barbeque at a *tsotsi*'s house in Soweto. That afternoon I found myself in a small sedan bumping furiously along the unpaved streets of Naledi in the northwest section of Soweto.

The mood in Soweto was electric and unpredictable, alive with the promise of fire. The Defiance Campaign was in full gear, moving up to the Transvaal from the Cape. Residents in townships all across South Africa were angry and mobilized, so much so that rents and mortgages hadn't been paid in over a year and the government was paralyzed with no capacity to act even as a collection agent for the landlords. The mass mobilization of people had sent shock waves up the spine of civil society. On July 5, 1989, three weeks before I arrived, P. W. Botha had been compelled to meet Nelson Mandela, not in his prison cell on Robben Island but at Tuynhuys in Cape Town. And fifteen days after the braai Khanya took me to, Botha would be forced to convene the members of his Cabinet—also at Tuynhuys— and resign; his replacement would be F. W. de Klerk, the cunning pragmatist who had already taken the reigns of party leadership in March of that year.

It had been a brutal year for president Botha and the Nationalist Party: he'd suffered a stroke in January; in February there had been the hunger strikes by political detainees, a Defiance Campaign, and the trouncing of his party at the polls; in March, the rise of his nemesis, de Klerk; in May he received intelligence reports of a clandestine South African Communist Party congress held in Cuba at which the first new communist program since 1962 was produced by South African reds. Now this, in July: another unwanted meeting with Mandela and the rising smoke of another Defiance Campaign.

Emblazoned on the walls of Soweto's buildings were portents of its coming: Socialism Is Our Shield! Kill the Farmer! Kill the Boer! MK Lives! Viva SACP Viva!

Richard was a tall and muscular Zulu man nearly ten years my senior. Shirley, Khanya's cousin, was a nurse. How a nurse and a gangster had come together was beyond me. But in the five days I'd been in South Africa this dilemma was not by any means the most vexing. Simple things like knowing where I was in space and time at any given moment; or asking a group of people to speak English instead of an African language that I might know what's being said; or wondering at what point a police dragnet would materialize and catch me in it and what to do or say when it happens…These were the most pressing problems of those first few days. Who was dating whom, and why, would have to wait until I learned my ass from my elbow. There were five people in the car: Richard at the wheel, Shirley beside him, Khanya, Botsotso, and me in back. Botsotso was a young man in his late twenties. He was Richard's lieutenant. We were on our way to pick up Botsotso's girlfriend.

A haze of toxic carbons hung in the air like San Francisco fog. It was shot through with the setting sun's blue-amber light. This beautiful swath of tinted translucence laced the garbage heaps where children played, like a saintly halo, and wove around the low brick houses where their parents waited. Shirley told me the pollution came from plants that powered the homes and businesses of Johannesburg, while forty percent of Soweto residents were without electricity. "The state coroner is forbidden to report levels of toxins found in the bodies of people who die here," she said.

We stopped at one of the countless small brick homes. Botsotso stood beside the car and whistled like a precious bird.

"You can't just go to a girl's house," Richard smiled at me in his rearview mirror. "'Now, who's this one and why is he coming for my daughter before I have my lobola?' That's what the father will say."

Everyone except me seemed to know why this was so funny.

"You can't even go out on a date without paying a bride price?" I said, effectively ruining the joke.

We waited five minutes or so. A light came on at the bathroom window. It went out, then came on again, and went out. Botsotso got back into the car and smiled. After a brief interval, a young woman stepped out of the front door and called some half-hearted promise, or lie, or both, to her parents inside. Mpo, a young woman who seemed as though she may have just graduated from high school, squeezed up front with Shirley and Richard. Now, here were six of us in the car as we drove up to Richard's house. Shirley and Richard, Mpo and Botsotso, and Khanya and me: two gangsters, a high school student, a young nurse, a young law student, and me.

Two Afrikaner policemen were in the lane, standing next to their car as we approached Richard's house. It had been raining. Richard cursed as he saw them and drew up to the front so fast that he splashed their pants with mud. They were furious. Furious White cops, I thought, in sheer terror, furious and drunk. One of them hurled curses at us in Afrikaans. Richard and Botsotso hurled curses back in Zulu. The cops drew their guns. Botsotso was sitting in the backseat—passenger side—in the middle was Khanya, and I was behind Richard, the driver. Botsotso leaned across both Khanya and me and, following Richard's lead, stuck his gun out the window. Insults ricocheted back and forth. Khanya and I were the only ones who seemed terrified. The police, the tsotsis, and Shirley thought it all quite normal.

Suddenly, and for reasons beyond my comprehension, it was over. The police got in their car and drove off. Botsotso and Richard climbed out of the car laughing their heads off. I was shaken but determined not to appear shaken. We went to the backyard, broke out the beer, and put steaks and chicken on the grill. The meat sizzled succulently as more and more people arrived. There were bus drivers, nurses, gangsters, and students. I marveled at this eclectic gathering and at how little my middle class, Kenwood, and Dartmouth College training had prepared me for it.

The streetlights in Soweto where Richard lived were three stories high. They rained down harsh garish beams on the residents like prison searchlights. As evening settled over Richard's backyard, most of the people left. Seven or eight diehards took the braai inside. We were all a little tipsy as we arranged ourselves in Richard's living room: Khanya, her cousin Shirley, Mpo, and one or two others. Richard, Botsotso, a couple of other men and me. When the conversation turned to politics the women went into the kitchen. They carried on a soft but animated conversation in Pedi or Setswana as they sat at the kitchen table, while the men talked about the Defiance Campaign which was sweeping north from Cape Town, and argued about whether or not F. W. de Klerk could really dethrone P. W. Botha. I felt a slight unease. It was as though anything could happen at any moment (like when Botsotso had thrust his gun out the window at the two policemen). There was an inner tension, mine. There was an outer tension, theirs. The source of their tension revealed itself in short order.

Khanya had remained seated in the living room. Not only was she still in the living room, but she was drinking Richard's good liquor with even greater alacrity than Botsotso, his own henchman. And, as regards the discussion, she was debating with the best of them, providing as much political analysis and as many cold hard facts about the Defiance Campaign as anyone in the room. Every so often Richard's eyes flashed at Botsotso. Botsotso mirrored his boss's exasperation. Khanya was oblivious to it all. She continued to hold forth. She explained why it was necessary for mortgage loan boycotts to run coterminous with rent boycotts. This, she pointed out, would force the cautious and conservative Black bourgeoisie to be carried along by the militant energy of the Black working class and not vice versa. And it would bring landlords and the government to the table more quickly. She said that P. W. Botha could afford to sacrifice a few landlords but a mortgage boycott would affect the banking industry more directly and would bring the economy nearer to a stock market meltdown—and bring *us* that much closer to victory. It was a brilliant analysis and it would have carried a heretofore-anecdotal debate forward, if not for the fact that Richard had grown cold and silent.

"Botsotso," he said, as he kept his eyes on me.

"Yebo, induna," Botsotso said, respectfully.

"Did I tell you I lived in Harlem for three years?"

"Many times, induna." I braced myself.

Richard had studied in New York to be a dentist. When he got back to South Africa, the apartheid government wouldn't let him practice. Well, he had thought, if I can't be a dentist, I'll fix them, I'll show them, I'll become a smuggler instead.

"Now, Botsotso."

"Yebo, induna."

"Remember what I said about the Black man in America—about his problem?"

"Some of us should hear it again, induna."

Richard thrust his drunken face closer to mine and said, "He can't control his woman."

I laughed at this. It was a nervous, fitful laugh but he thought I was laughing at him. No one else laughed, not even Khanya. But something in the laughter may have emboldened her for she launched into a long attack on African men and their lack of appreciation for the contributions of African women to the liberation struggle. The more she spoke, the more tentative I became. I felt that she and I were in a paper canoe being pulled toward the falls.

Richard was standing now, looking down at both of us. *If he hits her I'm going to have to fight him which means I'm going to die. Even if I could take him, Botsotso would jump in and that skinny guy with dreads sitting in the corner too—it'll be three against one. What am I doing in this country?*

Richard and Khanya were yelling at each other. She shook her finger in his face. I thought the walls would burst apart at any moment. I finally made an interjection that was heard: "What she's saying is true, Richard, and you'd know it if you'd read *The Handbook for the Black Revolution.*" That stumped him. I am only now beginning to understand what *really* stumped him. It was not the authority of a foreigner who "could not control his woman." Nor was it the reasoned and well-informed arguments of an African woman, her status as a law student notwithstanding. It was the authority of a book. For most of his life he had sweated and toiled at his kitchen table in the township while other boys were out playing soccer. He'd been studious, steadfast in his conviction that books held a mystical, emancipatory power that could break the shackles of apartheid. But it wasn't true. He'd found far more freedom in six years of gunplay than he had in sixteen years of study.

Nonetheless, the truth of guns had not shaken his faith in books. For he was still a traditional intellectual at heart. So the mention of a "handbook" which he had not read, and which challenged his basic assumptions, gave him pause.

"What handbook?" he said.

"*The Wretched of the Earth*, by Frantz Fanon," I said.

He regained his balance and was about to run roughshod over me when the silent dreadlocked man in the corner said, "Let him speak."

The room quieted. Botsotso looked at Richard. Richard looked at the slight but able-bodied man in the corner, who was no more than twenty-five years old, a good twenty years younger than Richard. A cultural axiom (a youth does not order an elder about) had been trumped... but why, I wondered. Who is this young man and who is he to Richard? Now, we could hear the soft jazz music from the phonograph that was heretofore drowned out by the roar of argument.

"I'd like to hear his views on Frantz Fanon," the young man said.

"Sure, Jabu," Richard said, "why not. Go ahead, m'china," he said to me, "speak."

Having taught Fanon's *Black Skin, White Masks*, as well as *The Wretched of the Earth*, I was in my element and all too happy to hold forth in the same way that Khanya had held forth. When I paused, Jabu said, "What, tactically, would Fanon advise in this dispensation; say, for the Defiance Campaign?"

"I don't know if he'd advise anything, he was a theorist not a tactician. But I know what he'd want."

"And that is?"

"For Nelson Mandela to be released immediately from prison." Everyone cheered and raised their fists, including the women in the kitchen, who had moved to the threshold to get a glimpse. It was as though the fight in the living room hadn't happened. They were all happy, in agreement, ready to forget the "woman question" and the question of "weak" Black American men and to celebrate the fantasy of Mandela's release.

"And then he should die," I said, "of natural causes, of course. But quickly, before he can do the revolution any damage."

Suddenly the sea changed. The room howled curses of anger and indignation at me. Even the women in the kitchen were enraged. Richard and Botsotso leapt to their feet. Khanya was wide-eyed and sober—torn between her affection for me and anger. *Well, there goes your chance with her.*

But Jabu was neither angry nor enthused. "Let him finish," he said, soberly, to Richard and Botsotso who were threatening to kill me lest I leave the house that minute. Richard protested. But Jabu raised his hand. "Let him finish," he said.

I told them that apartheid was no longer the problem; liberalism was the problem, laissez-faire White supremacy was the problem. Though it was clear that Mandela wanted an end to apartheid, it should also be clear that he would not help people like Chris Hani or Winnie Mandela usher in a socialist state. "How do you know?" retorted Botsotso indignantly, "Have you been visiting him in prison?" I said that all anyone had to do was read the symptoms of his letters to the world; those bits of pieces of his thought that have reached us from Robben Island. "The man's a Christian and a lawyer; that's the worst combination," I said. "From what I've heard from him, he'd take a jaundiced view toward rent strikes and mortgage loan boycotts. Sure, he's against apartheid, but how radical is that? It's like saying you're against starvation or torture. Hardly the grist of revolutionary thought."

"So, you're Mandela's pen pal," Richard laughed, and so did everyone else. "Tell us what his mail says, m'china."

"It's not what's in the letter that counts," I said, "it's who it's to: none of his letters are written to anyone in this room. They're written to liberals for a liberal consensus. His letters say we should have the right to eat in Hillbrow if we want to eat in Hillbrow. We should live in the suburbs if we can afford to live in the suburbs. But whatever we do we should go to work, pay our taxes, and get the same gold watch the Whites get at the end. He wants a White state with a Black face. Is that liberation?"

"You're lying!" said Botsotso.

"So what's the truth if I'm lying?"

"You can't come to our country and slander our leaders!" he blurted out.

"You're moving the goal posts."

Richard now sat forward on the edge of his chair and put his hand on Botsotso's arm as if to say, let me handle this. He shook his finger at me and the ice knocked about in the glass he held in his other hand and his drink almost spilled on the floor.

"Hey, m'china! You're talking about a man who's been locked up for twenty-five years. Who are you, anyway?"

"I'm no one." The liquor had gone to my head as it had to all of theirs; in my peripheral vision I noticed the women at the kitchen door listening to every word. Khanya touched my arm, as if telling me to come back to shore, these waters are too deep and too dangerous, Frank.

"I'm an uncredentialed kaffir," I asserted, unheeding Khanya's hand on my arm, "just like you, Richard."

Richard rose to his feet, his fists balled. I thought he was going to drive his fist through my skull. But the young man with dreads said, "You're suggesting we struggle to free Madiba from prison and then kill him once he's released—I'd like to understand the analysis behind such a provocative statement."

Richard was stymied by the question, and curious to boot, so much so that he sat back down. Still, he managed to thrust a finger in my direction and say, "We should kill him!"

"You're being provocative," I said to Jabu, ignoring Richard's latest ballot initiative, "needlessly provocative."

"Am I?" Jabu smiled, as though he alone knew where this would lead.

"I didn't say we should kill Mandela. I said it would be nice if he died of natural causes. He would be of great service to the revolution—dead. Just as he's of great service to us now—in prison."

"So, he'd be an asset to the Boers if were out of prison and lived too long?" said Jabu.

"Yes, but more to the Brits than to the Boers; and even more to US-style 'liberal democracy' than to the local Brits. Mandela will ripen the terrain for the 'peaceful' invasion of US multinational corporations. The Boers aren't the problem."

Botsotso was incredulous: "The Boers aren't the problem, he says." He motioned to Richard as he spoke, as if to say: I vote 'yes' on the referendum to take him out back and beat the shit out of him. "So those weren't Boers waiting for us when we arrived this afternoon? Those aren't Boers driving through Soweto *sjamboking* children and shooting at us?"

"The world is changing, Botsotso. The Afrikaner's hard line is isolating him. The sjambokings, the shootings—you'll long for those days if Mandela is allowed to usher in a liberal consensus."

"One of my professors says the English are as angry at the Afrikaner as the Blacks," noted Khanya.

"Yes," I said, and I felt how the sway of the room had shifted in my favor. It could not be registered at the level of agreement, not even the curious man in the corner had shown any signs of alliance with either me or the blasphemous oracle from which I read; but they all had shifted from aggression to curiosity, which meant that I had been granted the power to pose the question. *And the power to pose the question is the greatest power of all.* "But your English professor is not vexed with the Boer for the same reasons you or I are vexed with the Boer. Your professor is troubled by his own exclusion from a cosmopolitan West, not with your degradation at the hands of the state. Apartheid has isolated the Brits in this country culturally, intellectually, and economically, but most of all, at the level of esprit de corps from the rest of the Western world. In other words, he doesn't want to be the only White of Africa; he wants to be a *member* of a global Whiteness, the enlightened and cosmopolitan Whiteness of Europe and America."

"According to your theory," said Jabu, reflectively, but with a pinch of skepticism, either because he was skeptical or because he did not want to tip his hand at too great an angle toward mine, "Nelson Mandela is the White English liberal's only hope, not only for the rejuvenation of finance capital but for the stabilization of a more subtle, nuanced and, what you seem to be describing as international, form of White supremacy."

"That's it, in a nutshell."

"Is there anyone in our movement who you approve of," said Jabu, "since you disapprove of Madiba?"

"Chris Hani. Winnie Mandela."

"Anyone else?"

"You." This made him smile. "Khanya. Shirley. Mpo. The other women in the kitchen. Botsotso. Even Richard."

"A little late to be licking arse, m'china," Richard sneered and poured himself another drink.

"I'm not licking ass. I didn't say I liked you. I said I approved of you, politically. I'm making an analysis. Despite your reverence for Nelson Mandela, he would hardly approve of you. Chris Hani and Winnie Mandela may be the only people with Nelson Mandela's stature, but who aren't manacled by his vision. Their leadership is essential to a political project that Fanon would be devoted to; one that could validate and mobilize the energy and split-second analysis that you, Richard and you, Botsotso, showed when you drew your guns and made those cops stand down; one that can validate and mobilize the energy and split-second analysis that sprung from Khanya when she decided to stay right here in this living room and enlighten us as to the importance of a mortgage loan boycott as well as a rent strike instead of going quietly to the kitchen. Mandela would have paid lip service to Khanya's actions, told you two to put your guns away, and he damn sure wouldn't support a mortgage loan boycott or the meltdown of the stock market."

Richard appealed to Jabu, "Do you believe this nonsense?"

"It's a theory," said Jabu.

"Voetsek! I want him and his talking-woman out of my house!"

"Your words could precipitate internecine conflict within the ANC," said Jabu. "There's always that danger."

"The conflict already exists—my words would just make me a scapegoat."

"But, still, we don't want in-fighting in the ANC," said Khanya.

"I don't want in-fighting either," I said. "But it seems to me that a struggle for hegemony is inevitable. It's either our ANC or it's their ANC. We can't very well share it."

"Nor should we kill Madiba," said Botsotso.

"You're twisting my words again!" I said. "What I said was that if he's released from prison he'll use his biblical stature to sanctify an accommodationist stance through which cosmetic changes would be heralded as essential changes—and the revolution would be up shit's creek! We need his legacy but we don't need him."

In the kombi from Soweto back to Braamfontein Khanya was still unnerved by the way I'd spoken about Nelson Mandela. It was not my analysis that disturbed her, for my analysis had simply built upon what she'd said about rent strikes and mortgage loan boycotts as means of mobilization. Rather, she shared, with Richard and the others (except Jabu who never showed his hand), a feeling that whereas Mandela's ideas could be debated, Mandela the man was sacred.

"You talk like he's your father," I scoffed.

Her anger at my cavalier response prompted her to say: "He is my father!" But the look in her eyes that immediately followed was one of regret and embarrassment at her outburst.

We were silent as we walked from the kombi rank on Bree Street up the hill to her dormitory at the University of the Witwatersrand. The air was cool but not too cold for a midwinter's night in July and the moon was high and glistening. It was a perfect night for love. But love, I feared, was not in the air. To my surprise we kissed goodnight and promised to meet the next day.

—⚏—

It would be two years before Jabu would tell me how he had used one of the moments when Richard rose to his feet to throttle me to slip down the hall to Richard's bathroom and lock the door behind him. There he wrote notes about what I'd said on a napkin. He told me that he left the braai before Khanya and me, though I thought he was still there when we said our good-byes. From Naledi, he said he drove to a block of flats in Hillbrow just ten minutes walk from the bed and breakfast inn where I would soon lay my inebriated head after kissing Khanya goodnight. He slumped down in the car, so that his head would be lower than the seat, and watched anything and everything that moved in the mirrors. Thirty minutes later he got out.

The apartment, or Stimela's safe house, as I would one day learn to call it, was dark and empty. There were unwashed dishes in the sink but they were a reflection of no more than tea and biscuits, not a meal. The stove had not been used in ages, except to boil water. Beer and sodas huddled together on one shelf in the fridge and in the door there was a carton of milk for tea. All the curtains were drawn. As Jabu moved from room to room he left them drawn; he took care to turn off the light of the room he left and to turn on only one light in the room he entered. There were no pictures on the wall. He noticed an indentation on top of the bedding—has Stimela been here, he wondered, or Trevor, or Oupa? It could not have been Precious; she's been in KwaZulu-Natal and was just returning that afternoon. He sat down at the computer in the dining room and began to write.

Frank Wilders or Wilderness. Did not get the name clearly. Like all Americans he talks fast and swallows his words. He is a Black American. 26 or 27 years old.

Two years later I would let my vanity get the better of me as I read the report and thanked him for the inaccuracy, for I was 33 in 1989, not 26 or 27.

Occupation:

He typed *journalist,* then he said he deleted the word, for he hadn't heard me mention any affiliation with a newspaper or magazine. So he typed *writer.* He realized that the categories that they had used for these dossiers in the past didn't fit.

Met Wilders or Wilderness on the afternoon of July 30, 1989, at a braai in Soweto. He did not say he worked for an NGO. He did not say he was a student. He mentioned no organizational affiliations. Judging from the length of his hair (an afro), his dress (hiking boots and blue jeans—like a European tourist), and his demeanor (argumentative, dogmatic, erudite) he is not a salesman or a business consultant. He could be an artist but he argued politics like someone who would not be an artist. He came to the braai with a female student in the law faculty at Wits, Khanya. Her cousin is dating our friend. Wilders said he wrote but did not say what he wrote. His views on Madiba are provocative. Using Fanon's analysis of the national bourgeoisie (which he seems to have read quite thoroughly—perhaps he is a lecturer) he elaborated a scenario of compromises and sellouts, which, he suggests, Madiba himself will openly facilitate and encourage. The scenario is compelling and…

He said he deleted the word "compelling." There was no telling how far up the food chain Stimela Mosando would send this report—though he knew it might never leave the safe house. Still, no sense in having the wrong people—or the right people for that matter—in Umkhonto we Sizwe think that he thought that the scenario was "compelling."

The scenario is controversial and incendiary—perhaps. He claims to be staying at a bed and breakfast establishment in Berea. This is unlikely, Berea's accommodations are not multiracial. Therefore his address should be verified. He has a detailed knowledge of personalities on the National Executive Committee of the ANC and is eager to offer an assessment of their politics. Is he an agent or is he a comrade? Can we use him—and if so, how?

Later that evening, Jabu's cousin Stimela Mosando came in and found Jabu already there. Unlike Jabu, who was quiet and took a long time to warm up to people, Stimela was outgoing and friendly. They were nearly five years apart, Stimela being older; they had grown up in a township on the West Rand near Kagiso. In adolescence they'd gone their separate ways politically. Jabu had followed the Black Consciousness thought of Steven Biko and its affinity for Frantz Fanon's *Black Skin, White Masks*. Stimela had become a Charterist politically and a Leninist ideologically. Stimela preferred Fanon's *The Wretched of the Earth*, when he read Fanon at all. Jabu was still in school when Stimela slipped across the Limpopo River and began his odyssey of military training and political education: first in the secret camps of the Frontline States; then in Moscow; then in Sofia; then Tripoli; and finally in Pyongyang.

Then Stimela came back to Jo'burg and set up his network. There'd been a large demonstration where they'd grown up. Seduced by his fondness for mass action and eager for a chance to toyi toyi and chant again (he'd been living in the cold stiff tundra of the Eastern

Bloc for so long) Stimela had made the mistake of getting caught up in it. He was arrested along with more than a hundred others. That night he found himself in a cell with fifteen to twenty other men. Jabu was among them. The cousins' time in detention together was marked by fierce ideological debates (and constant fear of the guards who came in the night to take someone away to be tortured). When they were released Jabu had been converted; he quit the PAC. He became a Charterist and a member of Stimela's growing underground network.

I am told Stimela read the report and sipped his tea as Jabu slept in the next room, rather than wake him and rebuke him for being so unaware of his environment as to let someone enter unnoticed.

It might have been the night of Stimela's infamous fight with Heinus Bezeuidenhout, a large Boer in Special Branch who mocked Africans by drinking alone in their *shebeens* without any back-up on his off duty hours. Had it been one of Stimela's operatives (Jabu, Trevor, Precious, or Oupa) Stimela would have scolded them for pulling such a stunt—a stunt full of unnecessary theatrics and unnecessary risk, the stunt he had pulled. "You're not there to fight," he always said, "you're there to win. Attack him from behind when it's possible." But Stimela liked the way his advice looked on others more than it did on him.

The shebeen was no more than a long tin barrack with all the grace and charm of a wind tunnel. The tables were rickety but scrubbed and the splinters had been sanded. The male patrons outnumbered the women four to one. At the far end was a counter with several high stools in front and a small watchful Sotho-speaking woman standing behind it. She kept a gun under the counter and a cash box beside the cooler. Red Beard, as the patrons called him behind his back, was seated on one of the stools gulping beer from the bottle, imposing his jokes on an old man who'd only come there to drink, not to be held hostage by the humor of a cop. But the man knew what was good for him, so he laughed at Red Beard's jokes. Red Beard was demonstrating the technological splendor of a new fifty-two-channel walkie-talkie he'd just received from the Israelis. Its dials glowed. Its signals beeped. Voices spiced with static crackled from within. "Yeah, baas," said the laughing old man, "that's quite an instrument you have there, me baas."

Stimela seemed to glide rather than walk down the long runway of tables on his way to Red Beard.

"Excuse me, meneer, are you Colonel Bezeuidenhout?"

"You bet your ruddy arse, fana."

"That's a nice radio. Mind if I borrow it?"

"Of all the cheek, kaffir!"

"I'm Stimela Mosando. And I'll have that radio."

Heinus Bezeuidenhout had no time to curse himself for not recognizing the face from the book of Umkhonto we Sizwe suspects they kept at John Vorster Square. Stimela said Red Beard feigned as though he was simply going to take another swig of beer but then grabbed the bottle by the neck and swung it as hard as he could. Stimela was quick but not quick enough. The bottle caught him somewhere between his collarbone and his neck, but he managed to pull Bezeuidenhout from the stool and take him down in three moves. Two moves too many, he said to me, after I went to work for him. You're not there to fight, you're there to win.

Jabu opened his eyes to see Stimela standing by the dresser; setting his gun beside the radio he'd purchased at a 100 percent discount.

"Someone from Tel Aviv sent me this radio," Stimela smiled, "Who says the Jews are with the Boers?"

"I met someone from Minneapolis at our 'friend's braai," said Jabu, wiping cat butter from his eyes.

"Minne-how much?"

"Minneapolis."

"Which is?"

"In the States."

"New York?"

"No."

"I'll keep my radio, you keep your American."

Later that night the others joined them. Oupa, who would never learn to like me and who would never understand why Stimela kept me around; Trevor with whom I clicked from the start; and Precious

Jabulani who was always kinder to me—so it seemed—than Oupa, but who never allowed herself to be as unguarded with me as Trevor was.

—⁂—

In early September of 1989 I went back to the States, having met Jabu, but without having learned the significance of our meeting or what it meant for my future. I moved to Harlem and entered an MFA program at Columbia University. But I returned to South Africa in November of the same year, 1989, to continue my research, whatever that meant, and to spend two and a half months with Khanya, my fiancée. Jabu Mosando would come to the little flat that Khanya rented on Ameshoff and Jan Smuts, in Braamfontein, across the street from Wits. When I met Jabu on my second visit, he claimed to have bumped into me "by chance." He would invite himself up to Khanya's flat for tea or a cool drink with me while she was in class. Tea was a marker of just how Anglicized so much of Black South Africa was. I wouldn't have minded this if not for the fact that I could never find a decent cup of coffee. I remembered Jabu from the braai at Richard's house last July. I was happy to see him again. Here, I thought, is a true interlocutor. My easy hubris allowed me to think his visits facilitated my research, that it was I who was gathering information on him, that he was a specimen of mine. I learned that he was also a student and also a member of the South African Students Congress, SASCO.

SASCO was a member organization of the Charterist Movement; not a ragtag band of chanting, burning, and subversive Black students, but a national organization with branches on every campus of the Indian and Coloured universities, the Black universities, the English medium universities, such as Wits, and even at some of the technikons. SASCO had a mobilization capacity that the Student Nonviolent Coordinating Committee, even at the height of the Civil Rights movement, would have envied. They had a capacity to shut down a major university, or stage a national strike, that Students for a Democratic Society could not have imagined, even in Chicago in 1968. Despite this tempting analogy between SNCC and SDS on the one hand, and SASCO on the other, there were qualitative differences between them. Whereas SNCC and SDS had fought for equal rights within, and unfettered access to, civil society, SASCO was fighting to commandeer the entire university-industrial complex as a necessary step toward taking over civil society. Furthermore, a fair number of SASCO militants were already Umkhonto we Sizwe soldiers—student-guerillas, one might say. Unlike the children of White civil society in America, they did not have to agonize with their conscience over whether or not to pick up the gun. They entered the lecture hall with a gun in hand, a gun nearby, or a gun lodged firmly in their imagination. Jabu Mosando was one such comrade.

Jabu would sit in Khanya's living room and ask me endless questions about my political views and all sorts of sly things about my background. How did you vote in the 1988 Presidential elections? I don't vote. Why not? It only feeds my frustration. What political party do you belong to? I don't; I work with the Mozambique Support Network. How did you come to know so much about the ANC and Southern Africa? Research; and by reading the transcripts of the BBC newswires in the Dartmouth library when I was in college. What do you think of White students at Wits? They're smart but inhibited, they expose themselves politically but they won't take a stand. And African students? They could take this country down...if... If Mandela dies of natural causes, he smiled. I was drinking, I said, I spoke a little too freely. Not at all, comrade, he said, though I could not gauge his tone of voice; was it reassuring or just a placeholder between the space of my answer and his next question?

He had a knack for massaging my ego. I could discourse for long un-interrupted periods when he came by. He would listen to my impromptu lectures with great interest, but with neither assent nor disagreement, the way he had listened at Richard's braai. I was never suspicious of him. What's curious, however, were the things that I omitted, without plan or purpose: I'd worked almost ten years as a stockbroker and I grew up in a rich White Midwestern enclave. (Several months later, in 1990, when I would return to actually live in South Africa, he would ask me to write an article about Jesse Jackson's accommodationist bungling at the 1988 Democratic convention for the SASCO newspaper; to write an analysis of how and why he sold his entire constituency down the drain and got nothing in return from the Democratic Party centrists. Again, I was only too happy to oblige.)

—⁂—

In February of 1990, my second two-month trip to South Africa ended. I returned to New York, thinking, this, thank god, is the last time I'll see South Africa. Khanya will come to New York and from there we'll move to Brazil or Holland...live in peace, far away from both beasts—South Africa and the United States.

One morning before class I turned on the television. Crowds lined the streets of Cape Town and cheered, as the radiator lining the water-stained wall of my cold Harlem flat hissed and sputtered. Nelson Mandela and his entourage waved at me from inside my screen. Like the people in Cape Town I, too, was moved to tears on the day of his release from prison but I had a sinking feeling as well. Now, I thought, the compromise begins. I did not know that his demobilization of revolutionary forces inside the country would be so swift and decisive. Nor could I imagine that I would bear witness to it, much less contest it.

Khanya came to New York in July of 1990, but she left abruptly in February of 1991. Why, she said on the morning of her decision, should I trade one South Africa for another? After graduating in May, I followed her back to the one place I swore I'd never return. I'll be here no more than the year it will take her to finish law school; we'll be in Rio or Amsterdam soon. But a year and a half after Mandela's release, I was not living on a hill overlooking Ipanema or on a houseboat in Holland, but in Khanya's tiny Braamfontein flat across the street from Wits. I had no work permit, just another six-month tourist visa. I was married to a woman who could not get me permanent residency, for her sister's association with an exiled-PAC operative in Zimbabwe had put her sister under house arrest and caused Khanya to be stripped of her Bophuthatswana identity papers. I was a Black foreigner married to a Black ex-citizen of a Babes-in-Toyland state.

Letters of recommendation from my professors at Columbia, chief among them Edward Said, secured a teaching position for me at the University of the Witwatersrand. I was elated because it meant that I would be able to get a work permit and residency papers. I wouldn't have to continue working as a waiter at an Italian restaurant in Braamfontein—a job I'd held (illegally) since I arrived—and my legal status would then pass on to Khanya. We were about to turn the corner.

Several days before classes started I went to dean Elizabeth Rankin's office for what I assumed would be the first step toward getting the paperwork from the university that I would take to Home Affairs. Dean Rankin began pleasantly enough, but she was keen on discussing my syllabus, not the hiring forms (which were nowhere in sight). I engaged her with enthusiasm and energy, explaining the books on the syllabus and the approach I planned to take. She listened for a while and then said that there was a fair amount of Edward Said's work on the syllabus. I told her that there was only one book and an article, but that the course itself was in fact something of a replica of the Cultural Studies Project that he and Jean Franco had conducted at Columbia, and of which I'd been a part.

Rather briskly she informed me that Edward Said had come to South Africa the year before and caused quite a disturbance when he spoke on campus; Jewish students had launched protests and threatened civil disobedience. She had enough trouble with left-wing student organizations and she didn't need the Jewish students rising up as well. I told her that I failed to see what that had to do with the course I'd been hired to teach. Her look said, do you really now? I made some feeble mutterings about academic freedom, but I could feel my voice cracking. I could feel the floor falling away; I knew why there were no employment documents on the table.

She smiled and said that she believed in academic freedom as well. And she wanted me to know that this was not a matter of abrogating academic freedom—there simply wasn't money in the budget for hiring another lecturer at this point and she was deeply sorry that the chair of the department didn't know this before sending me to her for an interview. This wasn't supposed to have been an interview, I said, I was promised a job. That wasn't her understanding; she said goodbye and wished me all the best in my future endeavors in South Africa.

I went up to the department to confront the chair, for she must have known this was going to happen. But when I got there I found her with another professor. I had lost my will to fight. I simply sat down and told them both what had happened—without passion or protest in my voice. Then I said that if they let me go into the classroom I would teach for no pay, just to build up my résumé and keep my mind active. In the end, the two of them worked out a deal whereby I would teach but I would not draw a salary—dean Rankin had seen to that. Instead I would be paid a weekly check out of the department's entire external speakers fund… until the fund ran out. It came to roughly one sixth of what I would have earned had I been hired. It was not a job, which meant there would be no work permit and no residency papers. I went home and explained it all to Khanya over the wine and candles she'd bought to celebrate.

My life was at a low point. I found myself always thinking back on my two previous visits with a sense of longing and nostalgia. Those were visits, but this was immigration and I was an immigrant—of sorts. I fled a country whose anti-Blackness was an impermissible knowledge to one that wore its hatred on its sleeve. This don't make no sense! Sense or not, there it was. What makes this so different than the times before? It's the same country that I've been to twice before. What had changed? The air was still thick with the scowl of Whites and the rising militancy of Blacks, like rags and oil waiting for a match. In the shopping malls, by the newsstands, around the rotunda of the Whites Only entrance to Noord Street Station, one still saw Boers in khaki shorts, gun belts and revolvers braced against their hips. The number of political deaths still rocked steady at 240 per month. The same dread set with the same sun and rose with the same moon. So what had changed? What brought on this daily ministering to depression and a desire to leave, now, which wasn't there before?

On my two research trips, I had dollars and was always in transit. 1989: *Six weeks and outta here! Boom!* 1990: *Another six weeks and outta here!* A tourist in my own movie. Week one: *I could live here, sure why not.* Week two: *Not only could I live here but I could fight for this revolution.* Week three: *To hell with this place! The coffee's weak and the cinemas suck.* Week four: *These White folks are crazy and sadistic. Back home we got our White people trained.* Week five: *Time to stop playing at 'solidarity,' Frank. You can't hack it as a Black South African. Just put your greenbacks and your passport and your American accent front and center and get you some service, some air-conditioning, and some respect.* Week six: *At least they got one thing going for them—an airport with daily departures.*

But now, I thought, I'm neither a tourist nor a researcher. I don't have dollars in my pocket, only a few rand from the course I teach during the day and the tables I serve at night.

It is late. The neon sign at Luigi's has just gone out. There is no traffic on Jorissen Street. So why do I just stand here on the corner as though waiting for the light to give me permission? I wipe the residue of pesto from my hands and fold my apron. Behind me the Zulu cooks and dish-washers climb the restaurant's basement stairs to the street and drift into the night. I cross the street as Luigi and his Afrikaner wife ascend from the stairs. Luigi's restaurant is underground; one descends to dine. There's something prescient in that. They are laughing with the two Ro-manian waiters. The Africans follow them silently and then turn in the direction of the kombi rank.

Moon rings and lamp light winked and glimmered in the gutters. It had rained all through the dinner hour. The street was uncommonly quiet and uncommonly clean. I heard swishing of distant tires; still, no cars in sight. Fine, I thought, I'm here; here for the duration—whatever that means. I may as well call it "home." I waved goodnight to Luigi, his wife, and the Romanians (*racist bastards!* I hissed inside) and walked away, telling my-self, be happy, you're happy, if you say you're happy you'll be happy, if you call it home it's home. Braamfontein's banks and office buildings are all asleep. Tonight the university, closed and darkened on the hill above Jan Smuts Avenue, no longer holds me in its grip of subordination and awe.

My fear, even of it, has been laid to rest, and my night of waiting tables is over. I am free. I am happy and alone in a world whose lights and colors I alone command.

At the end of the block a tall White man is stumbling toward me. The corner is too far behind me for me to duck into a side street detour. He's too close for me to cross to the other side. *Why should I be afraid? Stop thinking like a South African. Walk on, Frank, walk on.*

As he grew near, I saw how his shirt was unbuttoned down to his belt; the tails were untucked as well. He strode down the middle of the side-walk. *Will he make room for me, and if so, what side of the walk will he claim?*

The drunk was now five feet away. In South Africa, as in Britain, cars drive on the left side of the street, so I held to my left side. When he swaggered to his left, I breathed a sigh of relief. But then he stumbled to his right, and our shoulders brushed.

"Are you blind, kaffir!" I felt his whiskey breath on my face.

"Who the fuck you callin' 'kaffir?' You wasn't so drunk, I'd slap you into next week."

He pulled a gun from under his shirttails and drew a round into the chamber. He rammed the barrel against the bridge of my nose. "And what would I be doing while you slapped me into next week?"

"Please, don't shoot me."

"I don't fancy next week! I fancy this week. You baboon. What if I fancy this week?"

He held the gun to my head. He pulled the trigger and a flurry of visions rushed into my head with the bullet. Scenes from a life which was surely mine but which, until then, I had neither known to be mine nor recalled. But there they were: my mother, younger than I had ever known her, pruning roses in the wind; my father asleep on cushions in front of a fire; a boy in Tangier who I'd seen for ten seconds ten years ago and forgotten ten minutes later; a couple kissing in a berth compartment of a passing train. Then there was a scent. *The scent of death?* No, it couldn't be, for I had never smelled death before and this scent was familiar. It was the whiskey breath of the man who shot me. I hadn't been shot. I'd mistaken the click of the safety for the pull of the trigger.

He laid his hand gently on my cheek, "I like you, kaffir. But Mandela's got you all stirred up." He belched in my face and turned to go.

"Welcome to next week," he added as I slumped against the building. Through a blue wall of tears he faded away.

I cursed and whimpered home. I sat for a long time on the steps in front of our building, trying to find someone to blame. *It's Khanya's fault. If she hadn't broken our agreement and left New York I wouldn't even be here. It's the chair of my department's fault. I wouldn't still be waiting tables if it weren't for her.* And then I cried like I cried the first night I arrived two years ago.

It was two in the morning. I went upstairs and rolled a joint and went out onto the balcony. I held the smoke at the base of my lungs and promised myself I'd leave this country by the end of that year, or kill a White man by the end of the next. Khanya's jurisprudence essay waited on the kitchen table to be proofread, along with essays written by my six seminar students at Wits. They had to be graded and returned by morning. I put a pot of coffee on. I changed into my robe and slippers without waking Khanya. I graded papers till morning.

—⁂—

Unbeknownst to me, Stimela had told Jabu to "hand" me on to Trevor. Trevor Garden became my handler—though I was still not aware of being "handled." I met Trevor at a Wits orientation tea for academics and graduate students in December 1991 or January 1992. He was a graduate student who ate his biscuits quietly and drank his tea politely and always deferred to another student when intellectual disputes (regarding, for example, the correctness of Freud's biological grounding *vs.* the correctness of Lacan's linguistic turn) occurred. I was to learn that his coalition-building dissemblance was all an act, part of his cover. Deep down he loathed the White students and faculty as much as he loathed his high school rector. But he would have to live among them if he was going to be in any way effective in destroying them. His facilitating dissemblance was a way to live with them and to laugh at them, if only inwardly, while he did. But it was also a way for him to keep his sanity in a room full of people whom he held in contempt.

He knew about my work and the political positions I'd taken in debates within the Hillbrow-Berea branch of the ANC but he didn't let on until he was sure of me. It goes without saying that he did not let on that he knew a certain Jabu Mosando in sociology across campus. None of the other literature graduate students or faculty knew what his political leanings were. He didn't let on that he was ANC and certainly not that he was Umkhonto we Sizwe.

The name Garden made no genealogical sense, for his mother, not his father, was of English ancestry. His father was of German extract like the haus frau at the bed and breakfast inn in Berea. The paternal family of this five-foot-nine-inch blond-haired young man hailed from Namibia to which his grandparents had emigrated from Germany between the Great Wars. His British mother had barred his father from being inducted into the secret world of the Broederbond—an aspiration shared by nearly every Afrikaner professional. Trevor's father would never stand in a darkened room with shrouded windows, with only two candles burning on a center table; with thirty Broeders lining the dark walls, their faces invisible and unknown to the inductee until he swore his ascent to each clause of the oath. Trevor's father never swore that oath nor did he hear the warning upon completion: "He who betrays the Bond will be destroyed by the Bond. The Bond never forgets. Its vengeance is swift and sure. Never yet has a traitor escaped his just punishment."

If Wilkins and Strydom's *The Broederbond* is to be believed, as an educator and influential man in the community, Trevor's father could have easily wormed his way through the seven hundred secret cells and one day found a seat on the Broederbond's Executive Council or on one of its watchdog committees. The think tanks were formed between World War I and World War II as a means of holding British hegemony at bay. The think tanks, by the time I arrived, were more than mere think tanks. The Broederbond's watchdog committees were shadow cabinets of the government: more secret and more powerful than the security police; more influential than the halls of learning, for key administrators (who were not English, of course) were Broeders; more official than the government, for the Cabinet Ministers were Broeders. In absolute secrecy the Broederbond made policy on Indian, Coloured, and African affairs; foreign relations, internal security against Africans, domestic relations with the English; the proper handling of the press; and made assessments of the relative threat of Black poetry and novels construed as "resistance" literature. The government transposed the Broederbond's watchdog committee's policies into law; the halls of learning turned the government's laws into ethics; and the police and the courts turned "ethical transgressions" into crimes.

But Trevor told me that scapegoating his mother had allowed his father to ignore the real reason why he never stood in a shrouded room to repeat the sacred oath—the fact that he was not an Afrikaner, but a German.

For his part, Trevor had disgraced the family not by marrying across the Boer line (or by being a German). "Crimes" which, supposedly, made his father unfit for the Broederbond. His betrayal was so unpardonable that neither the English nor the German side forgave him. What he did could not be repaired. They had done everything for him. He was not the eldest but he was the eldest boy and that was all that mattered. Each weekend they ferried him fifty miles from their sprawling house in the country to the gifted children's program conducted by educators at a teachers college in Johannesburg. "He's a genius," the proctor would exclaim, "truly a gifted child!" As an adolescent, he played rugby and acquired a fifth-degree black belt in karate. After school he would don his little army uniform with its sacred and indecipherable shoulder bars and carry his little rifle into remote veld and forests on Voortrekker expeditions where he and his male classmates were taught marksmanship and the danger of the *swart gevaar*, the Black Threat. There, in the bush, the children trained to hold the line for civilization itself.

But unbeknownst to his parents, his schoolmaster, his Voortrekker commander, *and even unbeknownst to Trevor himself*, Trevor had already been recruited by Umkhonto we Sizwe. It happened before he was even twelve years old. His nanny's brother was an MK operative, a man who had already left Umkhonto, when I met him, to study at the London School of Economics. This operative-cum-economist understood that what was needed were a cluster of Whites who could get close to targets that Blacks could not get close to. He enlisted his sister and several other nannies to work on the sentiments of youth to exploit the fissures of puberty and filial rebellion, thus "turning" their little White charges against their unsuspecting White parents and the state.

In 1977 the first televisions were placed in the living rooms of White families throughout the land. Trevor's hometown was no exception. His family sat in wide-eyed awe as his father turned the knob and watched as a line drew itself vertically across the gray silent screen and opened a new world of images and sound. But since the BBC would not run the risk of British television being shut down (Britain's actors had called for a strike should the BBC sell programs to South Africa), and since the Americans had not as yet filled the programming void, South Africans were not privy to much in the way of entertainment during those early days of television. Military parades were the highlight.

The Garden family and the children's nanny watched with pride as the armored personnel carriers, the rocket launchers that looked like open boxes of cigarettes mounted on jeeps, and thousands of troops marched past Prime Minister John Vorster and his generals looking down from the dignitaries' gallery.

It didn't last, for the parade was too long and the Gardens' attention span too short. They were bored. Meneer Garden went out to clean leaves from the pool. Trevor's mother and his siblings went to a friend's house. Only he and Nana remained.

"Look at the soldiers, Nana!" he said pointing at the screen. Then Trevor hoisted himself onto her lap and imitated a soldier commanding a rotating machine gun from the back of a jeep. "I'm going to be one, Nana. I'll be on the telly in my own parade. You'll see, Nana."

"Do you love Nana?"

He let the machine gun melt into the thin air and hugged her. Of course he loved Nana. If he knew with what power the English language could make distinctions he would have told her that he loved her so much he had little love left for his mother.

"One day," she told him, "the soldiers will hurt Nana."

"No, they're good soldiers, Nana. They won't hurt you."

"They're coming to hurt Nana right now—and Nana's family."

"No, Nana."

"I promise you."

"I won't let them. I promise you."

She would help him make good on that promise. If ten branches bore only one fruit, Nana's brother had told her, that one fruit would ripen into his parents' nightmare, a child who goes off to school and comes home a traitor. By the time Trevor was in high school he was a young man chock-full of dangerous questions about what his parents and teachers stood for; no one, save Nana, had answers. He set his questions in motion. The year before he graduated from high school he was disciplined by the rector for "subversive activity": he had started a jazz club whose members included students from his high school as well as students from the neighboring township high school.

—∞—

Trevor told me that his induction into MK was like a punctuation mark at the end of the sentence. He'd never been as happy as he was on the day of his high school graduation. All the girls were in their finery. All the boys were in their Voortrekker uniforms. The band played. The parents applauded as each child-soldier took the stage, received his diploma, and returned proudly down the stairs to the flashing bulbs of his parents' camera.

"When I went on stage, the rector was beaming like I'd never seen him beam. He held out my diploma. But something came over me and I couldn't take it. Instead of taking it, I ripped my shoulder bars from my uniform. Tore them right off. Then I left the stage. Walked right past my family; out of the auditorium. I went home. No one spoke to me that night. My little brother tried to but my father moered him just for coming to my room. Sometime later, Nana's brother came to visit her. When my family had gone she came up to the house and brought me back to her room. He was waiting for me. We talked, the three of us, long into the night. We spoke about politics and liberation in a manner that I'd never known was possible. He gave me MK literature written by comrades in the camps. And he gave me a name, Stimela Mosando, a Wits student whom I was to contact the moment I arrived. That's how I came to varsity: with my rugby shirt, my books, two grenades, and a name."

—⚭—

My own "induction" into MK was piecemeal but cumulative. Or perhaps I should say my entrée into Stimela's fold. For in 1990 Nelson Mandela unilaterally ended the arms struggle—without consulting Chris Hani. In 1993 he disbanded Umkhonto we Sizwe; from if not the first, then certainly the second, moment on our activities were those not of a sanctioned armed wing but of so-called "terrorists." Events and relationships came upon me and overtook me, with my understanding them only in hindsight. I seemed not to be the master of my own fate. *Are we ever?* When did it happen? How did it happen? The causal chain snuck up on me quietly, like the punctuation mark at the end of Trevor's high school graduation, when some inner force that was an outer force compelled him to rip the shoulder bars from his shirt.

In 1992, I was elected to the Hillbrow-Berea ANC branch executive committee. Soon after an ANC regional executive committee member named Barbara Hogan sent me to work for the ANC regional Peace Commission, a small group of people who were investigating township massacres perpetuated by the Inkatha Freedom Party (IFP)—an ethnically-based contra-like force armed and financed by the government, the police, and the army. I took photographs of people who'd been killed or wounded and wrote reports and sent them to Amnesty International and Human Rights Watch. Slowly, I came to see a cross-pollination between people associated with the Peace Commission and people associated with Stimela Mosando (and, by extension, Chris Hani). Part of the staff was involved in gun running to people in squatter camps who were being attacked by the government and Inkatha). At first I worked with these comrades as a propaganda specialist. I would accompany them as they ran arms to and from DLBs (dead letter boxes or arms caches); I would help brainstorm ways to "persuade" the Western media and human rights organizations that we were not smuggling arms: that we were not involved in self-defense, much less retaliation and our weapons were really being turned over to a transitional committee comprised of the Nationalist Party and the ANC. Sometimes I'd simply be told to bring one piece of paper to this person and another piece of paper to that person and not to open it, or to travel in a car with comrades without my knowing what was in the car, or to attend an interrogation of someone whom they were holding—either to protect that person or to get information out of him. Nothing was ever completely explained to me. I was privy to many fragments, but not to the whole picture.

One day Trevor came to see me and explained more than had heretofore been explained.

"Do you believe in the right of a small group of people to work clandestinely, that they might push the envelope, so to speak; in moments, for example, when mass mobilization is stalled?"

"Of course not. Clandestine operatives should secure their mandate from the people, not vice-versa."

"No doubt," he sighed, "but when reactionary forces have, how shall we say, stalled, yes, stalled or confused that mandate. What then?"

Such a question had never been put to me before. I didn't know how to answer.

"You're not a pacifist are you?" he said.

"There's no such thing as a pacifist."

"Explain."

"In the 60s and 70s a lot of activists in the States cathedralized nonviolence. All you had to do was ask them if they paid their taxes and watch their jaw drop. There is no space of the pacifist. There is no time of the pacifist. It's the time and space of laissez-faire backed by violence in reserve. Those who argue otherwise aren't pacifists. As a friend of mine says, they simply prefer the violence of the state to the violence of the people. The violence we should be concerned with is the structural violence," I went on, energized by his attentiveness, "of capitalism and White supremacy. In the face of structural violence it's unethical to cathedralize a tactic—whether civil disobedience, armed resistance, or writing a letter to the editor. In other words, violence or nonviolence should be viewed from a tactical perspective; not a principled one. The moment and a mandate from the most dispossessed will authorize the proper tactics. Umkhonto exists because Soweto exists."

"But Nelson Mandela insists we suspend armed struggle."

"Mandela exists because Soweto exists. He seems to have forgotten that."

"What exactly are you saying?"

"That Mandela is a man, not a mandate. He's elaborated by the mandate."

"Try telling him that."

"Yes, well, trying telling any of them anything."

"So, we're on the same page after all?"

"Yes," I said, a little surprised.

"We'd like you to meet someone."

"'We'?"

"Jabu Mosando and I."

I remembered Richard's braai from my first research trip, and Jabu's need to have tea when he met me "by chance" on my second visit. I had the sense of being halfway through completing a large jigsaw puzzle. "How, exactly, are you and Jabu Mosando connected?"

He simply smiled.

"Who's this 'someone'?"

"Jabu's cousin Stimela. There may be one or two others."

"Then what?"

"You like asking questions, don't you."

"A clue, perhaps?"

"Something interesting."

When I first met Stimela the Security Branch had not retrieved their Israeli radio from him, which meant Red Beard and his bloodhounds were still on his trail. Despite this, he boldly came to Khanya's and my apartment in broad daylight; it fit in with his penchant for the theatrical. He chatted with Khanya in Setswana. He played on the floor with Reba who was five years old at the time. He acted as though it were a social call. Not a word of skullduggery was spoken. Perhaps, I thought, he's been on the run for so long that he relishes this moment, that he'd rather play with a child and with Ginger, our cat, than speak to me. Presently, Khanya and Reba left. Stimela, Trevor, and I were alone in the living room (with Ginger, our carrot-striped cat, who was impervious to a hint). Stimela said he looked forward to what he called an "intellectual friendship and a political alliance" with me and to having many stimulating discussions about Gramsci, Marx, Fanon, and the writers I was teaching at Wits. Am I going into political education, I thought, or does he just want to hang out. What's this all about? Either scenario seemed unlikely. Something told me not to ask him to clarify, that he would clarify as time went on. He said he was pleased to meet me. He said that he had had to cut his own studies at Wits short "due to circumstances." What circumstances? I asked. He looked at Trevor who in turn frowned at me. Then he said, "The South African Police are not cooperating with my education plans." That made Trevor laugh. So, what the hell, I laughed too.

Now he was serious again. He said what the movement needed at this point was revolutionary internationalism to counteract certain "compromising" tendencies that were developing within the ANC. His words energized me and I thought about launching into one of my lectures on the subject, but decided against it. He said that he had been in the Soviet Union three months ago, in November and December of 1991, for a "special telecommunications course." His eyes lit up. I told him I'd been there as well, in April of 1973. We shared memories of Russian hospitality and how we both had felt the first time a man held our hand, the way men hold hands, when walking through Moscow. I had had an urge to say I'm a linebacker not a homosexual; then I looked into the man's eyes and realized that this was not a come on. It was simply a profound gesture of camaraderie. And I had wanted to weep. For at that very moment, as that man, who was willing to weave his few words of English into my few words of Russian, and I ascended the stairs to the cinema, I thought of the wretched children at Kenwood Grammar School who, eleven years before, had chosen to hold up recess until hell froze over rather than form a line where one of them would have to hold my hand. If communism will cleanse my hands, I had thought, then I am a communist.

Stimela said he'd almost fallen into the river along the Nevsky Prospect after a night of libations with his instructors. He had marveled at the artwork in the Tsar's palace, the Hermitage Museum, but what struck him most profoundly was how little security there was around the artwork and how many working people went each day to the museum. I told him that I had been a little tipsy along the Nevsky Prospect as well and had spent all night walking with a Russian, a woman who neither thought I was going to rape her nor thought she wanted to take me home. As morning approached she asked a question that she'd wanted to ask me since we met in the café. Here it comes, I thought. I told her that I couldn't imagine what there was that we hadn't already talked about (though I could, believe me, I could). She took a deep breath and said, Do you believe in god? I could tell by the expression on her face that my answer stood the chance of either solidifying or breaking irrevocably the bond that had been building all night. She had the look of a child who wants her parent or lover to care for the same thing she cares for. For the life of me I could not tell which answer she craved. No, I finally said, I don't believe in god, deciding it was better to tell the truth and be severed from my friend forever, than to lie and make my final gesture false. She breathed a tremendous sigh of relief. She smiled broadly. *Ocen horosho!* (very good), she said. For a moment I was worried. So many Americans are naïve, but I think you are not naïve. All night long we talk—about Nixon and Vietnam and revolution in Africa—and I think to myself, yes, yes, he is very intelligent young man; very intelligent for only seventeen, very much like young Soviet men. But, I also wonder, I wonder just a bit. He is so young, I think. And he is so American, I think. How intelligent can he really be? Does he know of our discovery? Your discovery? I asked her. We Soviets know there is no god, she proclaimed.

We have proven it scientifically! How's that? I asked her. We sent our cosmonauts up in space. They went up. They looked out into space and they saw no god. So there is no god! It's a shame your Mr. Nixon and your astronauts have kept this secret from you for so long. Stimela and Trevor found this to be hilarious. I told him that he should ask his comrades and instructors in Moscow if the cosmonauts ever found god.

At the mention of his Moscow comrades his eyes clouded over. Then, speaking not so much to me or to Trevor, but to himself, as though we were no longer there, he said how betrayed he felt by his instructors in the Soviet Union's Communist Party. Throughout the entire course none of them had given him any hint that what happened was about to happen.

"They saw it coming and said nothing to us. That's not the way you treat comrades," he said. "I went to sleep one night and woke up the next morning in a different country. Not the Soviet Union. Would this country still support us, I wondered. But I already knew the answer." He paused, allowing himself to become aware of our presence. "We need new allies, new relationships. Maybe Steve Biko was right," he said, without saying right about what. I knew it had something to do with the need for Black people to be on our own because on our own is how we always are. It was still too early in the struggle for a Charterist and a Communist to utter such thoughts aloud. Chris Hani would have to die first.

Before Trevor and Stimela left, Stimela said that he was enjoying the course "Intellectuals and the State" that I was teaching at Wits and that he hoped our relationship developed to the point where he could acquire the theoretical vocabulary that the course took for granted. "Funny," I said, with a smile, "I've never seen you in class—since they're only five students you'd be hard to miss." I was flattered that Trevor had been bringing him the books and my lecture notes.

Stimela laughed, "I'm at every class," he laughed, adding, "You're never alone." Was that, I wondered, meant to be reassuring? We shook hands and they left.

Several days later Trevor returned by himself.

"Stimela wants you to write out your biography, twenty or so pages. Here are some questions—guidelines."

"Then what?"

"Then he'll want you to write again."

"What will that prove?"

"You don't mind, do you?"

"No, but do you mind telling me what it's all about?"

"Something interesting."

"Thanks."

It wasn't long before he told me I'd passed a "certain level of mustard."

"So, I'm not a US agent?"

"We think not."

"Because?"

"Because you're too unsophisticated."

"That's reassuring."

"You live too much inside your own head. The dean tells you she doesn't like the books on your syllabus and you play Joan of Arc. Not the way one infiltrates an organization, is it?"

He said all this without a sense of irony in his voice, though the corners of his mouth seemed to draw up into a faint smile. It was simply an assessment of me. His? Stimela's? He wasn't trying to insult me. It was simply a report about my capacities, potentialities, and use-value; as though I were a small piece of a large puzzle he and others were putting together on the floor.

"If you had been sent here to establish yourself, your handlers would be cross with you, to say the least. You think you can hold an entire institution accountable to the ethics of the very people it destroyed to become what it is. And that scene with Richard two and a half years ago—he's a tsotsi for Christ's sake. He'd've killed you for sport. But you try to lecture him?"

"I didn't lecture him, I engaged him."

"You have no sense of your environment; and what's more you seem not to care."

"I'm supposed to backpedal when Fanon clearly states—"

"That's what I mean. It's called the intelligence community, not the ego community—they wouldn't have you."

"You're too kind."

"A dogged intellectual and social misfit. Stimela says you're perfect."

"Perfect for what?"

He opened the satchel he'd brought with him. One by one he plunked a manila folder on the bed and called out a name as he did.

"This is Nico Cloete. A policy wonk on steroids. A neoliberal wet dream. June Sinclair: legal scholar and an iron fist in a velvet glove— we'll have to watch out for her. Robert Charlton: Wits University vice chancellor, a bit of a disappointment to those who thought he'd help suture British hegemony once the Nats are forced down; think of him as the little engine that could—but probably won't. Charles van Onselen, the lone Afrikaner of the lot, the big stick boy who whacks them when he thinks they might jump ship. Eddy Webster and Etienne Mureinik, two sad puppies who want political change as long as it's not essential and as long as they can still be loved by the Blacks. Ron Carter, head of student affairs, a Black American from Boston—we think. We need more on him, we've got little to go on."

Each folder contained notes which had been written, presumably, by one of Stimela's people: articles and op-ed pieces written by the individuals named, newspaper clippings in which they were mentioned, human interest stories about them, news photos or more candid photos taken of them without their knowledge.

"These are people, the kind of people, we need to hit."

"Assassinate?"

"If it was that simple we wouldn't need you. It's simple and it's complicated. We want to isolate and emasculate them. The students and workers will then eliminate them, if need be. Stimela wants to help SASCO and the workers paralyze the university sector of civil society. That's where we are. That's who we are. Students. Lecturers like you. That's where we need to fight. We stand as good a chance of paralyzing the economy by paralyzing the universities—of keeping the drive toward revolution alive—as the Congress of South African Trade Unions does in the factories. More so, perhaps. Cut off the brain and the body falls."

I thumbed through Etienne Mureinik's file and said, resignedly, "These people are more likely to sit at the convocation of conquest with Mandela than you or Jabu or Stimela or Precious or me for that matter."

"I know. It's up to structures like SASCO—unskilled workers, squatters, and the Civics in the townships. If SASCO can really make the universities ungovernable and if the Civics can make the townships ungovernable—which means withstanding Mandela's pressure not to make the terrain ungovernable—then the architects of neoliberalism in these folders will show their hand and assume their police powers and act more like police than liberals. We must make them assume the violence that sustains them. Killing them prematurely would backfire because killing one of them isn't the same as killing a cop. Killing them won't kill their discursive capacity. We want you to help us come up with a way to unmask their 'democratic' values and force them out into the open; force them to act deliberately and with the force of arms they pretend to be ashamed of. That's the first step."

"What's the second step?"

"Something interesting."

"Could you be a little more vague?"

"Probably not."

—⁓—

Stimela had instructed Trevor to train me in the use of firearms. An AK–47 is an unwieldy weapon. I learned this the hard way. Gas generated, fully automatic, a banana clip with thirty rounds, and a hairpin trigger that can spit all thirty in ten seconds flat. The force of three bullets per second lifts the nozzle and can throw you to the side and make you paint the landscape with figures of eight. Any fool can paint a landscape, but it takes an artist to hold it correctly and aim. I was no artist. I wasn't even a draughtsman. I could never remember the simple things: the names of handguns and the list of their features or to take the safety off before you shoot or how to brace myself against the kickback of an AK–47, a weapon the Soviets built to rend the world of surplus value.

I saw Trevor several times a week in those days—at Wits, where the student/lecturer cover was above suspicion, and in the apartment where the student/lecturer roles were reversed (sometimes when Khanya was there, but often when she was in class). He'd often be arriving when she was leaving. She knew who he was and what he was; but she didn't say anything—that is, not until the day she found two rounds of ammunition while sweeping under the bed. She came to the kitchen where I was preparing the next day's lecture. She held the two bullets in her hand. Neither one of us spoke. I reached out for them. She drew them back.

"I don't want to know what you're doing," she said. "I just want to know if you're going."

"What?"

"The man I was with before I met you, Peter...he didn't say anything. He just left for training. We grew up next door to each other and he didn't tell me."

"I'm not going anywhere. And when I do, we'll go together. Trevor must have dropped those; though I can't imagine—"

"I don't need lies." Then she was silent. I didn't reach out for the bullets. I didn't break the silence. I didn't look her in the eyes. "I want you to remember that Reba's not even five years old yet."

"I know."

"And she stays here on the weekends."

"I know."

"She's coming to live with us one day."

"Khanya, I know."

"I don't want you to know, I want you to remember."

"I'll remember."

She gave the bullets to me.

I never told Trevor what had transpired between Khanya and me that day. I don't know if I knew how to explain it. He and I were developing a fast and rewarding intellectual and political relationship. I didn't want to jeopardize that. But nor did I want the thing I was finding my way into, Stimela's web, for lack of a clear way of naming it, to jeopardize my marriage. It would require a careful tightrope walk.

Looking back on it all, it seems strange that I should go to Africa and find that the person to whom I was closest, next to Khanya, was a White man. It did not seem strange at the time. The rush of revolution left little room for reflection. There was no time for the dust of stability to settle. One was either about the business of shoring up the cenotaphs of capitalism or about the business of knocking them down. Laissez-faire was not an option.

This, of course, is not entirely true, for Stimela's people all knew how the *tokoloshes* of laissez-faire—the faces in the files that Trevor spread on the bed—were hard at work. They'd been working invisibly since the day Nelson Mandela was released from prison. Eleven months later, in April 1993, when Chris Hani was assassinated, the tokoloshes of laissez-faire would emerge from their hovels in the knotty snarl of tree roots and say, "Now, yes, now, is the time of the trolls."

Leading ethnographers of trolls, specializing in tokologeology, have concluded that there are an estimated six hundred fifty-eight tokoloshes residing under rocks, in tree trunks, and beneath the beds of unsuspecting victims throughout South Africa. The tokoloshe is a small creature that stands about knee high to an adult. Some have very long hair, like monkeys; others have thick leathery skin, like trolls. "Their eyes are narrow and black and they have small ears," according to a renowned tokologeologist. Their long penises looks like tails and can be slung over their shoulders when running or walking briskly. Tokoloshes make themselves invisible and go into houses to harm people in their sleep or put poison in their food. "Many people put their beds on bricks so that the tokoloshe can't catch them in their sleep. It might be a good idea when you check into your hotel to ask if they can give you four bricks... just to be safe." If you sneak up on a tokoloshe, "He will put a magic stone into his mouth and disappear. He is also very scared of dogs, mousetraps and chameleons." Normally, if you are haunted by a tokoloshe, your sangoma can cast a spell for you, "And if the tokoloshe walks into it he will become paralyzed and visible. But if you shout 'Hey, tokoloshe, I see you!' then the spell will be broken and he will disappear."

But the laissez-faire tokoloshes, the ones in our files, were no ordinary tokoloshes. They were not knee high trolls with leathery faces who snorted and grunted as they rose up from beneath the earth to make mischief. They did not materialize under some unlucky person's bed and nibble at his toes in the middle of the night. They did not make dishes fly about the room and crash against the walls. They did not open doors when you closed them or close them when you opened them. They had no *muti* that made you itch or pull your hair out. We could have handled that.

We wouldn't have needed a safe house in Hillbrow to sort through their policy papers, their academic work, or the notes we had stolen from their dust bins—since most tokoloshes don't write. We wouldn't have needed a safe house in Hillbrow to study their movements and mount their photographs on the wall, since most tokoloshes can't be seen. We wouldn't have needed to bug their offices, bribe their secretaries to eavesdrop on their meetings, or send operatives to monitor their classes—since most tokoloshes are seldom heard and cannot be recorded.

The tokoloshes of laissez-faire were not tiny black creatures with gravel in their vocal chords, but grown men and women of average height—though some seemed tall and imposing like Charles van Onselen, the president of the academic senate, or Robert Charlton, the vice-chancellor of the university. Others seemed downright short, bespeckled, and sad, like Etienne Mureinik with his sharp, pointed, downward nose, a small and timid creature, what's known in Afrikaans as a *bang worsie* (scared kitten); Mureinik, the lonely law professor who just wanted the Africans to love him. Some were women. Like dean Elizabeth Rankin and professor June Sinclair, a law professor of some renown who held a Wits cabinet post one step down the food chain from Robert Charlton. I am not at all convinced that any of them had long tokoloshe penises—certainly not long enough to sling over their shoulders when they ran or walked briskly; though I must confess that in the five years in which I lived there, I did not actually see them running or walking briskly.

June Sinclair didn't curry favor with Mandela's people. Unlike Mureinik, she craved no feckless fawning from young Africans. No, these were not run of the mill tokoloshes. They lived in the suburbs, not in trees or under rocks. They dined at the Parktonian Hotel and not on the toes of children, for such delicacies as tiny tot's toes were not on the menu at the Parktonian Hotel. They vacationed in Europe. They dressed for success. And they were English not Afrikaners. The tokoloshes of laissez-faire were well-talcumed and well-deodorized little tokoloshes. You could not smell them coming. But oh, the stench when they'd gone.

Like traditional tokoloshes, they made weird noises when they spoke (they called this gargling "editorials," "policy papers," "scholarly articles," and "memorandums of understanding, compromise, and reconciliation"). And like other tokoloshes they wreaked havoc from the inside out and they vanished into thin air when you raised a broom to sweep them away or a fist to strike them down. They made poor targets, for they always said they wanted what you wanted, or what you would know you wanted if only you could want what they wanted, for example. They were all for Black participation within the existing paradigm—which seemed so reasonable that the paradigm itself could not be put on the table for critique and dismantling. And unlike normal tokoloshes who screamed and yelled and ran away in the night, the tokoloshes of laissez-faire were always willing to listen. They could listen for hours. They could listen for days. They could spend a lifetime listening. They liked to organize "listening sessions," like university transformation forums that would "listen" for the next ten years and never transform the university—never devolve power to the masses. Their favorite word was "stakeholder." Everyone was a "stakeholder" which meant nothing was ever at stake. Their second favorite word was "process." The process of negotiations had to be free of "intimidation" (their third favorite word), free from mass action, and from civil disobedience. The word they hated was "power." Talking about power was like saying, "Hey, tokoloshe, I see you!" It could make them disappear.

"We should just shoot one of them." I can remember that being said in the Hillbrow house. Was it Jabu? Was it Precious Jabulani or Trevor, as we pored over the writings of the tokoloshes, or was it me, who said it? At one time or another we all had said it. Some nights we said it together. Assassinate Robert Charlton as he leaves the Great Hall. Kill June Sinclair in her office. Audit one of Mureinik's classes and do the deed as he lectures on how to calibrate the rule of law with the discontent of the disenfranchised. Blow van Onselen away on the floor of the faculty senate. Make a spectacle of it. At the very least it would be good for student morale. We were joking...perhaps. Of course, we couldn't kill Eddy Webster, he still had friends in COSATU from his days as a labor union advisor. He was still a friend of the Negro.

We certainly had the capacity to kill them. Stimela kept an arms cache at another safe house on the other side of Hillbrow; per Chris Hani's wishes, not all of the weapons in the dead letter boxes scattered across the country had been handed over to the commission set up by de Klerk and Mandela. We had the will to kill them. Oupa would have hit anyone Stimela ordered him to hit; Precious and Jabu had proven themselves in retaliation against the police in the townships; as had Trevor. Jabu was trained in propaganda and psychological warfare—which is not to say he had no training in operations; he did. I only knew how he moved about the demonstrations, the rallies, the caucuses, and meetings; in the wee hours I knew only how he moved among the newspapers, the file clippings, the stolen memos, the photographs, some surreptitiously obtained, some cut from newsletters, yearbooks, and the evening gazette; and I only knew how he moved between a box of push pins and two computers. Peculiar proxies for live ammunition.

"Yes," someone else would say, as though testing the line between a joke and a plan, "why don't we just shoot one of them." We'd all be bleary-eyed by then. It might be one in the morning. The night's writing would be stale and redundant—how the hell would we get a pamphlet out by dawn? Or our analysis was on tilt and we'd be irritable and argumentative, instead of sharp and erudite. So we'd clear the bulletin board of our charts, our clippings, and our scraps of analysis. We'd take the photographs of the tokoloshes from their files and pin them to the bulletin board. June Sinclair leaving a restaurant. Etienne Mureinik shopping at the Rosebank Mall. A portrait of Charlton from the Johannesburg *Star:* Ron Carter, before he came to South Africa as an honorary White man, when he was at Boston University where he worked as the hatchet man for its neo-con president. Nico Cloete, whose work we interpreted as being tantamount to the evisceration of radicalism in the Charterist movement. Eddy Webster, striking poses like bargains with the workers he had turned his back on. Charles van Onselen, his head held high, his jaw thrust out like Mussolini, with neither irony nor shame. We'd pin them side-by-side, like figures facing a firing squad. We'd asked them if they had any last words. For the first time ever, none of these tokoloshes spoke. We'd implore them: "Honor us with something pithy about peace and reconciliation or the rule of law before you die." Then Precious and Jabu would draw bull's-eyes on them and I'd retrieve darts from the small room that was a bedroom long ago when someone lived there and it was furnished and in fee to domestic, as opposed to clandestine, needs and desires. "Ready!" said Precious, as I handed her the darts. She took ten paces back, "Aim!" Jabu, Trevor, and I stood beside her with darts of our own. "Fire!" One by one the tokoloshes slumped and fell.

Shooting them in real life might have been worse than letting them run amuck. Invariably, their deaths would spark rancor and indignation in the media; tears of sympathy from the Whites, long meandering speeches from the Black bourgeoisie followed by the criminalization of armed struggle and mass action in the press, the hue and cry for peace and reconciliation (a.k.a. anger management for Blacks). Yes, the tokoloshe dies but his laissez-faire lives on.

No one wanted to admit it but we were racing against time. We needed to capture as much territory (real and imagined) of the university-industrial complex before the ANC came to power as possible. Most of us understood, whether implicitly or explicitly, that Mandela's people would not be willing to use state force to take power out of the hands of the university councils and corporate board rooms, and to devolve that power to democratically elected transformation forums. Never mind the fact that such reluctance would be a betrayal of the Freedom Charter, Mandela's people craved stability. Many of them were against revolution altogether, weaned, as they were during decades of exile in the West on the "virtues" of liberal democracy. They were that part of the ANC "church" that had been fighting not for socialism but merely against apartheid.

We were caught in a vice-grip of time and we knew it. Once Mandela was on the throne, the game would be up; whatever portion of the commanding heights we'd managed to wrench away would be all we were ever going to get. Mandela and his people could not afford to be seen siding with the Etienne Mureiniks, the Charles van Onselens, the June Sinclairs, the Robert Charltons. But nor could they afford to be on record saying that the brain trust of the economy, South Africa's universities, would one day become liberated zones.

We were faced with the possibility of a scenario in which apartheid would end, and in its wake a Hydra would rise: English liberalism and African conciliation. What Khanya had said after Richard's braai was right, no one wanted an internecine war within the ANC. So it was necessary to move with unflinching resolve against their English partners-in-waiting. If a professor or administrator became so intoxicated with the rule of law or the sanctity of the campus that she or he felt compelled to identify student agitators on police videos in court, it was necessary to impress upon the individual the inevitability of his own mortality and the shelf life of his or her worldly possessions. So, you don't like "savages" running through the halls, destroying property, disrupting classes, muraling the walls with slogans—well, how do you feel about your office being burned from the inside out? And there would be one less witness for the prosecution and, perhaps, fewer still in waiting.

Once it became clear that SASCO was agitating not for access to power but for the complete devolution of power, then the liberals were forced to come out and fight; forced to call upon the police to whom they preferred to appear removed from. Such distasteful display of state power (distasteful only because they were the kind of people who prided themselves as being pacifists) were golden opportunities for us because they heightened the contradictions and allowed us to strike back with a greater range of tactics; furthermore, they helped radicalize more students and more workers, and secured for us a place in the hearts of Black people broadly—the same place that Mandela's moderates vied for. The moderates would have to go through us to share that space. But they could not go through us without being demonstrably against us at the same time. They were forced to publicly ask the tokoloshes to make more and more concessions, to be "transparent" in their governance, to set up the transformation forums first and worry about their powers (or lack thereof) later. But behind the scenes Mandela's people intimidated those students, workers, and radical lecturers who could be intimidated.

We let the darts stay where they'd stuck—on a nose, through a shoulder, in the groin, or, for Jabu who played darts in English pubs, right through the heart. We pushed the big table back to the middle of the room. We wheeled the two office chairs back in front of the two computers. Jabu put the kettle on. We opened the folders and got back to work.

Despite the good times and common purpose I shared with them during those long serious and sometimes silly nights, it was always clear that I was an outsider. They had been in the training camps together. They had been on operational missions together. They had grown up, if not together—for Precious hailed from a township near Pretoria, Jabu and Stimela from the West Rand, Oupa never told me where he came from (and I never asked), and Trevor was a White kid from the suburbs—then certainly in the face of the same dilemmas. They'd all fashioned themselves as enemies not of a state in the abstract, but of this state at this time. I had come along after they were already who they were. Regardless of how close I felt to them, they had ways of letting me know that I'd entered well after the show began, that they had had to scrunch back their knees to let me find a seat. How could I be trusted, completely trusted, with the ending when I'd missed the beginning?

When Trevor and I weren't working with the others, we would spend long hours discussing politics, literature, the future of South Africa and the world. Since I was a lecturer in literature and he was a student, our being together looked like the friendship I thought it was. This is to say our aboveground friendship didn't jeopardize our cover—unlike a potential aboveground liaison with Precious or Jabu would have. Stimela okayed it. I once told Trevor that he was the best friend I'd ever had. He looked at me as though I'd dragged a needle over a record.

"I don't have friends," he quipped, "only comrades." I didn't know what to make of this. I hadn't meant to make him cross. I let it pass. They all took care not to let me be seduced by an urge to bond and belong (though Trevor took the least care, his comment notwithstanding). Sometimes we would all be at the safe house, the flat in Hillbrow that Stimela sanctioned for the kind of work I did, not the one he used as a base for his own operations. I would be working on the computer and they might be talking, seated together at the long table. It was as though they'd forgotten I was in the room. The conversation would shift from English to Sotho (which Trevor spoke as well) at what I, straining to follow along, always felt were crucial moments. One night the conversation reached such a feverish pitch and the glee and laughter was so palpable and communal that I could not help but feel that it was meant for me as well.

"Hey," I chuckled, looking up from my workstation at the far end of the room, "what's the joke?"

No one spoke. Stimela dried his eyes.

"Something interesting," he said flatly.

"I just thought you were telling a joke, that's all," I said, with embarrassment.

Stimela considered me for a moment. Then he said: "Years ago, the first time I came back from training abroad, I thought I was going to build an airtight network of operatives who would one day roll past the Voortrekker Monument in Soviet tanks and North Korean jeeps. You know what I found instead?"

"No."

"That for every three people I jumped a fence with, one of them was an informer."

Then he and the others rose from the table. They stopped at the door.

"We're going out for take-away," he said, "Can we bring you anything?"

"Something interesting," I said, without looking up from my work.

ARRIVAL

I drive north along the river
past cane, corn, inland
oceans of wheat
away from a place
where my grandfather gave
his son shoes
that he might lose his accent
and marry my mother

a child kept in school during
the harvest
he opened his face
to words
a cowbird on a fencepost

says yes
it's true all true
as long as you get there first
then flies through
a hole
in my rearview mirror

4

When I was a boy, I heard my father talking to his brother about a plantation on the Mississippi River. My father had been sent to New Orleans when he was fourteen, where he lived nine months out of the year, attending high school while his siblings chopped sugar cane and went to school between the harvests. Dad was the eldest male child, so it fell to him to be educated in the city, that he might one day help the others. In the summers, when he returned home, his parents' shotgun house was still too small for two adults and six siblings, so he would be sent to live in the slave quarters of the nearby plantation that had owned us when we were slaves.

My father and my uncle were seated at one end of the dining room table. So lost in their memories were they that they forgot I was sitting at the far end of the table. So, that's where we came from, a plantation.

"What was the name of the plantation?" I blurted.

They both looked at me. My uncle eyed my father, then snorkeled back into his bourbon, as if to say, he's your child, not mine, you take it.

"The White Castle Plantation," is all dad said.

"My money's on the Packers," my uncle said to dad. "By a field goal. Whatchu think, FB?" He addressed his brother by the name people from their hometown had given dad so that they might distinguish him from my grandfather whose name was also Frank. "FB" was part of their "back home" lexicon; not a foreign language by any means but neither was it an invitation for me to go on asking questions.

"Vikings'll hold them to a hundred yards rushing," dad said. "And don't even think about throwing the ball."

"All Green Bay needs is a field goal, FB. That's what the smart money says."

Their effortless transition from slavery to sports sent me off on a daydream. *The White Castle Plantation,* I thought. *Why hasn't dad told me this before?* Then it occurred to me: *What if the people who owned the White Castle Plantation in Louisiana are the same people who own White Castle Hamburgers in Minneapolis? Man, I love White Castle Hamburgers. Maybe they'll give me a lifetime supply; seeing as how we were their slaves. Or, if they won't keep me in hamburgers for the rest of my life, maybe they'll give me a summer job...spring for a gift certificate? Some token of appreciation for all that work.*

That evening I found my father sitting at the table, staring into space.

"Since you were there," I said, knowing that he wanted to be left alone, but knowing as well that this might be my only chance to answer a question which Mrs. Olafson had put to us one day in class: where in Europe do our names come from? I recalled how, when the gaze of the class and Mrs. Olafson was turned on me, I'd been stricken with aphasia. "Since you were there, on the White Castle Plantation, do you know how we got the name Wilderson?"

He knocked back the last of his Jack Daniel's. The glass came down on the kitchen table a little too hard. He eyed me warily, then looked away.

"At the end of the Civil War the master came out and told the slaves that everyone in the free world had surnames. If they were going to live in the free world, they had to have surnames too. There were two rows of slave quarters. He waved his hand to the row on the right and said, 'I name y'all Wilson.' Then he waved his hand the other way and said, 'Y'all be Wilderson.'" Then he looked at me, that sullen-Wilderson-look that my mom always found so disparaging, but she was wrong, for the first time I knew she was wrong. It wasn't a Wilderson-look, for it could just as well have been a Wilson-look. He looked that look at me, the look of chance, and said, "Now you know."

By the end of the sixties, my parents' faces were remarkably open and full of hope for the future (the assassination of Martin Luther King notwithstanding). The Civil Rights Movement had breathed life into them; life which our first two years of isolation in Kenwood (from '62 to '64) would have otherwise sapped. And, it was true, Mrs. Proudwell and our good White folks, as Fawn would have said, had started to come around.

All throughout grammar school, my parents instructed my sister and me to clip articles on the events of the day, like the Cuban Missile Crisis, and discuss them, or at least the photographs, in seminars whose only participants were our parents. Jack Kennedy's assassination. The March on Washington. Malcolm X's assassination. Johnson's signing of the Voting Rights Act. King's assassination. Bobby's assassination. The launching of AIM—the American Indian Movement—in Minneapolis, just two miles from where we lived. If these moments were also experienced by the White kids at our school they were certainly not reflected upon in the same way; their parents, unlike ours, did not treat the events of the day with the urgency mom and dad thought they deserved.

"History is being made. You will never pass through this moment again," they would say, as though our souls would tumble into perdition were we to let the moment pass and go out to play.

In those days, the people with whom I felt most comfortable were not children my own age but an eclectic group of young professors, inner city organizers, poverty program workers, and no-nonsense civil rights activists who would assemble in our living room and share their dream to change the world. And with their dream they brought three things that I, in the rapture of narcissism that consumes every child, thought they brought for me alone. First, a vision of what that new world would be like (on this they debated from sunset to sunrise, since no more than two or three of them ever shared the same vision on the same day). Second, they each had a hypothetical timetable as to when Johnson's War on Poverty would be won, when Dr. King's dream for social justice and civil rights would be realized, and when the war in Vietnam would end.

Their points of agreement had less to do with timing than with faith: faith that poverty would end, faith that King's vision would be realized, and faith Johnson would leave Vietnam. The third and most lasting thing they brought me were books and a sense of the impact writing has upon the world. These books (amassed by my parents or sometimes left by a colleague having fallen from the pocket of a winter coat hung carelessly in the closet) I devoured between the ages of ten and fourteen. Tracts on community takeovers of the public schools; reports from the poverty programs; Freud's *Beyond the Pleasure Principle,* which gave me none of the pleasure promised in the title; the Moynihan report, which enraged them all and put me to sleep; Frantz Fanon's *Black Skin, White Masks,* which I pretended to understand by memorizing a few flamboyant lines and reciting them like poems as cocktails were passed around to everyone but me. This little trick—the capacity to utter ear-catching phrases from difficult and controversial texts—seemed to impress the whole lot and would focus the attention of the entire living room on me for five or ten minutes. There was Eldridge Cleaver's *Soul on Ice* which forced the Civil Rights agenda deep into the forbidden zone of sex and Black Power, a zone so forbidden, that my possession of the book was grounds enough for a severe spanking—so I made a point of reading it whenever I could. And finally, there was my old standby, *Invisible Man,* which I must have read ten times.

Once, while waiting with my father for a plane that would take us to one of several psychology conferences (children flew half-price and since my dad's tickets were paid for, he often took me along), five men in gray flannel suits approached us. I thought they were secret agents, so full of Cold War lore (from James Bond to *I Spy* to *The Man from UNCLE*) was my head. Dad stood and introduced me to Senator Walter Mondale and his aides. Dad told me that Senator Mondale lived down the street from us. I was impressed, not by the fact that dad knew Mondale, for he seemed to know everyone, but by the fact that Mondale had spotted dad from a distance and come over. Walter Mondale told my father about an education bill he was trying to write. He wanted to know if dad would help him with this while he and his aides waited for their plane to Washington, DC.

We all went to the airport bar. They ordered bourbon, so I ordered bourbon. Everyone chuckled, except the bartender. He blandly placed a Coke and a straw on the bar ("Are you deaf?" I wanted to say) and glided to the other end. For the next fifteen minutes, dad and Mondale huddled together at the bar, with two aides flanking them, and me, at the far end of the left flank—on the margins with a drink I hadn't ordered. Mondale asked questions and dad gave answers, not only answers but wording as well. Senator Mondale would peer around to one aide or crane his neck back to the other and say, "Did you get that, Harry?" or "Would you like Dr. Wilderson to repeat that for you, Bo?" who were briskly taking notes. Presently, they heard their flight being called. Senator Mondale asked dad for our contact information at the hotel in the city we were traveling to so that he could call if he had more questions.

That night, after the first day of the psychology conference concluded, I sat with my father in a bar at the New York Hilton. A slender woman with brunette hair done up in a pageboy was singing over by the piano. She wore a white evening dress and sang "The Days of Wine and Roses" or "When Sunny Gets Blue," a song of lost love that Nancy Wilson would have sung had Nancy Wilson been there. We discussed the day over cocktails (well, over my Coca Cola and dad's bourbon). I beamed with pride as I recalled our tête-à-tête with senator Mondale.

"So, you, like, make legislation, don't you dad?"

He smiled and sipped his drink. "Well, son, the senator just wanted my input on a small matter, that's all."

"Wait 'til I tell them in Social Studies!"

It would be the last time that my father and I would share a common political joy.

In 1968 I finished the sixth grade at Kenwood Grammar School. My father's sabbaticals cut deep into the next two years. This turned out to be a blessing in disguise. Whereas most children would have suffered from the disorientation of changing schools so many times in their early years of adolescence, I doubt I would have survived adolescence at all had I not found a world beyond Minneapolis—a world in the throes of Black Power. On April 11, 1968, just days after King was killed, when so many cities had begun to burn again, I turned twelve years old; I was a twelve-year-old Black boy coming of age in the snow-dusted pines and the cold "liberal" kindness at the top of the Louisiana Purchase. There were no Klan crosses blazing on our lawn, but "nigger" was as much my name on my way to school in Kenwood as it was my grandfather's on his way to work. In class, someone might one minute snigger, "Hey, Frank, where do we put the jigs?" and another ask innocently, "What is it like to be a Negro?" I got to the point where I had no capacity to distinguish between the coarse and the curious, the profane and the puzzled. I punched first and sought explanations later.

Mom came home one day and said that a district superintendent told her that my dad's forthcoming sabbaticals would be the best thing for me. Seattle, Detroit, Chicago, Berkeley; with each city she uttered, the superintendent had breathed a sigh of relief. He told her two things: one, that all of the fist fights I'd been in were becoming, "Well, how shall I put it, Mrs. Wilderson, problematic?" And secondly, that he was well aware that these incidents were "more often than not instigated by his classmates. But," he added, "either the entire school-age population of Kenwood is bussed somewhere else and your son is left in peace, or we bus your son somewhere else and leave Kenwood in peace. You folks go away for a while. That's the ticket. Come back when young Frank here is ready for high school."

Before we left town I did what everyone in sixth grade was doing. I gave love a try. I had a crush on a girl in my class named Jane Peterson. Walgreen's rings were all the rage in the spring of 1968. I went downtown to buy her one. For half an hour I picked through the rings lodged like real jewelry in felt display cases. The sales clerk asked me if I was buying a ring or molesting the display.

"I want one that looks like real," I said.

"He wants one that looks like real," she said to the ceiling. "Real what, sonny?"

"You know, real. Real diamond, real emerald."

"You're serious?"

"I brought two dollars didn't I? I need a genuine engagement ring," I said, mimicking something I once heard on a commercial.

"They're all genuine. Genuine Walgreen's. Now pick one and run along."

The next day, I slipped the "emerald" ring on Jane Peterson's finger. Jane smiled and kissed me half on the cheek, half on the mouth. Then she said she'd be my girl. I was in heaven. I knew I'd be back in Walgreen's next week for that genuine diamond. Two days later I saw her on the playground. Four or five children were clustered around her. I thought she was showing off the ring. I held my head high and joined them. But they didn't greet me. Jane wasn't showing them the ring. She was holding it out to me. More kids joined the circle. She didn't say anything; she just held it out to me.

"I can't go steady with you," she said.

"Why?"

"I just can't." Then she said, "My dad says I can't."

Her father had been mayor of Minneapolis several years earlier. What crushed me at that moment was the fact that I was an "A" student in social studies: I believed, like my father and mother, that whatever was wrong with the kids at school, elected officials in the North were fair-minded. They fought on the side of Lincoln. They were for civil rights, I thought, and the War on Poverty. Now, the former mayor of Minneapolis had told his daughter not to go steady with me. It was a cosmic betrayal that, to this day, I cannot fully explain. I stood before her and those kids with their smug condescension and I grew more sullen and more masochistic than I had ever been. The knife was in, it had hit an artery, the bleeding was profuse, it was only a matter of time. But that wasn't good enough for me. I was going to make her turn it, twist it hard with her own hands and tear it out. It is a pattern of masochism I repeat over and over again, almost thirty years later in Santa Cruz, with Alice. I draw close to her. I press and press against her until she has no other choice but to plunge the blade deep into me or turn her back on all her relations—kill them, so that I might live. Yes, it is them or it is me; the knife is in your hands. But they've always already made their choice. I know this even before I fold my hands over theirs to keep them from releasing the knife. Nonetheless, I grab her wrist and make her twist and turn the blade—she can only free herself from my grasp when I am too dead to hold on. With Alice, this would become a more reflective, though no less spontaneous, suicide; but on that day, when I faced Jane Peterson in the schoolyard, it was instinct, pure instinct. She waited for me to take the ring.

"What does your father have against me?"

"Nothing."

"You're lying!"

She hissed and tightened her white lips, the way Alice would hiss and tighten hers one day. How dare you, hisses the air from those lips, thrust your humiliation on me?

"You're a Negro," said Jane, and she made me take the ring, "I can't go steady with a Negro."

Now you can take out the knife.

But the wound, fatal as it was, was never fatal enough. It left me dead, but that changed nothing. I was already dead, if to be alive is to live with relations sutured by something more substantial than a wave of a hand to the right and a wave of the other to the left. The wound was only an incision into a corpse. It made a difference: the corpse flinched when it was sniffed (even if it were deemed fragrant); the corpse jerked when it was punched; the corpse stiffened when pressed with a ring; and its eyes dulled, murderously, when a nude White woman preened throughout the house and yard. These weren't signs of life for they had no translation for the living. What, after all, is the language of death? To prevent my mind from drifting to a futile contemplation of waking rigor mortis, I filled it with what, for lack of a better word, I called my life—with work and projects. Three jobs if need be, or one job and three projects; anything to keep moving, to keep running. That's what I did after I left South Africa, after the purges and marginalization of radicals within the ANC—when politics within the ANC seemed no longer feasible. I returned to America and filled my "life" with a thousand points of attention, a thousand evasions of waking rigor mortis.

My younger brother Wayne was a working actor in Hollywood. He let me live with him in Los Angeles until I could get myself together. I sat on his living room floor long hours night after night rummaging through my suitcases that had more books and papers in them than clothes, picking through the debris of my life in South Africa. I organized all the business cards, addresses, and correspondence from visiting Americans I'd met when I lived in Jo'burg. One by one I called them. There was a book of W. S. Merwin's poems that had been sent to Khanya and me as a thank you gift from a woman who'd been on sabbatical there in 1992. The inscription on the inside was addressed to both Khanya and me. It was signed, Alice Wilson. But she sent it to you, Khanya said, as we divided our belongings during those last few days together in South Africa. There was no jealousy or reproach in her voice; I, at the time, for no other reason than the fact that the woman was White and twenty-two years older than me, could not imagine that I would fall in love with Alice. I had packed the book in one of my boxes and thought nothing of it.

I took a break from telephoning contacts and went into Wayne's kitchen to make myself a late night snack.

I returned to the living room with my sandwich and coffee. I arranged myself on Wayne's sofa and read the book of W. S. Merwin's poems from cover to cover. The next morning I awoke, still on the sofa with the book turned down on my chest. She lived in Santa Cruz County. I remembered that much. I looked on the map and saw that it was only four hundred miles up the coast from Los Angeles. A stone's throw when compared to the distance I had come. I picked up the phone and called her, I told myself, in search of no more than a job.

—⁂—

From 1998 to 2002, I seemed to always be in two places at once, one night at my Berkeley apartment, the next night at Alice's house in Santa Cruz County. One day teaching at Cabrillo College in Aptos in Santa Cruz County, the next day lecturing at UC Berkeley, or UC Santa Cruz, or at any number of the small colleges where I managed to find work. I was one of many in that army of adjunct lecturers—"flexible" laborers who know only the flexibility of a reclining car seat. They haunt the highways between San Francisco and Santa Cruz; Los Angeles and Long Beach; Sacramento and Stockton; Bakersfield and Merced. Punch drunk and fatigued, they call a student in one town by the name of a student they taught the night before in another town. Their filing cabinet: the trunk of their car. Their grade books: shelved on the backseat, passenger side. Their spare (clean) shirt: on top of their grade books. Their syllabi, books, and handouts: shelved on the back seat, driver's side. Pencils, pens, paper, chalk, and spare eraser—for who knows what conditions will be like where they're going: on the back seat, driver's side, on top of the syllabi, books, and handouts. Music for the journey: on the passenger seat Beethoven, Schubert, and Vivaldi cassettes inside the Stevie Wonder, Sly Stone, and Martha Reeves cassette cases. Sandwich and water bottle for the journey: on top of the Beethoven, Schubert, and Vivaldi cases, where the Stevie Wonder, Sly Stone, and Martha Reeves cassettes are to be found. They catch their forty winks in the car—sometimes parked, sometimes not. They are punctually late. They have no faculty parking space. They arrive when the lots are full. But they always find a space and a thirty-dollar ticket when the day is done.

I was in three highway accidents during this period, one that totaled my car. It was a miracle that no one but me was ever hurt. On top of it all, Alice and I were going for the Guinness record of splits and mending. Our love affair was like an earthquake that rent the earth twice a year...or more. Then, like two taxis colliding at rush hour, we'd be back together again.

If you hate me, why do you fuck me! Alice's words would echo in my ear each time we fought, even when she chose to omit them. I would storm out. Leave, when I knew I was too exhausted and distraught to drive eighty miles back to Berkeley. Leave, when I knew I wanted to stay. Leave, rather than face her question—her accusation—and answer it. Yes, I hate you. But not nearly as much as I hate myself—black, big-lipped, ugly, and menacing. I am gargling speech. I am AIDS. I am larceny. I am dirt. I am deceit. I am vulgarity. I am the dereliction of integrity. You are health, honesty, cleanliness, piety, and plentitude. I rub against you that you might rub off on me. And then I can't stand to look at you. I left knowing that I did not have the stamina to drive the winding highway over the Santa Cruz mountains; knowing that yet another accident had already packed its bags and was heading south down Highway 1 to meet me.

I drove to the pier at Seacliff, five miles north on Highway 1. I parked the car as close to the water as I could. I lowered the seat and closed my eyes. *If we're lucky, we'll wake up and the ocean will have swallowed us up.* But even then I could not sleep. The words we'd slung back and forth across the kitchen would sling back and forth across my mind. As I sat in the car I could still hear her ruminating at the kitchen table, as she'd done one night when I'd gone upstairs to pack and she thought I was out of earshot. "I'm a sixty-five-year-old grandmother," she said, to a wide-eyed but unsympathetic cat, now, her only interlocutor. "I should be mending scarves or something. What am I doing with a Black revolutionary?" *If you hate me, why do you fuck me?* But I didn't throw her words back at her when I came back downstairs with my bags. I pretended not to have heard her as I closed the door behind me.

The sea was shimmering and calm. Too calm to rise and crash upon the windshield and drown our words. I turned the ignition on so that I might heat up the car and listen to the radio without running down the battery. But there was nothing on the radio and I feared idling away the gas. Maybe, I thought, if I breathe calmly and listen, the rhythm of the waves pulling back and forth along the shore will be enough. Maybe the moonlight will be enough.

To my right, running out in an imaginary line that extended from the headlight to the water, was a long dark pier. At the end of the pier stood an old hulk, one of those concrete ships built during one of the "Great" Wars. In the 1930s, a nightclub owner anchored it at Seacliff. He turned it into a dance hall. It's a dance hall no more. It is vacant and unlit. And when you get close, you come upon a sign that reads

"Danger, do not board." But people are always curious. People want to go wherever they've been warned away from.

At Dartmouth College, we ridiculed Black men so smitten with Snow Queens they couldn't say "no" to "the poison." I carried my dog-eared copy of Frantz Fanon's *Black Skin, White Masks* around and was superior to them. One day I'd grow up and marry a good Black woman, have good Black kids, live in a good Black neighborhood, and all the rest, I used to think as I watched them through my lens of condescension, watched them as they slithered across the campus at night, thinking no one knew. But that was before she came to me, flaunting her White nudity and Mother Earth mantras.

I'll sleep here, in the car tonight, I thought. But another voice told me that it would be better to drive back down the coast to her house than to catnap and try to drive over the mountain to Berkeley. You always return, why prolong the inevitable? Why, I asked myself, did I ever break the silence with her? When we first met I kept my mouth shut. I offered no critiques of the body politic in which she was so blithely ensconced or her display of her body, the body politic's most prized possession. I wanted in, in every sense of the word; and I'd had enough of speaking out. Left all that in South Africa. It was time to settle in, and be happy. That lasted a year and part of another. Then the air grew thin and I couldn't breathe—but I had no faith in the proposition that I could breathe anywhere else. The first faculty meetings at Cabrillo College were like that as well. And whom could I call upon for air? What would I say to Alice? She'd been instrumental in getting me the job. I need the money but my throat is tightening and my thyroid is pulsing, I'll die if I have to show up for work. So I smiled and nodded and nodded and smiled my way through the meetings, fearing all the while that the corners of my mouth would rip the skin around my cheeks to the back of my neck or that the bobbing assents of my head would force it to fall like an apple. I wanted in.

—⚏—

Are you awake, not wanting to open your eyes…or are you still sleeping, still in the throes of a garish dream? A dream in which you and Barbara

Bush are lovers, though in this dream you feel more like a refugee than a lover. She peers out at you from her bedroom: her cotton candy puff of silver hair: her translucent nightgown shielding her sex. She stares at you sharply. You have no right to look at her, to see through her negligee—you feel dirty and criminal. You want to say, friends should open up to each other, but dread consumes you, your palms are sweating, the glands in your neck are pulsating—you avert your eyes. You're psychotic, she says—but her lips don't move. She won't stop staring at you. She looks at you as though you are a creature she should run from. She goes into the bedroom and closes the door. You rush forward and knock and knock...

You lie there for a long time. At first, you keep your eyes closed hoping she'll open the door and say all is forgiven. But the knocking persists.

Outside a deer's antlers are knocking against Alice's wall as it tries to eat her winter flowers. You open your eyes and listen. You are a long way from South Africa. It is too early in the morning to remember how you got from Johannesburg to this bed. She stirs and turns and drapes her arm across your chest. Now you remember, you met her eight years ago: you were thirty-six, she was fifty-eight. You were married. She was divorced. She was just another American on sabbatical who had drifted your way, the way so many of them did. You would have written a report on her and passed it on to Stimela Mosando, the way you did on so many others, but she was just passing through, gathering research for her "World Literature" course. Besides, she was too undone from her divorce to be a threat to anyone but herself.

Now you're in bed together. She turns over and smiles. You press yourself against her. You make love. Today is her sixty-fifth birthday. November. Early winter in northern California; the beginning of summer in Jo'burg. She dashes out of bed completely nude: through the living room, now prancing around the kitchen with no curtains on the windows. She sits down nude at her computer and starts to prepare for class. A workman can come to check the meter; a neighbor can come to give her mail. It doesn't matter, she displays her sacred body without a trace of self-consciousness as though she's never been disrobed on an auction block; just stripped down, loose and breezy in her hot tub with her colleagues—and called it not slavery, but the other thing: or stretching and yawning, nude at her computer with the world rushing by: or rushing out the back completely naked just to feed a hungry cat. No it wasn't slavery. It was the other thing. It is the quintessence of freedom. She exhibits her freedom in the raw and whoever doesn't like it be damned. No matter how many mornings you encounter this spectacle, you are amazed and mortified at how she spreads her sexuality so effortlessly across the world. Your glands are throbbing. You want to fuck. You want to kill.

She drips out of the shower and dances into the kitchen and puts breakfast on the stove. You and your wide incognegro grin make like nothing's amiss. But you won't breathe properly until she's dressed. She stands in the middle of the kitchen and throws her butt into the air as she bends over. Her long brown hair falls forward to the ground. She brushes it down to her toes. You say, honey, you'll make us late. But what you really mean is, *Stop airing your ass in front of the window you skanky White bitch!*

She thinks she's doing you a favor: found you a job at a nice college, given you a home where you can lick your South African war wounds and write and make love day and night. She thinks her world is your refuge and you let her. But her refuge makes you long for apartheid like you've never longed for anything before.

As you drive down the service road that leads to Highway 1, she reaches over and places her hand on your thigh. You try not to flinch.

"You were tossing and turning last night, was it a nightmare?"

"Well, yes, sort of."

"South Africa?"

"What...uh, well, yes. South Africa."

"You should be able to relax here in Santa Cruz away from all that."

"Well, yes."

"I love you."

"I love you too. It's your birthday, we should celebrate or something."

We stop for gas on Highway 1, a mile or two south of the college. Wet, salty air drifts up from the sea. Gulls swoop in from the shore and perch on the gas pumps, on the hoods of vacant cars, on the roof of the station itself. I would have loved to have had the calm to transpose the image into a poem, but I was in a state of heightened agitation—I was still knocking at the door.

Last night I could find no way to write the memoir. My hatred of the world had been too profound. It seemed to have nothing to do with—or bear no singular relation to—my life in South Africa. It was nearer at hand. Alice liked to think the reasons for this did not flow, like the most deadly exchange of kinetic energy, between her and me, but were to be found instead in the substance of South African flashbacks, like flashbacks from an acid trip. And when her well of "foreign" reasons ran dry and forced her to find reasons closer to home, she chocked it up to the overwhelming minutiae of "culture shock" experienced upon my return, such as novel advances in consumer technology that expatriates are known to be awed by after years abroad. She was too clever to see what was in front of her.

The gas tank has been full for at least a minute, but I am still standing with my hand on the pump. I am still watching the sea gulls.

"Stop daydreaming," she calls. "Now who's making us late?"

As I settle back behind the wheel, she laughs at me, compassionately, the way one laughs at an old uncle who has lost his hat.

"It's almost the twenty-first century," she says as her fingers stroke my hair, "and you still marvel at gas pumps that take credit cards."

"Well," I say sheepishly, so grateful for her touch, so repulsed by it. I always start with "well" (whether I'm well or ill), it gives me time to say the right thing, the thing that will give her image back to her, that she might give mine to me. "Well, they still didn't have gas pumps that take credit cards when I left Johannesburg."

In the Cabrillo College parking lot, I tell her to go on ahead. "I need to sit in the car for a moment. Compose myself before class."

She reminds me that there's an English department meeting before classes today. I am squeezing the steering wheel the way I want to squeeze her neck and the necks of her universe of people. To hell with English and everything it stands for. The steering wheel is gasping its last breath and my knuckles are in pain, for it dies hard.

"Well…okay. I'll be there."

We lean toward the middle.

"Should I save you a seat?"

"Whatever you think."

We kiss.

"Should I get coffee and a muffin for you?"

"No, I'll see what's on offer." *Why won't this steering wheel die?*

"I love you."

"I love you too."

As she gets out of the car I have an urge to drive away. But where to? I'm lucky to have this job, I think, to have any job at all. I take a deep breath. I exhale long and hard. I walk down the hill to the courtyard and enter the classroom…

People are still arriving as I finally enter the large classroom where the English department's meeting is to be held. I make my way to the breakfast buffet in the back of the classroom. I rush to it pretending to be in search of juice or coffee, anything that will keep my "colleagues" from mobbing me, from asking how I'm getting on, how my classes are going or, worst of all, from saying, "Welcome to our little family"—but it's no use…

Here they come: Darcy Graigallan. Mousy and diminutive, but don't let that fool you. Like Alice she lived near Oakland once. She thinks she knows the deal. She thinks she got the score. She's hip as hip can be. And like Alice she, too, had a Black lover up there in Oakland. This she told me during our first encounter, pushing her life story on me like a summons. My lover was a woman, not a man, she clarified before I could ask her anything at all. They loved and they fought, she elaborates now as she smears her bagel. She's careful not to say how or why they broke up. I'm careful not to ask. She wants me to know how rich and rewarding her love affair with that Black woman was (now her summons becomes a gift). I'm glad to hear it, I say. *What else can I be?* "It was good in the end. Even our fights." *Good for whom? No, Frank, don't ask.* "It put me in deeper touch with my Jewish roots and my Jewish identity." *And they say alchemy is a lost art.* Culture and all that are great, she says, but her new passion is whales. A passion greater than sex; she's remodeled all her writing courses. I have them write on whales now. Gray Whales, Blue Whales, Minke Whales, Fin Whales, Killer Whales, and Humpback Whales—they enter my class knowing nothing and they leave with a sense of urgency. Just thinking about the urgency exhausts her. She looks over the table without finding what she wants. Now, she looks across the room at Herby, the chair, as he writes the agenda on the blackboard. She whispers to me: "We're planning to put a woman in his place then things will change—for one, we'll finally get some chamomile tea around here."

Here they come: Herby Wilson, Alice's ex-husband and chair of the department, approaching fast from the podium. Robert Mitchum, someone said of his likeness, if not for that double chin. A paperback writer, I can almost hear the Beatles, singing his song as he moves toward me. The faculty once toasted him with heartfelt gratitude for never becoming a literary success, for not leaving them behind. He's got a firm, longshoreman's handshake. He talks like a straight shooter. So, why are two voices coming out of his face at once? His lips say, Welcome to our family. His eyes say: Are you fucking my ex-wife? His lips say, How's your classroom? His eyes say: How big is your cock? His lips say, Got everything you need? His eyes say: She's still my wife! His lips say, Any problems, let me know. His eyes say: How many times a night?

Here comes Rick Norbert, Herby's best friend. Late fifties. Balding. Athletic. "I love women and Greek mythology," he says, as though handing me a business card. "But women most of all. Women, even more than the Greeks. I worship them." Everything he says is a double entendre. He sees breasts in the hills, vulvas in the stars. He gives off heat. He touches me as he talks. He leans in when he speaks, like a man about to open his raincoat. He was Alice's lover after Herby. No big deal, we're all family, right? But now that she's sleeping Black he wants her back. Doesn't he know, once you've gone Black you never go—no! no! he mustn't let himself think that. She must come back. He wants her more than breath itself. He can hardly breathe for his rekindled desire. When he can no longer take it, he'll rush to her house. Sweating. Panting. Grinning ear to ear. "Now what does that cucumber on the counter remind you of, Frank?" And: "What dazzling muscles you have, Frank. You could help rry wood." Then to her: "Remember, Alice, the splendors of oak?" either one of them will translate this snippet of erotic memory for me. See, he seems to be smiling at me, she and I still have our secrets— our family secrets. Alice will serve lunch, but there won't be enough food to keep his mouth closed. Alice will get up to fetch him condiments and, two minutes later, to fetch him a knife. "I just love to make her get up and down," he will wink at me. Days will pass before I can muster the courage to enter his office and tell him how offensive he was. "Yes," he will say, boyishly; he's a man on the prowl but a boy when the chips are down. "That was such a black day for me. I'm sorry." My blood pressure will rocket through the roof. "No," I'll say, "it was a white day, just another white day."

He'll say nothing as I leave his office for class. Then he'll storm into Alice's office: "I don't like your new boyfriend's conversation."

But all that is still to come. This morning he can't sing my praises enough. He can't get close enough to me. I step back. He steps forward. I step back. He steps forward. Now I'm backed against the buffet. I recoil from his moist familiarity. Even glazed and inebriated Rick can spy his prey. As at the retirement party when he spied a lone Black woman who'd had the misfortune to be invited and who had lacked the clairvoyance to decline the invitation. As though no one had warned her that, any moment now, the people in the room might take off all their clothes and howl at the moon or strip her of hers and howl at her. Rick slinked through the undergrowth of chamomile tea and dry martinis, and suddenly he was upon her. She thought it was a party so she didn't draw a gun. She said, "Hello." He grabbed her breasts and turned them like knobs. That's ole Rick! Someone roared. Rick's just being Rick! The party was just getting started.

Here's Belinda Ritz, a lesbian, but not the "ethnic kind" like Darcy she'll have you know. Irish stock, she is. Salt of the earth, she is. Old school, she is. Mz. Ritz doesn't teach creative writing or take her students on a journey in search of their inner child and whales are fine but they're not her passion. Mz. Ritz can mix it up with Herby, Rick, all the boys. Mz. Ritz doesn't need a woman's handout. Her latest crusade: to stop the hemorrhage of grade inflation. No more hanky-panky handholding of immigrant students. Don't care what they speak at home. I'm running a classroom not the Salvation Army. The last time I checked, the name of the class was English. And the man's name was Shakespeare, not Salvador or Gustavo—maybe they shouldn't be here if they don't know the difference. Herby once raised his glass in her honor and lamented, "She's the last White man in the department."

Here's Bo Dowd, who thinks he's Pablo Neruda and thinks I'm "cute." Here's short Edna Shultz and slender Ginny Nair, long time conspirators in the feminist plot to take power from Herby, Rick, and Bo. Much like Virginia, Alice's daughter, Ginny is tall and aloof with long stringy hair that she washes in the morning and air dries in the meeting. It blows wild in the afternoon wind. She's free. She's breezy. Edna is more serious and a trifle slow on the uptake. Jokes and punch lines don't come easy for her. But dialectics do: "Did I tell you, I'm an online Marxist—they're more of us than you might imagine. You'd be amazed at how many hits our site gets each day."

Here they come: Helen and Andrew, at long last the college couple, now that Herby and Alice are divorced. "Mustn't call her a secretary," I'm told before they're in range, "it's 'office manager.' She runs the place not Herby. And she's Jewish, too. But Andrew's Canadian. Or is he from Brooklyn? I can never remember. But they're like you." What am I like? I ask. "You know, into issues. They're into issues—like you. He teaches journalism and mentors the school paper. He'll want you interviewed. The school paper needs more issues. I'm sure he'll want you interviewed. They've been talking about doing a story on Shelleen and her southern roots for years. She's into issues too."

Here they come. They laugh. They joke. They solicit. I am a magnet for their pious confessions and excess libido. They flatten plate glass against my face and make themselves up in my reflection. They emerge from their glib, uninhibited encounters with me feeling refreshed, as though they've rediscovered something vital within themselves. And I emerge transformed from a black hole in black space to a star with a sacred place in their constellation.

There are two Black women in this department, Shelleen who, like me, is "into issues" but who, unlike me, has tenure, and Gladys who, like me, is an adjunct. With me, that makes three of us out of seventy. Shelleen and Gladys are smart. They have their survival strategies down pat. They wait 'til the meetings are almost underway before they enter. They manage their encounters so that the rush of welcome and goodwill storming down on me from every corner of the room doesn't trap them.

Now Herby takes his leave of me and calls the meeting to order. At last, they stop coming and take their seats.

During the meeting, I raised my hand and, with pristine diction, spoke on a curriculum matter. I used the word "we" a lot. What do "we" want from the new curriculum? How will "we" feel if this or that is added to or subtracted from "our" curriculum? Where are "we" going as an English department? Where are "we" going as a community? A reverent silence fell over the room. Heads nodded before anyone even knew where I was going. Chins were stroked in contemplation. Quiet now, the Negro is speaking. I seemed to cast a magic spell on them. Smiles broadened. More than a few people looked not at me but at Alice, with raised eyebrows and approving nods, one man even stroked his beard and smiled at her, as if to say, Fine catch, Alice. No, really, I mean it. When Herby left you for that little co-ed, we thought, well, we thought it was the end for you, but you bounced right back, you spry old bird you. Went to South Africa and bagged yourself a Negro. That'll show Herby. You're so liberated, so full of surprises.

By the end of every day I am disgusted with myself—horizonless self-loathing: my endless pandering for approval and recognition; the disturbing remembrances of a nude White woman self-contained in her nudity, in her house high up on a hill while in the Watsonville valley below Black people are hunted and Chicana/os at labor are raped in the fields; a woman oblivious to her signifying power but claiming it as her birthright; the department meetings with her "family" and their terrifying pleasures. If they ever forced me to clarify my rage—for example, they might ask with that wide-eyed wonder, the way they often ask, What did we ever do to you?—I'd have to tell them the truth. You were laughing. You were loving. You were living. You were there.

After one such meeting, I snapped. I took my rage to class, where "their" children awaited me. I stood before them, twenty-six students, thirteen laced around the walls, another thirteen laced around the table. I stood at the podium shuffling and re-shuffling the papers from my briefcase—anything to catch my breath and to stifle my contempt before I began.

The fog had cleared and with it went the morning sea gulls. Through the back window I could spy the hairline fracture of sea and shore. The sun shimmered on the water. There was a glimmering thimble floating on the water: a barge, inching north along the coast. *I must leave this place. I must get far away from this precious beauty that sputters and chokes. And go where…where would I go?*

Somehow I find myself talking to them about South Africa. It has happened before. I make the linkages. No one seems to mind. On the contrary, they're always intrigued; it works like a cocktail party gimmick from my adolescence. I am talking about Chris Hani and Winnie Mandela. We came this close, I am telling the class, this close to winning a revolution.

"If it was so great," a voice calls from the back. He is blond and freckled, a sun worshiper, his T-shirt advising me to Surf Free or Die. The tiny barge disappears behind his head. There is nothing now to look at but him. Only in a place like California could "surf free or die" stiffen the general public's resolve against all enemies foreign and domestic. "And if America's such a…a…what's the word he used?" he asks, turning to his friend. "Bastion," the boy beside him offers in assistance. "Yeah, bastion! If America's such a bastion of anti-Blackness—which frankly, I don't see, 'cause I mean, dude, you're here, teaching at this college, you've got a good job and you're Black, so what's up with that, huh? I mean, how come you came back, why didn't you just stay in South Africa?"

The others nod their heads and look approvingly at the sandy young surfer; it is the same group affirmation Alice was showered with at the meeting. You got that Negro, they're nodding at him. You got that Negro, they had nodded at her—blurring the line between custody and target practice. I smile at him, appreciatively, the way I do when someone makes a cogent insight about the reading. Fuck you, Beach Boy.

"Excellent question, Chad," I say, smiling, "excellent question, indeed. But my fidelity to a policy of infinite suspense in this class compels me to table it for a few weeks."

"Like dude, that's a cop out."

To think, there are two hundred-forty million more of you in this country alone. The mind boggles.

"On the contrary, Chad, it's not a cop out, it's a shrewd pedagogic move on my part. Now, there's a paper due next week. We should talk about..."

It was then that Dana Sole, a young woman from up near the Oregon border, sincere and loquacious Dana, raised her hand. I stopped talking and called on her. Maybe I was stymied by the fact that she had actually raised her hand. She seldom raises her hand, just blurts out whatever she feels whenever she feels.

"I have a question," she asked with none of Chad's sarcasm in her tone, "but I can discuss it with you after class if we need to get on to other things."

I told her to continue.

"Why did you go to South Africa?"

I answered her question in a flatfooted way by telling her that I had studied Southern African politics and liberation movements at Dartmouth College in the 1970s. I waxed on about the literary awards I'd won in 1988 and 1989, a pile of money that let me travel freely without having to work. I said I met a woman there named Khanya. We tried to live in New York. Then we tried to live between New York and Johannesburg. In 1991, we gave up on New York and moved to Johannesburg. At the end of 1996, I returned to America.

"Why there and not somewhere else?"

The question unnerved me; I held onto the small rostrum and told myself that none of them were the wiser. I tried to smile at her the way

I had smiled at Chad, a smile to give me time enough to burrow another tunnel and flee, but it wasn't working. For when she rephrased the question, I was suddenly overcome with the memory of Mureinik. I remembered his face pinned to the wall of Stimela's safe house along with the other tokoloshes. And I heard his thin anxious voice once again from the "chance" meeting I'd orchestrated at the Rosebank Mall—I'd wanted to get close to each of the tokoloshes, to feel the touch of their breath, to see the movement of their eyes, to know firsthand the enemy I plotted against in Stimela's safe house in Hillbrow. And I remembered how Mureinik died; how I cheered with the students and workers upon hearing the news. *I can't tell them all of that...can I?*

"Why did I go in the first place?" I see Mureinik's body, now airborne, now wingless and fluttering, now falling from the 23rd floor. "Well...I wanted to kill someone White."

There's a gasp of horror in the classroom, followed by the angry closing of notebooks and anxious shuffling of feet. A young woman to my left whispers to her friend, "I'm dropping this class. This isn't English." I pretend not to hear her.

Above the din, I declare, "Class is not dismissed!" They settle in. They're sullen but they're scared, so they settle in. "Yes, I wanted to kill someone White." *There'll be hell to pay for this, but I have never felt more alive.* "I know what you're all thinking." I look around the room at them. "That I could have stayed right here and killed someone White." Apparently, they are thinking no such thing. *This is so much fun! Good, clean, sadistic fun.*

"Well, yes, I could have stayed right here and done just that. There are as many White people in California," I pan the room again; they brace themselves against the slow rotation of my gaze, "as there are in South Africa. But South Africa, in the throes of revolution, provided me with something I didn't have here; a narrative of legitimation through which I could return the gift of murder to the world—the gift the world gave me: that gift of creation that brought me into existence on the plantation...no...before that...at sea. I can see by your expressions that you don't understand. Let me put it this way. Here, I'd be just an ordinary criminal. A murderer. A dot on a graph. A number at San Quentin. But there I could have a story. The deed could be recognized as a deed. Sides could be taken. One of those sides could be mine. The other could be yours. I would, in effect, be placed; and once placed I'd gain recognition—not fame. Recognition. You see what I'm saying?"

The only thing they can see is the door.

"We'll let it ferment. Class is dismissed."

The following week half the class refused to return. The other half, for various reasons (some because they needed the course for their major, others because the thought of boycotting an instructor was even more upsetting than the thought of being the objects of his homicidal fantasies) stayed on. Dana Sole (who sat up front and who had put the question Why did you go to South Africa? to me, and then waited till everyone had left and I was stuffing the debris of the lecture into my briefcase, to ask me, Did you kill one?) was among those who returned. Whether out of fear or out of a desire to understand, I'll never really know; but she stayed on and engaged me and the issues I raised, with sincerity.

During this period an unexpected but perhaps inevitable thing occurred. Herby, Alice's ex-husband, stepped down as chair of Cabrillo's English department. The Ginnys, the Ednas, the Darcys, the Helens, and even Belinda Ritz, "the last White man in the department," in a dazzling display of what they no doubt would have described as a counter-hegemonic maneuver, canvassed and cajoled the tenured faculty until they garnered enough votes to elect Shelleen Johnson the new chair of English. By the time "my students" (for lack of a more appropriate euphemism) got it together to take their case to "the man," "the man" was no longer "the man" but a Black woman.

As I approached her office, however, I was too anxious about the consequences of their petition for the knowledge that the guard had changed to sooth my anxieties. I was working on my PhD at Berkeley and teaching there as well and I had child support responsibilities in South Africa. I needed both jobs.

When I entered Shelleen's office, my exterior was cool. I'd learned in South Africa how to not show fear. But I was almost as on edge walking into

Shelleen's office as I would have been had it been Herby's office. In addition, there was this: I would have been frightened of Herby and therefore more apt to pounce first and call him a racist; get the jump on him before he got the jump on me. But toward Shelleen I felt an intangible anxiety. I did not want to offend her in any way (two of three Blacks in a squabble, a spectacle for them; that wouldn't do) but nor did I want to be disciplined for speaking my mind. Somehow, someway, I would have to strike a delicate balance. But "delicate" and "balance" were words I could hardly spell.

The letter from the students was on her desk. Some of their complaints were that the secondary articles I assigned were too theoretical. *Okay, fine, I'll dumb down the reading for them.* The letter also cited objections to the research project I assigned on the literature of US political prisoners. The letter stated that there was no such thing as a political prisoner in the United States—only criminals. It objected to the project's requirement that they write group research letters to US political prisoners as part of their research. It stated unequivocally that anyone who had taken up arms against the United States government deserved to be in prison, or worse. Those were among the complaints in their opening salvos. Then came the main attraction, their collective animus toward me in particular. Shelleen pushed her glasses up the bridge of her nose and held the letter aloft.

"It says here that you told the class you went to South Africa in 1991."

"I went there on extended research trips in 1989 and 1990. I told them I immigrated in 1991."

"Yes, okay, Frank; you told them you immigrated in 1991." She looked up. I nodded my affirmation. "Because you wanted to kill a White man." She put down the letter. "Frank, did you really say that?"

"No."

"No?"

"I would never discriminate by gender…that's wrong."

Shelleen picked up the letter and sighed. Turning to the second page she paraphrased, "In your class you disseminate 'subliminal communistic propaganda.' Is that true?"

"No."

"No?"

"There's nothing subliminal about it."

With her elbow resting on her desk and her chin resting in her hand she said, "How did I know you were going to say that?"

Then she chuckled, quietly at first, now with openness and abandon. I began to laugh as well. We might have laughed ourselves silly and floated out the window together, far away from that miserable place, if Helen hadn't come in. Helen was still the office manager—not the "secretary." Shelleen had inherited Helen from Herby. Helen looked at us as though we were two kindergarteners making a ruckus at naptime. This after all was to have been a disciplinary encounter not a house party.

"Shelleen, is everything alright?" she asked. *The same thing the cop asked Alice on the highway that night.*

Shelleen and I came to attention as though Helen was faculty and we were secretaries, er, office managers. Shelleen dried her eyes.

"Everything's fine, Helen, thank you."

Helen cast a disapproving glance in my direction and departed, closing the door.

"These people," Shelleen said, shaking her head, "I swear."

She suggested that we get out of there. Grab some lunch. Fine, I said, let's put it on Cabrillo's tab. "You's da chair, now!" At this she laughed again and we laughed into the general reception area where Helen sat.

In those days Shelleen and I didn't know each other very well so we spoke openly but carefully to each other. Black professionals do that. Neither one knows the exact nature of the danger that lies ahead. But both know where they are and whom they are up against; which is to say that both parties know that danger does indeed lie ahead. The question is how either party will act, or react, when danger rears its head. Do I have your back? Do you have mine? These are questions soon to be answered. Our conversation unbundled, with uncharacteristic ease, however, because Shelleen, on the cusp of an existential decision (to discipline me or not), had chosen laughter in lieu of punishment.

She placed a healthy dollop of pad thai noodles on my plate and then served herself. An hour and a half later we were still at the table. She asked me whether I was missing any classes. "My students have defected to the West," I said. I asked her if Helen was likely to send a posse out looking for her. Shelleen shook her head in resignation.

"She acts like she doesn't know you're in charge," I said.

"They all do," Shelleen said, "Belinda Ritz, Ginny Nair, Edna Schultz." And this was not only true of a plethora of English instructors and Helen (supposedly Shelleen's subaltern) but it seemed to have been sanctioned by Judith Chrisp, the vice president for academic affairs. And there were others, she said, by which she meant the old guard, people like Rick Norbert, Bo Dowd, and Herby Wilson, the men who had lost the struggle for hegemony to the feminists. Nothing would surprise either one of us about them. But what hurt her the most was the role the women played. Shelleen explained how, now that "her feminist sisters" had placed her in Herby's chair, they were working behind the scenes to dismantle the heretofore-unquestioned authority of the chair.

Her voice ached as she recalled their deceit and skullduggery, which she knew they would never admit to. For more than a decade she had struggled alongside these women against sexism and gender discrimination at Cabrillo. Their collective efforts had spawned reforms such as the Women's Center; the use of "she" as well as "he" in the curriculum and official documents; and the hiring of more (White) women to the point where White women now seemed to hold a numerical advantage. They had needed Shelleen and had not been bashful in expressing their need—what struggle doesn't need a beautiful, articulate, and righteous Black woman? Most of all they had desired Shelleen; desired her in ways they were bashful about; desired her in ways they weren't. They had hoist her up into the air, sometimes to parade her through the streets of their sham aesthetics and fake liberation; but more often than not, to turn her sideways and use her as a battering ram to bludgeon down the door of male supremacy. Now, the door was down. The dust had settled around it. They were inside now. The fortress, or at least a corner of it, the English department, was theirs. With the fervor of Allied troops staking the flag at Iwo Jima, they staked a cardboard sign on Helen's desk: "Girls Rule!" was the first thing people saw when they entered the main office. Everything had changed.

"I thought we were sisters," Shelleen said, "but they don't act like sisters."

I waited to hear if Alice's name would come up. It didn't. Still, I wasn't completely mollified by the omission. There were several circumstantial, as opposed to noble, reasons why Alice would not have been in the mix of the maneuvers that were chipping at Shelleen's power and eating away at her soul. To begin with, Alice was in her sixties. Though she had helped start the Women's Center and nurtured and guided the women who were now coalescing in a bloc against Shelleen, she was nearing retirement and somewhat out of the loop. However, like some elder stateswoman, Belinda Ritz and Ginny Nair continued to make meccas to her doorstep for counsel. I consoled myself for a moment; then it dawned on me that in point of fact Alice's allegiances could very well have been in line with a reorganization of White power along gender lines, and in line with this crowding out scenario of Shelleen, if in fact she were still young and still in the loop. A profound unease overcame me. I felt like a traitor. As I listened I realized how difficult it would be to mount the kind of political struggle against them that we had launched in South Africa against tokoloshes of laissez-faire; for the simple reason that here we would have to prove that these maneuvers were in fact racist, rather than the effect of "administrative wires being crossed."

Shelleen, Gladys, and myself, in English, and Lisa in Dance...the four Black instructors throughout all of Cabrillo....What painful and complicated lives we lead in Santa Cruz County by the sea; so painful and complicated that we seldom ever spoke intimately about our lives. Each one of us was partnered with a white-skinned lover. Shelleen's partner was a white-skinned Puerto Rican woman, who was often—upon visual rather than auditory contact—taken for a White woman. Gladys's husband was White. Lisa's partner was a White woman and so was mine. We all knew the ecstasy of soft white skin, or supple white breasts, or a firm white cock. We knew the psychic whiplash catalyzed by each encounter with that epidermal schema; the enchantment of possessing and being possessed by its charm; the feeling of robust worldliness; the orgasmic transcendence which offered something more immortal than the simple promise of sexual release. Thirty seconds later the world comes rushing in. You lie there, wet and breathless. Never more together. Never more apart. You pray that she (or he) is satiated enough to doze off before witnessing the frieze of anxiety that once was your face. You press your body to hers. A tactical move that lets your chin rest on her shoulder and gives your nerves time to recover. But sometimes she senses the tension in your body and asks, "Is anything wrong—didn't you come?" You take a deep breath. You let the air out slowly. You might lie and say, "No, nothing's wrong." Or perhaps you speak only to the second clause: "Yes, I came." Or you might say, "I love you." You will say whatever it takes for the moment to pass unnoticed.

We were so miserable, Lisa, Shelleen, Gladys, and I, which is why we smiled so much and told folks how fortunate we were. And the more miserable we became the fewer words we seemed to have to express our misery. Our misery seemed illegitimate, even to ourselves—especially to ourselves. How could four Black professionals, who lived by the sea where the climate was always temperate, where the food was organic and plentiful, where the people all had smiles and tans, where we held esteemed degrees and good jobs, be so miserable? How could our misery be blamed on anyone but ourselves?

Shelleen once told me: When I walk down the street in Santa Cruz, when I walk into a store, when I ask to be seated at a restaurant, I must be a whore—that's what they see, that's all they see. I can be nothing else. I wait in vain for one morsel of human recognition to rescue me, she said, but the world is stingy. Shelleen had a PhD. Shelleen was chair of the English department; didn't that count for something? She had left the South behind so why hadn't her imago stayed in Mississippi? Why was her imago so eternal?

A life of stasis was too much for any of us (Shelleen, Gladys, Lisa, myself, and so many like us in Santa Cruz County) to be burdened with. Sleeping with a white (or yellow or brown—anything but black) skinned lover, was an act of rescue—ours: a desperate gambit for life over death. These White beings flaunt their sex, because they have sexuality to flaunt; they hide their sex, because they have sexuality to hide. But Shelleen is a whore before, and whether or not, she flaunts her sex—what sex? Unlike Helen or Virginia or Alice, she has no sex to flaunt. And Frank, much the same, you are an ape a priori. It is not a question of discrimination, it is a question of being.

We love them because they alone can give us life. We hate them for the same reason. Shelleen and I cannot call the White women of Santa Cruz "whores" for throwing their clothes off with such reckless abandon, for their group sex and orgies; that would be "uncivil" on the part of the whore and "sexist" on the part of the ape. They would try to teach the whore and the ape a thing or two about women's liberation: Our bodies, ourselves! they would shout. They'd even spell it out for us if they had to. But that would be an act of bad faith on their part; another performance of the arrogance of power. What they should really say is this: How can the a priori whore and the a priori ape presume to assess us at all? We are alive. We are the world. It is not just "our bodies, ourselves;" it is the fact that we have bodies—we are not reduced by the violence of our imagoes. Show a little common sense, nigger; don't let your mouth get your ass in trouble. They should put it like that, plain and simple, and not confuse matters with their "rights" discourse, their fancy talk. That would be the ethical thing to do. And we could respond with an ethical gesture of our own, the slitting of their throats, and salvage the clarity that we lost in the spring of 1865.

Words always get in the way, dragging desire and confusion behind them. Through words we share their illusions and move through their day. What else can we do? We need someone to love. Don't look at me, I say to Shelleen and the others. And don't you look at me, Shelleen and the others say to me. We are all too familiar with our own repartee. We've heard it all our lives in the subterfuge of our parents' "issues." There was no particularity to their "issues;" least of all when they insisted on the particulars; just an a priori rupture. We've been there and done that ourselves—Shelleen and I, Lisa and Gladys—we'll not be fooled again. We must love someone who can be loved, that we might be loved in return.

And we'll each take good care of our someone. We'll make them laugh or cry like they've never laughed or cried before. We'll keep them vibrating, keep them pulsating, keep them alive. We'll make love to them again when they come down. And when they catch their breath, when they wipe the sweat from their brow, they will look into our eyes and say, "I love you." Not "I love you, whore" or "I love you, ape" but "I love you! you! you!" We are forever hopeful. A loved captive is better off than a hated one.

Jim Stevenson, the chair of the sociology department, came into the restaurant, followed by a gaggle of sociologists. From their table across the room, they took far too much interest in my liaison with Shelleen.

"Better get out before they call the riot squad," she said.

I suggested we move to the Ugly Mug coffee shop down the road. As we left I thought, has Shelleen left Alice's name out of the mix because it doesn't belong there or is the omission a gesture of deference to my feelings? But I didn't ask.

That night I had a dream, not of Barbara Bush, but a dream that transposed the nude hot tub rituals of Alice and her colleagues into a prelude to an orgy of sex and violence. It was one of those dreams in which I could feel the presence of my body though I could not witness myself as being present. I neither spoke nor appeared in this dream but I was there...trying to escape. The naked nymphs frolicked in the steaming water: Rick, lewd as usual, gregarious as usual. Herby, resting his head back against the edge of the tub, holding his cocktail above the water. Alice, looking triumphantly upon the nude bodies she had assembled. She laughed, not too enthusiastically, however, at Rick's lewd jokes. Belinda Ritz, sitting in the water, saying nothing. And Helen, emerging late from the kitchen, with a towel around her, which she finally threw aside like proverbial caution to the wind. Alice sat uneasily opposite Herby, lowering her body from time to time to submerge her breasts when he opened his eyes. The others were empathetic to her dilemma. Two people recently divorced, nude and communal in the same hot tub. We're all family here, said Helen reassuringly. Rick topped it off with an off-color joke and they all laughed and splashed each other.

They all felt better, now. There was a long, silent interlude. Well, said Rick, what should we talk about now? Belinda Ritz suggested, Let's talk about the faculty. All at once they said boring! and were quiet again.

Then an eyeball bubbled to the surface of the steamy water. With its optic nerve as a tail, it jiggled on the surface like a squid. Blood inked the water around it. In the hot water they all shivered in their nakedness. The vibrations of their bodies caused such a tempest of waves that the eyeball and its severed nerve darted back and forth. It lit upon Helen's nipple. She started to scream. This is your fault, Belinda Ritz scolded, sternly, to Alice, it's entirely your fault! Herby's lobster red body rocketed up out of the water and onto the deck. The water lurched back and forth as he left, sending the fat ocular squid slithering toward Rick and Alice who beat the water to keep it back. Rick wretched into the steaming soup of bodies. He climbed out leaving the women and his slime on the water.

I awoke with a start, drenched in sweat.

Alice was already awake. "You're sweating," she said.

"Yes," I said. What else could I say? I reached down and grabbed a towel from the nightstand on my side of the bed. I asked her to wipe my back. But her touch was as terrifying as the dream.

"What's wrong?" she said

"Nothing."

"Why did you flinch?"

"When?"

"Just now, when I touched you."

"I don't know."

"You were having a nightmare." I grunted, affirmatively.

"About what?"

"I don't remember."

"You don't remember?"

"No," I lied.

"Fine. You don't remember."

THE LUCKY ONES WITH SHADOWS

sometimes in a country where
torture is rife
I think how lucky the school children whose
denial is truly plausible
whose sleep is dependent on screams
of what they may not become
a nostril punctured by a favorite math pencil
a vulva pinched with shop tools from the floor of seventh grade
testes crushed by new teachers
part pupils part objects of pain
in rooms darkened with sunlight where
they alone are the only students
sponging knowledge free of texts the lucky ones
they may never know this
fraternity of fragments these dim
and flickering lamps at night
truant in the streets
insuring their future their safe return

5

—⚟— WEDNESDAY, FEBRUARY 26, 1992

There are days when the poverty, men with missing teeth and scarred faces and holes in their shoes, women with large and bloated ankles and dresses worn as thin as the fabric of their smile, standing, sitting, some sleeping on the sidewalk, days when encountering humanity with such sharp dependence on a sale or a handout that make me long for the shade of Wits's campus trees under which I eat my lunch while reading Gramsci or Foucault. Long for the four libraries I live in; for the noontime lectures by visiting scholars from all over the world the hush of my office; the graduate students; and the faculty tea room. A Shangri La lowered from the sky by ropes into a bog of state terror.

I must write my friends back home and tell them not to believe what they read in the New York Times. *Socialism is alive and well in the hearts and minds of the South African people. Mass action is happening on a scale that dwarfed our wildest expectations in the sixties and seventies. Not a week goes by when I am not in a march or demonstration, when I don't hear the chanting and singing of workers—three hundred of them some days, three thousand of them other days—just outside my window. I stop what I'm doing, I leave the office,*

I go down into the street, and we jam the traffic for miles around, we let them know as we march through the streets that you shall not pass, that we won't be turned back. Khanya is at home here in South Africa in a way that she never was in New York. Since school began she is buried in her law books—not really though: she attends the rallies, she marches when she can, and she works diligently at the Workers' Library. And she defends workers in the trenches of the Labour Dispute and Relations Board in Pretoria. She never tires of making a connection between her course work and the radical transformation of an entire society. I love the nights we sit beneath the stars on the Wits University lawn, sharing a bottle of wine, talking of revolution and the future. Or the times when Nadine Gordimer takes us out for coffee, or invites me to read at the Market Theatre or the Johannesburg Art Gallery or somewhere in a township near Pretoria. Times when we take Reba and her little cousin Dudu on picnics atop the grassy knoll above the cricket pitch and I, blinded by the gleam on those white, imperial trousers, try to make heads or tails of cricket as the children squeal with joy and tumble down the hill. Times when I ask myself, could I live here, am I not living here now?

But then there are the other times, tide upon tide of time that climb the levee and rush in...

...with the victims of the squatter camps

...with the dead on the trains

...time that washes over me with the absence of the six women I was searching for yesterday, abducted by Inkatha: dead? alive? Nancefield station was thirsting for witnesses...

I was in Hillbrow last week eating ice cream with Reba. The sound of her pocketful of coins jingled like wind chimes as we walked. At the corner a casspir, a police personnel carrier, pulled up beside us. The ice cream cone fell to her feet. She holds her pocket and silences the coins. She squeezes my hand. Her little face is twisted with fear.

"Daddy, will they take our money?"

"No, pumpkin, they won't take our money." What possessed me to lie to a four-year-old child?

"Have they come to get us?" The casspir is now blocks away, but still she speaks in the present tense.

"I won't let them get us, pumpkin." Like hell you won't.

...at times like these, I tell myself if we had three plane tickets we would leave.

Nostalgia for a homeland that was never mine creeps into my thoughts at times like these. If I'm lucky I write a letter, an essay, a vignette, and I'm pleased with the terra firma of the page. I wish the people on the page were all the people in the world.

—⁓— SATURDAY, MARCH 7, 1992

You're a Black man. You're a strong Black man, goddamnit. This ain't nothin' but a thang, go out there and kick some ass. Nothing terrified me more than going out there; than leaving the flat each morning. Lost and alone. A stranger in a strange land. Don't think like that, you can handle it. What, exactly, is the "it" that I can handle? Is "it" the daily sting of apartheid? Is "it" my cultural dislocation, or worse, the realization that whereas Khanya's *culture has been displaced (from arable land to dust), my capacity to make culture (the very apparatus that one needs before one can even name his displacement) had been obliterated centuries before I was born? Khanya's loss can find its verb and make a sentence. For her, the "it" is having* this, *when she used to have* that. *"It" means being relocated* here *when she used to live* there; *but for me there was no here, here; no there, there. They kicked me off my plantation and sent me to town? What an absurd formulation. My loss has no language because "it" has no grammar.*

—⁓— MONDAY, MARCH 9, 1992

Reba has none of Khanya's social graces. Instead she is amply endowed with her grandparents' penchant for criticism. But unlike her grandparents who are critical behind my back, which is to say their observations are tempered by a superego, Reba was all id.

Yesterday I'd been calling Reba to come and eat lunch while I attended to something like the early stages of a soufflé that could not be left unattended. Her food was getting cold. I stood on the balcony calling out to her then I went to the door and did the same. I was under the impression that she spoke very few words of English (but Christ-almighty, her name is the same in English and Setswana!). My nerves were frayed and I was tired from working a late dinner night shift as a waiter at Luigi's. This is not my idea of a houseboat in Amsterdam. Our money's running out. The job at Luigi's sucks—who taught these White people how to tip? In a hot minute my tourist visa will expire and I'll be here illegally.

The South African government has revoked Khanya's passport. Her "homeland" identity card has already been confiscated as a result of her sister's house arrest. All this takes on a surreal quality when I consider she was born just outside Pretoria. She has a student ID from the University of Witwatersrand which is only good for one more year. I have a student ID from Columbia University (whoopee) which had expired a year ago and a tourist visa in which a clock ticks.

I know Reba heard me calling her. The whole complex heard me. Finally, I gave up and went back to the kitchen.

Then I heard, "Dumela," and looked up from the stove to see her, the kitchen door swinging back and forth behind her. She is a beautiful child, I thought. The kind one sees in commercials. Those child stars who stomp their feet and walk their parents around a toy store the way most people walk their dogs around the block.

"I've been calling you for hours." She stared at me, that wide-eyed unblinking stare of hers. I've felt more protected during an x-ray. Stop staring at me little girl. *"Didn't you hear me?"*

"It hasn't been hours."

"So you do speak English after all. And you can tell time as well. Sit down and eat please."

"I'm playing."

"Eat, then you can go back to play." On the freeway.

"I'm not hungry."

"Why have you been coming here on weekends, pretending that you don't speak English?" She just stared at me; that wide-eyed unblinking stare. "Never mind, just...please...sit down, okay? Eat your food."

"What is it?"

"It's vegetarian lasagna, from the Moosewood Cookbook.*"*

"My grandfather says you must make pap and fleece."

"I'm a vegetarian. You can have pap and fleece when you're with him."

"I said I'm not hungry. Are you deaf?"

"I beg your pardon! You're going to eat not because you're hungry, young lady, but because your mother and I have a deal—"

"Hey, wena, speak 'Swana."

"My name is not 'wena.' In America not even the most belligerent children walk up and down the house calling their parents 'hey, you.' Try 'father' or just try eating." And blink, damnit.

"My grandfather says you must speak 'Swana."

"He does, does he? Well, I've only just arrived."

"You were here before, I saw you."

"Those were research visits." Can you believe it? I was plea-bargaining with a four-year-old.

"Listen," she said. Yes, the little runt said, *"listen." Her hands were on her hips like her grandmother, "When I'm at my grandfather's house and he says 'Reba do a thing,' Reba stops and Reba thinks 'Does Reba want to do a thing?' If Reba wants to do a thing Reba does it and if Reba doesn't want to do a thing Reba doesn't do it; and that's the way it's going to be here."*

Lord have mercy, I need a divorce.

—⌇— TUESDAY, MARCH 10, 1992

As soon as Khanya left for school, Trevor knocked on the door. He said he'd been watching the flat since before we woke up. Khanya and I had eaten breakfast on the balcony but I didn't see him or any car like his. He came in with a boy from Mozambique. I say "boy" because he was at least 15 but not quite 18. They both smelled musty and unwashed. He said the boy (don't remember his name) is to be a material witness for a special commission on violence and massacres. They needed to stay here until it was time for Khanya to return. He's been transporting this young man from place to place for almost a week. Trevor's dorm room isn't safe. This young man's father (I'll call the boy Howard…what kind of name is that for a Mozambican?)…his father is a mercenary for the South

African Defense Force (SADF). Trevor thinks his dad and the other soldiers at the base are guilty of genocide. To the best of my understanding there is a secret military base, somewhere northeast of here (I think Trevor called it 5 Recce). Transport helicopters airlift Mozambican mercenaries and their White officers off the base. They carry out atrocities against civilians, whether ANC or non-aligned, in the outlying areas. Three electric fences ring the base. How did Howard get out? Trevor didn't explain this to me, or if he did I don't remember. Howard works in the kitchen and told Trevor that he had not left the base since he, his mother, and his father arrived after fleeing the civil war that the SADF instigated in Mozambique. Several days ago he found his mother washing his father's uniform in the tub. The water was mixed with blood. His mother freaked out when she saw him and told him to get out and close the door. Later, all she would tell him was, "something went wrong." Howard has been disturbed by what he sees on the news; the deaths remind him of his own country. He will testify—provided the generals don't get to him and Trevor first—that:

1. Certain massacres have coincided with his father's absence from the base.
2. Though his access to restricted areas on the base is prohibited he knows that when he has seen news reports of atrocities in outlying areas, he and the kitchen crew have peeled only 3,000 potatoes. They normally peel 5,000 potatoes. The days when 2,000 potatoes are not peeled would indicate that on those days two large battalions have left 5 Recce and gone somewhere. You can't move two battalions without there being records of where they went and why. Perhaps his testimony would be enough for the Goldstone Commission to subpoena those records from the SADF. Then the Goldstone Commission can investigate.

After Howard took a bath he ate the chicken curry I made and conked out on top of the bed. Then Trevor washed and stretched out on the couch and asked me to sit on the balcony, to pretend to be grading papers, and to note anyone who comes in and out of the building. Trevor's already missed a week of lectures at Wits. There is no telling when the commission will call Howard to testify. Its calendar is backlogged.

I am thirty-six years old today. I wonder what that means. Here's a milestone: I have been elected to the executive committee of the Hillbrow-Berea ANC branch and I have been appointed to the executive committee of the sub-region, making me a political commissar for the city of Jo'burg, which means, as far as I can tell, nothing. I'm like one of those Great Migration Negroes; the one who called home to tell his people he'd gone up North and got himself a big im-poe-tant job: "I'm ova five hunnid White folks, mama." He wasn't lying; he mowed the lawn down at the cemetery. That's what it means to be an ANC commissar for the city of Johannesburg. Mowing the lawn at the cemetery.

Since February I have been active in the ANC's Pretoria-Witwatersrand-Vaal (PWV) regional structures. After ten years in prison and a stint in exile Barbara Hogan, a White woman, returned to Jo'burg and was elected to the third highest post in the ANC's PWV regional executive committee; the position of Secretary. And since the national executive committee (Nelson Mandela, Walter Sisulu, Oliver Tambo, Ronnie Kasrils, Gil Marcus, Joe Nhlanhla, Winnie Mandela, Chris Hani, Joe Slovo, Jeremy Cronin, and about seventy others) sits in Shell House, just a few blocks away from Hogan's office, the PWV regional executive committee may be the most influential and important regional committee in the ANC. Not because of its ethical embodiment of power, but because of its physical proximity to power.

Barbara Hogan spoke at our branch meeting in Hillbrow. She asked for volunteers to assist fieldworkers on the ANC Peace Commission desk at the regional office. She explained the disarray that the ANC regional Peace Commission was in:

* *Only one coordinator.*
* *Only two field workers.*
* *Only one secretary.*
* *Violence everywhere. Inkatha, the police, and the army are murdering two hundred to three hundred of our people per month. Most of the violence is occurring around Jo'burg, the rest is in Natal. That means twenty percent of the country is burdened with eighty percent of the violence.*

"Comrades," she said after raising her fist and shouting, Amandla! *"We, at the regional office, want you in the branches to volunteer. Comrades, you are needed to go into the squatter camps where the massacres happen. You are needed to ride the trains where the shootings and abductions occur. Go among the people and bear witness. Take statements from the victims and their families. Work in the regional office and write reports for the human rights lawyers, the Peace Commission Bulletin. Take the international press into the unrest areas. This is Jo'burg, comrades; some of you are artists and educators, professional people who have free time and resources. Who owns a camera?"*

Before I knew it, a reflex in my shoulder had raised my hand.

— MONDAY, APRIL 13, 1992

I work for the ANC regional Peace Commission three days a week. Each time I interview a victim in Boipatong...an eighty-year-old man who hid beneath his bed while his neighbor of ten years, the seventy-year-old woman in the shack next door, screamed as her limb was hacked off, screamed until she could scream no more and there were only moans flowing quietly out with her blood. A thirty-five-year-old woman whose daughter and husband languish in the hospital from multiple stab wounds and whose four-year-old daughter was stabbed through the head—this she told me while still in shock, as I photographed her body's patchwork of stitches—spoke through a fog, as though any moment she would drop her bundle and the eggs would smash at her feet. A woman of eighteen who stares through me answering none of my questions. What has happened to her? *I put my steno pad on a rock. I try to hold her hand, but her hand has forgotten how to summon dexterity; she stands in the sun—please, come into the shade, I say, beckoning to her shack—she won't go back into the shack where her parents and sister died last night; she gazes into the distance; she doesn't bat an eye. She didn't move when I came. She didn't even hear me greet her. She makes no motion when I leave. This is a war. I pray I get no closer to it than the day after or the day before.*

Eleven ANC comrades that I am close to get death threats as a matter of course. They are followed. Detained. Their flats are ransacked by men unknown. Ten to twelve people close to them have been murdered execution style. They were educators, intellectuals, labor union organizers, peace commission workers, and university students. They were also members of Umkhonto we Sizwe. It goes deeper than that: activists who aren't "officially" part of the armed struggle (Khanya's school mates from Bophuthatswana or civic leaders in the townships) are being targeted as well. And there are the township people who sleep in their meager shacks in shifts—or only in the daytime if they live alone—and the commuters who, even in winter, in the wind and the rain, keep the train windows open ready to bail out if a man suddenly shouts something in Zulu and pulls an AK-47 from beneath his long, suspicious coat. Now more than ever I am convinced that we must take the fight back to them. I am tired of affixing the faces of the dead to film. Mandela implores us not to strike back, to climb the moral high ground. How does a corpse roll up hill?

—∿— SUNDAY, MAY 31, 1992

Khanya and I just had a fight. I was settled on the sofa with my books, a cup of coffee, and a delicious New York Times *that I found for the first time in ages at the kiosk in Hillbrow.* Delicious *is not a word I would have used to describe the* New York Times *when I lived in New York. In fact, I've always turned a Chomskian nose up at the* Times. *But when I lived in New York I didn't have to hunt for it. Never mind the fact that this one is a week old. It's been almost a year since I've read one.*

I was settled, okay? I had just stretched out. I was happy. For the first time in a long time I was content. Then, she walked in and told me her classmates Naledi, Ntombi, and Gladys were coming over to study immaterial property with her. But I just stretched out, I said, it's Sunday; and for once we don't have Reba for the weekend. (Now, let's not lie to the diary, you know you didn't say that last part. You feel guilty because you're supposed to be filled with joy at the mere thought of Reba's coming to spend the weekend, when the truth of the matter is all you really wanted was to take this woman on a fifty-year date. Better scratch this out in case she snoops around and finds it.) What am I doing here? What-what-what! Why can't she stop trying to prove she's a responsible mother? And she would say, Why can't you grow up? She told me I would have to go to a café or to the bedroom with my books and my newspaper. Why can't you guys go to the library? I said. She said the law library closed early on Sunday. I told her that there's nothing in Braamfontein but banks, hotels, and businesses—there's nowhere for me to go on Sunday. Go to Hillbrow, she said, something's open there and everything's multiracial. I don't feel like walking all the way to Hillbrow; why should I have to leave my own living room just so the Pointer Sisters can rehearse, y'all ain't on tour no more. She didn't laugh at that. She's having adjustment problems where my humor is concerned. Now she's pissed. She said when I moved here we had agreed her studies come first. How can I argue with that?

There are only two miserly rooms here, excluding a bathroom and a matchbox kitchen in this little flat. I'm ten pounds overweight—well, five, but it feels like ten. It's the end of the month. I don't get paid until tomorrow. As usual we are completely broke. I'm craving a koeksister or some ice cream. She's going to invite the Pointer Sisters all to stay for dinner. I can feel it. I can just feel it. A study session, my eye. Just listen to them in there yucking it up. Speak English, okay? Probably talking about me. Immaterial property. Yeah, right. Sounds like a damn Tupperware party.

I'm so depressed. Brazil or a houseboat in Amsterdam. That was the plan. I remember distinctly, even if she *doesn't. We agreed. I wrote it down, I wrote it down right here in the journal the night we talked about it. Why, okay, just tell me, whyyyyyy can't they keep their voices down? Go out there and tell them to keep it down. You're the man of the house, aren't you? And this is Africa where such things are well known and respected. Would her father put up with this? Would Richard, that tsotsi from Soweto? Hell, no. At Richard's house the women went to the kitchen and spoke quietly, you dig, hushed tones, dulcet voices, made little bird steps when they served the drinks. Now, really, would Richard's woman send* him *to the bedroom? You're a chump. Face it. You're a pussy-whupped chump. That's your destiny in life. Here lies a chump who died of acute chumpitus after being sent to his bedroom.*

I'm homesick. Can't believe I just wrote that. What a chump. What a fucking *chump. Only a chump would say some shit like that. But it's true. I'm homesick even though "home" is more and more intangible as the days go by. Yesterday I spoke with Reba on the phone. She was calling from Mmabatho. I did my best to speak the little bit of Setswana that I've managed to learn. I told her that I loved her. Was this a false gesture? I hate false gestures. I live in dread of sentimentality. But there you have it. I told her that I love her. She responded in English, "I will teach you father." Last week she turned five. Next year we're going to have to face the challenge of finding a school for her if we're still in Jo'burg. God, I hope we're gone by then. How are we going to find a decent school in this hellhole? The only schools that are multiracial are the Catholic schools. I can't think of an institution I despise more than the Roman Catholic Church. A lifetime of kneeling and genuflecting and no in- surance for knee surgery. I'm a recovering Catholic. Yep, taking those Twelve Steps to Sobriety. Hi, my name is Frank and I have a Jesus problem. Welcome, Brother Frank, you've taken the First Step. Let's hear it for Brother Frank. (Whistling and moderate, heartfelt applause.) Somebody get Brother Frank a cup of coffee (Yeah, and let me drink it in my own goddamn living room). We've all stood right where Brother Frank is standing now. Why Brother Jim here had a Jesus problem that lasted ten years but, knock on wood, he's been clean for the last five. Let's hear it for Brother Jim! (More whistling and mod- erate, heartfelt applause.)*

I—am—so—fucking—bored. There's not enough room in this diary to say how bored I am. Nothing sucks like Sunday in South Africa. Nothing. I used to love Sunday. Riding the subway to Greenwich Village. Hunting for second- hand books at the Strand. Then back uptown to the Hungarian Café on Am- sterdam and 114th where I'd sit and read my newfound treasures with a cup of Turkish coffee and a cheese Danish. Fat chance of a cheese Danish here. This is such a fucking Christian country. Nothing is open on Sunday. I'd welcome another Boer War—hell, let the Brits nuke 'em!—just to get a Starbucks in Braamfontein.

The violence at Phola Park—a camp for homeless people east of Alber- ton—was in the news this week. It's just on the other side of a field from the townships of Thokoza and Katlehong which together form the second largest Black township in South Africa. The army and the police launched their most murderous raid on the squatter camp since the 32 Battalion Affair. I saw the winter dust billowing up from the long line of hippos silhouetted by the sun as they advanced upon the squatter camp. Soldiers spilled out from their bel- lies and made house-to-house searches for ANC organizers and for weapons.

I saw a woman being dragged by her hair as the commander stood by and watched. He told the reporter, "No one goes in and no one comes out until order is restored."

Go into the living room. Greet everyone. Ask them about law school. Be genuine. Their lives are no easier than yours. Then, take your New York Times *and go to Hillbrow. It's not that far. There'll be peace if you do.*

Khanya is depressed as well. She is trying to make it through an extremely racist law program. Twenty percent of all the students at Wits are Black, whereas Blacks make up eighty percent of the country. And professors like Etienne Mureinik, Charles von Onselen, and June Sinclair act like they're do-ing this twenty percent a favor. Everyday she gets treated as though she should bow down with gratitude just to enter the classroom. She is also trying hard not to think about the gruesome murder and suicide that just occurred on her father's side of the family. A cousin who was light enough to "go Coloured" moved to one of their neighborhoods, changing his name and the name of his family to Fritz. Last week he snapped. He murdered his family and then killed himself. This is the kind of political violence that doesn't register as "political" violence. What would it take for such violence to make the news?

—⁓— MONDAY, JUNE 1, 1992

This morning I went back to Phola Park with Thabo Nkosi, a fieldworker for the ANC regional Peace Commission. Before Thabo came to work at the Peace Commission he was a labor union organizer for the Congress of South African Trade Unions. The ANC has "borrowed" him from COSATU. People love and respect him because he doesn't write two different letters to two different constitu-ents. Like Stimela, he is one of Chris Hani's people. It is this trust and respect which the ANC needs in squatter camps like Phola Park. F. W. de Klerk knew that by orchestrating and escalating township violence, the ANC would be forced to call upon the most radical comrades in the ANC-SACP-COSATU Alliance. These are the only people with any street cred in the townships. They now work like triage doctors. As a result, their political organizing has been stunted and often put on hold. This is good for de Klerk. This is good for Gatsha Buthelezi. It's also good for Mandela and the internal bourgeois reorganization he is trying to preside over. This revolution has four fronts: (a) the Afrikaner State, with de Klerk at the head, (b) the Black contra forces—Buthelezi's Inkatha, (c) the White English speaking "progressives"—tokoloshes of laissez-faire, and (d) Mandela's people. But we seem to have the political will to fight only the Afrikaner and Inkatha.

This morning when I arrived at the ANC regional office, Thabo told me that there had been trouble at 6:00 A.M. in Phola Park. We walked six blocks to the municipal carpark. We recorded the mileage on the small Japanese import. We headed east, past the low, red clay plateaus with their sides carved out by miners long ago.

Thabo and I check in with the local ANC official inside a shack at the entrance to Phola Park. I am always staggered by the difference between this office and ours. Our office: carpeted floors, clean and plentiful bathrooms, telephones and fax machines, computers, and most of all our central heating for it is early winter. Their office: this hut made of corrugated tin, this ceiling too low for a tall man, these walls that hold no heat, this floor of dirt or cement depending on where one stands, these tattered chairs around the desk and lining the wall, no kettle whistle calling us to tea. Here membership dues are not brought to the bank, but put in an envelope and tucked into a drawer.

There is an ANC attorney seated in one of the chairs along the wall. He is tired, angry, and distraught. He writes on a pad on top of his briefcase. He is taking notes from the woman behind the desk. She is a member of the ANC Phola Park Branch executive committee. Near them is a young man taking membership dues from an elderly woman. It is 10:00 A.M. The lawyer has been here since eight; just two hours after the raid. He knows how useless this exercise is—though I cannot understand him since he is Xhosa and speaks to the young man and the two women in Xhosa. All six of us, Thabo and I, the lawyer, and the residents are Black, though I am not a mother tongue speaker. Only Thabo and the woman behind the desk know this about me, which is why the others greet me in Xhosa. I return their greeting in Xhosa and sit in one of the folding chairs along the wall as though I am in fact Xhosa.

When the lawyer is finished, Thabo and I will want to ask this poor woman the same questions. She is willing. She says she'll tell this story one hundred times if need be. Someone must know. Someone must help us. She's been talking all morning. First, to the press. Then to the police (the very police who launched the raid, no doubt). Then to the ANC attorney. Now she will help us with our report.

"At 6:00 A.M. the hippos drove into the camp. Once inside the camp, the rifles and shotguns were thrust through the windows of the hippos. They shot into the shacks of residents. They shot dogs wandering in the streets. They shot the windows of the few. They only got out of their hippos once, to make an arrest. Rarely do they alight, comrades, you know this. They don't want to engage us on an equal footing."

That is all she can tell us. She escorts us out the door and to our car. She points in the direction of the areas of the squatter camp where the most damage was done. She tells us to go take statements from people in those areas.

The road is a pastiche of potholes. We drive at two miles per hour, dipping and rising like a billy goat. I fear we will get lost in this labyrinth with no street signs and no landmarks. But Thabo has been coming here for a long time. He lives across the field in the township of Thokoza. For him there are numerous landmarks. Now, the road has narrowed too much for the Nissan. We get out of the car. We will walk from here.

Today we made it to Phola Park and back to Jo'burg unmolested. But Thabo is often stopped and harassed by the police; detained for hours, sometimes over night; his firearm for which he has a license, is often confiscated without rhyme or reason. At night, the police sit in their cars outside his house. They never leave their cars. They simply arrive at night and sit. In the morning they drive away.

—⚂—

The kombi chokes and sputters out of the taxi rank at Noord Street Station. In the park beside the station: the squatters, always the squatters. Whole families lounging amid the litter and thread-bare turf: women selling fruit and vegetables which would be difficult to give away in New York; men listening to music or talking in clusters, the language of which I still can't penetrate. Perhaps I never will. The sign on the seat behind the driver says: 15 maximum. We are eighteen or nineteen.

Early autumn leaves lack the luster of fire to which I'd grown accustomed in New England and New York. Here, at the bottom of the world, the inversion of seasons debauches all expectations as though some vaudevillian lowered his sham aesthetics from the sky by ropes. *Go to Africa,* a friend once laughed, *you'll see how goddamn First World you really are.*

In my first year, I took no issue at gutter-swells that eddied in September when they should have raged in March; didn't pine for the mastery of December's snow-dusted fir trees as the Transvaal sun beat down day after day after day. No, it isn't, I think as the van rocks back and forth in one of Noord Street's potholes, the throes of time-ass-backwards that defeats me, but the way these seasons gather a different steam, hobble along indifferent to my memories, lack any notice of my presence.

Sardined between nineteen others black as me, I seem to travel alone. Jo'burg's mustard-metal skyline shrinks in the rearview mirror. For my sins, I once spent two years in Chicago. Johannesburg and Chicago are enough alike to convince me of the longevity of bad karma. Chicago is a brown, polyester town where power's hunched beneath the rumpled raincoats of balding men whose names end in "-ski," who buy their suits at factory outlets and forget to have them altered, who remember the surnames of their long dead cronies and the maiden names of the long dead mothers of those long dead cronies. Richard Daley and de Klerk could switch places without a skip in the heartbeat of the world.

We pass the last vestiges of factories and stores as the highway breaks toward the sky. Beside us now the open veld and its pylons swooping past. Here the dry monotony of grass breaks with a matriarch and her children sitting in the middle of nowhere on the remnants of upholstery someone discarded; further on, too far for the woman to have come from or to reach with all those children, stones the size of kneecaps hold down tin roofs against a corrugated sky; ahead, the free will of brush fires crackles in the low dry grass, the sky won't shed a tear— and my head is the only one that turns. Even my spectacles are viewed in isolation.

Jo'burg is a face of scars, I thought, an hour ago in the ANC lift where someone'd left the front-page picture of Winnie emerging from Rand Superior Court, this time without Nelson at her side. On the street, a man with a question mark carved into his nose. In the foyer to our office, Ma Mpume scrubbing stairs beneath the weight of someone's razor in her face. Not a day goes by when I don't count five people on my way through the city with the memory of knives drawn across their faces. I am supposed to think revolutionary thoughts, but all I register is pathology as though the entire terrain was polymorphously perverse, its only aim to offend my sense—of what?

Shell House: a thirty-odd story building that Shell Oil gave to the ANC, the government-in-waiting, a down payment on future legislation. Thabo Nkosi meets me outside a meeting room on the 18th floor. We go into one of the private cubicles by the window. I sit on the ledge by the window. I am nervous due to his note left for me at the regional office. "I'm at Shell House. Come at once. Urgent." Beneath me, the squatters of the park look like ants milling about in the aftermath of a picnic. The kombis scurry in and out of Noord Street like moving thimbles.

"Has there been another massacre?" I ask.

"Something's happened. We don't know what."

"What else could have happened? They killed thirty-two people last week."

I had just come from a job interview and planned to spend the day in the regional office writing the Amnesty International report on the military's last foray into Phola Park. A suit and tie is no attire for a trip to a squatter camp, pinched on one side by an Inkatha stronghold, pinched on another by a makeshift military base, and with a large open veld where corpses are dumped between it and the township.

"Three..." he says, "thirty-three. Ma Kekana died in hospital this morning."

"My god. Why comrades in intelligence sat on our reports..."

"Because anything approaching 150 deaths a month is good publicity for the ANC; anything more is a tragedy."

"If I'd said that, you'd put me in my place as a foreigner."

"That's why you can't say it. By the way, I hear you received 81 percent of the vote for a seat on the ANC Hillbrow Exec. Why don't you join the Communist Party as well?"

"When did they start letting communists into the Communist Party?"

"What have you got against the Party?"

"Nothing. Fifty-thousand dedicated militants. The workhorses of the ANC. Just one blemish."

"Which is?"

"The Central Committee."

"You're worse than Winnie Mandela."

"What have you got against Winnie Mandela?"

"She's *ungovernable.*"

"That's a red herring, comrade. Ungovernability has been one of our most sacred principles for more than a decade."

"She speaks out of turn."

"Like Chris Hani? Like Harry-Communist-Party-Gwala? Like Madiba himself?"

"They have legitimacy."

"Thabo, that's pathetic. If you were an ANC policy wonk or a mixed-economy moderate like Thabo Mbeki, I'd shrug my shoulders and walk away—*they* really believe what you just said, it fits them well, like the blue suits they wear. But you, Thabo—you! Do you have any idea what's going to happen to your Communist Party if Nelson Mandela is allowed to consolidate power? You're gonna need more than Chris Hani on your side. You'll need Winnie as well."

"And what will you ultra-leftists need?"

One of us had to stop our debating a future that we could not control and get back to the business at hand. So, I let it go. He told me that the situation at Phola Park needed looking into and that there was another emergency in Soweto where Inkatha had kidnapped more women from the trains at the Nancefield station. We still had not located the other abducted women, though he believed that they were held as sex slaves in the men's hostels, which were guarded by the police from any rescue attempts by MK. He and another fieldworker were going to Soweto to investigate. He wanted me to wait for his return and then we would go to Phola Park together. In the meantime I was to make a series of phone calls to see if there was anyone (journalists we knew, media people) who may have been there this morning. When he told me that he'd already been doing that and to no avail, I volunteered to go to Phola Park myself.

"We're not supposed to travel alone," he said. " You'd be breaking protocol."

"We can't manufacture another person out of thin air. Besides someone has to go. Tell me how to get there by kombi."

"The army has built a wall of razor wire around the entire camp and we think—"

"You can't put razor wire around ten thousand people."

"You can in South Africa, com."

"How many entrances and exits?"

"Last report: one."

"Remember how many men and women lost their jobs after the last massacre? What's going to happen to people whose only excuse is they stood all day at a checkpoint?"

I was at the door when he asked me to shut it and sit back down. He reminded me of a few "extra-curricular activities" that I had been asked to perform by Stimela Mosando. One of the "activities" involved hitching a ride from Phola Park back to Jo'burg with a *New York Times* journalist named Bill Keller. It was simple enough; I was to schmooze with him and feed him a bunch of lies about how the people in the squatter camp were completely unarmed and how the stories he'd heard about gunrunning into Phola Park were lies. I had done that, as I had all along with other Western journalists. Bill Keller was just back from a stint as Bureau Chief for the *New York Times* in the Soviet Union, which had collapsed last Christmas. He thought the fall of communism was a necessary and ultimately good thing. He seemed like a wolf licking his chops after a meal. And Keller didn't seem to like Winnie Mandela either. We had argued, amiably, but argued nonetheless. In the car I fed him all the information from all the reports I'd help write that went to Amnesty International and Human Rights Watch and I had steered him away from any discussion of ANC self-defense units or dead letter boxes in Phola Park. The next day I returned and saddled up to other journalists. I sought out easier marks than Bill Keller, many were all too happy to talk to a fellow American who was a card-carrying member of the ANC and more predisposed than Keller to have me paint a sad portrait of us as victims who didn't fight back.

Thabo Nkosi said he had another "extra-curricular" task for me. He told me that when I got there I was to meet up with the young comrade who was collecting membership dues the last time we were in Phola Park. and bring back some other information besides that pertaining specifically to human rights abuses on the part of Inkatha. Indeed, we had been smuggling arms from the Transkei into Phola Park and they were hidden in various dead letter boxes among the residences of the squatter camp. There was a chance, a strong chance, that during the last incursion into the squatter camp the military and police had discovered the whereabouts of some of those DLBs. If this was true, it would not only mean that precious weapons, weapons which since the fall of the Soviet Union were increasingly harder to come by, had fallen into the hands of the state but it could lead to an embarrassing public relations crisis, and an internal ANC political problem, since Madiba did not want us supplying squatter camp residents with arms.

"Find out from the comrade if the weapons are safe," he said.

As late as 1989 I rode these kombis to the rock and tumble of people singing their favorite Motown songs, or the reckless glee at speculations of Nelson Mandela's imminent release, or the unbanning of the ANC, or talk of a wedding at home in the "homelands." Now, since the massacres in the townships, the shootings on the trains, and the ambush of commuters in kombis such as these, people ride in silence with only the echo of their thoughts. What can be said in these days of uncertainty? In July 1990, as Khanya and I were being wed in New York, Gatsha Buthelezi, with help from de Klerk, sent 100,000 "soldiers" from Kwa-Zulu, in Natal, to the townships surrounding Johannesburg. First, they commandeered the multi-ethnic single-sex hostels on the outskirts of the townships and began their "ethnic" cleansing. When the hostels were solidly Inkatha, the army and police smuggled guns and food into them, sustaining them as they launched raid after raid upon the residents of the surrounding townships. They spread like a virus, killing people in the houses that surrounded "their" hostels and gutting the homes with fire so that those who fled could not return. Many fled to Phola Park.

De Klerk bemoans "Black on Black violence." Nelson Mandela calls for "Peace and Reconciliation." Last month the jokes at the ANC regional Peace Commission were all about Gatsha Buthelezi. This month the joke is about recruiting: Join the ANC and sign your own death warrant.

In March a group of residents from Soweto's Meadowlands marched on Nelson Mandela's home, demanding something be done about the Inkatha Freedom Party hostel and its nocturnal raids. Mandela came to the door in slippers and pajamas and gave a pitch for the angels. Go back to your homes. Peace will come when we have the vote. Remember, the eyes of the world are on you.

Still in her flannel nightgown, Winnie pushed past him, walked through the crowd without a word; now across the lawn, now fumbling with the keys at the door of the garage, now throwing it up to the moon. She stepped inside. Handed AK–47s all around.

Here, in this taxi, on the long East Rand road to Thokoza township, it's not safe to speak of such things. The driver could be a young man who's worked this route or another just like it for years and has no political affiliation beyond his daily fee. He could be a police spy. He could be a thug who fought in the internecine taxi wars, did the killing for a fleet owner, was rewarded with this job. He could be one of Gatsha's impimpis from KwaZulu. And since he's not talking, we're not talking.

Suddenly the sound of machine gun fire rattles the inside of the taxi. My head crashes into the window as the taxi swerves across the highway. The bullets keep coming and I duck again, this time smashing my forehead against the seat in front of me. A baby falls to the floor. An old man may have pissed his pants. I cannot tell which screams are mine and which are someone else's.

The kombi rattles slowly along the shoulder of the road. I taste blood seeping through my teeth and I know that I am dying. It is the same blood I tasted this morning when I fought with Khanya in the kitchen. I see her in her nightgown at the kitchen door.

"In my culture, it's just not done," she said. She had arisen early, before I left, to ask me not to confront her father. He drank and gambled away the money for Rebaabetswe's childcare. Word came from Mmabatho that Reba's nanny had not been paid and so had gone back to her village, leaving Reba alone in the house with Mr. Phenyo's drunken cousin Thebe. There is no food in the cupboards, no milk in the fridge. No money to pay the nanny or the nursery school fees. And we are behind in our rent here in Braamfontein.

"In my culture a deal is a deal," I responded. "'I'll see that Reba is fed and taken care of until you graduate. I'll even pay her school fees.' His words, am I right?"

"That's not the point."

"Then what is the point?"

"Frank, please."

"Next thing you know they'll be sending Reba here to live with us before you finish law school and before I find a decent job."

"Then we'll have to take her."

"When I moved here we had a deal!"

"What can we do?"

"We can sit down with your father and—"

"It's not done in our culture."

"It's not done because I haven't done it yet. After I sit his ass down, and straighten his ass out, then it will be done. You know why? Because—I—will—have—done it."

"My father always said you're not a real African."

"I often wonder if it's you I'm having sex with or some proxy for your parents."

Within seconds her legal mind had translated "proxy" from English to Setswana. She slapped me so hard my teeth tore into my tongue and my eyes glazed over. I faced the window. Tried to regain my composure. The tinny taste of blood seeped through my teeth.

I turned and found Khanya trying not to cry as well.

I grabbed my suit and tie, stuffed my reports on Inkatha massacres into my briefcase along with the photographs of Ma Kekana and her naked wounds—and opened the kitchen door with my fist.

She followed saying, "It's words you strike me with. English words. You don't try to learn my language."

I took my rage into the street where it mingled with the rage of others, fed on the angst of traffic, apathy, and apartheid, grew large and communal.

Now, in this taxi hobbling to a halt like a broken mule, this morning's blood swells once more in my mouth and I ask god for a life long enough to say *I'm sorry.* There are no atheists in foxholes.

The driver knows what we will know, only after one by one we search ourselves and then our neighbors in disbelief at the absence of blood, that the automatic weapon unleashed upon us is a piece of garbage, a plastic bag caught first by the wind and then by the driver's side view mirror. Everyone laughs, except the embarrassed old man.

As we lumber back onto our side of the highway, I'm certain the driver is not Inkatha. *A Zulu would've made the old man walk.*

—⁂—

Within the hour we arrived at Thokoza township's taxi rank under the shadow of a local hospital for Blacks. Here the victims of last week's massacre were brought to heal or to die. *Thirty-three.* Thabo's words echoed as I disembarked and made my way through the makeshift queues of kombis. I was trying not to look conspicuous in my Brooks Brothers' suit and wing-tipped shoes. I'd've drawn less attention in a clown suit. *Ma Kekana died this morning.* The sun dipped into the rooftops of Thokoza's prefab houses and shacks. "Don't ask anyone for directions," Thabo had said. "Just find the taxi stand for Unit 6 and take that taxi to the end of the line. From there you'll see the veld where Inkatha and the army dump the corpses. On the other side of the veld is a road into Phola Park. Don't tell anyone where you're headed. Look straight ahead in the taxi rank. Look as though you know exactly where you're going. Look stern. Like you live there. Let no one hear that American accent."

"But I'm not armed."

"Better to be unarmed than caught as an ANC activist with an unlicensed weapon."

And I don't *live there. I live in Johannesburg, in Braamfontein, surrounded snug and safe between banks, businesses, high rise apartments and Wits university. How I can be stern with the sensation of shit oozing through my bowels? How can I look straight ahead with so many faces looking at me, with the click of kombi doors standing in for clips clicking into guns? And for your information, comrade Thabo, this is Thokoza, not Jo'burg, and this is the Thokoza-hospital-rank, a matchbox-and-mud rendezvous thrown up on a prayer, and not the Noord Street Station. And Ma Kekana died this morning.*

I walk on.

I walk in a straight line toward the hospital at the edge of the taxi rank. *Walk too far and you'll be out of the rank. Then you'll have to turn back and start searching again. It's then that they'll know. The fraud-police will come to take you away. If they're not already here. What do I do? Walk around in circles in this suit and tie? You'll be suspected of being ANC or the press. Walk up to a group of taxi drivers? Again: In this suit? With my accent? They'll suspect you of being some human rights investigator (which you are) nosing around in Inkatha's business (which you are) or the taxi wars (which you are not). Heads you're dead. Tails you're dead. Get in a taxi and go back to Jo'burg. Yeah right, and get labeled a foreigner unwilling to take risks which ordinary South Africans take everyday. Ma Kekana died this morning. Fuck it. I'm going to ask someone for directions.*

The earth stands still as a cluster of taxi drivers stare at me. Three or four beats of silence. Then one of them asks me to repeat the question.

"I'd like to know which taxi goes to Unit 6."

"What business do you have in Unit 6?"

"Well, I don't have any business, per se, I'm simply going to pay a friend a visit." *Don't be a cheeky bastard, Frank, just answer the question and live.*

"Which friend?"

None of your business, fat boy. You gapped tooth square-back-sedan-head muthafucka. "Well, er, his name is Thabo."

They look at each, one to the other. "Thabo's" as common here as "John" is in the States. Someone has turned off the radio. Marvin Gaye was asking "What's Going On?"

"Thabo how-much?"

"Thabo...Thabo Kekana."

"Thabo Kekana, eh?"

"Yes, that's right." *Be stern!* "Thabo Kekana. I'd be grateful if you guys could point me in the right direction. I mean." *Stern, Frank, stern.* "Thabo's going to be real worried if I don't make it by dark. I mean he'll probably call my wife or something if I'm not there within thirty minutes at the latest."

"Now you say this Thabo—Thabo how much?"

"Kekana, Thabo Kekana. Please, I really do need to go."

"This Thabo Kekana lives in Unit 6. And when did he phone to say you must pay a visit?"

"This morning. I really don't see the relevance—"

But *they* see the relevance: As of 3:00 A.M. that morning, Unit 6 was no more. All these drivers knew it. Some may have known it first hand. They may have been the very impimpis who tore into the homes of Unit 6, the unit at the edge of the veld between the township and the squatter camp. Some of them may have toppled the kerosene lamps, which gutted the houses; some of them may have pumped their .45s or driven their stakes into the hearts of people half-asleep.

I stood there in puddles of mud that reflected the low sun's light, playing out my role in this absurd little repertory. Unit 6 had been destroyed. Everyone knew that but me. I was worse than the fool waiting for Godot. Godot is before me, his round stomach testing his T-shirt, and I am insulting his intelligence.

"When did Kekana phone and tell you to come?"

"He phoned this morning."

They look at each other again.

Now Godot straightens. He's had enough of me. He's made his decision. "Who will take him to Unit 6?" Most of them look away. To the one young man who doesn't look away he delegates the task. "Sipho, you take him. See that he gets to where he's supposed to go."

"Sharp! Sharp!" Sipho responds, a little too eagerly. Nothing in his sloughy ambiance instills confidence in me that he is a driver for Unit 6.

"If he's not the regular driver, I wouldn't want to put him out of his way. I mean, for that matter, I wouldn't want to put anyone out of their way."

"Go with him!" barks Godot.

"What is it you do?" Sipho asks.

"I'm here...I'm here on holiday."

"You're here on holiday?" Godot is being sarcastic. "In Egoli? In winter?"

"Well, it's summer in America. The only time I could get off."

"Uh-huh. Go. Sipho will take you."

I followed Sipho to the queue for kombis where eighteen or so passengers waited in a line next to the door. He told the last two passengers, an elderly woman and her granddaughter, to go away or wait for another taxi to fill because I was to take their place. Without protest they stepped aside. I tried to give them an apologetic glance. They'd have none of it.

The mood of the passengers was more subdued than that of those leaving Noord Street. We jostled anxiously for the best seats. I found myself in a middle row beside a man in his fifties and a young woman.

When Sipho stopped for gas, I had an urge to bolt from the kombi and run. But in which direction? And in this suit, with these shoes? How far would I get? Better to stay among people for as long as possible in the hopes that they could be transformed into witnesses.

I broke the code of silence and asked the passengers: "This is the taxi for Unit 6, isn't it?" There was a short collective gasp. But no one said a word. Some looked at me, but quickly turned away when I looked back at them. Others looked at Sipho pumping petrol, then at me, then back at him. Sensing something amiss, Sipho struck the window with his ring, motioned for the window to be rolled down, demanded to know what the fuss was all about.

No one spoke.

"Hey, people, somebody better answer me!"

A woman twice his age spoke reverently to him: "Nothing *Tata*, it's just that some of us have been waiting a long time already."

"You'll take longer if you have to walk."

"Yes, Tata."

Now I'd begun to panic. "Sipho, if Unit 6 is out of your way, I could just as easily get out here and phone my friend from the petrol station; have him come get me." Everyone shifted uneasily; it seemed as though the man beside me wanted to move as far away from me as possible.

He gets back in and guns the engine. We bolt from the drive into the street. Only now, as we turn into the street, do I see what I should have seen before. Three of the men from the cluster of Godot's drivers are behind us in another kombi. They have followed us here from the taxi rank.

Cover your breasts. Words I wish I'd spoken to Ma Kekana the last time I saw her. Cover your breasts before I take the picture; who knows where it will appear, who will see you half-naked and in shock. It's your wounds which we want the world to see, not your breasts. But I said nothing. For a moment I simply watched as she undressed. Stared in disbelief that she would take her shirt off, to show me a knife wound below her shoulder, above her heart. I wondered whether or not I was getting aroused. She's too old, I told myself. Her two long brown melons unfolded from her blouse. Not a hint of shame, modesty, exhibition, seduction, or dare glimmered in her eyes.

I raised my camera to my eye and asked her to remove the bandage. She did so and looked through me. To where? To yesterday and the kerosene lamp overturned on the floor; to her two-year-old granddaughter taking blade after blade into her pin cushion belly; to her daughter in Thokoza hospital's intensive care unit; to her husband shuffling aimlessly in the dust outside their gutted shack; to where she sat on the springs naked to the waist. As the bandages peeled away I tried to focus the lens on the tributary of rage stretching from her collarbone to her armpit and I heard her husband's feet stirring the Rand's red clay dust beyond the vacant tooth that was once their window. I imagined him as he was when I entered: his dry eyes focused on nothing. His open hands hung down at his sides. I held the camera steady and tried to crop her nipples from the frame. I tried to think of other contexts in which one who is neither husband nor lover—a doctor, a Nazi, a cop, a stud— gazes upon the breasts of a woman while the man who is waits outside. Pa Kekana paced back and forth outside the burnt window ruminating in tongues. I took the picture. Earlier that day, Ma Kekana had undergone the gaze of a doctor. His gaze had done as much good as mine. For neither of us realized that beneath her blouse, beneath her bandages, beneath the lens of my Miranda, Ma Kekana was still bleeding. This morning she bled to death.

The kombi continued to shadow us. Stopping several yards behind us each time a passenger in our kombi called out, in his or her turn, to disembark. Each time I looked back to see where it was, I looked forward again to see Sipho looking at me in his rear view mirror. *I'm an American. They can't do this to me. They wouldn't be that stupid. Americans don't just disappear. Someone calls the US Embassy. Then someone else calls the State Department. Then someone else calls the president. Then the Marines come in to rescue you. It's a fact. Everyone knows it. Just go to the movies. These impimpis don't want to fuck with the Marines. And my dad's a friend of Walter Mondale. They must remember Walter Mondale from the 1984 presidential elections. All I have to do is drop that name and these fools'll raise up, quick! That's right! Kidnap me muthafucka! Shit. There'll be an international incident like you won't believe. Shut down the whole taxi industry. Destroy Inkatha as a party. Put Gatsha Buthelezi to shame. Don't be no fool, now.*

Cover your breasts. Why didn't I say that? It was the decent thing to say and I'm a decent person. Instead, I stared and placed the camera over my eye and observed her nipples as closely as the lens would allow, drawing each speckle, each goose-bump in the breeze into focus and snapped the shutter; preserved the moment of her nakedness so that others might see it and go out and "do good."

When I return to America I will be unable to explain how death falls like rain here. How we watch and wait for it the way folks back home watch and wait for inclement weather. I will sit in a turn-of-the-century manor on Minneapolis's posh West Side. Sit cross-legged on the floor in a neighborhood once reserved for the city's founding fathers. Sit beneath a poster of a hooded man smoking a pipe over the words "Subcomandante Marcos for President" and try to explain South Africa to my friends: young activists, students, musicians, and organic gardeners who have turned a mansion into a commune.

"It's the death *toll* that has political resonance in South Africa," I will say, "not the names of the dead." Bisho. Nancefield. KwaZulu-Natal. Boipatong. Phola Park. These place-names are the only names we give to our dead before they are buried and forgotten. Place-names and numbers. But they will tell me how and why each individual death matters— the sorrow of the parents and the value of the name as a touchstone of memory; personal and political.

I find myself wanting to go home—with no idea where that might be. Ma Kekana died this morning.

The population in the taxi has dwindled to three. A nursing sister with tired feet, judging from her weary eyes, another woman much younger than I but obviously no longer in school; and myself. Now Sipho's eyes and mine meet more frequently than before. Time and again he checks his rearview mirror. He stops to let the nurse out. I don't even bother to check the kombi behind us. It's still there. It has to be. It's come this far. What can I do but see this thing through? Bolt now? Jump out with the nurse and run away? I don't even know where I am.

I am sitting perfectly still.

The door of the kombi slides open. The nurse gets out. For a moment she looks at me. I look away. She slides the door shut. The kombi sputters, coughs, jerks back onto the road. We are off again.

It's been more than a year since I last spoke with my father. Unable to stomach the smooth mendacity of our family, I left without saying goodbye; no more than a message on his answering machine: *Tomorrow I am moving to South Africa. Good-bye.* Now, I wonder who will take it upon themselves to explain my death to him, make it comprehensible, put it in its proper context. What will my body look like when it finally reaches him? Assuming it reaches him.

The young woman next to me slides her hand across the seat and holds mine. I give a start, but know better than to turn my head in her direction. Through my peripheral vision I see her looking out the window.

"*Dankie*, driver!" [Next stop please!]

The kombi hobbles to a halt for her. She crawls over me, slides the door open and gets out. The kombi that's been following us draws up to our fender. Sipho stares at me in the rearview mirror. I hear the idling engine of the kombi behind us. The young woman starts to cross the road. She has left the door open. I have yet to move.

Safely on the other side she turns and yells: "Aren't you coming?"

Sipho looks at her, then at me.

"This is the stop you wanted," she yells. "Come on! Get out of the kombi."

Sipho waves a warning finger at her: "Hey sisi! Mind your own business. He wants Unit 6."

"No, Tata, *this* is his stop," she yells, firmly, but reverently.

I hear the doors of the kombi in back opening. Someone next to it yells, "Mind your own business, bitch!"

"It's true," I tell Sipho, sensing that this, the moment of indecisiveness on all sides save the young woman's, is the time to act. I slide toward the door. "While you were getting petrol, I told her where I was going and she said it wasn't Unit 6 at all—that she'd let me know when we got there."

"Hey!" he yells at me as my foot dangles out the door, "Hey, *induna*! Get back in here."

The young woman continues to yell: "Why do you want to take him somewhere he doesn't want to go?" Her voice is gathering onlookers. They stop and cluster around her. Some have started to come out of their homes. From the kombi in back someone yells, "I'll *moer* you, bitch!

"Tata, why must you abuse me?" she asks. "I'm merely trying to help this man find his friend." Then to me: "Come brother, cross the road. It's okay, cross the road. These people know where you're going. We'll all help you find your way," to the others, "won't we?" None of them seem too eager.

My legs are jelly as I stand on the gravel. In a split second I decide not to close the door behind me. *Make no wasted movements.* To my left, the men from the other kombi glare but don't approach. From the graveled shoulder I light upon the tarmac. I start to cross. What must it feel like, a bullet to the spine? What do you feel when the wound has healed? Numbness in the thighs? Feet forever floating in ether? A mouth that will not close? A hand that cannot write? Bowels that run at will? A life forever indebted to others?

Now I am beside her, shaking.

"Walk forward," she says, "don't look back. If they see you're scared they'll come for you."

"Where are we going?" I ask.

She looks at me and says, "I don't know."

—⁂—

Crossing the veld between Thokoza Township and Phola Park I was almost as tense as I was in the kombi. In that field I was alone with myself and I didn't like what I saw—a coward, a fraud. My only thoughts were how to get into Phola Park and how to get out before dark. I was not thinking of the woman who had just saved my life. When my thoughts did go to her—*How is she doing, what is she doing, did she make it home safely, and what of tomorrow, how will she get to work, will she ride in those kombis, and what will happen to her if she does*—I put them out of my mind. *You're an armchair activist. They'll be coming for you soon, the fraud police. When they do, it won't be pretty.* As I realized how scared and uncertain I was not only of my role in the struggle but of my capacity to act, I became disenchanted with myself. *Do I have what it takes to go on?*

The ground was uneven, the grass had never been cut and was well above my ankles in places making it impossible to judge the terrain. I knew good and well that I could not return via Thokoza but I didn't know another way. I didn't relish the thought of sleeping in the squatter camp for the night either. What if tonight is the night that it gets attacked?

I was suddenly aware of yelping dogs. They were less than thirty yards away. I was straying too close to them and they let me know it. They clustered together, most of them seemed to be jockeying with each other for position that they might feed on something dead. I couldn't tell if what they fed on was human or beast. One of them snarled at me as if to say, *walk on pretender, this is what we do to frauds.*

—≈—

Having reached the edge of the field I had only a mile to go down a dusty road. In the distance I saw what was either a large company or a small battalion of soldiers. There were armored personnel carriers with mounted weaponry clustered at the entrance and patrolling the perimeter of the squatter camp. I would have to run the gauntlet of those soldiers just to enter the camp for they had unfurled a long coil of razor wire that was as high as a grown man's thigh. It wound all the way around the perimeter of the camp like a giant slinky. The squatter camp was now a prison camp. *How did they lay all this wire? What malevolent mind could have done this?* As I walked down the road, the tiny spikes of the razor wire sparkled in the light of the setting sun. I could have been Dorothy entering Oz.

—≈—

The young man, who'd been collecting membership dues when last I was here, guided me through the camp. This time we went everywhere on foot. It was exhausting. The adrenaline rush from my ordeal in Thokoza had long since left. I needed to sleep. I needed to go home. My notes looked like the cursive of a drunkard. I'd have one hell of time writing my report from them:

Section E.

Home of Johnson Malgus. (Xhosa with English name). Police alighted from hippo. Now, door will not close properly. Searched house. Took R1000 in cash, a generator, and a wielding machine. After entering they found his wife asleep. Held her at gunpoint and forced her to wake up. (Raped? He claims not. She will not testify.) Were in his shack for one hour. Says they did not hit her. Broke glass in his car outside.

Section E…still…I think.

Home of old man: Joseph Sibonyoni. Phola Park resident since 1986. One of the original squatters. Door is completely damaged and off the hinges. Police broke in and didn't say anything except, "We're searching for weapons." Continued a house to house search up and down his street. Broke all of his dishes. Took all the money he had (R270). Nothing else was taken. Says they did not hit him or threaten him.

Section F.

Shack #F13. Front wall caved in by hippo at 8:05 A.M. Woman's name is Rose. Also: Mrs. Yoliswa Cabu arrested nearby.

Shack #F69. Fifteen bullet holes fired into the front wall.

Shack #F44. At 8:15 A.M. Shots fired through left window. Two bullets. One went all the way through the house, ripping a dress in a wardrobe.

Shack #F18. Pulled down wall of Alfred Magxala's house. He worked as a security guard but was fired when he could not get to work this week due to the razor wire. He was turned back at gunpoint when trying to go to work. Demolished the inside of his house. Took his uniform and his belts, plus R50 in cash. Destroyed his entire wardrobe. Destroyed his bed and his bureau.

Shack #F48. Home of Mandla Mangeni. Put him outside. Kept his brother inside. Beat his brother for fifteen minutes. His brother had been wearing a "Mass Action" T-shirt. Poured 2.5 liters of fish oil on floor.

Shack #F???. Pumza Gibixhego. Was not at home during raid. At work. Returned home at 2:40 P.M. Police had demolished his door. Door cannot be fixed. Wall is also torn. Took R100 from his drawer.

Section J.

Shack #J90. Home of Mrs. Noxolo Zila. Put powder on her cooking stove (hot plate). They didn't say why. Used fire extinguisher on her belongings (nothing was on fire). Belongings damaged. Hot plate no longer works. They didn't take anything.

In street near Section…not sure where I am right now…fill in later.

Met James Mobela. Says he was arrested during the raid. Just walking to his home. Had R700 in cash on him when arrested. Police still have it.

More people (don't have all their names): say police arrived in this part of camp at 9:30 A.M. Said they were searching for arms caches. Found no weapons. Stole drink, tobacco, and cash from residents. Police had no forms of identification on their uniforms—no names or rank recorded. Two Mozambican women with Transkei identity documents were arrested. No one knows their names. Rubber bullets and live ammunition were used to disburse the crowd. The two women were taken away.

Met Mandla Qikwa. Lives in Shack #L53. Was arrested in the street. Police took him to vehicle BHK172B. Says other police took R50 from his shack. They hit him with butt of a rifle on forehead. Kept asking him where weapons were buried. Asked him about marijuana as well.

Total killed: not sure. Must find out. Maybe none this time.

Miscellaneous.

Police stopped water trucks from entering the camp. Turned them away. Delegation of residents went to the police station. Water was still refused. Curfew has been imposed. No meetings or gatherings are allowed. License number of one of the hippos: BHL168B. Police who attacked Section A wore camouflage fatigues. Sprayed unknown substance in people's homes and in their faces. Caused women to cough. Sprayed in face of two babies, one eleven months, the other one month old. Spray comes out in huge clouds of smoke. Is normally sprayed from open door of an armored personnel carrier. No cameras are allowed in camp, except police cameras.

Total arrested: not sure. Have 9 names. One is a five-month-old baby.

—៣—

It was more than I could bear. Wherever we went, a throng of people would intercept us. The young comrade would tell them that I was from the ANC Regional Office and then it would start, wave upon wave of atrocity from everyone around. If we could, we would duck into a nearby shack of one of the victims and take the testimonials one at a time as the people queued outside. Many had been so badly beaten that, as I wrote I tried not to look at the bandaged arms, the bruised and swollen lips, eyes closed and puffy; I tried not to be overwhelmed by the shock and trauma that they had been overwhelmed by and to which they were opening their bodies once again as they spoke. *What are they doing to us?* My hand was aching from non-stop note taking. I was aching somewhere else as well. *Be compassionate but don't break down. That's not what's needed here. You're more than a pen and a steno pad. The regional office is hope and redress. Don't jeopardize that.*

I felt my lips trembling. I focused my eyes on the steno pad. *If I look up at this old woman, she'll see my eyes. Just look at the pad.* She had the countenance of my mother's mother. Sharp decisive words and quick eyes. I could tell that despite her abject poverty she had been gay once and that she liked to speak with her hands. Now she couldn't because one of her hands was wrapped in a large bandage. When she tried to move it, she winced. She was telling me how they barged in and woke her. My grandmother used to play the piano at jazz clubs in New Orleans. *How will you play now?*

She asked me why I had stopped writing. I said I needed the loo. She directed me to a communal outhouse in back of her shack. It stood like a coffin on its hind legs. Inside it was dark and small and putrid. So much shit and urine in such a shallow hole. The whole decaying world swelled through my nostrils. I couldn't stop my body from shaking. *Don't...don't, Frank! Hold on.*

The young comrade was standing outside her shack when I returned. He asked me if I was alright. I assured him that I was. She's from the hospital just this morning, he said, now she's asleep. Should we wake her and complete her statement? No, I said, perhaps a little too vigorously. I asked him what had happened to her hand. He didn't know. He suggested we find someone who knows her. I said I'd come back another day.

—⁓—

He stood with me at the checkpoint where the coiled razor wire gave way to the opening at the road. I looked down the road and across the field, back the way I had come. I felt paralyzed. *I can't go back that way. I'm bound to meet those taxi drivers.* I looked at the battalion of soldiers patrolling the outer perimeter of the wire and those bunched together by their hippos at the entrance just ten yards away from where we stood. I told myself that I couldn't spend the night in Phola Park because there was no way to let Khanya know where I was; after our fight that morning she would be worried. It was a charitable rationalization that let me off the hook from having to think of myself as someone who would do anything to remove himself from the threat the people around me faced every night.

It was getting late. The sun was slowly setting. My shoes, my brightly polished wingtips, were caked on the bottom with mud or feces. On a patch of grass beside the wire I did what I could to clean them. The comrade was waiting patiently for me to announce my departure. His ubuntu kept him from being the first to depart.

"The weapons, the ones brought in from the Transkei—did they find our DLBs?"

"No," he smiled, "they'll never find them. You can tell Thabo and Stimela the weapons are safe."

"Good. Well, I...I guess I should be going?"

"Travel safely, com."

"Is there some other way back to Jo'burg," I said looking down the road and across the field.

"Isn't that the way you came?"

"Yes, but you see...It's...I had a spot of trouble on the way."

"Oh, I see."

"I'm not armed and I don't know the territory. I'd be lost in the dark."

"You can spend the night here. In the morning we can organize some comrades to escort you."

This place won't be here in the morning.

Then, a mile or so down the road I spotted a caravan of shiny BMWs approaching the checkpoint. Two large oil tankers trailed in the dust that billowed behind them.

"Not petrol," said my friend, smiling, "water. Winnie Mandela is bringing us water."

The armored hippos that stood at the checkpoint crunched and groaned as they turned around and went out to block the caravan's advance. They stopped the lead car fifty yards or so from the checkpoint area. The commanding officer, a lieutenant colonel, climbed out of one of the hippos and walked over to the first car. Winnie Mandela rolled down her backseat window. The words they exchanged could not be heard. But their demeanors seemed tense though reserved. The commanding officer told the soldiers to reverse the hippos enough to let the cars pass. Then, as the cars came forward, he commanded them to close ranks again so that the water carriers could *not* pass. The four BMWs swooped into the checkpoint area. Winnie Mandela and an entourage of four women from the first two cars and one driver, who was also a bodyguard, entered Phola Park without pausing to be searched or questioned at the opening in the razor wire. They walked past us and nodded or greeted us earnestly, but without stopping. They then went to Phola Park's tiny ANC branch headquarters where several members of the local executive committee met them on the steps. I recognized one of the drivers as an Umkhonto we Sizwe operative whom I had once seen Jabu Mosando speaking with. From this I concluded that all four of the drivers must be MK as well.

Peter Mokaba was in the car that Winnie had been riding in. He was the president of the ANC Youth League and an MK soldier of some note (though his high public image had more than likely forced him to lessen his role in the latter capacity). It is said that in 1988 he fought valiantly with the Popular Movement for the Liberation of Angola (MPLA) and ten thousand Cubans in Angola at the Battle of Cuito Canavale, the battle which crippled UNITA—the União Nacional para a Independência Total de Angola—and the South African Army; the battle that led to the settlement in Angola, that led to the demoralization of South Africa's standing army, that led to widespread resistance by young White conscripts like my students at Wits.

The women in Winnie Mandela's entourage were leading members of the ANC Women's League, a wing of the ANC whose first president and founding member was a Black American woman, Madie Hall-Xuma, the wife of Dr. A. B. Xuma, who was president of the ANC in the 1940s. Like Mrs. Hall-Xuma, I too had followed my spouse to South Africa and had been swept away by the events of the time, though not at the commanding heights that Madie Hall had known.

The ANC Women's League entourage that entered Phola Park that afternoon, fifty years after Mrs. Hall-Xuma had presided over the League's first meeting, were nether young nor old; they all appeared to be in their forties and fifties. They were dressed in bright and richly colored traditional garb, replete with splendid head wraps. Two of the women remained outside the building. The other two women and the bodyguard went inside with Winnie Mandela.

I asked the two women who remained outside if I could ride back to town with them. They told me that they didn't know who I was, that I could be anyone. I told them I was with the regional office. They said, "No," and something like only authorized people were allowed to ride in those cars. I was so frantic trying to get my ANC membership card out of my wallet that I spilled a number of other cards on the ground. I gathered them in the darkness and held out my Minnesota driver's license by mistake. They were underwhelmed.

"Sorry. Here's my membership card." They considered it as though it were a little more legit than a Mouseketeer's Club Card, but a ride was still not on offer. "I am on the executive committee there, you can ask Stephanie Kemp—Albie Sach's ex-wife; and her son, Michael Sachs." One of them nodded in recognition of the name, but a ride was still not on offer. "And Janet Love." Everyone knew Janet Love because she was an MK operative who had been captured during Operation Vula, a bold mission to smuggle huge quantities of arms into the country in 1990. She was a White woman who lived in Parktown and worked in the ANC Parktown branch with Nadine Gordimer. She was now head of the five person ANC sub-regional executive committee. "I've been seconded to the sub-regional executive committee as well. She'll vouch for me." I kept pulling more rabbits out of my hat. "And I work for the regional Peace Commission. They sent me out here today."

"Why can't they transport you to town?"

"I'm on my own. I don't have a car."

"How did you get here?"

"By taxi. From there." I pointed to the veld beyond the road and the tiny houses further on, emptied of all inhabits by that morning's massacre. "I can't go back there."

"Where in town do you live?"

"Braamfontein. Across the street from Wits."

"We can't ferry you to Braamfontein!"

"I'll get off in Kensington or Jeppestown. Anywhere in town."

"We're going to Shell House."

"That's even better. I can get a taxi at Noord Street...please."

I heard loud, angry, talk and commotion coming from the clearing, from the checkpoint beyond the wire. I'd been vaguely aware of it all along but had been too caught up in my pleading with the two women from the ANC Women's League to pay it any mind. Now it was too vitriolic to be ignored. I hurried back to the razor wire and asked the young man what was happening.

"The Boers are insulting comrades. Trying to intimidate them. Comrades are getting furious, com."

"How did it start?"

"Like it always starts."

Soldiers on foot had converged on the first two BMWs. They were pointing their rifles at the window of both cars. Some of them were in front where they trained their guns on the windshield. Others were at the sides. They were yelling curses and insults at the passengers, primarily in Afrikaans with only a phrase here and there in English.

Throughout all of this Peter Mokaba, who was seated in the lead sedan, was matching the soldiers' insults and expletives measure for measure—but he cursed in English. Without knowing what we were doing—I certainly did not know what I was doing—the young man and I found ourselves walking through the opening in the wire. I drifted, as though floating in ether, over to Peter Mokaba's car. Mokaba was now out of his car. He wore a suit, dark blue like mine, but his shoes were sleek, Italian, far more sophisticated than my wingtips caked with mud or feces. With their rifles in his face they ordered him back into the vehicle.

"Voetsek!" he said. "We can shoot too. You know we can shoot. We shot back at Cuito Canavale! One day we'll shoot back here."

They barked at him repeatedly. I simply stood next to him, trying to maintain my balance for my legs were uncertain. I took care not to make any movement that would get me shot as I put my hand on the hood of the car and tried to steady myself. The hippos that were back a ways, blocking the passage of the water trucks, lumbered back into position. The gun ports slid open and barrels were extended from them. I saw one of the women I had asked for a ride scurrying up the steps of the small shed where Winnie Mandela was meeting with the branch executive committee.

"Yes, you know we can shoot back, don't you," Mokaba yelled.

I felt nauseous and dizzy standing there next to Mokaba. There was yelling and pandemonium coming from so many directions and, with the sun setting behind them, it was hard to see the expressions on the faces of any of the soldiers except the two or three that stood directly in front of and closest to us. All I could see of the other soldiers were their silhouettes, which made their voices seem transcendent and disembodied. But there was also a hint of apprehension in their voices—both fearless and terrified. The soldiers inside and beside the hippos had been calling Peter Mokoba a kaffir. Now one of the soldiers who held us at gunpoint called him one as well.

"Stop your nonsense, kaffir!" He spat the words into our faces.

This seemed *not* to enrage Peter Mokaba but to energize him. His cavalier demeanor expanded and he pushed the barrel of the rifle out of his face. The soldier went berserk. He screamed obscenities and thrust the rifle at Mokaba as though he had a bayonet on the end. *It's like a firing squad.* That was all I could think. *We're facing a firing squad. I don't want to die. Not here. Not like this.* Peter went on with his repartee about the Battle of Cuito Canavale. I didn't know how much more of this the young conscript could take. Whether he lived on a dirt farm in the Karoo or whether, like my students at Wits, he lived in the tree-lined tranquility of Parktown where his nanny followed him from room to room picking up after him, I could not tell. His rage had transcended class. One thing was certain, he had never been spoken to this way by an African. Peter Mokaba was forcing him to encounter a battle from a war he might not have even fought in, but one whose defeat he had surely inherited for it had been tethered to the army's institutional memory. What kind of rejoinder was available to this young man; what was *his* claim to fame? The grandmother whose hand he mutilated? The man whose collarbone he broke with his rifle butt? Those doors behind him that will not close? He could shoot this kaffir dead. That would shut him up. But he couldn't finish the war of words that he and his squadron had started.

I did not see Winnie Mandela leave the meeting. I did not see her walk down the four or five stairs or approach the razor wire and enter the clearing of the checkpoint. I simply turned and she was there, making her way quickly and cautiously through the throng of soldiers. As she made her way, the lieutenant colonel emerged from somewhere near the hippos and barked an order which was immediately repeated by the command sergeant. All of the soldiers seemed to lower their rifles. *Where has this joker been all this time?*

I am not completely certain what happened next. I had lost my capacity to concentrate. Winnie Mandela must have said something to Peter Mokaba. If I heard it I either don't remember it or she spoke in Xhosa. I remember seeing her and the lieutenant colonel somewhere near the hippos, speaking with one another. The women whom I had been speaking with, and the ones from inside the meeting, filed past me to their cars. "Come," one of them said as she passed.

I sat in the back seat. I was trembling. I put my knuckles to my mouth. The woman beside me gently lowered my hand to the seat. "Not now," she said, "later."

The hippos made enough room for the water trucks to pass. Their long silver cylinders rolled past my window and into Phola Park. Lined along the razor wire the dark twilight residents watched. No one cheered. *It isn't over. It never is.*

—◊—

I stood in front of the door to our flat. I had a key but I was too broken down to use it. I don't know if I knocked or if Khanya sensed I was out there and opened the door. I just stood there incapable of movement. Tears were streaming down my face. I felt her pulling me by the hand. I was making grotesque, indecipherable sounds when I tried to speak. Reba was asleep on the sofa. Khanya put her hand over my mouth. She led me to the bedroom. She held me as she sat beside me on the bed. She tried to remove my jacket. I wanted to help her, Lord knows I wanted to help her—*what kind of man can't even undress himself*—but my arms were wrapped around my sides.

"Your father was right," it was hard to talk through the embarrassment of tears, "you married a forgery."

"What happened, Frank?"

"Fraud police came. Said they had a warrant."

"Frank, oh, Frank."

"We don't need another fake ass nigger. Another nigger by Mattel. That—is—what *happened*. Christ. My christ. Who did I think I was?"

What do we make of black men at this point? How does a hole with a penis work in this situation?

—Lewis Gordon
Bad Faith & Antiblack Racism

two

PASSAGE

they smile tip their hats lower their
shotguns and let us
cross the mississippi line
legs dangling from the pickup in front i don't recall
the guns mom remembers dad
doing the nothing he could do
like him i'll make a
career of it

6

[JOURNAL ENTRIES: SANTA CRUZ COUNTY]

—ᵚ— *FRIDAY, MAY 25, 2001*

Last night Naima asked me a disturbing question. Would I ever be with a Black woman again? The question startled me, though I tried not to show it. I pretended it was as ordinary as the other questions that had been bandied about the living room that night. But it wasn't an ordinary question. I knew that Naima wasn't making a pass at me. That would be too simple. Not that a twenty-year-old Black woman and a forty-five-year-old Black man was an unknown phenomenon. It was much more common than my four-year relationship with Alice (a sixty-seven-year-old White woman and a forty-five-year-old Black man). Nor was Naima making a veiled demand like, you best leave that White woman and get yourself a proper Black woman if you want to keep organizing with us. That would be too easy and not her style. She was too sincere for that. And there was something in her sincerity that made Lisa and April, the other two women in the room, look up. They waited. They seemed to hold their breath, waiting for me to answer. But then Selma, April's mother, came in from the kitchen with the cup of coffee she'd warmed in the microwave. She looked at her daughter. April was sitting on the living room floor near Naima and me. Then Selma looked at Lisa, who lay on the sofa with her legs fully extended. No one said a word.

"Okay, who died while I was in the kitchen?" Selma asked. We all managed to laugh at this.

"Naima was teasing Frank," said April, hurriedly. She and her mother were both students at Cabrillo College, where Lisa taught in the dance department, where I had taught off and on in the English department, and where Naima, like Selma and her daughter, was a student. April was a fun loving young woman but she had a way of assuming the role of ombudsperson when she and her mother were together. Moving to Santa Cruz from Oakland had been the only way Selma had been able to put herself, April, and April's brother—whom I never really got to know—through college. But it hadn't been a picnic. Like Lisa and Naima, they had become the targets of institutional racism that had even spilled over into vigilantism, as on the night when their car was demolished and the words "nigger" and "KKK" were scrawled across it. Selma continued to help lead our organizing efforts despite the fact that it became more and more dangerous. We could never tell whether or not things like her damaged car, my being accosted by skinheads in a public toilet in downtown Santa Cruz, and all of our problems with the police were isolated incidents or if they had some strange connection with the work we were doing at the college. And this not knowing made us even more anxious. It all seemed so random, like the night a group of Black students were attacked in Santa Cruz by Whites and Chicanos wielding baseball bats. A young man's jaw was broken; he left school, went back to Oakland—where, they said, he "belonged." It all seemed coordinated like Selma's car coinciding with her most severe confrontations at the college. Whether random or coordinated, it had had the effect of making Selma be about business when it was time to be about business—after which she and April would go straight home.

"Teasing him about what?" Selma said, with only a teaspoon of interest.

Lisa bent her knees and pulled her feet back so that Selma could sit down at the other end of the sofa. As she sat down, Selma was careful not to step on any of the documents which Naima, April, and I had spread out in three concentric circles: formal complaints of racism, job discrimination, and institutional neglect which Lisa had filed primarily against Virginia, Alice's daughter, and also another White woman named Trish. Both were co-chairs of the dance department. Both were Lisa's bosses. Naima's question could be read any number of ways because Frank was sleeping with Virginia's mother and Virginia was the number one problem that evening.

"I wasn't teasing him," said Naima. And she meant it. She had once told me that she valued our friendship; that I was someone she felt she could talk to, to whom she felt she could ask anything. No, she wasn't teasing me. Nor had she put the question to me the way I was used to it being put to me, for instance, by three or four sisters nursing their drinks on girls' night out, looking at me and Alice as cruel reminders of how often it has to be girls' night out. Once, as we passed the bar, I'd heard the sound of sucking teeth as someone murmured, "salt and pepper, I declare."

"Let's get back to Lisa's case against Virginia," Selma said, "it's getting late."

Selma was tired and needing to go home. And there was the little one to think of. He was a teenager and could take of himself, which is what she might have been afraid of.

We had scaled down the day: in the morning the rally, and the march on and occupation of Sesnon House. Sesnon House served as a sort of faculty club where, that morning, key faculty and administrators had held what they thought was a closed meeting on college policies—it was "closed" until we arrived. We'd organized a coalition of Blacks, Whites, Chicanos, Asians, moderates, and radicals. Two hundred strong was the conservative police estimate. We needed anyone who'd come with us, for numbers to buffer us against the police and to prove to the press that we could mobilize a mass demonstration at the drop of a hat—even in Santa Cruz County, a void of masses; our distance from San Jose, Oakland, and Berkeley wasn't a handicap we could not circumvent. We simply bussed people in from San Jose, Oakland, and Berkeley. In the afternoon, there were the workshops and teach-in. For the most part, the Asians, the environmentalists, the liberals, and the moderates had gone home and we were left to contend with the Chicana/os and a few White feminists, who all thought they wanted to get down, really get down, when what they wanted most of all was to get into the system, make it spread its arms wide and make room for them like it had made room for the others who'd just left.

They'd imposed upon the workshops and teach-ins a structure of feeling that could not be reconciled with the structure of feeling of slaves. Their structure of feeling was different in content but the rebar was the same: the Asian and Chicana/o's immigrant desire for greater access, the environmentalists' desire to protect "their" natural world, the White feminists' desire for equity of pay and power with White men. Two hours of "rights" talk about a system that has no right to exist. That's what we, the Blacks, had endured all day long.

Naima and the other Black women at the post-rally teach-in had been impatient, but polite. We had kept quiet, waiting for the accommodationists to peter out and leave. Finally, night came. Now we were alone. Lisa; Naima; Selma and her daughter April, the mother/daughter dynamic duo from Oakland who'd been two of the original organizers of the Coalition Against Institutional Racism just over a year ago; and me. Five Black folks who'd washed up on the shores of Santa Cruz County like driftwood. Now we could speak freely. Now we could speak openly. We could say how we wanted to tear it all down without fear of that reproach that comes, always comes, that had come during the day's meetings, comes from the others: What would you put in its place? Those seven little words that stifle Black desire and make it a crime for us to be mad at the world. But now Naima had spoken a little too freely when she asked me, Would I ever be with a Black woman again? And had there been reproach in her voice I could have found my sea legs and steadied myself and answered her. But instead of reproach I heard the timbre of abandonment.

It was a difficult moment. April, Naima, and I, sitting on cushions on the floor; Lisa stretched out on the sofa; Selma sipping coffee at the other end. Four Black women. One Black man. One Black man who's been sleeping with one White woman for the past four years; a White woman whose daughter, Virginia, is the focus of this evening's scorn. That much I remember, for the feeling in my bones was unmistakable. I can see the documents arranged on the floor; I can see April, perhaps a little unnerved or embarrassed on my behalf, or on her own—for the sense of abandonment in Naima's voice is something they share, though none of them would have spoken it as she did. April is picking up the clipboard with pages of my scrawl on it. She begins to read aloud the bullet points from the minutes I've taken thus far:

"One, Lisa is the only Black instructor in the entire dance department. Two, Virginia and Trish are two White women who are co-chairs of the department."

"We know this," says her mother, imploring her to cut to the chase.

April continues as though her mother hasn't spoken. "We have before us," she says, sweeping her free hand across the folders on the floor, like Perry Mason introducing new evidence into court, "various affidavits, photocopies of grievances, extensive narratives and testimonials—"

"April, please," she implores.

"—of the institutional racism which Virginia and Trish have subjected Lisa to for...how many years?" she asks Lisa, as though the answer is not right there in my notes.

"More than I care to count," says Lisa, looking not at April, looking not at any one of us, but staring up at the ceiling.

"Four hundred years!" Naima laughs.

To which April says, "Amen. We have a chronology of the college administration's refusal to even consider Lisa's claims."

"I'd write Judith Chrisp's name beside that point, she's the vice president for academic affairs," Naima instructs.

"It's already here," says April, "but you're the one who said we need an institutional analysis more than complaints about individuals."

"We need both," says Naima, "we need both."

April continues. "And we have the sonic boom! The makings of a propaganda coup! A former student who happens to be White."

"What else would he be?" quips Lisa.

"Who is almost primed to come out—"

"Heavy on the 'almost,'" I demur.

"Who will testify—"

"He never said 'testify,'" Naima interrupted.

"Okay, report, confess—whatever the verb is, if we can work him right he'll let it be known that he was hired to take classes and spy on 'problematic' teachers and that Lisa was one of them."

"It'll be great," I tell them, "if he was also hired to spy on Shelleen when all that mess went down last year. That means that two of the three Black *women at the college have been the victims not just of institutional racism, but of state surveillance."*

What's his name, someone asks and we all look at Naima. She tells us that her source has not produced a name as of yet. But a face-to-face meeting is in the offing.

"Let's not count this chicken before it's hatched," Lisa says, "We not only need to know who he is but we need him to commit his story to paper." And, someone else adds, we need to know if Virginia and Trish were in on it.

It was a strategy session in which we were to have worked out ways and means to fight the disaggregation of Lisa's grievances so that the burden of proof was no longer on her, but on Virginia, on Trish, on the administration, and on the police. We set out to construct a narrative of our rage and brainstorm ways to bring our "coalition partners" on board. Then if all went well, and if, above all, we are lucky, the liberals who ran Cabrillo College and Santa Cruz County would have to come out into the open and fight; fight the way they're not used to fighting, fight with all their fire power to preserve their institutional power. If we could make them fight in the open then we would have won; not an institutional victory—that was never our intention—but an organizing victory. When we've been able to do that, the two percent Black population who live in the county and the two percent at the college would come out of the woodwork and morph into a force to be reckoned with.

It was a tall order. But a simple step by step agenda. No, it wasn't that simple. Not that night. There were unspoken issues waiting to be spoken. CAIR (The Coalition Against Institutional Racism) had been in existence since the spring of 2000, a full year now, when a young White woman, Dana Sole, a Latina student of mine, Sonia Rodriguez, and Selma and April launched it with my help. That was the year of the public screeds: open letters, public missives, attacks and counter attacks in a solidarity campaign for Shelleen who, like Lisa, was a Black lesbian trying to survive here in Santa Cruz County. Everything had been straightforward then. Alice had been on board in the fight for Shelleen. Now where was she? I wondered. And now, where was I?

Tonight things were murkier than they were a year ago. A night laced with complications. Earlier in the evening, I felt that the question on Lisa, Selma, and April's minds was: Were Virginia and the dance department off bounds last year because I was sleeping with Virginia's mother? I wished they had asked me this last year. I would have had a straightforward and simple answer for them: No, they're not off bounds. I'm not even aware of the situation. They would have known that I didn't know Lisa or anything about the years of strife she'd gone through in the dance department. At some point during the evening, Naima put this complication to rest by explaining that, like me, she too hadn't known Lisa then. They'd met only recently, in the parking lot, by accident. Lisa had seen Naima's picture in the paper as she led a demonstration. She'd told her her story. And Naima had called me. But this clarification only catalyzed another complication, another layer of suspicion: Did Alice know last year? And if she did and chose not to tell us, how can we trust her? And that would be a question I too would want the answer to. No. I did not really want the answer to it. And not wanting the answer returned me to the pendulum of trust and mistrust that swung in the air that night. And then, Naima, not waiting for these intangibles to find tangibility, not waiting for what was already unspoken to be spoken, had asked, Would I ever be with a Black woman again? Had it not been for April's grabbing my clipboard and reading aloud, I don't know what I would have said, for it demanded a response that was more essential than yes or no. It was a question about my life, or even Naima's life, in the future; it was a question that interrogated our very claim to life...not will you be with one of us...but can you be with one of us...can we be with ourselves...can we be at all? That was the question inside the question, which is why she had not put the question to me the way I was used to encountering it by sisters on the street or in a restaurant. Here comes Sambo, their eyes are saying, prancing through the club with Sally on his arm—making a mockery of our isolation; Sambo and Sally, heartless and vain, stomping on our guts. Maybe Naima had twenty years to go before she would ask the question that way. A way I could have handled.

"When not teaching," April is still reading from my notes on the clipboard, "she manages a Buddhist retreat."

The end of the twentieth century found Virginia in her mid-forties with no sense whatsoever that, like that French benediction at the altar of civil society— equality, liberty, fraternity—there were in fact three constituent elements to the badge of entitlement worn by Second Wave feminists, her mother's cohort: free,

White, and twenty-one. Free and twenty-one was all that Virginia seemed to have inculcated. I say this, not in an effort to cathedralize her wisdom. On the contrary, her forty-something "innocence" with respect to race, her incomprehension of the antagonism between the seaside towns where she and her mother offered their languid limbs to the sun and the eviscerated ghettoes of Oakland (where, in the sixties, her mother's generation had put in their time and then escaped, with no more exertion than the recitation of two small words, "I do," to a White man and a house in the suburbs)—in short, Virginia's refusal to acknowledge her pleasures being bound to our suffering made casual conversation with her feel like a forced march to Disneyland. Alice, on the other hand, was too intelligent to feign incomprehension of the essential antagonisms. She'd seen the cities burning in her rearview mirror as she drove down the coast to Shangri La. She knew what she'd run from. The antagonisms were still lodged in her preconscious, not merely her unconscious, which is to say that this knowledge was available for speech. Virginia, for her part, knew only in her unconscious that Black people could not be reconciled with her world. Which is to say she did not know what she did know. She seemed to abuse Lisa with an administrative violence that was as blithe as it was severe. In this way she was more White than her mother, White in a way that would have embarrassed Alice's generation: the Betty Friedans, the Gloria Steinems, and the Bella Abzugs who, through their activism, had midwifed the conditions of Virginia's possibility. Unlike those women, she could never have dreamed the things Black folks had said about her in such late night meetings, having grinned in her face all day long. She did not know she could be hated on sight, for she had no appreciation of the forces, the arsenal of death that assembled across the landscape each day, that she might rise and shine and take her morning piss and teach her midday class, choreograph her evening recital, and return home each night without so much as a flesh wound. Innocence looked good on her.

"Buddhist my ass," April says, looking up from the notes, "Virginia's a straight up racist." She handed the clipboard back to me and said, "That's what I hate about Santa Cruz—these New Age façades. The way these people hide behind 'spiritualism.'"

Two of the women slapped five. Sounds like you hate her, as well, I said, as though talking to myself. We feel like we hate her, I was told by either Selma or

Lisa, but we don't let our thoughts catch up with our feelings. I told them that I didn't know if I could manage that. It's easy, April said, just turn on the radio. Or call a friend and talk about something else, said Naima. Or put your head under the pillow until it passes, said someone else, because if your thoughts ever caught up with your feelings, you'd have to kill them. This made me think of my grandmother and a game we used to play. A game she called Mad at the World. *We used to sit together and watch all kinds of sports on television—football, basketball, baseball. But our favorite sport was the riots. We could watch the riots all day and all night, without getting bored. She'd have her pig foot and her bottle of beer, I'd have my milk and cookies, we'd be having us a good ole time watching the riots. Look at that grandma, I'd shout, pointing at the tube, he got himself a stereo! And look there, they're shooting at the National Guard! Yep, she acknowledged, almost got one, too. She'd sip her beer and say, Negroes are hopping mad, child. I'd dunk my cookies in milk and say, Why are we mad, grandma? Before she could answer I'd run through a litany of reasons logged from "The Riot Report" on the nightly news. We mad because we don't have jobs? No, child, we're not mad 'cause we can't get hired. We mad 'cause they won't sweep our streets? No, child, we're not angry at the brooms. We mad at the mayor? Not mad at the mayor, sugar. The governor? Not mad at the governor, either. Are we mad at the president? Everyone's mad at the president, but when he's gone we'll still be mad. So, why are we mad grandma? She'd smile and wipe the milk mustache from my mouth and we'd shout out together, We're* MAD AT THE WORLD! *then bust out laughing while thick flames licked America's windows and walls.*

"Some of us have to teach in the morning," Lisa is saying, sleepily. It's our cue to leave.

April and Selma were driving. Naima wasn't, so I offered to drive her home. She lived near Scotts Valley, ten miles out of town. I was quiet in the car. It had been a day of rallies, teach-ins, and then the night's meeting. I begged off conversation, claiming fatigue. Finally, when we were out of the city and the highway was so dark we could no longer see each other's faces in the car, I said, "I never answered your question."

"No," she said, "you didn't."

"I'm not sure I could have."

"I understand," she said, as though she really did understand; but I don't know if she did. I didn't understand myself.

"I didn't want to lie."

"And this wasn't a night for lying," she said, as we stopped in front of her house.

No, it's not a night for lying, I thought. Yet all I could do was lie...

—⁂—

One Sunday morning, when I was 12—a Sunday not long after the Tet Offensive—I walked into my parents' bedroom with a copy of El-dridge Cleaver's *Soul on Ice* and handbills I'd picked up from various militants I'd met, largely through my parents. As they sat up in bed and wiped the crust from their eyes I told them that the Roman Catholic Church was responsible for the slave trade; that I'd learned all about the role of the Pope in our horrifying sojourn from Africa to the New World; that my sister Fawn (age 11), my sister Amy (age 7), my brother Wayne (age 3), and I had discussed the matter among ourselves and decided that as of today we were all communists and atheists; from that day forward we would not be attending Mass. Then with boundless generosity I told my parents that as they were both adults, it was not my intention to demand that they boycott Mass just because we were.

"You're both free to go on attending Mass, if you feel you can live with the contradictions. But my comrades and I are going to stay home and hold anti-imperialist teach-ins."

For several seconds they said nothing. They stared at me, perhaps in disbelief. Then, my mother spoke.

"You must be crazy."

"The *very* idea!" my father trailed in behind her. "Go to your room and get ready for Mass."

I went back down the hall to inform my brother and sisters about our "collective" decision, though I had not discussed it with them before I informed my parents.

"Look, people," I said to them, "we have a situation here. The Establishment is being irrational. Don't freak out; that's to be expected."

Wayne and Amy looked at me like I'd just landed from Mars. Fawn was nodding but her heart wasn't in it.

"Dare to struggle, dare to win," I said, "Mao. Can you dig it? What we have to do now is to remember to keep the word 'protracted' in front of the word 'struggle,' or else it's just a meaningless slogan."

"What does 'protracted' mean?" Amy asked.

"It means what it means," I told her, "protracted. Like, if it's not protracted it's like meaningless, ya dig. So, everybody hold the line. No matter how hard they come at us."

Frank and Ida-Lorraine came at them hard, indeed. They threatened each of their other three offspring with the belt, the switch, and the yardstick. Before I knew it they were all in their Sunday best—white gloves for the girls, black missals for them all—and waiting dutifully in the downstairs foyer. I crawled back into bed and padded my backside as best I could. I knew the drill. I'd been down that road before: my parents beat me until they were tired.

Through my gasps and tears I managed to tell them that their belts would fray and their yardstick would break long before I did. They were livid. Crazed with fury. In their madness I took delight. Finally, they were exhausted. They limped back into their bedroom and dressed themselves for Mass. When they have gone, you get up and go to the bathroom. The mirror offers your ruined face and you start to cry again.

You are an anxious, almost chubby boy pushing through puberty, pushing through the war in Vietnam, pushing through anti-colonial struggles in Africa, pushing through the Black Revolution at home. Never too fat to play sports, but never slim enough to maintain some semblance of yourself as "the Mack." Your hair is always a problem. Your parents won't let you grow it long enough to be a proper Afro, so you keep picking it out in the daytime and blow drying it at night. You may very well go bald with all the deforestation you carry out from one side of your ear to the other. You try to comb the Afro forward to cover your zit-peppered forehead but all you manage to do is leave scratch marks from your Afro pick, turning your forehead into tabula rasa for tic-tac-toe. Your embryonic Afro goes home in the rain: it curls up on your head into tight tiny naps and you cry alone in your room and stay inside.

Your mood swings are seismic. You talk with your hands and stamp your feet when grown folks don't listen to you. And that voice of yours: caught between puberty and a nervous breakdown. Like Mickey Mouse doing Mao Zedong.

They chuckle when you enter the room—but with you or at you? They sip their martinis and tell your mother what "a curious little boy" you are—how, they ask, did you come to be so informed? In an effort to either steal your thunder or put you in your place, your mother tells them, Don't encourage him or he'll draw a zillion connections between the tetanus shot and the Tet Offensive. Oh, how they laugh, to the point of almost spilling their drinks. Now they turn away and forget you altogether; the spotlight is on your beautiful mother. You are bursting at the seams. You, who wants to go and fight a revolution somewhere, have let this humiliation get the best of you. You're as angry at yourself as you are with them. You stand there, too short to look them in the eye, which is the really awful thing. You bide your time. You wait for them to stop laughing at something witty your mother has said. You hold back the tears as the room relieves itself of the jest. Now all that remains is a lingering chuckle and the clinking of ice. Now that they're quiet, you begin again: For your information, the average Vietnamese wakes up in the morning wondering whether he'll have napalm or bombs for breakfast while the average American wakes up wondering whether he'll have poached or scrambled eggs. You stole that line from *Soul on Ice*, but they don't need to know. Bet you guys didn't know that! you say. Touché, you think. You sip your Coca Cola, suavely. You wait. They look at you. No one says anything; they just look at you like you are the only exhibit in the whole museum without a name tag. So, you look back at them. Well, you say, what do you think about that, huh? There's mild mumbling but no real engagement. And mom, for the record, I never drew connections between the tetanus shot and the Tet Offensive; you're just making fun of me. Okay, Frankie *(don't call me Frankie, my name is Frank!*—it's the thing she does when she wants the last word), time for bed; say goodnight to everyone. *Frank! Call me Frank!*

One moment I was in Minneapolis being shunned by my mother at my parents' cocktail parties, the next moment I was in Detroit in a fistfight with Smooth, trying to get some respect. Then I found myself standing beneath Chicago's snow-covered L, holding my "girlfriend" Jocelyn Brown as the hawk whipped around our ears and the train clicked and clacked on the tracks above. Finally, I was walking beside my father up the esplanade of warm sun-drenched stairs that led to a Spanish courtyard, squared on all sides by bright red mission-tiled roofs and beneath them the open air corridors of Willard Junior High, on Berkeley's Telegraph Avenue. Sitting in the assistant principal's office, I looked about his room searching in vain for his overcoat.

"It doesn't snow here?" I asked.

The assistant principal put his pen down and laughed softly, as though I'd asked something ridiculous like how do you feed your hamster.

"It doesn't snow here," he said. "Well, come to think of it, my grandfather remembers snow, once back when he was a boy. But that was in the City," by which he meant, San Francisco. "You're safe here in Berkeley. There is a fair amount of rain this time of year." He might have told us all about Berkeley, or snow and his grandfather, had dad not cleared his throat.

When it was decided how far I had gone in the new math in Detroit at Spain Junior High and then in Chicago at St. Mary's, and after I was told by my father that I could take neither "US Imperialism and the Viet Cong" nor "Rock 'n' Roll and the American Woman" for either of my electives, the assistant principal offered to take me to my new homeroom. But dad told him to take my sister Fawn instead. He told me to walk with him back to where the courtyard met the street.

I don't want to walk with him. I want to be rid of him. I want to get on with the struggle, that's why I came here in the first place.

My father is not speaking as we leave the office and walk out into the warm California sun. At the edge of the schoolyard he turns to me.

"You're to study and look after your sister. You're not here for 'the revolution.' Don't let me get any reports like I got from the nuns in Chicago, you hear? I'm on sabbatical and your mother is completing her language requirement so she can advance to candidacy. Don't have me have to come up here behind you and your foolishness."

"Dad, I do not intend to be on the wrong side of history."

"Boy, don't mess with me. Not this morning. *Not this morning.*"

We stood on the steps glaring at each other. I stared at him as long and as hard and as evil as I could, taking full advantage of our presence on the school ground near the street with school personnel walking to and fro behind me and cars and pedestrians passing behind him. He would have to beat me out in the open. He quieted his breathing. He looked at his wing tips. He blinked once or twice. He walked down the last remaining steps.

"I think I've made myself clear," he said over his shoulder.

At moments like those I told myself that I'd won. I crossed the open courtyard and scuttled through the cool shadows of Willard Junior High's outdoor corridor. *That fool can't mess with the kid. Shit. Jive turkey best step off the property and give a revolutionary his space!*

It was in this period, between 1969 and 1970, that my parents' outlook and demeanor began to change. The sixties had bequeathed them with a certain kind of outspokenness and attention to injustice that I had admired and tried to emulate. It had changed the way they walked and the way they talked. It had changed the way they looked; the way everyone looked. The Black women who sang R & B no longer wore their hair fried-died-and-laid-to-the side. And the Motown men had unconked their hair. Even Diana Ross had an Afro. And so my mother, not one to ever, *ever*, believe that nappy hair could pass for good grooming did not put her hair in an Afro but did go out and get an Afro wig. Dad had an Afro—albeit short and "respectable"—he even grew a beard and smoked a pipe. James Brown's "Say It Loud, I'm Black and I'm Proud" could be heard in the streets and in the halls of universities long before he recorded it. The Viet Cong, the Algerians, the Cubans, Che, Mao, the Angolans; the fighting men and women in South Africa, Rhodesia, and Guinea-Bissau; *but most of all Huey P. Newton and the Black Panther Party* had stiffened the spine of the Black American petty bourgeoisie so firmly that they found themselves looking like and sounding like something other than themselves. Or, perhaps, they were themselves for the first time in their lives. But as the hand of Black Power pushed them from one side, the hand of an anti-Black state pushed them from the other. And though they had welcomed the cultural transformation, they had not bargained for the political fight and brutal repression that came with it.

I remember the joy of anticipation in my parents' voices as they spoke on the telephone with professors they soon hoped to meet at Wayne State University in Detroit, at the University of Chicago in Hyde Park, and at UC Berkeley. But each arrival went awry, as though we'd boarded a plane for the tropics and landed in Antarctica. There were no departmental receptions, no barbecues at the homes of the chairs. Dad and mom tried to shrug it off: Everyone is quite civil on campus, dad would say. And it's not like we're helpless, mom would add. We're of strong Louisiana stock, they would both agree. Our hands aren't broken. We can certainly thumb through the Yellow Pages and find a motel for a few nights, and then an apartment, without their help. And we can certainly find schools for the children on our own. It's not like they haven't given you an office, Frank. Where is it written that folks on sabbatical have got to have their hands held? Weeks would go by, and then they would say: You've got to give folks time. What, with the riots and these Black students acting like they 'bout to take the riots to class? Who wouldn't be cautious? They came around in Kenwood, they'll come around here. But when we reached Berkeley, our last whistle stop, dad and mom may have given up hope of anyone coming around. It was as though there'd been no real movement in their lives from the time of Jim Crow to the time of the Kenwood Committee to the time of the sabbaticals.

When I stood in the morning glint of the Berkeley sun and told my father I would not be on the wrong side of history, my parents had all but abandoned history. Or maybe history had abandoned them. In this they were way ahead of me.

Halfway through our time at Berkeley, the Kent State murders did make some folks "come around." After Kent, one of dad's Berkeley colleagues must have thought, It's happening to us like it happens to them. Compelled, as he was, by what was being called the "niggerization" of White youth (though, seemingly unfamiliar with the heretofore niggerization of niggers), he approached dad and apologized. One never *really* knows which is more severe, the blithe disregard one suffers at the hands of White Americans or the pious remorse through which they purify themselves.

It was late in the day and the halls were silent—not even the echo of dust. There were no students in the halls. Some were preparing for vigils and candlelight marches. Some were in the streets throwing stones. Some were in the basements making bombs. Dad passed the open door unsure as whether to speak or walk quietly by. The dilemma was solved when that White colleague's voice calls out to my father asking him to come in and sit down.

He told dad that the killings at Kent State had jolted him as never before: four of our kids...*dead*. He said it was time for him to break the silence. We've done you and your wife an injustice, he said; he was deeply sorry that our family had been "blacklisted" by the faculty in Detroit, Chicago, and even here, in Berkeley, he said, as one might say, even here in heaven. He kept repeating "blacklisted" in an effort to describe a process no Black person had had a hand in. Before you arrived, he said, FBI agents interviewed some of the faculty. They wanted to know what we knew about you...about any allegations or rumors...or rumors of allegations...I don't know, Frank, it was all so confusing...was there a chance, they wanted to know, a chance that you and your wife were using the sabbaticals as a cover to run guns across state lines for the Panthers...or some group like the Panthers... it was all so confusing. He added, It's crazy, I know. I should have told you long ago.

My father was stunned. He came home and told my mother. Together they were stunned (and afraid) for days. Then their shock turned to paranoia and, as they slowly came out of their daze, to disbelief. Like other young mandarins of the Great Society, my mother and father had thought of themselves as an American couple simply moving with their American family from one city to another. They would not have characterized our sojourn as *crossing state lines*, like bootleggers, gunrunners, or jailbait brides. So bound by the promise of their dream were they that they never looked back to see how the fantasy that they pursued along the yellow line was a different fantasy than the one closing in on them. Was this nation so fickle that it cared not whether it hunted down "good" Negroes like Frank and Ida-Lorraine Wilderson or "bad" Negroes like the Panthers? Did it make no distinction between the two? Were such words as "good" and "patriotic" void of adhesiveness when attached to the Negro? Now, with this accusation, this, "official" rumor, they felt like they'd been slapped with a nasty gym shoe. Accepting their status as objects in a world of subjects wasn't what they had bargained for. *Transporting guns across state lines?* Could they really say *that* about *us?* they wondered. Is this our destiny, willful misrecognition, callous fungibility? Even after the brutal assassination of Martin Luther King they had not joined the tumult of Black Power. They had remained loyal Americans. This made it all the more cruel and ironic. Their loyalty had been scorned without their knowing it. Not until late in the day, in the wake of the Kent State murders, in an office of captain's chairs and dust-flecked light falling on unmarked papers, did someone tell my father what he'd gone to school all his life to unlearn: that while a "nation's destiny" is often uncertain, a "nigger's destiny" is an oxymoron.

On the eve of the Kent State slayings I entered the Black Panther Party headquarters in Berkeley on Shattuck Avenue for one of their after-school teach-ins. I had no idea that this visit was on the eve of the bombing of Cambodia, the murders at Kent State in Ohio, and at Jackson State in Mississippi. Ralph Ellison's *Invisible Man* was wedged in the pocket of my windbreaker like a baseball or slingshot in the pockets of other boys. A slightly irritated brother wearing a black beret watched me through the door. He looked at his comrade, who looked at me, then looked back to him and shrugged his shoulders as if to say, I told you, youngblood is hopeless.

He said, "Look here, youngblood. Yeah, I'm talking to you. Everybody else in here is grown so I must be talking to you."

I had no idea where this was leading, and being the center of attention in this room did not swell me to the same egoic proportions, as did being the center of attention at my parents' cocktail parties. I couldn't con this dude.

"Every time you come in here you got this book." He tugged the Ellison from my windbreaker and damn near broke the counter with it. "This Ellison book! Haven't you finished it by now?"

Now my apprehension turned to pride, for I thought he was scolding me for being a slow reader. This would be a great opportunity for me to tell him how each year the teachers wanted to skip me up a grade, how last year they wanted to skip me up two grades, and how when my parents refused—citing social adjustment issues—I was given a reading test that showed that I did not read at a seventh grade level but at a twelfth grade level. But this was not the thrust of his inquiry. What might have held me in good stead with the new mandarins of LBJ's Great Society in my parents' living room did not mean a thing to this Panther. Having figured none of this out, however, I charged ahead as though courting a round of praise.

"I've read it five times. I'm now on my sixth reading, at the point where he takes the White trustee to the Golden Day Saloon and the vets—"

He picked up the book, ran his eyes over Ellison's picture, muttered "trifling-ass Tom," and tossed it in the trash. He scrunched down behind the counter. He rummaged through the lower shelves ruminating to himself about how that trifling-ass Tom was shucking and jiving the people. He rose with Frantz Fanon's *The Wretched of the Earth*.

"No after-school lesson for you today. Go home, read the first chapter, and come back tomorrow and tell me what it says."

The next day I returned to the Berkeley Black Panther Party office. Before we started he apologized for being so hard on me yesterday. He had Ellison's book on the table where we sat and he asked me if I wanted it back. Rather cautiously I asked him if it was alright to read both Fanon and Ellison. He laughed and said, "I was wrong. You should read everybody. Hell, even read Hoover." To which someone yelled from across the room, *especially* Hoover! Then he asked me why he was just now seeing me, why he hadn't seen me at the teach-ins in the fall. I told him I'd been living in different cities over the past year or so, Seattle, Detroit, and Chicago and that I was relatively new to Berkeley.

"Where did you live before all that traveling?" he asked.

"Minneapolis, Minnesota."

"Oh," he said, as though I said I was born and raised in Sing Sing, "that's too bad."

I told him how I'd been called "nigger" throughout grade school and how I fought everyone who looked at me cross-eyed; the authorities had said either Kenwood would have to move, leaving its buildings, infrastructure, and instructors to me or I would have to move and leave Kenwood to them.

I was being serious, but he thought it was funny.

His name was Darnell and he told me he'd never expected to see me again; he was surprised that Fanon had interested me. I bragged that it captivated my attention because I read at a second-year-in-college-level (which was pushing it by two years) and that my father had caught me with it last night and beat the living daylights out of me—so I knew it must be good. That had never happened with *Invisible Man*.

Then, using one of my old cocktail party gimmicks, I quoted a passage of Fanon from memory: "'From birth,'" I began, "'it is clear to him that this narrow world, strewn with prohibitions, can only be called in question by absolute violence.'" I told Darnell that for some strange reason that had made me think about Kenwood, but why, I didn't know; nor did I know why my father had beaten me when Fanon's other book, *Black Skin, White Masks*, was nestled on his bookshelf beside the works of Sigmund Freud.

Darnell pondered this, but offered no insight. He told me to read more (in bed with a flashlight) and think about my own questions some more; to come back in a week and tell him what I'd come up with. I came back not in seven days but everyday that week, hoping against hope that he would simply lay it all out for me. But this period was the height of

COINTELPRO's war against the Panthers, and Darnell and the others were as busy with fortification activities as they were preoccupied with dread. There was tremendous hustle and bustle in that office and fewer and fewer after-school lessons on anti-imperialism and police brutality. One day I arrived after school wide-eyed and ready, only to find that the office was no more. The storefront windows were demolished. Glass and bullet casings were strewn across the sidewalk. The crippled interior of the office looked like the remains of Fanon's world strewn with prohibitions. Yellow tape prevented my friends and me from getting as close as we would have liked. An older woman who lived in the neighborhood stood among us in the crowd.

"What happened?" I asked her. She looked down at the hunger in my face.

"It's the *police*," she said, "nothing but the *police*." She started to leave but I had taken hold of her hand.

I wanted to cry, but my posse was with me and they weren't crying. "Where did he go?" I managed.

"Where did who go?"

"Darnell."

"Who?" she said again. Then she understood. "I reckon he went to Oakland. I reckon they all did. More of us there than here."

"I wanted to tell him something."

"Tell him what?" she asked.

But I was too choked up to answer. I just stared at the jagged glass dangling like loose teeth from the window frames, at the bullet-ripped posters of Eldridge Cleaver and Huey P. Newton, and at the crystals and cartridges glistening at our feet like gems. *You left me bullets and glass in Fred Hampton's place in Chicago,* I thought. *You leave me glass and bullets here.* The woman who held my hand was savvy enough to know that though I needed her to hold me, to press me tightly to her, my ego could not bear that much love. She eased closer to me and carefully and clandestinely put her arm around my shoulder—so as not to stir my friends. Without turning to look at me, without taking her eyes off the yellow tape drawn across the ruin, she said, "You've got to learn if you want to stay alive."

It was then, at the age of fourteen, standing in the ruins of the second Panther dwelling that I'd seen riddled with gunshot in less than a year, that I began to inventory the things I had learned in my brief time on the planet; as well as the things I had yet to learn. The list was meager and elusive. Meager because, how to stay alive was one in a seemingly infinite number of lessons that I had yet to learn and, until a moment ago, I had not even known it was on the list. What else was on the list? I could only inventory this particular lesson (and categorize it as "to be learned") because its omission had been brought to my attention. And what of the things I had already learned?

In Kenwood, I had learned how to be against White people (or that they were against me), but I had not learned how to be *with* Black people. Had it not been for the political training which I was giving myself through the reading of so many books my parents brought home from the Civil Rights front, and the sense I was making of the riots and the images of Black Power on television, I would not have been able to process the shock that came when I was transplanted from the sanitized calm of Kenwood to the ghettoes of Detroit (our first whistle-stop before Chicago and Berkeley).

Detroit was burnt hollow from the riots, or rebellion, when we arrived. Buildings scarred with third degree burns; dried blood on the sidewalks; here and there vacant windows in wait of plywood. We moved into the St. Antoine Projects across the street from Wayne State University. I had not lived in such crammed and crowded quarters since my parents' first year in graduate school when we lived in student housing, a period I had no recollection of because I was three years old. I thought the St. Antoine Projects were made of papier-mâché, a huge piñata waiting for god to crack open its walls.

On the first day of school, dad and mom sent me to register alone. I was anxious, but not scared. Though I'd heard gunfire the night we arrived, and though it seemed the whole papier-mâché complex was alive each night with the shouting of voices, the pounding of walls, and the beat of music, none of this seemed to spell chaos for me. Even so, looking back on it all, I could have done with a little warning, a brief conversation about what I was about to encounter at Spain Junior High: someone could have at least told me that though I might have been a bad mutha-shut-your-mouth in Kenwood, Kenwood was not Detroit.

I walk down the corridors long after the homeroom bell has rung. The halls are still full of kids. The first thing I notice is that there is not one White kid in sight. This is strange but I don't have time to parse it out. I'm late. I must register in my new school and get to class. Everyone is laughing and having a good time. Over by that locker the cutest girls I've ever seen in my life are listening to Archie Bell and the Drells on a transistor radio and doing the Tighten-up. I've got to learn the Tighten-up; in Kenwood they can't even do the Twist. I'll marry one of these angels and take her back and Tighten-up in front of Jane Peterson and say, *so there!* I walk into the office, fully expecting to leave the din of the dance music behind in the halls, only to find more carnival festivities going on inside. A group of eighth grade boys have commandeered the main office for what can only be described as Soul Train Central. I ask (that is asking no one in particular, for it is impossible to see who's in charge—the group of boys or the three White secretaries) whom should I speak to about registering? I'm new, but I have a transcript from my former school in Minneapolis. The boys get quiet. Now a flurry of whispers spread tiny wings and flutter from ear to ear. One of the boys repeats my words in an exaggerated tone, mocking my diction.

Then he says, "He talk White."

His friends start to laugh. The three secretaries brace themselves.

The boy who mocked me is sitting on one of the secretary's desk cleaning his fingernails with a file he has taken from her purse. Both his feet are in her chair. He rolls her chair back and forth with his feet as he cleans his nails. She stands by the file cabinet, four or five feet away.

"Come here," he says. I push through the swinging partition between the benches where students are to wait and the desks of the three secretaries. "Why you talk White?"

Foolishly, I interpret the question to *be* a question. I am thinking to myself: *Do I talk White?* and *That's a good question, why* do *I talk like I'm White?*

"I don't really know," I say, earnestly, "do I talk White?"

He stops cleaning his nails. He has taken my response as an affront. He looks at me hard.

"Is you a gumpy?" he says, accusingly.

Again, I think this is a genuine question, worthy of a genuine answer.

"Well," I say, mulling over a word I've never heard before, "I can't say for sure. What is a 'gumpy'?"

His whole posse paints the walls with their laughter. One of the boys yells, "Hey, Smooth, he's shuckin' and jivin' you man!"

Another one chimes in, "He's fuckin' with you *good,* Smooth. Nigga must not know who you is."

Continuing on down my blind alley of sincerity I say, "Well, who are you?" and the room howls even louder. I see one of the secretaries leave the office while she still can.

"Ahhhh, shit!" somebody says. "Nigga called you out, Smooth. The shit is O-N-N *on!*"

Smooth grabs me by the shirt. "I'll beat the black offa you."

I suck my teeth and roll my eyes. "Oh really, now." His posse laughs harder and keeps yelling, "It's on, man, whatchu gon do, Smooth? The shit is on for real!"

"I said is you a gumpy!"

"And I said you'll have to give me a clear definition of the word gumpy before I can answer. And I'll thank you to unhand me."

Smooth snaps a switchblade from his pocket. He opens it against my throat.

"This is *school,*" I say, "you can't bring a knife to school. It's against the rules."

By the filing cabinet where the secretary who couldn't get away stands, a door that reads "Principal" creaks open. A bald, portly, White man with hollow eyes wearing a factory outlet suit peeps through and clears his throat. He looks at Smooth and the knife. He looks at me. He stays where he is with the door half-cocked. He looks at the secretary. She tells me I may go in now. Smooth closes the blade and puts it back in his pocket. As I step toward the door Smooth touches my arm.

"I ain't forgot you," he whispers.

In the weeks that followed, Smooth and one of his posse would jump me the moment I hit set. I'd cross the vacant lot between the St. Antoine Projects and the school looking all around for them, wondering whether they'd come from the east or from the west. It was hard to believe that what was happening was really happening, but it was *really* happening: they would jump me in the hall, right in the middle of school. No one did anything and, if asked, no one would have seen anything. I'd cross the threshold and he'd come out of nowhere, grab me, press his blade against my throat, run me backwards on my heels until the back of my head slammed into the lockers, hold me there, stiff, long-necked and scared against the lockers, one hand holding the blade to my throat, his other hand ferreting my pockets. He'd find a nickel, the maximum nickel each kid could bring for milk money—find it in my pockets, find it in my socks, find it in my Afro, wherever it was hidden, he would find it. Then he'd press the blade harder or he'd slap me and say, "Dimes! Dimes, gumpy! Don't bring your ass up in here 'less you got dimes!" And I would recite chapter and verse how school rules prohibited us from carrying anymore than five cents on our persons at any time. And besides, I said, trying not to cry, my dad won't give me dimes.

I tried to tell my dad about it, but he had his own problems: his notoriety as a runner of guns he'd never seen, to people he'd never met, his life inside a rumor he had yet to hear.

Dad said, "Don't come in here and tell me somebody took money off you."

"But he fights," I'd whine.

"Fight back."

I'd plead and complain and whine some more.

"What do you want, for me to come with you to school?"

"Yes," I told him.

"Everyday?" he asked, hoping I'd see how bizarre that was. "Look, you stand up to Smooth. Not only will he leave you alone, but the rest of them will know not to mess with you. When it's all over, you and Smooth may even become friends."

"The kids I stood up to in Kenwood didn't become my friends and they didn't stop messing with me."

"They were White. These kids are Black."

"I don't see the difference."

"You will. Every friend I had when I went to school in New Orleans I had to fight. That's how we *became* friends. I went to New Orleans all by myself. And my aunt didn't have time for every little thing that happened to me. Kids came at me hard, the way Smooth's coming at you. One by one I had to fight them. By Christmas we were all friends. Now deal with it."

The next day I caught sight of Smooth before he could reach for his knife. I slammed my fist into his face. He flew against the lockers. He would have fallen to the ground if one of his boys hadn't caught him. He was winking and blinking, seeing stars. My stomach turned to jelly. I knew I was dead. He sucked the sliver of blood from his lip. He straightened up. He looked at his boy and said, "What's wrong with him?" And that was that. They walked away as though nothing had happened.

A week or so later, I saw Smooth and his friends in the schoolyard. We looked at each and said nothing. They all turned away from me. I got closer to them and they kept talking, ignoring me. One of the boys was talking about the Algiers Motel incident, which occurred two years prior during the riots of 1967. At the ages of 11 and 12, Smooth and his friends had all been part of the riots that took place on 12th street and Clairmount, just east of Spain Junior High. I had watched the rebellion on TV with my grandmother and I had read about them in my parents' copy of John Hersey's exposé *The Algiers Motel Incident.* It gave chapter and verse on the killing of three young men at the Algiers Motel during the Detroit riots.

On the morning of July 26, 1967, as much of Detroit was rebelling, heavily armed policemen, state troopers, and National Guardsmen patrolled the ghetto. National Guardsmen said they heard shots. They later claimed that they believed themselves to be under sniper fire from the Algiers Motel. The police and the National Guard rushed into the motel. Inside they found no guns, but they did find ten Black men of varying ages and two young White women. Soon three of the Black men were dead and the others were badly beaten. One of the men had his face blown off, an eye beaten out of his head, and an arm nearly severed by buckshot. No one was ever convicted of the murders. The policemen got off because it was determined that they had not been properly advised of their rights before they filed their report.

Now one of the boys eased aside and let me join the circle. They went on talking in a serious and concentrated manner. Like singing in a round, each boy told a story about where he was the night that the police and the Guard vamped on the Algiers Motel—what he'd seen, what he'd looted (they called it "affirmative shopping"), how he ran, what he threw at the Guard from up on a roof, and all the blood that flowed in the streets.

Smooth pulled his shirt down around his collarbone and said, "See. See that shit? A Tac Squad pig did that shit."

The Tac Squads were Detroit police units made up of four, usually White, officers who had a reputation for harassment and brutality. I had never seen a scar like that before and would not see one like it for twenty-three years until I photographed the flesh above Ma Kekana's breast the day before she died. I didn't ask him about it, in part because everyone else already knew. Smooth asked me had I ever been to 12th and Clairmount, where the rebellion had started.

"No," I told him.

"Come on," he said.

"What about school?" I said.

"Some things are more important than school."

Just like that we left the schoolyard. On the way Smooth and his friends bought me a slice of bean pie from the Black Muslim bakery (presumably from the nickels and dimes they'd "borrowed" from other kids).

"If the National Guard hadn't shown, we'd've taken this whole city," he said. "Took eight thousand of them to stop us." He wiped some piecrust from his mouth and said, "We still ain't stopped; we just taking a rest. We can take this whole damn country down." Then he turned to the other guys and said, "He ain't no gumpy."

When I left Detroit and moved to Chicago, I could fight; I could almost dance. I couldn't quite rap to the ladies—not like Smooth, anyway, but I sure wasn't no gumpy; I knew why we were mad at the world.

—⁓—

After Alice and I had been together for a while, I convinced myself that the looks we got from people in Santa Cruz when we went out were starting to change. Perhaps I'd just been paranoid. Perhaps she was right, I told myself, when she insists that the looks meant no more than, Aren't those two so in love. Or: Isn't that cute, a forty-something man and a sixty-something woman. Or: He's no ageist. Or: She's really *lucky*, a second chance at love (not to mention the sex!), when all is said and done, love conquers all. Maybe they didn't see me as King Kong screeching from atop the dome when they saw us together. In fact, it seemed as though they liked me. But more importantly, they seemed to trust me. I was soon called upon to counsel. I was called upon to heal. As at an End the War march, when you hear your name being called. Huffing and puffing, she pushes through the crowd and catches up to you. Can I march with you for a little while? she says. Sure, Dorothy, it's good to see you. Another hour and your lungs are tired from chanting, Hell no we won't go, we won't fight for Texaco! Look, she says, pointing to a park bench across the street. She takes you by the hand and together you minnow through the flow of demonstrators to the other side of the street.

On this march the two of you renew your pledge to keep fighting that Son of a Bush! Arm in arm, hand in hand, Black and White and all the Rainbow colors in between are marching with you down the street. You and Dorothy catch your breath on a park bench. You let the sea of signs, towering puppets, and noisemakers flow past. Mind if I ask you something, Frank? I'm troubled. Deeply troubled. Ask me anything, Dorothy. She tells you: I couldn't even dream of saying this to you if I didn't know how you and Alice are. You're the perfect couple. Well, you say (your signature well), we work at it; that's the key, Dorothy, hard work and commitment. Then you take her hand and you ask her what's troubling her. It's really embarrassing, but I've got to get it off my chest, she says. You place your other hand over hers. It's Erica, she says, my daughter, you remember Erica. Frank, I don't want you to take this the wrong way, but I feel so empty. Dorothy, you say, just breathe deeply, let it all out. Erica's pregnant, she exclaims, and...and the father is Black. She won't have an abortion. What is this *fixation* of hers, Frank? It's not that she's with a Black guy, we all dated Black guys in the sixties, it's not a racist thing with me. But Erica *only* dates Black guys. It's unhealthy. A fetish. And now this. I had to talk with you, Frank—anyone else would've called me a racist. I'm not a racist. I'm a mother. It's a mother's pain, Frank; that's not Black, or White, or Red or Yellow. That's human nature. No mother wants to think of her daughter falling in and out of bed with a fetish. Tell me, Frank, lay it on me like folks laid it on each other back in the day: Does Erica need therapy? Is she psychotic? She must be psychotic. Frank? Frank, your palms are sweating.

A week goes by. You return from Alice's house in Santa Cruz County to your apartment in Berkeley. There's a message on your answering machine. It's Barbara. Not Barbara Bush of your dreams—that would *really* be strange—but Barbara from school. She needs to talk. Are you there...Frank...c'mon...pick up if you're there...none of this, I'm writing my memoir shit...I need to talk to you. Paul and I are going through changes. I really don't like talking to your machine. I'm not trying to violate your space or your writing time but I'm in a jam here. Frank? You're not sitting there listening to me, are you? Call me, okay?

You call her. You explain to her that you were indeed working on your memoir but you weren't working on it at home, you'd gone to the library—to do research on South Africa, you say (instead of saying you wanted to get away from the phone).

The next day, with your low-fat decaffeinated latte and your Sunday *New York Times*, you wait for her at a small café on Telegraph Avenue. You're wearing penny loafers, no socks, of course. Khaki pants from

Banana Republic. Pierre Cardin shirt. Cashmere sweater tied around your neck. You're so clean you wish you had a mirror. She arrives thirty minutes late. She's been crying. Her blonde hair is disheveled; her cheeks are red from the rush. She says, It's Paul, we've been together longer than you and Alice, but lately he seems, I don't know, tormented, yes, that's the word, tormented. It's as though I torment him. I'm closer to him than his own mother. He's sullen and moody. Suddenly he's full of that Black Power rhetoric that he was full of back when, well, you remember, back when everyone was full of it. He isn't changing with the times. I won't go back to the way things were. Federal agents knocking on my door, looking for him. You tell her that she needn't worry, there's no chance of Paul getting into any revolutionary activity, all that's come and gone. Times have changed, you tell her. *I* know that and *you* know that, she says, but try telling that to Paul. Before I married him I lived a simple life. All I knew about the Feds was Elliot Ness and *The Untouchables.* Then, I married him and spent seven years on a first name basis with them—seven years. That's what I've been through with Paul. And not for his sullenness, not for his moods, not for his hatred. I always thought that what he hated was out there, outside our house. I thought that he and I stood shoulder to shoulder against it all. But it's in here, Frank, he's brought it in here! He's turned against me. Because I'm White? Is that it? Is it that crude? I feel so betrayed. I've wasted my whole life with him. I'm fifty-five years old. Who wants a flower child halfway to one hundred? And he calls himself a revolutionary! I've done nothing, Frank, you hear me—nada. I don't deserve this. It's like he wants to kill me. *Me.* After all I've gone through with him. I'm White, you know—*can we talk here or what.* Could've walked away a long, long time ago. Just walked away from all the shit that comes his way. Could've said ciao, Mr. Low-n-Moody, I'm going back to Evanston. I never said that, Frank. Frank, I never, never, said that. Could've walked right back into my White life just as easily as I walked out. Where's my recognition? The way he looks at me when he gets out of bed in the morning. If looks could kill. It's no cliché, I'm here to tell you, it has real meaning. Why can't we make it like the two of you make it? That's what I tell him. Look at Frank and Alice. Do I deserve the same contempt he has for the Feds? What did I do to him? Nothing. What have I done for him? Everything. You'd think it was the sight of my body, or the way I comb my hair. I don't know *what* he's contemptuous of. Damned if he knows. Maybe I'm the fool, the blind, the deaf, and dumb; the one who should've seen it coming. I'm rambling, I know. But I needed to talk with you. Now she looks you in the eye and says: I thought you were avoiding me. Then: No, no, I take that back, Frank. I know you wouldn't do that. You should talk to him; he'll listen to you. I ask myself, am I a racist, is that your problem, Barbara? I have those thoughts. Who wouldn't with Paul and his angry Black man routine? Sometimes I wonder, are all Blacks like Paul? I scold myself for having such thoughts. You're not like Paul. You know I know that, but the thoughts are overpowering. I wonder if all Blacks hate like he hates; if Black hatred isn't a deep well. I drop a stone into it and listen, waiting for the sound when it hits the water. It's a sound I never hear.

Whenever you and your bedside manner meet a friend in need like Dorothy or Barbara, you feel like you've made the world a better place. But for some reason you don't tell Alice about these encounters when you spend the night at her house. That's not exactly true, you tell her, but you tell her days later. Why? You're not sleeping with these women. Full disclosure would go a long way toward endearing Alice to you. After a week or so you feel strange as you replay the conversations in your mind. You try to decipher who you were in those moments. If, as Dorothy and Barbara and the others have implied, by the mere fact that they are there with you, you are not a hulking monstrosity like the others, who were you? Who are you in those transactions if you are not Paul or that Black fiend who makes unwanted babies even more unwanted with his tarred stroke?

It is not a matter of having simply traveled incognegro. You lost yourself completely in those moments. You go to bed, worried. You hold Alice in your arms, worried. You lie there, worried. You want to tell Alice everything, but you're worried about the consequences. You want to tell her nothing, but you're worried about the consequences. You are waiting for her to drift off to sleep, so you can roll over to the far horizon and be alone with your thoughts.

You want to sleep but there is no telling what horrors will steal into your dreams should you sleep. You cannot, however, keep your eyes open forever; soon, despite your efforts, you are asleep. In your dreams you wonder how it is you came to be in the living room. From the bedroom a voice calls: you're psychotic, it says, that's how you got there. You know that voice, the voice of Barbara Bush. She's leaving you, she yells, leaving you to put on her clothes! Then she starts reciting a poem you haven't heard since you were a child; you'd forgotten it years ago. "You may talk of gin an' beer/when you're quartered safe out here." Then she laughs, you won't be safe for long! That's not how it goes, you try to tell her, adding, why can't I come back to the bedroom? And you laugh, that a little levity might make you lovers again. You, with your sweaty hands? she says.

Morning. You lie awake and wonder why this dream moves like a comic strip, picking up where it left off and ending with no sense of resolution. You'd like to go back to sleep, but sleep is such a minefield. Presently, Alice wakes up. She draws herself to you. You stiffen—not where you should, between your legs, but where you shouldn't: all over.

"What are you thinking about?" she asks.

You take your time, then say that you have been thinking about class and your lectures.

"You're lying," she says.

You stiffen more. "What makes you say that?"

"Because I know you had bad dreams."

"Did I?"

"Did I," she mocks. "And I know what they were about."

Oh shit, you think, here it comes. We need to be up and dressed, we need to have at least the span of the kitchen floor, if not the distance of telephone wires, between us to have this conversation. But she plunges ahead.

"About South Africa and what you went through there."

You breathe an extended sigh of relief. She smiles, thinking that you've been calmed by her clairvoyance.

"Well...yes, that's right."

"Maybe you should see someone," she says, "I'm only saying this because I love you."

"Yes, well," (*well, well, well!*), "I love you too."

That evening after school she says it's hot outside and even hotter inside. She takes off all her clothes in the middle of the kitchen and throws them over the chairs. She goes into the bathroom and showers. You are seated at the kitchen table writing longhand, as you do with your early drafts. You think you are writing about South Africa, at least that's what the words on the page would indicate, about the dead massacred in the squatter camps and the ordeal in which you were almost kidnapped. You remember trying not to step in the feces of children as the young ANC comrade guided you through the devastation of Phola Park. *How can I describe the knife wounds drawn just above Ma Kekana's breast?*

She flits back out into the kitchen, half dry, half dripping. She says she needs a cold drink before she dries off. *Goddamn you, woman!* You mean, goddamn you White woman, don't you? The kitchen door is open to whoever passes by. The front door is open and the windows have no curtains. This is one White body you will never claim, the way White bodies claim you. You can't write the memoir. Not now. But if you stop so abruptly, she'll know something is wrong. She'll see you're rattled. She'll ask why. Then what will you say? You switch. You put the description of Ma Kekana into a manila folder and take out a blank sheet. Your political theory and film studies research is nearby on the table. It's a cinch. Just start writing the other book, the one on cinema and White supremacy. Chapter Three: The Dissonance Between a Theory of the Human Subject and a Theory of the Black Object. *No, too awkward, even for a chapter title.* Chapter Three: The Human Subject and the Black Object. *Yes, okay, go on. Try not to look at her. Just ignore her. Hope against hope that no one comes to the door; that she dries off and gets dressed. Now write:* Nudity and sex are at issue in the film *Monster's Ball*. *Shit. You're repeating yourself; the whole chapter is on this film, the reader already knows this. Focus your mind, Frank. Write, just write:* Nudity and sex are at issue here...the flaunting nudity of White people in cinema, and in civil society more broadly, manifests itself as one of White feminism's many dramas. What White nudity signifies, what politics the contestation and performances of its codes generate, whether exploitative (see Judy Chicago's screed on pornography) or liberatory (elaborated by the White feminists cry: it's my body, I'll do what I want with it)...*the shit Alice would say...*these are the tiresome and aggravating questions through which White women (and men) perform their intramural dramas. *You can't write tiresome and aggravating in a scholarly book—what if the editor's White; they have their limits, you know.*

She stands before you toweling herself off, sipping her cool drink.

"What are you writing, your memoir or the film book?

"The film book."

"Read it to me while I comb my hair."

"It's not there yet."

She bends forward. That full head to knees forward bend of hers. She lets her hair fall over her head to the floor. She brushes her hair down to her toes. *They can even rule the world with their ass in the air.*

"Go on, read me what you've got."

"It's tiresome and aggravating." *Like you!*

"I'm sure it's brilliant."

"When it's there," you say, "I'll show you when it's there."

Keep writing: The rub, of course, is that everyone, even the slave, or Black, must contend with the force and fall-out of these naked White dramas; for the simple reason that the logics of a White woman's body are in fact indexical of...*is it of or to?...of...okay...*of a shared historical and anthropological—that is to say, a shared ontological—capacity between White women and White men. This ontological capacity of Whites is also a constituent element, however diminished, of their junior partners in civil society, which is to say, non-Black people of color. (Footnote: The liminal position of the Native American is taken up later, in Chapter Four.) The White woman is the most frequently narrativized trope of this ontological inheritance, not just in cinema, but also in civil society writ large. *Yes, good, this is what we want.* Nonetheless, there exists a structural democracy (where this capacity is concerned) between White men, White women, and non-Black people of color—indeed between all Humans, between everyone but the slave. And, conversely, there exists a structural democracy where this incapacity (the absence of being) is concerned, between Black men and Black women: a prohibition against performing similar dramas because...because...*because what...because the kitchen and the auction block are not the same. Put your clothes on.*

She comes up behind you. She presses her damp body to your back. The scent of lemon soap arouses you, a maddening blend of sweetness and rage. She clasps her arms around your neck. Now she kisses you.

"That's nice," you say, though you can scarcely breathe and your thyroid is on fire.

"I'm not a harsh critic. I know it's a draft."

You cover the page with your hand. "Yes, well, I'm sort of mind mapping. When I type it up...that'll be the time." *So put some fucking clothes on, you White bit*—But you don't want to call her a bitch, not even in your mind, for fear you might say it out loud.

She tells you she loves you.

"Yes, well," (the obligatory well) "if you love me you'll hand me the Williams' biography over there." *God almighty, someone's bound to come to the door; this is my White body, this is my White body, this is my...*

Just keep writing: The Civil Rights leader Robert Williams recalls his first encounters with the performance of White bodies as an anecdote from his childhood, when his father worked at a railroad house in North Carolina. Williams writes:

> Black women walking from Newtown crossed the railroad yard on their way to work in the kitchens of white families.

Robert Williams would have sense enough not to write in a White woman's kitchen.

White [male] workers using the washroom "would walk around the railroad yard nude. They would do that," according to black workers, "just so that the black women would see them." White workers acted this way, African American men felt, because "the only thing they had was their white authority, the power of their white skin." (Tyson 19)

"What are you scratching out?" she says. "You act like you hate it. It can't be that bad. Let me see."

You cover it up.

"Okay, don't let me see."

Write! The semiotic play of nudity as a drama of value is an expression of Whiteness as Human capacity—this stands in stark contrast to the "monstrosity" of Blackness. (Spillers 229)

"Alice, you should get dressed, you'll catch cold."

"I told you, I'm hot."

"You must be dry by now. Look, the doors and the windows are open."

"What's that got to do with anything?"

"Forget it."

Write! White Nudity and its disparate valences within civil society, elaborate a myriad of performances that separate the living from the dead.

That's enough—can't write anymore.

You wait for her jiggling behind to start up the stairs before you muster the courage to say, "I am so sick and tired of your flaunting White nudity." But your voice is cracking as you speak.

She turns and faces you: none of your hesitant flicker is in her eyes; none of your quaking is in her voice. She's cocksure of herself.

"You're psychotic!" she says.

Psychotic? Did she say that? What one Barbara said about Paul; what another Barbara called you from the other side of sleep? *Psychotic?* What a "fetish" made of Dorothy's daughter? She says it again. Psychotic! She stands at the top, her glorious hair, her glorious bosoms expanding.

She is being-in-itself and being-for-itself. She is her own sun. Down the stairs she hurls a litany of all the things she and they—the immortal *we*—did when they were young. We gardened in the nude! We hot tub in the nude! We sunbathed nude! We have our nude beaches! Our nude forests! If her skin wasn't wrinkling, she yells, she'd still be doing it—and you can be damned, she is saying as she extends the infinite litany of her conquests of pleasure. Yes, she says, turning to go, you're psychotic. You stand up from the table. *Psychotic: of or having the nature of psychosis.* This tells you nothing. You float up the stairs, taking them two at a time. You lunge at her. *Psychosis: a major mental disorder in which the personality is very seriously disorganized and contact with reality is usually impaired.* Your hands grasp the reality of her thin white throat. *Psychoses are of two sorts, (a) fundamental (characterized by lack of apparent organic cause, and principally of the schizophrenic or manic-depressive type).* They close around her neck. *Yes, that's you: a Fundamental Psychotic! And (b) organic (characterized by a pathological organic condition such as brain damage or disease, metabolic disorders, etc.).* Or is that you, the second one: an Organic Psychotic? Which one is it, damnit! You must choke the answer out of her. Which one does she mean?

But you stop. As your hands press down on her throat, you stop. Why? Unless you kill her, the answer will always loiter in your midst but elude apprehension. But *if* you kill her, the answer will die with her. You won't even have a place in the story of psychosis.

—⁂—

"If you hate me," she said as I left, said as she'd said before when I'd left before, "why do you fuck me?"

—⁂—

...all I could do was lie.

"And this wasn't a night for lying," Naima had said, as we stopped in front of her house. Then she said, "Is the answer so horrible?"

The answer wasn't really so bad, I lied, but it's late and we've spent all night talking about Lisa's case against Virginia and there were still all those solidarity requests from groups fighting the prison-industrial complex and the Merritt College strike up in Oakland—we needed to meet about that stuff tomorrow. She nodded, but she reminded me that I had once told her that I had wanted someone to explain "the structural antagonisms of race" to me when I was a college activist like her; I had told her I might not have made so many mistakes in life if someone who'd been through it all had explained it all to me.

"So what gives?" she said, playfully, but firmly.

Naima, I said, the truth is…then I looked at her in the dim light of the car and I knew I couldn't say what I wanted to say. How does one speak the unthinkable? I asked her if she would think too badly of me if she let me wait until the time was right for me to answer her question. Some things, I said, are as hard for me as they are for you. I'm not smarter than you I've just had more time in the foxhole. She agreed to a rain check.

As she walked up the stairs of her building, all the things I would have said to her came flooding in. I never told you this, Naima, but I tried to kill her once. No, that's not true. I *wanted* to kill her once. Even that's a lie. I wanted her dead. I wanted for her to have never been born. I wanted her to live forever and fuck me that I might live for a moment. There. It is said, if nowhere else but my mind.

Now, all that remains are unspoken scraps scattered on the floor like Lisa's grievance. I am nothing, Naima, and you are nothing: the unspeakable answer to your question within your question. This is why I could not—would not—answer your question that night. Would I ever be with a Black woman again? It was earnest, not accusatory—I know. And nothing terrifies me more than such a question asked in earnest. It is a question that goes to the heart of desire, to the heart of our *black capacity to desire.* But if we take out the nouns that you used (nouns of habit that get us through the day), your question to me would sound like this: Would nothing ever be with nothing again?

That night I lacked the courage and the integrity to speak such words. I can hardly write them now.

THE POLITICS OF EVERYDAY FEAR
  for Khanya

Since we've parted I've become one
of those people who sat
never more than once a
childhood at our diningroom table
the day after or perhaps two days before
a life in some far off and unpronounced place
I could not imagine
over broccoli, roast beef, and early bedtime
they were all ten years younger
or ten years wiser than their age
they lived sideways
    between stories
they laughed the loudest talked the most ate the least and
drank well past
the hour of civilized departure
as though they who'd lived
everywhere had nowhere to go
and would sleep on our doorstep
to not be turned out into the world

7

In South Africa I put my shoulder to the wheel of rational and coherent struggle and tried to forget America. Despite the daily violence that filled those transitional years or perhaps because of it, there was an existential groundedness to my life in South Africa. When we lived in New York even Khanya felt the jolt of anti-Blackness. For her it had been a sudden unexpected shock to the system. It did not seep into her gradually like it seeped into me: the slow accretion of a childhood in Kenwood. She was, so she thought, both Black and an immigrant. But as the months wore on, she found it increasingly harder to hold on to the "immigrant" portion of her self-image, as though "Black immigrant" was a private joke to which everyone but she knew the punch line. After a while the joke became so clear and the punch line so potent that she couldn't bear it. Certainly, the *idea* of a Black immigrant existed in the minds of many of those who, like her, had come ashore wide-eyed and hopeful. But it was only a matter of time before she realized that such fantasies could not bring about a durable coupling of Black with immigration, not in America. She left, returned to South Africa, for other reasons as well. She was homesick in America. Though in South Africa, she had been sick of home. More than anything, however, I think she was fearful of becoming what one often became when one was Black in America: sullen and coiled.

From 1989 to 1991 we had shuttled between New York and Johannesburg. It was during one of our "layovers" between here and there, while trying to live and love between four narrow walls in Harlem, that she made one of her more disquieting observations about me.

"You have many White friends," she said, "but you hate them all."

The declaration was so piercing and unprovoked that I reeled in disbelief. I stuttered and fumbled for some kind of rebuttal but before I could fabricate a disclaimer, she said, "In that way you're like most Black Americans I've met since I've been here." What I finally cobbled together by way of a response escapes me and is not worth scratching for now. I remember how she held up her hand as I spoke.

"You're like that homeless woman," she continued, "who stands on the steps at Columbia University and yells at the students and professors as they race by trying not to see or hear her."

I dismissed the analogy. "She's incoherent."

"I stood near her one day and listened."

"What was she screaming about?"

"Slavery and how somebody repossessed her sofa."

"What does she blame the professors for, slavery or the couch?"

"Both."

"And this is supposed to be some kind of metaphor for me and my friends?"

"No. You're too self-possessed for that. But it's in your eyes. You have a way of being charming with White people, but I notice your eyes that instant before you smile, just as you extend your hand, I see it there..."

"See what?"

"A flicker of hate like that woman on the steps of Columbia. When we were in South Africa I used to think you had a mental problem. I wondered how I could live with this volcano that had no way to explode. But now, I think it's in all of you."

—⁓—

In South Africa I could forget the rank intangibles that dogged me in America, the psychic instability of Black life there. But there were times when America would creep back in. In New York they used to say that the best way to admire Manhattan was to look back at it from across the water, in a little restaurant under the Brooklyn Bridge. They—whoever they were—no longer say this, now that New York is missing its two front teeth; who wants to look back at wreckage, dreck, and waste? But sometimes Stimela compelled me to look back when he had me take journalists into squatter camps or mix with the growing throng of Black American expatriates and write dossiers on them.

Late one evening he and Trevor came to our new apartment in Bellevue East, a middle-class enclave nestled in the northeastern corner of Johannesburg between the jazz clubs and trendy restaurants of Yeoville and the quiet mansions of Observatory. It was 1993, and it must have been February or March because I remember how it felt like autumn and that Khanya had finished law school and now worked for an NGO and Reba had come to live with us. Trevor and Stimela were armed, which had never sat well with her since we lived in Braamfontein where she swept their bullets from underneath the bed. Two bullets, she had said, that Reba might have found. They came armed, nonetheless; Trevor with his Glock 9mm tucked under his shirt, Stimela with a small Berretta strapped to his ankle. And an AK–47 in the boot of Trevor's car, over which there was good-natured dispute as to whom it belonged. Though Stimela was a Motswana of Khanya's clan, and though he was officially enrolled as a student at Wits, there was no evidence of a budding friendship between them. She didn't like men whose vocation was lying. Once, Stimela invited us to his wedding—sometime in the indeterminate future. "Do you really think that one is getting married?" she said when he'd gone. And she was right; I had met one or two women through him, but for all I knew they could have been like Precious, not intendeds, but fellow operatives or cover. Around the corner Precious waited in Trevor's car watching the street for suspicious activity. How and where she was armed I have no idea. Everyone was armed except me.

"These are your weapons," Stimela used to laugh, whether with me or at me was never clear, as he pointed to my array of computer discs on the desk in the pantry Khanya and I had converted into an office with an overhead light, a smooth piece of plywood that folded down from the wall to form a desk, an office chair on wheels. "Besides, we don't trust you with a firearm." This indicated less my status as a security risk and more my status as a klutz. It was a joke that he and Trevor each had their own versions of. Remember Frank on his ass in the high veld, when the AK's kickback knocked him down? The target, of course, is bullet free! Or the time I took him to the firing range in Norwood, Trevor would recall, passed him off as my houseboy being trained to protect my home from Black terrorists. Open your eyes, mate, I'm yelling, open your goddamn eyes, the bleedin' Glock can't see the target. And the manager, a big red-faced Boer from the Karoo, khaki shorts, safari boots, the whole bit, I promise you, a live one, right there in Norwood, get this, this bloke comes over to me and says, Never mind the terrorists, you need protection from your houseboy. What I lacked in precision, I made up for in laughs.

Khanya emerged from the bedroom into the foyer buttoning her robe. She nodded to both of them. No words were exchanged between her and them. Nor did I say anything as I passed them on my way to the pantry. Conversation might wake Reba who was asleep down the hall. Khanya wanted to see me off in case—though she never said it and tried not to think it—she was seeing me for the last time. It was better Reba didn't know; she fretted when she would see Khanya and I leaving the flat wearing ANC T-shirts on our way to a rally. "Inkatha will kill you," she would say, and try to mask her fear with a lilt for she wasn't a child who risked sounding vulnerable. To this day she still may not know. I was told to keep it all even from Khanya. Say you're having an affair, Stimela had advised me when I asked him how I was to explain my nocturnal absences. I'd heard stories of husbands and wives in different units of Umkhonto we Sizwe who'd kept it from each other for years, who were captured and tortured together, and who, in those moments of searing pain, had revealed to each other the only secret of their lives.

Why I asked Stimela for permission to tell Khanya is still a mystery to me, as is why he agreed.

The moon was high and it had recently rained; jacaranda petals had yet to fall and turn the damp sidewalks into glimmering pools of purple. This was good. We could walk to Trevor's car without our shoes crunching the petals and waking the downstairs tenant's dogs. For fifteen minutes—the time it had taken Trevor and Stimela to scale the fire escape, tap on the window and slip through, for me to collect the discs and files of the work I'd prepared and to kiss Khanya goodbye—very few words had been spoken.

We climbed into Trevor's car. Precious nodded. Silence clamored all around. The key turned. The engine sparked like a soft explosion. We were off.

Hillbrow's Strydom Tower shot above the high-rise apartments like an exclamation mark. As we passed beneath it I recalled my first night in Jo'burg, nearly four years ago, when a woman with whom I shared a taxi and never saw again told me how Strydom Tower had once been to Johannesburg what the Space Needle was to Seattle. But MK had detonated enough bombs to make the Boers too skittish to keep it open. Now one wondered what it still signified, if one noticed it at all.

The revelry on Pretoria Street was a menagerie of disco music and sidewalk carousers. Two cars in front of us revved their engines as they waited to jump the light and drag race down the street. It was almost eleven, but the sidewalks were still teeming with people. Outside the Fontana Deli two young hotheads squared off for a fist-to-cuffs. The girlfriend of the larger, more aggressive one tugged urgently at his shirt, reenacting, no doubt, a familiar ritual of their evenings out. A street parson with a bible also tried to keep the two gladiators apart. Precious shook her head as we watched them and waited for the light to change.

"Now, I ask you, *wena,*" she said, in a voice that seemed to mock the woman I'd shared a cab with on the night I arrived, "are the Whites ready to govern?"

Stimela laughed.

"Please! Please!" the parson was saying to the smaller man, "We're Christians! Save your fury for the bloody kaffirs and the communists."

The light turned green. We moved on. I knew that neither the girl-friend nor the parson were a match for the gathering crowd. This is Hillbrow, I thought, they want a fight, a *lekker* fight, and they won't go home without it.

When we reached the safe house, Oupa was already there. He was in bad humor, which was normal. From what I understood, he seemed to only be in good humor when I wasn't around. Some time ago Trevor and Jabu had asked me to accompany them to an interrogation of an in-formant from the homeland of Bophuthatswana. The session took place in the offices of an NGO in Braamfontein, just around the corner from where Khanya and I were then living. Oupa had been against my pres-ence at the interrogation, but Stimela and Precious, neither of whom came along, okayed it. One of the people who worked for the NGO let us in and told us to lock up when we left. (I suspect that he may have also been one of the people who were rumored to pad the books for various NGO projects so that money could be siphoned off to Stimela for essen-tials, like the rent on the two safe houses in Hillbrow and the purchase of small arms when the Soviet flow dried up.)

Trevor and Jabu said that I was to sit at the interrogation table and listen to the informant. That only Trevor, Jabu, and Oupa were to ask questions. My role was to sit there and look imposing. They didn't put this in the form of an "order," and as the night wore on the story told by the man before us (a complicated narrative of an alliance forming between the Bophuthatswana army and the right-wing paramilitary organization known as the Afrikaner Resistance Movement, or AWB) became more and more intriguing. But it also became impossible to fol-low. At one point I slipped and asked the man we were interrogating a clarifying question. His eyes lit up. He looked at me with great interest. He smiled. Oupa had taken my head off during our internal debriefing that followed. If that man was not on the level, if he was a state agent, then he now knows there's an American working for us. You ignorant fool! he admonished. He wanted Stimela to jettison me on the spot. But

n his tirade, he raised other issues as well. He let it be known that he
was not at all pleased by the fact that the propaganda and psychological warfare activities, of which it should be noted he was not a part (for
he was an operations man with ten to fifteen kills under his belt), were
pushing us further and further down in the ledger of Nelson Mandela's
good book. Are we soldiers, he asked Stimela rhetorically, or agent provocateurs? I had something to say on this issue, but held my tongue. I
felt too ashamed of my blunder, too unworthy of their consideration.
Fortunately, Oupa had struck a nerve with Stimela, which took some of
the attention off of me.

Now as we entered the flat, I saw Oupa and Jabu seated at the table in
the front room. Oupa's eyes met mine, briefly. I hung my jacket on the peg
by the front door and slipped quietly into the kitchen to put the teakettle
on. In the car they hadn't told me he would be there. Nor had they mentioned anything about Jabu, who was seated across the table from him.
We'd all been too amused by the two toughs squaring off in Hillbrow. Not
that I would have asked if we hadn't been. I was happy to see Jabu.

Precious chaired the meeting. She asked me to give her the files I'd
been working on. Dossiers of low-grade intelligence gathered mainly
on American expatriates living in the Transvaal and on people who
were passing through and inquiring about the ANC. The word had
gotten out that I was an elected official in the ANC and people would
want to meet me. I'd become something of a tour guide, or tourist attraction, for Americans on business, Americans with NGOs, American
academics on sabbatical. A certain counsel general had sought me out
with a litany of questions on the ANC. There was also a young woman
from the state department whom I met at a cocktail party and whom,
after having one too many, said, "I work on the ANC and the PAC.
I know *all* about them." Then she smiled, "But I could always know
more."

The political acumen of the average American visitor couldn't fill a
petri dish. They didn't know the difference between a social democrat
and an anarchist. How could they possibly disentangle all the myriad
tendencies *within* the Charterist movement? Whenever I met anyone I

pretended to be nothing more than a good democrat, small "d." All I had to do was stroke them for being so brave and so righteous for visiting South Africa (without pointing out that they didn't have to come to South Africa to find a good hotel) and pretend that my idea of liberation was no more controversial than the demand of one person one vote. They liked that. That, and a few drinks, worked wonders. I was to listen to what they said, note where they steered the conversation, and write summaries of their questions and points of attention.

Anyone who asked questions about the ANC economic policy—were we going to nationalize the banks and the mines; would we renege on past IMF and World Bank loans; would Mandela keep Chris Hani on a leash; what were the chances Chris Hani could one day be president on an ANC ticket—were to be noted. Special note was to be made of anyone who asked questions which showed evidence that they understood the very thing most Americans didn't understand: the fault lines within the ANC, the fact that weapons were still being smuggled in from places like the Transkei, the names and political leanings of regional ANC leaders. Chris Hani had written at least one article in which he pointed out that ANC leaders who were most at risk were not the members of the National Executive Committee and not elected officials at the branch and sub-regional levels, like me, but the intermediate leadership of the regional structures. People like Thabo Nkosi and Stimela Mosando. These people, he suggested, were not only the most militant and outspoken leaders but they were also the most effective organizers; the strata who, more than any other strata, had secured the mandate of revolution and were best placed to mobilize the masses. This, he suggested, made them the primary targets of state-sponsored assassinations. Any American who could drop these names and bios was someone to be put down in my files and followed up on.

In my five years in South Africa I only met Chris Hani once, though I saw him at rallies and spoke about him often with Precious, Stimela, Jabu, and Trevor—but not with Oupa. Whereas the others were clearly working not for Hani as a person per se, but for the revolutionary vision he personified, Oupa was not. He respected Hani, to be sure. He recognized him as his commander as well. But unlike the others, Oupa did not believe Hani's ethical and political authority trumped Mandela's. Unlike Stimela, he was not close to Chris Hani, personally. And unlike Trevor, he and Chris Hani did not exchange literary insights when they met.

Chris Hani had soft hands. That was the first thing that ran through my mind as he followed his bodyguards out of the van and took my hand in his. *How could such soft hands have fought their way across the entire arc of the Frontline States, wielded an AK-47 in Angola, Mozambique, Zimbabwe, Lesotho, and the "homeland" of the Transkei?* I beamed like a schoolboy when he called me "comrade." It was April or May, autumn in the Vaal Triangle, an hour, maybe more, south of Jo'burg. Though winter was approaching, the midday sun was still intense. Perspiration beaded on his forehead. I was still working for the ANC regional Peace Commission when Hani's van pulled up to where I stood on that potholed highway in the Vaal Triangle; I was with Thabo, for whom I had gone to Phola Park less than a fortnight ago. Like Stimela, Thabo had trained under Hani in the camps and had been deployed by him on cross-border raids from the Frontline States into South Africa. Now Thabo drew a paycheck from the Peace Commission.

But Chris Hani was not in the Vaal Triangle that day to see how our reports to Amnesty International and Human Rights Watch were coming along. Nor was he there to check on the flow of weapons from the Transkei to the Transvaal. He was there because no one else—not Mbeki, not Mandela, nor any of the other "moderate" members of the National Executive Committee—would come.

There were two hostels a mile to a mile and a half apart from each other on that neglected highway. In each hostel lived several hundred men, but I had also seen women and children in them. Nearby was a massive Iscor facility, one of the quasi-state-and-private corporations that the Boers had taken from the British when they came to power. It was a bulwark of Afrikaner socialism, institutions that had lifted the Dutch farmer out of the dregs of poverty. Men from both hostels worked at Iscor or had once worked there. But now, lurking on the far side of the factory there was an Inkatha stronghold of Zulus who'd been transported to the Transvaal from KwaZulu-Natal and who wreaked havoc and death on people in the surrounding area. To go to work was to risk one's life. And of course, where there was Inkatha, there was also the army. I don't know what caused the war we were supposed to be fighting against the state and the IFP to turn inward in the Vaal Triangle that autumn. Perhaps I never will.

Both of the hostels in question were solidly ANC. But one hostel was loyal to the labor unions and structures of the Mass Democratic Movement (MDM), while at the other hostel, Umkhonto we Sizwe sentiments were hegemonic. Two old men whose allegiances had now diverged to the point of being irreconcilable governed them. Whatever the details of the feud, five people had been killed in the last two weeks; two from one hostel and three from another, which meant that there was still a score to be settled. It all struck me as being ridiculous because, in my experience with Stimela's people underground and with the branch and sub-regional structures I served on, it had become clear to me that the lines dividing COSATU, the ANC, the SACP, and the Organs of People's Power of the MDM were always blurred. Many people belonged to so many different structures at once and we were all adherents to the Freedom Charter. I myself was an ANC branch and sub-regional executive member who did work on various regional committees aboveground, but I also gathered information on Americans and worked on psychological warfare, propaganda, disinformation, and general political analysis for Stimela's underground. In one of the two safe houses that Stimela had secured there was a rotation of the same five or six people who could be said to be MK because they worked for Stimela at night and may have even been trained by someone like him at a base in the Transkei or across the border in the Frontline States. But one could just as easily encounter them in the daytime as shop stewards for NEHAWU, the National Education Health and Allied Workers Union, or as student agitators in SASCO. The same people cross-pollinated so many different structures that it would be difficult to determine where they belonged and where they did not. How a division within the Charterist

Movement could become so trenchant as to lead to the death of five people was beyond my (admittedly naïve) grasp.

But these old men had too much grit in their craw for compromise. The week before Chris Hani's visit I traveled from the regional Peace Commission office and told those gray heads that comrade Nkosi said, Call it off. The first one heard me out, politely taking in all the points I'd been sent to convey—even nodding his ascent to each clause of Thabo's message. A sense of authority surged through me as he escorted me out to the highway the way one should treat an important emissary from the regional office. As I turned to leave he smiled and warned me not to return.

The decorum of his nemesis, a mile or two down the road, could not have been more different. I'd hardly finished the first sentence when he interrupted and said I was always welcome, yes, comrade, always welcome, yes you must come back anytime. Anytime you're tired of breathing.

I reported all of this to Thabo Nkosi. That's what I thought they might say, he chuckled. Then he picked up the telephone and called every big wig he knew on the ANC National Executive Committee. He stressed the need for someone from the NEC to come to the Vaal Triangle and stop the bloodshed. No, they told him: too busy with negotiations at CODESA; too busy taking pictures with a British MP; too busy with a membership drive in the northern suburbs; too busy...too busy... too busy. Then he called Chris Hani, who said, Where and when?

We were on the shoulder of the highway outside the first hostel. As Hani shook my hand and smiled at me I wanted to say, "Hey, I know Stimela, I know Trevor. They told me all about your *Wretched of the Earth* project." Chris Hani had wanted the two of them to write a new Handbook for the Black Revolution in Africa, one that would be based on the South African struggle the way Fanon had based his on the Algerian struggle. I chided myself for such an adolescent need for recognition. Thabo apprised Hani and his bodyguards of the situation. Tokyo Sexwale (who, in the new republic, would become the premier of the Gauteng province) was also with them. We followed Hani's entourage through the gate and to the main hall. The first old man, the inscrutable one who treated me like a "dignitary," came out to greet us. Behind him were seventy-five to one hundred men and women armed with *pangas,* pistols, old rifles, *knobkieries,* and sticks. Hani spoke calmly and quietly to the old man. Everyone listened intently. He spoke in Xhosa, not English. I could follow none of it. Then we turned and left. Beside us were the old man and his lieutenants; behind us, his entire congregation, armed to the teeth, was following. As we walked down the road they sang joyous political songs in Xhosa. When we reached the second hostel, Chris Hani asked them all to remain on the shoulder of the highway. Thabo and I followed Hani and his people into the second compound to the entrance of its main hall. A similar group of armed men and women came out to greet us, clustered, as they were around the old man who had invited me back when I no longer fancied breathing. Now, however, he paid me none of the attention that I was paying him. When Hani had spoken to them, they too went with us out to the highway.

As we walked down the road something happened which I had not expected nor thought possible. The procession from the first hostel mingled with that of the second. They were all walking together. There was no telling the two groups apart. And they sang the same songs.

Chris Hani led us into an old soccer field. The grass had not been tended in ages. Nor had its benches been sanded or painted. The people billowed out onto the field. Hani, a stout but sturdy man of forty-nine (young by ANC top leadership standards) ran up into the bleachers as though racing to light the Olympic torch.

"The leadership will speak to the people from up there," Thabo told me.

I was going to join the people down on the soccer field when Thabo said, "Where are you going? You're part of the leadership."

"No," I said.

He beckoned me up the bleachers. Looking down on the people in the field, Hani was flanked by his bodyguards and Tokyo Sexwale. One row up and behind them I stood with Thabo Nkosi. The crowd quieted as Hani held up his hands. Standing on the field in front of their mingled constituents the two old men looked up at us. One of them carried a knobkierie. Our eyes met. He winked at me. *You old buzzard! Just last week you threatened to kill me. Now you're all smiles.* But his wink and smile were so that I smiled back.

Thanks to Thabo, who whispered a simultaneous translation, I was able to follow Hani's speech. It was stirring and sacrilegious—soaked with none of the hedging, equivocation, and generalization that characterized the speeches of so many National Executive Committee members. First he criticized CODESA, and the whole notion of negotiating with de Klerk, with sharp wit and sarcasm that made everyone howl with laughter. He said that we revolutionaries were only at the negotiating table in deference to Madiba. Madiba wants to try it, so we'll give it a try. For now. For now, he repeated. The people stirred in anticipation of what he would say was to come after "now." He said that he did not believe that the Nationalist Party could ever negotiate in good faith. The changes we demand cannot be won through negotiations! There was pandemonium and cheers of ascent. They have something to salvage, but we have nothing to lose! Again, the ground and the stands seemed to shake from their response. Yes, comrades, we will give CODESA a chance, a chance in deference to Madiba. But will we give CODESA our guns? And now they waved their weapons in the air. Noooo! they answered. He chuckled garrulously; he could hardly speak for his own ripples of laughter that ran on ahead of his words. It is no secret, comrades, now he leaned back and his rotund frame arced up and out, that we are going to *need* those guns! They were with him, laughing, toyi toying, chanting. When this charade is over, comrades (by which he meant the charade of negotiations at CODESA), when all the parlor games are finished, comrades, he laughed, yessss, we'll need those weapons. He was signifying now, signifying on CODESA, signifying on de Klerk, signifying on Mandela, because it was Mandela who had in fact ordered MK to stand-down. Here Hani was insinuating what everyone knew but dared not say: that his people were bringing weapons into the country and keeping current DLBs intact, and that he, like those who were gathered there, was still committed to revolution. We must be ready! We must be vigilant! Poised for the moment when we confront these Boers and confront them decisively! There was continuous applause and cheering, but I sensed something else in their voices as well. Something I had been aware of, but which had been so incongruous it had not registered. They were cheering him and jeering him at the same time. Sometimes the howling could not rightfully be translated as empathetic but as rude catcalls or heckling. How could they be cheering his call to arms and berating him for it, at the same time? And why was he not disturbed by this discord? Not only did Chris Hani not seem to mind being jeered, he reveled in it.

"Why are they cursing him?" I whispered to Thabo.

"They're not cursing him," he touched my elbow that I might turn around and look at the scene in back of us, behind the fence. "They're cursing them."

"My god!"

On the other side of the chain link fence was a company of South African Defence Force infantrymen. They must have followed our procession as we walked from the hostels to the stadium. I had been in the front of the procession with Hani and the two old men and had not seen them. How had Hani seen them? Now I realized he had been speaking in a skillful relay not only to us, but to *them* as well, threatening the SADF even with his back to them.

He turned around calmly and faced them.

"We are not afraid of you," he hurled his voice through the slats in the bleachers and through the chain link fence beyond. "The time has come for *you* to capitulate." The people on the field erupted once more into an uproar.

Then Hani, his bodyguards, Tokyo Sexwale, Thabo Nkosi, and I went down onto the field. He embraced both of the old men and like a minister wedding a bride and groom, he presided over them as they in turn embraced each other. Before him they each vowed to end the internecine violence. Then they raised their clasped hands and clenched fists into the air.

We all filed out through the gauntlet of infantrymen. They were so close we could see the color of their eyes. The front of our procession was halfway through the corridor when I was sure I heard a voice from the back say, "Kill the farmer, kill the Boer!" Then it came again from someone else—or maybe it was the same person yelling out again. I thought Chris Hani would turn around and call for calm, but he made no such move. People were not simply walking but they were toyi toying as well, which meant it would take nearly twice as long to move through this death trap. Hani seemed to slow his pace. The soldiers could have cut us all down—it would have been over in minutes. But they didn't. They let us pass.

We marched with each group back to their respective hostels. Then Thabo and I walked quietly out to the road where Chris Hani's kombi was parked. We thanked them all for doing in a few hours what we could not have accomplished in two years. They didn't make us feel small for being unable to broker the truce by ourselves. Nor did Chris Hani give us the impression that this had been a waste of his valuable time. In fact, he seemed energized by the whole affair, as though he'd just come in from an invigorating swim.

"The effort," he said, "not the outcome. History will judge us by our efforts."

—⁓—

I handed Precious four files and my computer disks, the fruits of several weeks' work. She asked me for a general diagnosis. I wanted to tell her how utterly bored I was with this kind of work; how much I hated getting all hugga-bugga with expats.

"Universal suffrage, equal opportunity liberals," I said, colorlessly. "These people wouldn't bust a grape in a food fight. If we lose, and Mandela's people win, *then* they'll be dangerous. There'll be a threat to the future of a Hani presidency."

"What do you mean, 'Mandela's people?'" questioned Oupa, coolly.

Trevor broke in quickly. "Any one of these files we should be particularly interested in?"

"I marked two of them 'military backgrounds,'" I said, politely extracting the two files in question from the stack that Stimela had started to peruse. "Two men in their early- to mid-thirties. They seem not to know each other. In other words, I've followed them on their daily routines and they've never rendezvoused. But that's what puzzles me. They both arrived within a week of each other. They're both Black. They're both from the east coast. One from Jersey City. The other from Philly. And get this: they're both supposedly 'diversity workshop facilitators.'"

Jabu asked if either one of them had saddled up to any leaders on the National Executive Committee or asked about anyone further down the food chain.

"Not to my knowledge," I said.

"Not to your knowledge?" said Oupa.

"Bob Thornhill's file has two résumés in it, along with notes from my conversation with him over coffee at the Parktonian. One is the résumé he gave me. The other is a résumé he gave an executive at ABSA." ABSA, the Amalgamated Banks of South Africa, was a banking conglomerate created by the Broederbond after 1948 when the Nationalist Party came to office. Much of the money soaked in the blood of government conspiracies was supposedly handled by ABSA. "We're having coffee and he gives me *this* résumé," I continued, pulling it out of the file and handing it to Oupa. "If you know of any local businesses that want to make their workplace more humane, he says, please pass it on to them."

Trevor laughed, "I love it, he's playing you for a bloody employment agency."

"But what he doesn't know is that I already have his résumé. This one." I gave Oupa another, almost identical, résumé. "The one he filed at ABSA when he first arrived." Then I asked Oupa to turn to page three of each résumé. From either side of Oupa, Precious and Stimela drew closer so that they could see as well. "Notice anything different about the two?" I asked

"On this one he's a former US Treasury agent," Precious said excitedly.

"But on this one he's not," finished Stimela.

Oupa let Stimela have the file. He wasn't the least bit interested. "And from this," Oupa said, "you've uncovered a grand conspiracy."

"I'm a clerk," I said sarcastically. *Now I really didn't like this job.* "A note taker. Isn't that something you said? It's a note, that's all. Maybe it's noteworthy. Maybe it's not. Two Black Americans comes to Jo'burg at the same time. Both have special training. One tells the Broederbond about his training and tells me, his homeboy, nothing. It's a note. Okay? I wrote it down. Okay? Which is what I'm supposed to do."

"So, what does it mean?" Oupa pressed.

"I don't know what it means."

"Did you try to find out?"

"Did I try to find out? This is low-grade intelligence."

Precious, Stimela, Trevor, and Jabu showed genuine interest in, and appreciation of, my findings. They were unfettered by Oupa's needling. But I was undone.

"What about the other man," said Jabu, "the one who arrived a week after this one; why did you mark his file 'military'?"

"Special Ops," I said.

"Do you have a second résumé on him as well, one with a different font perhaps?" Oupa chimed in.

I ignored him and spoke to Jabu. "I told him that my uncle fought in Korea and Vietnam. We bonded right away."

"Special Ops," repeated Trevor, warily. "Vietnam?"

"Zaire," I said.

"When?" Precious asked.

"Not sure. But judging by his age, if you do the math, it's gotta be right after Vietnam. Say 1975 to as late as four or five years ago, the late 80s."

"Doing what?" she asked.

"Are you ready for this?" I exclaimed. "Training Mabuto's people."

Precious massaged her weary eyes. "That's all we need, American advisors training Gatsha's impimpis."

"Have either one of them made contact with anyone in Inkatha?" Jabu asked.

"I don't know."

"One would think whoever gave you the second résumé should be able to tell you that," said Oupa, pushing the envelope and my blood pressure. "It's a simple question, comrade."

"There was no second résumé, *comrade*—not on this guy." I could feel the blood rushing to my neck. "We saw a show at the Windybrow. We had drinks at the bar. Finito." I could feel my voice rising and I wished that it would level out. Stimela frowned at me. He didn't approve of rancor between comrades. I tried to hold my tongue. I didn't want Oupa to know he was getting to me. But he *was* getting to me. "Who's asking the question here, Oupa—Mandela, Mbeki? Or some new sell-out we haven't heard of yet?"

He shot to his feet. He had a knife in his hand. Stimela and Jabu stood up as well and implored him to be seated. Stimela told me to apologize. I did. Precious used her prerogative as chair to move to the next agenda item.

"I'm sure we're all pleased with comrade Frank's files," she said with genuine appreciation. "And I'm sure we're in agreement that we don't want comrade Frank taking any unnecessary risks." She took a quick poll of faces. Everyone but Oupa nodded. He was cleaning his fingernails with the tip of the switchblade he'd fished from the garter that held his sock up. She smiled at him.

"Don't hurt yourself, Oupa."

I breathed a sigh of relief.

—⁊⁊⁊—

Sometime in 1993, Stimela began allowing me to share the files with Zachary Richards (who, as far as I could tell, was not in his network). But Zachary and Stimela were on the same side much the way Oupa and I were on the same side—we were all fighting apartheid. So when Stimela had finished with my files he let me pass them to Zachary Richards—who was not to be told he was getting hand-me-downs.

Unlike Stimela, Zachary never brought me to his safe house, if indeed he had one. We would meet at a quiet restaurant in Kensington. That night was no different than any other. I had penne arrabiata, whereas Zachary, in honor of his fifteen years of marxist freedom from the orthodoxy of a Judaism strewn with culinary prohibitions, ordered the prosciutto and provolone platter followed by the pasta primavera.

We finished our coffee and walked down the hill to a thicket of trees in which his car was wedged. He got in on the driver's side. I offered him the files that contained my reports.

He waved his hand. "Give me the gist."

I turned on the overhead light. He switched it off.

"You should know what you wrote," he said. Had I insisted on the light I might have seen the gun on the seat between his legs.

I looked out over the dashboard into the dark, impenetrable shroud of trees and started to tell him what I knew about one of the men who was promoting himself as a diversity-training entrepreneur. But he was caustic and abrupt that evening.

"Just get to the point. Is he or isn't he an American agent?"

"No idea. Not in my job description."

"Is ruining Mandela's economy in your job description?"

I laughed because I didn't know what else to do. I had no idea what he was talking about.

"Think this shit is funny, huh?"

"Comrade Zachary, first off, it's not Mandela's economy."

"You sanctimonious—"

"What's eating you?"

"You know damn well what's eating me. It's in the *Star* and the London *Financial Times.*"

But I didn't know. I'd lectured at Vista University in Soweto all morning and held office hours in the afternoon. After that I'd zigzagged on various forms of public transportation: from Soweto to Bree Street, doubling back to Mayfair from Bree Street where I tried to lose myself in the fabric stalls and food courts of the Indian bazaar and lose whoever might or might not be following me. I'd wound up in the lobby of the Carlton Centre Hotel in a stuffed chair where I could watch the door. I only pretended to read the paper; from there I went down to the garage where he waited in his car. Then we dined. And now, we were here in these dark woods. I had not seen the newspapers.

The *Financial Times* had run a small but potent article on Operation Litter, the South African Student Congress' campaigns of coordinated disruption at universities in the Transvaal. Simply put, Operation Litter was a campaign to make the university-industrial complex of South Africa ungovernable for White administrators and to make esprit de corps and stability untenable for its White faculty and students. These objectives were pursued through rallies and marches which morphed "spontaneously"—so went the disclaimers of SASCO leaders—into mass disruptions by chanting Black students toyi toying in the halls and in the lecture rooms leaving a swath of upturned garbage bins and strewn debris in their wake. NEHAWU, the union of Black service workers, cafeteria workers, and custodians, would then sow the seeds of *their* discontent into this compost heap created by the students, and demonstrate their solidarity with SASCO and their desire to devolve university power downward from the university councils to democratically elected transformation forums by refusing to clean up the mess. Zach said there were even press photos of these old men and women singing and toyi toying in the university halls around the strewn garbage, broken glass, and debris—sanctifying the disturbance when, "As elders," he said, "they should have condemned it." And as the afternoon had bled into evening, NEHAWU workers had met with the students of SASCO for teach-ins and to plan the next day's campaign.

According to the article in the Johannesburg *Star*, vice-chancellor Robert Charlton placed the blame for yesterday's episode of Operation Litter on a certain Frank B. Wilderson, III, former lecturer at the University of Witwatersrand who is currently lecturing at Vista University in Soweto. According to vice-chancellor Charlton, Wilderson gave a speech at the SASCO rally that incited the Black students to launch their destructive rampage. The *Financial Times* of London said that foreign capital should put all plans for investment in Mandela's future regime on ice until it was clear he could bottle this discontent and send it back to class.

"Hey, this is great!" I said, when Zachary finished reading, "Think we can still get copies at the newsstands?"

"This your idea of development, scaring off foreign investors?"

"As a matter of fact, it is. If the small parasites won't come here we'll have an easier time giving the middle finger to the International Money Fund and the World Bank."

"Mandela's agreed to a mixed economy—not to socialism."

"You sure found a new religion, fast."

"We're not voting for a socialist state, we're voting to end apartheid."

"Says who?"

"Says Nelson *Rolihlahla* Mandela."

"Oh, I know him. Isn't he that li'l peg leg man who sells veggies down on Noord Street?"

"Stop your nonsense."

"The woman who cleans Robert Charlton's toilet?"

"You're taking your chances."

"A Twilight Child caked in soot, sniffing glue. Look, last time I checked we were the masses and he was one man. He secured his mandate from *us*. Trust MK to get it ass-backward."

"Cheeky bastard!" He grabbed my neck and yanked me down to the steering wheel. A burst of angst blared from the horn. He quickly repositioned my head on the rim, silencing the horn. He pressed his gun against my temple. It was ice cold. It was hot as a branding iron. "I'll show you ass-backward."

Breathe, Frank, breathe. I knew that he had a black belt in karate and I could feel it in his firm, expert grip pinching my neck. *Guess you don't do Jesus jokes in Jerusalem.*

He went on a tirade about how the Ultra-Left would ruin the economy—isolate us more than Cuba or North Korea were isolated; bring the US Marines to our shores. "Is that what you want," he snarled, pressing the gun to my temple, "huh, huh, is that your idea of development?"

I stayed as still as I could. As he spoke, I heard a tremor in his voice that I'd never heard before. It all happened so fast that I would be lying to say I fully understood this tremor at the time, but it would be correct to say that I intuited a deep conflict brewing inside of him, as though his tirade was running ahead of his heart. He had always believed that to fight apartheid only to suture another racial and economic relationship with the West was wrong. Like Stimela Mosando, Zachary Richards had been trained to fight, to infiltrate, to subvert, and to dream of the day when thousands of Black guerillas, with a sprinkling of Whites like him, would march past the Voortrekker Monument in Pretoria to the cheers of the liberated masses. But now, caught between the ashes of apartheid and what they said was coming, he'd been ordered to turn his back on that dream—and to "neutralize" those who wouldn't.

"Zach...you'll get blood on your shoes."

"Shut up!"

"I'm not worth shooting unless you kill me. And according to the papers, you can't afford to kill me—not yet."

"Like hell I can't," he said. But I felt his grip lessen. Still, I didn't squirm. His trigger finger might be more impulsive than his soul.

"Kill me, Zach, and what do you think'll happen on campus tomorrow...and the day after? You're ignoring the objective conditions. Not very materialist of you."

He squeezed my neck harder than before.

"I had bronchitis yesterday, no one heard a word I said. Robert Charlton should be my booking agent. "

He squeezed me harder still.

"Zach, let me up, I've got a crook in my neck. Zach. Much as I'd like to suck your dick—"

He released me immediately.

"Thank you." I turned my head slowly from side to side and massaged my neck. When he grabbed me and pinned me down, the files with my reports had fallen to the floor. They were at my feet, half in, half out of their folders. I reached down, cautiously, retrieved them and put them in order as best I could in the dark. Only then, after the fact, well out of harm's way one might say, did I become scared and angry. I was struck by the horror of what had just happened and I was more angry than scared. Zachary lit a cigarette.

"Could you please not smoke, asthma runs in my family."

"My car."

"I did say please."

"Get out of my car."

"You know, Zach, the asymmetrical balance of power between us is disconcerting."

"Three seconds, then it's bugger the objective conditions. One."

I clutched the files to chest. "Guess I'll sell this high-grade intelligence to the highest bidder."

"Two!"

I jumped out and left the files on the seat.

"You're a grouch, Zach, what can I say."

He revved the engine and put it in gear. I closed the door. *He put a gun to my head. This White boy put a gun to my head.* I tapped on the window. He leaned over and rolled it down.

"Look, Zach, if you're going to bring a salad, let Fiona make it, ok? And not that stale lettuce from Noord Street. Get your produce at Checkers, mate." He was nonplussed. "You've forgotten? Sunday? Zach and Fiona? Frank and Khanya? No kiddies. Just couples. Dinner at our house? Never mind. Just bring wine. And nothing white. You know I hate white."

He plunged the car into reverse and damn near snipped my toes. "Toodle-oo," I waved, "cheerio. That's a good chap."

Damn, I thought, as his taillights vanished. *He was going to give me a ride.*

It should go without saying that Sunday dinner with Zach and Fiona was rather peculiar. Zach and I were wound tight as Swiss watches, which made us gallingly polite to one another. We let our wives do most of the drinking, which they did, if for no other reason than to ease the illegible anxiety. Though we'd finished eating long ago, neither Zach nor I made any moves to retire into the living room, despite the fact that the women had suggested it twice.

Our new flat, in the upper quadrant of an enormous fourplex in Bellevue East, had French windowed doors that opened onto the living room with polished hardwood floors. Down the hall was a kitchen large enough for a gazelle to lope about freely. It was the emblem of the middle class crossing we had worked hard to achieve. In the center of the kitchen were a large table and four comfortable chairs. Most nights they hosted Khanya's legal papers, her briefcase, her pager, and her briefs that documented acts of political violence and intimidation she'd drawn up for the NGOs and commissions she did freelance work for. But tonight they were stacked neatly in the pantry, which had been converted into a small office for my early morning and late night journaling, for the eternal wheel of paper grading that I was chained to, and for my writing of reports for Stimela...and for Zach. There was a bright-checkered tablecloth on the table and a bouquet of flowers that, as the evening wore on, Fiona had placed gently on the floor. Khanya had wanted the evening to be one for adults, so Rebaabetswe was sent to her grandparents in the "homeland" of Bophuthatswana and Doreen, the young Pedi woman who looked after her and kept house, was given the weekend off. Zach and Fiona lingered well past the hour of civilized departure as though they had nowhere to go.

The night lengthened, and with it a fog thickened between Khanya and Fiona. Khanya had said she had a bone to pick with Madiba for allowing Winnie to fall from grace over the Stompie affair. This, however, did not mean she believed that Stompie's death was justified, far from it; she grieved for the boy. But she wasn't entirely convinced that Winnie Mandela was guilty of murder. More importantly, she resented Mandela having let Winnie twist in the wind. Think of all the murders ANC big shots ordered at long range from exile and prison, she noted; the ANC didn't turn *them* out. How could he turn The Mother of the Nation over to the Whites and their courts?

Fiona, who shared none of Khanya's identification with Winnie, said, "It's not Madiba who's hanging her out to dry—if that's what's happening to her. It's Mandela's people."

"Then why doesn't he sort them out?" said Khanya.

Zach interjected a non sequitur which, after all these years, is impossible for me to remember—something about how there was a lot of mess from the Old South Africa that needed to be cleared up if we were to move into the New South Africa as one, nonracial nation; a platitude that said nothing and went nowhere. It only fed Khanya's frustration. I knew that she had not raised the issue of Winnie's marital woes, her public humiliation, her criminalization in the press, and her ostracism by her own comrades so that we might spend the evening kneeling at the alter of institutional stability, the rule of law, or the vague promise of a vague future.

She pushed back a bit from the table, unconsciously perhaps. "They're hanging Winnie out to dry," she repeated.

"What if she's guilty?" said Zach.

Fiona nodded.

Khanya looked directly at Zach and said, "She wouldn't be the first person in the ANC to kill someone."

The coils in Zachary's inner watch tighten but he held his tongue.

"The way they're treating her is the way they're treating women at every level," Khanya continued. "What's the use of being a woman in the ANC now?"

Khanya did not clarify her remarks by saying "Black woman." But I'd heard her and her friends clarify this many times before: how ANC branch chairmen bent over backwards to be so nonracial, a White woman could make the same proposal that a Black woman had made just minutes ago (while the plenary's eyes were glazed with ennui) and be showered with nodding heads and the shit-eating grins of obliging African men, followed by a quick motion from the floor to adopt. But that evening she did not frame her remarks in the way she would have framed them with her friends. And this collective of three non-African-women (a Black man, a White man, and a White woman) at the kitchen table was more than a little relieved by the canyon of misrecognition into which her meaning fell. Her discontent, couched in the universality of unracialized gender, allowed Fiona's voice to take root and grow.

"The new constitution will sort out these men who think they can keep us down," Fiona pronounced. The flower of White womanhood spread its tendrils across the table and strangled the life out of Khanya's words.

Khanya bristled at the word "us." I shit on the very inspiration, she seemed to be thinking, of your presumptuous personal pronoun. She looked to me for a lifeline. But I did not throw her one. The rage that simmered in her eyes could have torched the world.

Fiona asked me why I wasn't drinking. I told her I didn't like white wine. She turned accusingly to Zachary.

"I told you, he likes red, but you insisted on hock."

"It doesn't matter," I assured her. Then I smiled at Zach, "It's the thought that counts."

It wasn't long before Fiona slid unselfconsciously into the realm of their marital affairs. She reenacted Zach's arrest, which was not a breach of security for it had been in the papers: he hadn't told her the panels of their car were laced with grenades when they returned from vacationing in Swaziland. The next morning dozens of police swooped down through their front door; slithered up the stairs with automatic weapons; pounced on them (I imagined them both shocked and bleary, with cat butter crusted in their eyes and drops of dried sex between their legs); and herded them and their terrified child down the stairs and into the living room. She said that she would be glad when we could all go to the polls and vote an end to "this wretched cloak and dagger business," as she put it. But she was talking about Zach's life, the only life that had given him meaning, made him an actor on the world stage. Putting an end to it would mean putting an end to him.

"I thought Zach's arrest, the trial, and his suspended sentence would make time stand still," she said, appealingly to both Khanya and me. "You two live such ordinary lives. I envy you. I keep asking him, why we can't live like you two, now that it's over...it really should be over."

"Fiona, please," Zach pleaded. He started to light a cigarette.

"Not in the house," I said. "If you don't mind."

He shook out the match.

"We saw a film," Fiona said, "a French film called *La guerre est finie.*" She poured herself another glass of wine and sipped it intensely. "It's about this man who grows old fighting a guerilla war and loses all sense of proportion."

"That's not what it's about," said Zach.

"He still thinks there's a revolution and yet there's no more revolution to fight."

"That is *not* what it's about."

"Am I allowed my own interpretation or are you the only intelligence officer here?"

He sat back and pulled out another cigarette. His eyes met mine and he put it back.

"Frank," Fiona said, touching me lightly on the hand, "this man is trying to fight Generalissimo Franco from *Paris.* Franco's in Madrid and he spends three quarters of the film in Paris. I said to myself, That's Zach, I promise you. And I saw myself in that woman, his wife or mistress, who ends up...I don't know."

"Who ends up taking his place," said Zach, "joining the resistance and crossing into Spain herself."

"That's not the point, Zach."

"What's the point?"

"The point is they have a child together and they never see each other and she spends the whole film covering for him and raising their child alone and—and she wanted to be normal."

"What's normal, Fiona?" Zach wasn't shouting and neither was she, but it seemed like only a matter of time.

"Normal is knowing when it's over. It—is—over, Zach. Don't you agree, Frank?"

"Well, Zach, Madiba has suspended the arms struggle, you know," I said.

Fiona clapped her hands. "See there! I'm not the only one with a clear head."

Zach was speaking to her but he was looking at me: "When the revolution *is* over, Fiona, there'll still be agent provocateurs to sort out."

"Let someone else sort them out. Am I being unreasonable, Frank?"

"Frank?" Zach exclaimed, before I could say how perfectly reasonable she was being. "Frank's a bloody stranger. Why are you asking him?"

"He's a friend of the family," she insisted.

"Yes, Zach, I'm a friend of the family." *You even let me blow you, remember?*

It was all too subtextual for Khanya to weigh in on, so she had stayed on shore, nodding yes, sometimes, but not knowing exactly to what. Zach was glaring at me now, as though any minute he'd reach out and strike me or put me in another headlock.

Fiona was drinking steadily now. The wine put her in the mood to settle unsettled scores.

"He still goes out at night," she said, indiscreetly, "playing spy games."

"Fiona, it's time to go."

"Then go," she said, not looking at him.

She sat there, reading the label on the wine bottle she'd emptied. The table fell silent: a defiant silence for Fiona; an anxious silence for me; a furious silence for Zach; and an irritated silence for Khanya, for she had been ignored by the repartee, excluded from the bond between me and Fiona, and was unable to decode the aggression between me and Zachary. Khanya rubbed the stem of her wine glass between her thumb and forefinger. Zach quietly corrupted the art of origami with his napkin. Someone might have sighed.

Shouting and harsh words floated up from below the kitchen window where more Zulu families than Khanya and I were willing to imagine lived in a row of four garages. The voices grew louder and unrestrained. First a man's, then a woman's voice; now both voices shouting at once. Dry, angry voices; voices at their breaking point. We tried to ignore them, but the shouting rumbled up the fire escape, forced open the windows, squatted on the table like the call of nature, and flung the cups and glasses amuck—as if to say, *How's your dinner party now?*

Then, the voice of a young boy wove itself into the fray. We looked across the table at one another, but still no one spoke. The boy was pleading for mercy. Fiona and I knew that much but no more. Both Zach and Khanya could have unraveled the mystery for us, because they both spoke Zulu, but if they had wanted to they would have done so long ago. Khanya was not one to translate Black family dysfunction for Whites, even Whites within the revolution. Now we heard the snap, snap, snap of a belt biting into the boy's flesh. The boy screamed as he was beaten; both the man and the woman seemed to be shouting at him. *Are they both beating him?* I wanted to know, but I didn't dare ask; nor did I dare go to the window. He screamed and screamed. Fiona and I watched our spouses wince as they translated the words of the man and the woman for themselves and themselves alone.

Had Fiona and Zach been a Black couple (though not a Zulu couple), someone might have motioned toward the window and said, "Natal cockroaches," a quip of bigotry that a gathering of non-Zulus could rationalize by recalling the violence of Inkatha impimpis; a "joke" that could get us over the hump of discomfort and mask our mounting fascination with the beating of the boy. But Zach and Fiona were not a Black couple, so no such intimacy could be exchanged. The beating stopped. The boy was no longer screaming. His moans retreated into the garage and all that was heard were snippets of grown-up voices restored to normalcy.

No one knew how to resume the conversation, or what it had been about. The coffee was cold. The glasses were empty. We had nothing to do with our hands.

TET

In a gray veil of drizzle
she clears a space where
tombstone tongues lick wet leaves
lays the wire & cloth poppies
survivors sell.
The last war pushed this graveyard out to the street.

He used to laugh down there down
there the rain never
chills your bones
then hoist his ladder two eyes of stucco
patch them pronto those
eyes bleeding in the rain.

Windshield wipers erase his
face each time he laughs
or cries
or says what's so special
about the dead he'd trade her.

8

Jocelyn Brown bundled out the back door of St. Mary's Junior High. She held the collar of her hand-me-down coat closed against the hawk. She stopped to button her coat against the icy wind that clicked around the building from the north. Now she pulled a pigtail out from under her collar. She looked around, as though trying to find someone in the empty schoolyard where for two years running, she'd led Creamella, Shantay, Yvette, and Troy to back-to-back Double Dutch Championships for Hyde Park and South Shore. This schoolyard was hers if it was anybody's.

At the end of the schoolyard, just out of range, I sunk back into the shadow of the wall. I loved her, but damned if my stomach understood. Wolfman stood next to me, but he wasn't trying to hide. He took a hit off the roach we'd been nursing and held his breath for maximum effect as he passed it to me. Smoke sputtered from his lips as he spoke.

"Here comes your girl."

I'd been waiting for Jocelyn for almost an hour, but now that she was here, now that the beautiful girl in the very next row in homeroom, the girl I'd wanted to get next to since we moved from Detroit to Chicago was rolling this way, I was frozen with stage fright. That wind was as wicked as the hurting Reverend Mother had laid on Wolfman and me that morning. Sister O'Meara had run from homeroom and fetched her herself. Reverend Mother had come and given us one more chance. We refused, just like we had refused Sister O'Meara earlier.

"Very well," said Reverend Mother, "we'll handle this the Jesuit way."

First Wolfman, then me: she placed our hands in the door where the hinges met the wall. Slowly but steadily she closed the door on my hand. The pain was greater than anything I'd ever known. I screamed and tried to tear it out but only tore the skin on my knuckles. Jocelyn had shocked the room, and even herself, when she stood up and called the Reverend Mother "evil."

I kept my back against that wall hoping its shadow would protect me. Growing up in an all-White neighborhood, I had no rap whatsoever, and the little bit of game I'd picked up in Detroit before we got to Chicago had failed to turn me into Marvin Gaye. The school's long sooty brick wall blocked the last light of the day so that Jocelyn had to strain to see us. I took a long hit off the roach and flicked it into the snow.

"She had your back this morning, man, and you can't say hello?"

Wolfman jabbed my ribs with his elbow. I stumbled out into the light.

She waved and called my name as she came. In spite of all that had happened that day, she managed to smile. "I ain't afraid to talk to no female," I whispered. She was forty feet away. My heart pounded so loud it drowned out the L train as it rattled across the tracks from Hyde Park to Chicago's Gold Coast. "All I *do* is talk to females; women always following me around." She was thirty-five feet away. "Talk to so many females, don't hardly have time to study. I *got* some conversation, now." She was twenty feet away and closing. My voice came out the side of my mouth and dropped into my chin. "*You* the one who don't have a rap. Yesterday I had to help you talk to Creamella. Every chick up in this mug want some of *me*." Suddenly, Jocelyn was upon me.

"Hey, brother Frank."

My heart hit my gut, pulled on the rope, and yanked all that conver-*say*-tion I'd been bragging about down with it.

"It's so good to see you. Mussolini took her time with me. I didn't think you'd still be here." ("Mussolini" was the Reverend Mother's nom de guerre—according to us.)

It was December 1969 and I was thirteen. Jocelyn would be fourteen on the first of the year. I would not be fourteen until April. Still, it seemed that she was two generations older than me. This unnerved me and tied my tongue like a pair of old shoes tangled on a wire. Not only did it seem that Jocelyn Brown had grown twenty-six years in the past thirteen, but she was quiet-spoken and wise in a way that was neither showy nor strange. When she said *hello, brother Frank,* she sounded as grown as those soft-talking Muslim women or those sure-footed women in the Panthers, those grown Black women who touch your face or hold your hand and speak your name like they know how bad you hurt inside because once upon a time they were hurting inside just like you and now they're into a movement that takes away their pain—something you always wanted to be a part of but couldn't name. That's how Jocelyn Brown sounded when she spoke to me. Something inside me felt warm and loved and something else inside was all shook up and running scared. I knew that I had no persona that could match what she expressed with little or no effort: not my down-revolutionary-self, not my jive-got-some-conversation-for-ya-baby-self, not my big-bad-football-self, none of those could balance the scales with this little girl who greeted me like she cared about me. I was speechless in the face of such integrity.

"How do you feel?" she asked. "How's your hand?"

"Yeah," was all I could say, as though *yeah* was a feeling that described the human condition.

Wolfman smiled at her, "Hey now, sweet pea, how you making?"

"I'm alright, Wolfman, how you doing?"

"I'm cool." Then he looked at me and said, "He's cool, too. What happened in there?"

"Il Duce was all over me, man. But I didn't care; not after what she did to you two." She took Wolfman's hand and then she took mine. "Does it hurt?"

"Naw," said Wolfman, "we a couple of superheroes, it don't hurt."

Maybe we called him Wolfman on account of the hair that made him look like Jimi Hendrix. Or maybe it was because, unlike any of the other boys at St. Mary's, he was already shaving. Or perhaps it was because he was the only eighth grader who was taller and bigger than any ninth and tenth grader. Word was the high school coach wanted him to start at middle linebacker as soon as he hit ninth grade. No junior varsity for Wolfman.

His father was not in his life. His mother was White. This, Wolfman, told me one day from the depths of a reefer haze, was the same as having no parents at all. Wolfman was politicized in a way few other kids at St. Mary's were, except Jocelyn. He knew Black folks were on the move and he was ready to seize the time. This strained relations between him and his mother. "Black folks are on the move," Wolfman used to say, "Whitey better get with it and get behind us." His mother, however, was not convinced that her destiny was to follow her son into Nation Time. "Rather than waste this precious revolutionary period trying to tell her what time it is," Wolfman explained to me, "I spend as much time as I can away from her." To which I would nod and say, "I know that's right. It's the same shit I go through with my mom, and she ain't even White; at least your mom's got that melontonic-pigmentation-thing as her excuse, know what I'm saying?" I may have been the only one who could offer such erudite commentary on his mother without getting knocked into next week. We would stand in the shadows of St. Mary's schoolyard and talk about our parents and talk about Huey P. Newton and Eldridge Cleaver and try to decide who was right between the two of them, and talk about Mao and Ho Chi Minh and try to decide who was the baddest between the two of them; we'd be so high we could predict the exact date, the exact time, and the exact place that would set off the Revolution. Our repartees were so righteous and the reefer was so good that we'd forget how cold it was and where it was we were supposed to be.

Jocelyn looked into my half-yam eyes. "You some superheroes, alright; couple of stoned out superheroes. No wonder your hands don't hurt." It wasn't all that funny but somehow me and Wolfman got the giggles from what she said and it wasn't long before we were all laughing at god knows what.

"So, come on, Jocelyn," Wolfman said, "what did Il Duce *say?*"

Jocelyn stopped laughing and looked away. I followed her gaze down the buttonholes of her secondhand coat with its frayed and truant threads to the same patent leather shoes her sister, Olivia, had worn in this very same schoolyard five winters before. She didn't cry. She hadn't even cried this morning in homeroom when she walked over to the door and held my wrist and told the Reverend Mother to leave me alone; nor when the Reverend Mother said for her to let go of my arm or risk being expelled.

I was so angry I forgot how tongue-tied I was. "She better not kick you out! Is that what she said? Tell me, Jocelyn, what did she say?" Jocelyn said nothing. "We gonna straighten that heifer out."

Wolfman put his hand on my shoulder, "You've smoked yourself into a fit of temporary insanity."

I went on like he hadn't said a word. "She wants to expel you, she best look like expelling me and Wolfman, too." I made a snowball and threw it against a window that I knew was nowhere *near* Mussolini's office. I shouted: "Don't let me act a fool up in here! 'Cause I *will* go off on your ass!"

Calm as ever, Jocelyn looked at me and said, "She won't expel you," and then to Wolfman, "and not you either."

Why not? we asked her, as though we'd been summarily stripped of our street credentials.

"Because your daddy's a rich professor and a deacon in the church," her words cut through me like a blade of ice, "and she won't expel you because your mother is White." I'd seen Wolfman cold-cock a big ass tenth grader who had simply signified about his mother being White, but he didn't as much as flinch when Jocelyn laid it on him raw like that.

"She said, up till now, I've never been a 'discipline problem.' She even laughed, you know the way she laughs. She said holding your arm did not contravene the archdiocese's code of conduct. And she said she *wouldn't* expel me for sitting down when she told everybody to stand up because then she'd have to expel you, someone whose parents brought 'prestige' to the parish." I couldn't bear the way she looked at me when she said "prestige." "Or someone like you," she said to Wolfman, "whose mother was part of the parish when it was 'still halfway decent.'" Jocelyn wasn't signifying she was just telling it like it was.

"Damn," I said in complete disbelief, "she actually said all of that?"

"And more."

"What more could there be?"

"'So you see, Miss Brown, I'm in a predicament: I cannot very well bring a student conduct case against you for holding on to young Wilderson's arm and I will not expel you for remaining in your chair when I distinctly told you and the rest of the class to stand.'"

"Well, goddamn," I said, holding out my palm to Wolfman, "we put Il Duce in a trick bag!"

"She put those funky spectacles on and started to read the Catholic Bulletin like I wasn't even there. So I put my coat on. I got up and I walked to the door. Just as I got to the door, she called my name and didn't even look up from her desk, just reading as she spoke to me. 'Despite what you people think—'"

"You people? Naw, naw, I'da been all over her if she'd said that shit to me!"

"Let her finish, Frank."

"'Despite what you people think, the Roman Catholic Church is not Fort Knox. You, Miss Brown, have blossomed due largely to our philanthropic embrace.'"

"Philanthropic embrace! Shit, let that big square-back-sedan-head wench say some shit like that to me!"

"Just ignore him, Jocelyn, go on with your story."

"I started crying. She told me that the time for tears had come and gone. She said 'South Shore is teaming with underprivileged Negro girls far more deserving of scholarships than you.' Then she said I was free to come back to St. Mary's after Christmas break if the money for tuition and uniforms finds its way to her door. 'Who knows what you will do in lieu of your scholarship, Miss Brown. Our Lady works in mysterious ways.'"

With cool precision Jocelyn told us what Mussolini said. She didn't even cry when she told how she cried in the office. When she finished, me and Wolfman just looked at her in our stoned-out stupor. Il Duce had won by taking the fight away.

"Oh, yeah, I almost forgot: she said that she had thought I would turn out differently than my sister Olivia, who graduated only to waste her Roman Catholic education on Black Power. She said 'Perhaps H. Rap Brown will hold a bake sale for your school fees. Is he any relation, Miss Brown'?"

We all left the schoolyard together but somewhere in Hyde Park we separated from Wolfman. I cannot recall if he really and truly had to be somewhere else or if he saw how much I loved Jocelyn and knew that I would never make a move as long as I remained in his capable hands. I remember saying something like, "They murdered Fred Hampton." "Yeah," said Wolfman, "they coming at us, they coming at us hard." "And Mark Clark," Jocelyn added. She must've been the one to have said this because she was not only up on all the news from the Front but she knew all the names, names that weren't in the newspapers, the names that weren't in the songs, the names that did not give the speeches. Her sister, Olivia, was a field worker for the Student Nonviolent Coordinating Committee. Olivia was one of those names.

I said that we should all go over to West Monroe to see the apartment where Hampton and Clark had been killed. I didn't want to go home where Frank and Ida-Lorraine would be on me like light on a wall for what happened that morning in homeroom.

Fred Hampton, deputy chairman of the Illinois Chapter of the Black Panther Party, had been shot in his sleep several days ago; a victim of a COINTELPRO hit. A secret FBI/COINTELPRO directive had called for "imaginative and hard-hitting counterintelligence measures aimed at crippling the Black Panther Party." The federal government's use of an infiltrator to drug Fred Hampton, and its use of the Chicago police to execute him, was certainly "imaginative," "hard-hitting," and "crippling." Hampton had been successful in building alliances between the Panthers and Students for a Democratic Society, the Panthers and poor Whites in Chicago, and, most threatening of all, between the Panthers and street gangs like the Black Stone Rangers. The government had tried everything to stop the Black Panther Party of Chicago: pre-dawn raids on their West Chicago office; the burning of cereal boxes for the Panthers' Free Breakfast Program; the leveling of trumped-up charges, in which, for example, they sent Fred Hampton to prison for two years. The charge: stealing seventy-one dollars worth of ice cream bars from an ice cream truck and giving them to kids in the street. The raid at his home took place at two or three on the morning of December 4, 1969. The police used shotguns and machine guns. They turned the walls of the apartment, the door to his bedroom, and even his bed into Swiss cheese. Mark Clark was shot through the heart before he opened the door. Deborah Johnson, who was eight months pregnant with their child, Fred Hampton Jr., at the time, and the others, whether wounded or well, were lined up against the wall in the kitchen. They heard the cops talking in the bedroom, *Is he dead, is he dead? He'll barely make it.* Then the sound of two more solitary rounds being fired followed by a verbal confirmation: *He's good and dead now.* For some mysterious reason the Chicago police took the bodies away and arrested the survivors but left the premises open and unattended. The Panthers turned the apartment into their own crime scene, and folks from all around filed in and out one after the other. The police did not seal off the place until December 17, 1969, eleven days after the raid.

I got it in my head that we should have a look-see. To my surprise, Jocelyn said this was a good idea. At which point I panicked. I'd get home not only late, but late at night. The beating that waited for me would have two justifications instead of one: disruption of a Roman Catholic ritual and a patriotic pledge that morning in homeroom, coupled with my violation of Frank and Ida-Lorraine's curfew. As the anxiety bubbled up inside me, I stayed cool and copasetic. I displaced my anxiety onto Jocelyn. "Probably not a good idea, your mom would tear into you if you went to the scene of a Panther/police shoot-out."

"No she wouldn't. Olivia's been involved in talks between SNCC and the Panthers. They might even merge."

"Well, what I mean is, you being a girl and all, she'd probably be all in your shit for being out so late. Not like dudes, ya dig, who can just come and go and nobody trips."

"My mother rarely comes out of bag," she said matter-of-factly, "and she doesn't whup me."

For a while I walked in jealous silence.

"Your parents whup you?"

"Shit, they ain't crazy." I looked away.

"Your parents down with the Revolution?"

"Of course, I'm surprised you'd ask me a question like that. Everybody at my crib is down with the Revolution. My four-year-old brother be shouting 'Off the pigs!' on his way to nursery school."

"I didn't ask you about your baby brother, I asked you about your parents."

"And I told you. They're down with all that shit. Even took us to Jesse Jackson's church for an Operation Breadbasket rally. The Cannibal Adderley Quintet played at the break."

Olivia said, "Jesse Jackson is no Fred Hampton. And Operation Breadbasket is not the Black Panther—"

"Fine. My parents aren't down with the Revolution."

We reached the corner and waited three hundred years for the damn light to turn to green.

"Since King died," I confessed, "I don't know if they're down with anything." We crossed the street. "Tonight they're going to beat me for what I did this morning in homeroom."

"What *we* did." She held my wounded hand and I welcomed the pain of her grip.

I began to cry. We were standing at the bottom of the stairs, under the long iron tracks of Chicago's L train.

"We should run away together," she said holding me in her arms trying to stop me, if not from crying than at least from shivering, "crash at the Panther pad till we've saved enough money to go find my sister Olivia in New York." The rock and tumble of the train rambling above our heads ceased. "Or you could come live at my house." She led me by the hand up the stairs. "Mama's always saying how we need a man around the house. And you're just the kind of man she means. I know it, I just know it."

On the train she reads from a letter she received from her sister. Olivia writes her all about SNCC and the growing pains of an organization that started off agitating for voting rights and integration and now finds itself struggling with the next phase, the revolutionary phase. Olivia is angry about the murder of Fred Hampton. She asks if there were really ninety bullet holes in the apartment. Jocelyn is emboldened. She has a task. She has a responsibility to get hold of vital information and then pass it on to her big sister. At the end of the letter, Olivia says that she is writing from New York where the Panthers and SNCC are holding talks. She says that she visits the United Nations whenever she can and that she might send for Jocelyn next summer. She writes that she met a man from South Africa at the UN and he was as distraught by the murder of Fred Hampton and Mark Clark as she was. *The brother is from a place called Guinea-Bissau, Jocelyn, where the Revolution has matured. He informs me that the ANC, that stands for African National Congress, has written an official letter of revolutionary condolences and solidarity to the Black Panther Party and all Black insurgents in the United States.* As we come to our stop Jocelyn folds the letter and asks what the ANC is and how they had heard about us.

—m—

Berkeley in January was light-years away from Chicago in December. In Berkeley the mornings seemed fresh and cool with the scent of rain-moistened grass in the air. There was no snow, no unkempt playgrounds of uneven asphalt and ice. Willard Junior High was a huge Spanish hacienda with open courtyards, mission-tiled roofs, sun-drenched sports fields, two swimming pools, and large classrooms free of mold and free of the sputter and hiss of run down radiators—and there were no nuns. St. Mary's in Chicago couldn't hold a candle to Willard Junior High. I used to walk up Alcatraz Avenue to Telegraph, then east on Telegraph to school and pinch myself: was I really here, in Berkeley, I would think, and feel it was all a dream as though any minute the sky would fall in and the hawk off Lake Michigan, having chased me halfway across the country, would descend upon me like it descended upon Jocelyn and me, whipping its wings across my face. The hawk never came to Berkeley. Not, at least, the hawk I was expecting. I remember the day that it finally hit me—I'd come to the light at Shattuck and Alcatraz—and I just started yelling "I'm in Berkeley goddamn it! I'm really here! I'm here in Revolution Central." To my chagrin the early morning street was not as empty as I had assumed when I closed my eyes and started to howl. But the hippie who was watching me seemed to understand. "Yeah, man," he said to my gap-mouthed surprise, "you're in Berkeley. That's for sure, man, that's the deal. And it's groovy, it really is groovy." All around me was the absence of polyester suits under long burly coats and mufflers and galoshes. Here the White cats sported beards and sandals. The White women wore peasant dresses and jeans. On Telegraph they sold T-shirts of Che, posters of Mao, pins and medallions of Lenin. They were "demonstration-ready" with their football helmets and construction hats near at hand. And the sisters seemed to all have beautiful Afros and strong clenched fists that spiked the air and fast strong words for whoever came at them anything but correct. The brothers looked serious and ready for the get-down with their sunglasses, their berets, and their side-to-side strut that was all about bizzz-ness.

Could it be, however, that in the first two days of my arrival I saw what I wanted to see, and felt what I told myself I should feel? Was it all as wonderful as I told myself it was as I walked to my new school, or was I simply trying to keep suppressed in the manholes of Telegraph Avenue the memory and the longing for Jocelyn Brown? When she held my hand and whispered my name I could beat back the wind and melt the snow.

As with Fred Hampton in Chicago, the East Bay had seen its share of the slaughter of Panthers. In Berkeley we lived on Adeline, two feet from the Oakland/Berkeley border, six or seven blocks from where Li'l Bobby Hutton was slain and Eldridge Cleaver was wounded in a shootout with the Oakland Police. But somehow it didn't have the feel of killing fields. There was too much music and the sweet perfume of reefer in the air. Chicago was America in a way that Berkeley wasn't. They comin' at us, Wolfman used to say in the days after Fred Hampton's death, they really comin' at us. In Berkeley I felt that though they were coming at us, we were coming back at them. But none of this euphoria staved off my longing for Jocelyn.

I spent too much time at the Black Panther office on the morning of my third day in school. *What the hell, I don't need homeroom anyway.* A guidance counselor, who looks like no guidance counselor I've ever seen—a tall man sporting a large Afro, a sliver of a goatee beneath mischievous eyes, a silk shirt, and bell bottoms—catches me reading the Black Panther newspaper in the outdoor corridor.

"Contraband, I presume," he chuckles. Then he says he wants me to meet some folks. *Ah shit, here it comes, a trip to the principal's office and an ass-whupping when I get home.*

"Contraband" is what the nuns of St. Mary's called the pamphlets and underground newspapers that broke in on their cloistered space and turned our heads from Jesus Christ to Chairman Mao. "Contraband" is what Sister O'Meara hoped to ferret out in homeroom as she rushed toward me down the row of desks. She leaned over me and her long black rosary clattered on my desk.

"Young Wilderson, open your desk."

"Why?"

"Because I said so."

I raised the desk with its exhausted hearts and crippled arrows, its penknifed declarations of love and profanity carved into it over the years.

"I will not surrender this classroom to Ho Chi Minh," she declared. She rummaged through my belongings. "I swear by the bridges of Dublin I will find your contraband." And as she finished her oath some of the more adventurous little chocolate drops at the safe end of the room (for though all the nuns seemed to come from Ireland, all the kids seemed to come from Mississippi) met her at the bridges of Dublin and sang out to the end. It sounded like a jam session between an Irish folk singer and the O'Jays. Sister O'Meara was not pleased with the recording, nor did she seem willing to take it—one more time—from the top.

"Silence, you Cretins! Mother above, I'm surrounded by Cretins and communists." She let the top of my desk fall without warning; an old trick she'd used in the past. I pulled my fingers back in time. "Now, Young Wilderson, for the *very last time*, will you stand and pledge and pray with the others."

I looked up at her. An uncertain, "No," frogged its way up my throat.

She changed her tone from ironside to bedside: "Tell Sister O'Meara what it would take for you to stand and pledge and pray?"

"I want Nixon out of Vietnam," I said with all seriousness, as though I was not in homeroom but at the Paris Peace Talks.

Her iron side manner returned, "Is that all?"

"No, that's not all."

"Pray tell, what else?"

"We want all Black men to be exempt from military service."

"Now he speaks for *all* the Cretins!"

"We want an end to exploitation by the demagogic politician and the avaricious businessman."

"Button up!"

We were talking at the same time, now.

"We want Fred Hampton and Mark Clark—"

"—I said button up—"

"—to be alive, again."

"Quiet!"

"We want—"

"I will not tolerate this insolence; you stand and pledge and pray right now!"

I shook my head. My hands were trembling but I shook my head.

"Come with me." I followed her to her big, sprawling desk. "You are the master of your own fate." She pulled out a ruler. "Palm." I held out my hand. "Your right hand, please. Let this pain be a source of divine reflection as you move through the day."

The sound of the ruler smacking my palm snapped against the multi-colored map of forty-eight states that hung over the blackboard; rippled in the taciturn folds of the flag to which I would not pledge; stung the statue of the Virgin Mary gathering dust on her desk. *Don't cry. Revolutionaries don't cry, damnit. Did Che cry when they shot him? Did Bobby Hutton cry when they shot him? Did Fred Hampton cry when they shot him? Don't cry.*

But the sting was so incredible that if water did not fall from my eyes it would surely fall between my legs. Faced with the Hobson's choice of crying in front of the class or peeing in front of the class, my throat choked and sputtered like a spent carburetor. I sniffled and groaned and finally cried.

Seven. She was finished. I stood there unwilling to turn my ruined face to the class. I dragged my nose over my sleeve (to her utter disgust). She looked at the class and they all stood up and faced the Virgin Mary on her desk and the flag that hung above the Virgin.

I went back to my desk. I sat down; *damn your flag.* Recalcitrant to the end. A collective gasp went out. At that moment, for the first time that morning that I can remember, I made eye contact with my sister Fawn. She is pleading with me to stand up. She is tired of the fighting between dad and mom since this sabbatical started. She is tired of all my antics and all the strife and spankings that go along with them. She wants, one night, just one night when there is peace and quiet at home. I ignore her. Sister O'Meara calls me up for seven more lashes. What am I going to do? Perhaps I'm no revolutionary. I can't go through that again, plus more tonight at home. The stinging from the last episode has not subsided. *What have I gotten myself into?*

"Right now, Young Wilderson!"

My hands were pressed to my desk. Was I going to stand up and pledge and pray or was I going to stand up to take, once again, her wrath into my hand? The question will never be answered. For at that moment, Jocelyn Brown, who'd been standing with all the other chocolate drops, waiting for contraband to be discovered, waiting for my lashes to end, waiting for me to stand, that we might all pledge and pray together, sat down and folded her arms.

It was one thing for Sister O'Meara, or Batman, as we call her behind her back, to tear into the flesh of this egoic little Black boy who had more affectations of Whiteness and more arrogance of Blackness than her immigrant baggage could carry; who talked back to her with words and references to events she barely comprehended. It was quite another thing for her to be confronted by the refusal of a little Black girl with whom she watered the marigolds each morning before homeroom; a girl she had hoped would one day convert and become a nun like her.

Sister O'Meara has come undone. The chocolate drops have also come undone but in a different way. She had always thought of Jocelyn Brown as a sponge for her loquacity. She feels the world spinning back on its axis. She tries to utter the word: Jocelyn. Why can't she say this simple word? Now she gathers herself. The word comes out and with the force and authority and the power to beat back all the Cretins in the world. "Jocelyn!" But before anything else transpires, Wolfman sits down too. She leaves the room to find Mussolini.

—◊—

The bell ending homeroom rang. Doors opened. Students poured out like water through sluice gates. The goateed, bell-bottomed guidance counselor yelled down the hall, "Rebecca! Harold! Garland!" Then to me, "The folks I want you to meet."

When they came to us he said, "This is Frank, 'scuse me, Frank B. Wilderson, the third—did I get it right, partner? He's new. Eighth grade like you. And righteous. Transferred here from—where are you from?"

I almost said, St. Mary's Roman Catholic Junior High School, but I saw how beautiful and sophisticated Rebecca Jones looked with her neatly trimmed Afro, her hoop earrings, her yellow miniskirt and sandals with leather straps laced around her ankles. I saw how ready for the get-down Garland Shiloh looked with his cap tilted to the side and his tinted shades; how serious Harold Milton looked with his long blonde hair pulled back in a ponytail, his thick reading glasses, and his button of the flag of North Vietnam. Harold had all the latest books, like *The*

Student as Nigger, in his book bag and, through his mother, who was an academic at UC Berkeley (or "Cal"), he had met many of the authors. No, I thought, we need something more for real than a Roman Catholic junior high school if we was going to run with this posse—*and* get next to Rebecca. So, I said, "I'm from Chi-Town." There was little to no reaction, so I said, "South Side" which was a bit of a stretch. Hyde Park is indeed south of downtown but it is not the ghetto. What the hell, it did the trick. Their eyes lit up.

Rebecca shook my hand and said, "Did you know Chairman Fred?"

"I wouldn't actually say we hung out, but yeah, I knew him. I was all up in it, so you know I had to, like, know him, you know. Me and him was cool, not tight, but cool. He called me Young Wilderson."

"What are Chairman Fred's views on the speech Rennie Davis gave when they bound and gagged Bobby Seale?" Harold asked me.

I couldn't answer.

"What I mean is what are Fred Hampton's views on the White mother-country radicals who are on trial with Bobby Seale? For example, does Hampton put Rennie Davis in the same camp as I would assume he puts David Dellinger, that of a misguided pacifist and, if so, why did he allow Rennie Davis to speak at the rally?"

I looked at this little White dude as though he was talking pig-Latin.

Garland Shiloh said, "You are from Chicago, aren't you? You are hip to the Chicago Conspiracy Trial, I take it?"

They're just jealous. I was trying not to panic. *They see how Rebecca's diggin' on me.* I copped an attitude. I turned on Harold because he seemed an easier mark than Garland.

"Actually, when me and Fred talked about White folks we mainly talked about the Beatles." The joke was a dud. Harold and Garland exchanged glances. The glow was slipping from Rebecca's eyes. They did not think this was either funny or righteous.

"Well," said the tall Black counselor, "perhaps you all should go to first period. What do people have?" Rebecca, Garland, and I said social studies; Harold was on his way to the new math. The counselor told us to hurry along and then left us.

"I never met Fred Hampton," I said, looking down.

"So," Garland sneered from behind his shades, "Fred didn't really call you Young Wilderson." Rebecca told him to shut up, but I could tell I'd be seeing little of her after today.

"Yeah," I said to Harold, "all I know about the conspiracy trial is what I read in *Ramparts.*"

"Did you ever even see Fred Hampton," asked Garland, "I mean you are from Chicago, aren't you?"

"No, I'm not from Chicago; I'm from Minneapolis, Minnesota."

Garland sucked his teeth.

"My dad is on sabbatical and my mom is a graduate student. We lived in Chicago for a few months. I went to a Catholic school where nothing really happened."

They started to move in the direction of class. I followed them, praying for one of those California earthquakes to pull me down and bury me. Speaking more to myself than any of them, I said, "I never even went to hear him speak. The only place I went to was his crib, and even then it was after the pigs had offed him."

They stopped dead in their tracks. They turned around. They gathered around me like Socrates' chosen few. I hardly knew what had happened. They were throwing questions at me left and right. Tell us about the bullet holes. Tell us about the blood. Tell us about the people who waited to get in. Tell us what was said about the investigation. Suddenly, both my memory and my erudition were in vogue again.

Rebecca had a great idea: we would go to social studies and she would tell the teacher that today was no day for all that imperialist nonsense. That instead I would give a lecture to the class about my trip to the home of Fred Hampton. Harold said, screw the new math, would it be alright if he came along too? So, to social studies it was.

Rebecca stood in front of the class and called for a vote—right there in front of the teacher, who didn't reproach her with Sister O'Meara's kind of talk about Cretins, contraband, or communists. For the next twenty minutes I passed off a lot of "ums" and "ahs" and repetitious descriptions as a lecture. No one seemed to mind. Everyone had questions.

The only thing I am ashamed of is that I did not mention Jocelyn in my talk. I was dreaming of my marriage to Rebecca Jones, which I knew would take place in a month, maybe two.

—m—

Garland was the one who introduced me to the Black Panthers in Berkeley. They were a group of brothers who could care less what my name was or where I came from except to tell me that Ellison was a Tom and that I should get with Frantz Fanon. Garland's parents were also righteous. Even though he was under 16, they signed a release allowing him to go through armed struggle training—not just the after-school political lessons that I went to—with the Panthers; something my parents wouldn't have entertained if they were tripping on acid. It was Harold Milton who I had the most consistent contact with. Rebecca had a boyfriend and he was a hundred years more mature than me; she was too busy giving speeches and organizing rallies to take me on as a backdoor man. Garland was always able to stay late at the Panther office, long after it was time for me to go home and we didn't have a lot of classes together. Harold Milton and I had more classes in common (I took the classes the counselors made sure White kids took), and we were both avid chess players. We played chess each morning in the courtyard before homeroom and discussed *Ramparts* magazine articles.

When Rebecca had interrupted the teacher and called for a vote to let me speak, I learned that not only was she superfine and outspoken but she was also the president of the Black Student Union. My crush on her swelled to cosmic proportions. I fantasized walking her home and singing The Originals' song "Baby I'm for Real" to her. Unlike Jocelyn Brown (who was a "good" Methodist girl in a "good" Catholic school, a girl whose network of relations extended no further than the Double Dutch Championship team, her circle of homeroom classmates, and the letters her sister sent her from the front where Civil Rights merged with Black Power), Rebecca Jones was swimming in a sea of adult relations. Rebecca knew women in the Black Panthers. Rebecca knew all the teachers at Willard Junior High and called them by their first names. Rebecca knew the radicals of SDS from the University of California, just six blocks up the street from our school. When Harold asked me about Fred Hampton's views on Rennie Davis, Rebecca not only knew who Rennie Davis was but she knew what Harold was talking about. From time to time, she, Garland, and Harold even invited the Cal student radicals onto Willard's campus. They turned that place inside out and called their teach-ins Anti-Imperialist School and told our teachers they could stay and become part of the solution, or they could go home and be part of the problem. I loved to see her standing on stage next to Harold, who was the president of the People's Student Union, the organization of White kids who did not want to be called "White," and next to the presidents of the Chicano and the Asian Student Unions.

Rebecca would lay it on us: "Nixon is bombing Cambodia, so SDS is dealing on Rot-see [ROTC]!" "Right on!" we'd shout. "And just last year the Indians vamped on Alcatraz and held that shit, you hear me, baby! They took their shit *back* and held it! Said, up against *the wall,* muthafucka, it's a hold up—we come for what's ours!" And when we finished cheering, Rebecca would remind us that the pigs still had our sisters and brothers in the Panthers up against the wall. "But that's okay," she'd say, "you can kill a revolutionary but you can't kill a revolution." I doubt if there was ever a time in US history when junior high school auditoriums rang out with so much political passion; although many of Rebecca's words have faded from memory, I can still close my eyes and feel the shoulder to shoulder sway of all those bodies, young and alive, pressed against mine, I can still see our small fists thrust in the air. And *right on!* still rings in my ears.

Then Harold and Rebecca and the heads of the Chicano and Asian Student Unions would stand shoulder to shoulder in front of the podium and raise their fists high in the air, shouting, "Hell no, we won't go, we won't fight for Texaco! All power to the people!" And then, the obligatory, "Off the pigs!"

Now Rebecca and Harold and the other two are chanting and each thing they say is being drowned out by the din of our cheers; blurred by the vision of our fists reaching up like theirs. We follow them to the exits and into the streets.

A cool breeze from the San Francisco Bay welcomes us as we march from the school. Nothing can stop us. *Tricky Dick, where are your tin soldiers now?* After four or five blocks we get tired of chanting, Hell no we won't go, we won't fight for Texaco! And tired of singing the words to Edwin Starr's "War." And the pigs have not even seen fit to show themselves. *Okay, okay, so it's like that, huh, so it's like that. Y'all think we playing 'cause we're half-sized. Well, we may be half-sized but we ain't half-pint. And just in case you don't believe it...*We break into a run, sprinting up Telegraph Avenue toward the University of California; overturning garbage cans and breaking all the windows we can break without breaking stride. At the corner of Dwight and Telegraph we stop to catch our exhausted little breaths. One of the boys looks up: gasping for breath, his hands on his knees. He sees a Mercedes Benz. No owner in sight. He takes another breath. He straightens his spine. He points. No words are needed. Anarchy descends upon this lone Mercedes. A hundred little munchkins—some with long hair, some with big afros, some in mini-skirts, others in blue jeans—press against the car and rock that bad boy from side to side until *boomshakalaka!* It flips over on its side. Ah shit! Here come the sirens. I start to run, then stop and see that none of these kids are running with me. A young White girl steps up with her bandana. Some other kids step up with matches. The sirens are getting louder, and I am thinking, these Berkeley kids are the real thing. God-damn, nobody's running. Now *whoosh!* The Benz ain't lonely no more: it's got all kinds of fire keeping it company! Garland says, "Didn't that blow your mind, baby!" *Yes,* I am thinking, *it blew my mind.* Flashing red lights are screaming down Telegraph. The sirens damn near drown out our laughter, our cheers, and our primal dance of fire. Garland says, "Hey, Slick, it's time to boogie," but I am transfixed by the fire. *Damn, we did that shit! I've never done nothing like this before. We set it off. This IS Revolution Central.* "Frank," he yells, "we got to hat the fuck up!"

Our retreat is racially choreographed: White kids and the handful of Asians cut through People's Park on their way to the Berkeley hills.

Black kids and the handful of Chicanos head downhill to the Oakland/ Berkeley flats. It's all I can do to keep up with Garland, who holds a junior high track record in the 440. The pigs are only chasing the downhill crowd. They're coming full speed down Dwight, gaining on us. I am losing Garland and losing breath. He turns and yells, "Cut left on the first one-way going right." "Why!" "Just do it!" It's brilliant: the pigs are still in a moment in history when they obey street signs. We are safe on this one-way street (safe until they circle the block). Here the Black kids break up into ones, twos, and threes. Some double back to Telegraph Avenue. Others hide behind dumpsters. Others duck into the foyers of apartment buildings. I follow Garland to a huge dumpster behind an apartment complex. We slide to the ground and catch our breath.

"This was the hippest shit I've ever seen," I tell him. "The way we *all* got away. It's almost like you've done it before."

Garland Shiloh takes a joint from under his cap. He fires it up. He passes it to me. The smoke slips serenely from his lips as he speaks.

"We do it all the time."

I get home high. Sweaty. Exuberant. Late.

Mom looks at dad, his cue to start snarling.

"Where have you been?" He snarls on cue—amazing.

I really, really want to answer him, but baby, let me tell you, Garland's Acapulco Gold ain't in no mood for conversation.

"Well, answer me!"

Gumpy, you fuckin' with my high. I swear, Spiro T. Agnew got more sense than you.

"I asked you a question, Frankie...where were you?"

Frankie? My name ain't Frankie. Is your name Frankie? Why I got to be Frankie. You startin' to sound like Mz. Lemonade over there.

"Are you deaf?" he says.

If you must know, I was out offing pigs, and you can call me Fidel.

"I said, are you deaf!"

"I was...ah...I was," *damn the floor is rollin' like a sailboat. Let me sit my ass down.*

"Stand up and answer my question."

"I was, um, playing…playing basketball."

"I thought football was your sport, since when do you play basketball?"

Since you been a pain in the ass. "I do too play basketball."

"I distinctly recall telling you to walk your sister home from school during the first two weeks you're here."

"Hey, man, like I'm sorry, okay."

"'Hey, man, like I'm *sorry'?* Have you lost your mind?"

I shrug my shoulders, "It's your world, Slick, I'm just one of the squirrels." *Holy fuck, did I just say that? Tell me I didn't just say that.*

"Say what!" He jumps up from his easy chair.

"I said, fine, fine, I'll walk home with her—I'll walk her home tomorrow."

"Boy, you may be in Berkeley, but Berkeley better not get into you. Understand?"

You got it, Smokey. "Yes."

"Yes, *who?*"

"Yes, dad."

He's seated again.

"Get some gumbo."

—∞—

As Jocelyn and I left Hyde Park on the L, I didn't know that SNCC was dying as an organization; that the Voting Rights Act and federally mandated busing had thrust her sister Olivia's organization to the brink of a crisis of purpose. Jocelyn Brown knew all the names of SNCC leaders: Stokely Carmichael, Bernice Reagan, Kathleen Cleaver (who was now a Panther), Julian Bond, Marion Barry, and James Foreman. She knew the songs and she told me she had the pictures, those black and white photos of SNCC demonstrations and meetings, in her room. Looking back on our journey to the house of Fred Hampton's assassination, I have one regret, one biting regret. I wish that I had had the confidence of a grown man and not the shy anxiety of a thirteen-year-old boy; enough forward motion as we stood beneath the columns of bolted steel that held the rambling train above us to draw her close and kiss her. Instead, I asked her if she had change or tokens for the train.

It was music, sweet soul music that saved us from ourselves. It came from within a place that would not have announced itself as anything more than a beauty shop, a barber shop, or a storefront church if not for the speakers clipped to the awning, and the sound of Martha Reeves and the Vandellas painting the sidewalk with watercolor love. In Detroit I'd developed a new theory of evolution. The way I saw it, Berry Gordy created the world. On the first day he made the Temptations, on the second day he made the Supremes, day three it was the Four Tops, then came Smokey, followed by Mary Wells, and when on day six Marvin Gaye stepped out of his cloud, ole Berry stopped for a moment to catch his breath. On the seventh day the world got down.

Jocelyn took my hand and we went inside. A handsome, slender man with conked hair came from the back room and leaned on the counter. A toothpick balanced between his teeth. The sign above him read Jimmy Mack's/45s Back to Back.

She walked over to the register and kissed him on the cheek.

"Hello, uncle Jimmy."

"How you makin', Brown Sugar?"

"Mussolini vamped on me."

"Why my sister sends you to that school—I swear." Then he looked at me and broke into a fifty-two teeth grin that embarrassed us both. "So, when's the wedding, Brown Sugar?"

She gave him a *forget-you* wave of the hand.

He walked to the end of the counter where the Martha Reeves's 45 was scratching round and round in the groove, he lifted the needle.

"Ain't got to be J. Edgar Whoever to see you two in love. Yes indeedy. Son, you gonna marry my niece?"

I almost had a heart attack.

"Don't mind him," she said, "he can be as tired as a two dollar bill. That's what mama says."

"It's a question, son, two dollars or no two dollars."

"You're embarrassing him, uncle Jimmy."

"Embarrassing him. Ain't that a blippty-blop."

He searched the shelf for another 45. He found what he wanted. He kissed the record, then put it on and said, "You two love birds groove on this." It was Martha Reeves and the Vandellas's "My Baby Loves Me," a sultry sure 'nough slow jam.

"Don't you have any Sly Stone?" said Jocelyn

"I said groove to this, lest you want me to keep at your little man here. Go on girl, take Jodie in your arms. He sho' ain't gonna come to you—jes look at him."

"His name is *Frank!* Frank B. Wilderson, the third. And he's from out of town."

Her indignation tickled Jimmy Mack. "You don't mean *the* Frank B. Wilderson, the third? The big time shipping tycoon? *From out of town?* Where you from, boss, New York? L.A.?"

"I'm from Minneapolis, Minnesota," I said proudly.

The toothpick flew from his mouth as he laughed. "And you mad 'cause I called him Jodie."

"He's probably high," Jocelyn whispered, "we'll dance, just humor him."

"But I can't dance," I whispered back.

"Now don't lie, Jodie," he shouted over Martha's searching moans, "You Black ain't you? Then you can dance. What they do up your way, the snowshoe? Go 'head on and do a little snowshoe for me. I swear girl, you gonna marry this fool and have a rhythm-less baby."

She held me and we slow dragged.

"Just ignore him, he talks more shit than a radio," she said softly, "he'll tire out in a minute or two."

"You wish," he called back.

Jocelyn and I held hands on one side and drew each other close around the waists with the other. We moved slowly and easily, as though we'd done this before. The record was reaching a soulful crescendo and all the while Jimmy Mack was leaning on the counter, smiling, chuckling to himself, singing backup, as though Martha Reeves had signed him as the fourth Vandella. When the record stopped, Jimmy Mack told us not to move. We were fine with that. We liked holding each other, and it gave us an excuse to keep holding each other. He put on Etta James's "At Last" so effortlessly you'd think he had it up his sleeve.

We slow danced, lord have mercy, how we slow danced. I took her in my arms, no handholding now. I held her like I'd wanted to hold her under the L. We turned slowly, twining into each other with all the longing we could muster until, *at last*, Etta James called down from heaven and told us to stop.

—⁂—

We didn't walk from *Jimmy Mack's 45s/Back to Back* to Fred Hampton's house, we glided. We soared. We sailed. Once in a while we landed on a runway next to some unknown someone's snow-tapered steps. There we refueled with kisses; hungry, grown-ass kisses. And that unknown someone's grandma raised the window and said, "Stop all that Filthy-McNasty-carrying on! You two ain't grown!"

We were still holding hands chirping like sparrows when we ran up against the backside of a middle-aged couple. The man and the woman turned abruptly. They looked like Mississippians who had fled Jim Crow with one-way tickets on the Illinois Central. The man's face soured as he looked down at us, but the woman smiled discreetly.

He spoke sternly to us.

"You children need to stand in line quietly and wait your turn. This ain't a playground, two men have died inside. Brutally murdered."

I peered around him. We were indeed at the end of a line that was almost a block long. A line running up the stairs and into the building. The whole community had turned up and the icy cold evening was chilled like a wake.

I was not prepared for what I saw inside Fred Hampton's apartment.

I remember a voice ringing in my ear; a distant and incessant voice from across the room, the voice of a young Black Panther explaining to the procession, as it flowed into one room and out the other side, how the pigs had vamped in the wee hours of the morning when the folks inside were asleep; how they came with murder on their minds; how they shot Mark Clark in the heart—through the door he was going to open for them; how they burst in and scrambled over his body with machine guns blazing; how another contingent came up the back stairs across the porch, into the kitchen, then broke into the bedroom and lit the bed up—the bed where Chairman Fred slept with his pregnant wife—lit that sleeping bed up with bullets, like fireworks lighting up the sky.

Did he say that, did he really say they fired into the bed of a sleeping man and a pregnant woman? Tell me he didn't say that. They yanked her from the bed and threw her up against the wall in the kitchen? They went back and shot him in the head? He's dead, did they say, he's good and dead now?

I held Jocelyn's arm and looked around the room where the voice of the guide folded over me like veils of water. I saw the bullet holes: ninety-nine bullet holes, machine gun, shotgun, handgun bullet holes, in the walls, in the door, in the bed, that bloodred bed where Chairman Fred was pronounced "good and dead." *Jocelyn, protect me; protect me from all of this.*

Sensing something frightened and chaotic in my demeanor the sour-faced man from Mississippi touched me and said, "Breathe, just breathe." Then he said, "We got to move into the kitchen, let folks behind us come through." He nodded toward Jocelyn. "You got to protect her."

I looked down and said, "Yes, sir."

I wish I had a different memory of my arrival home that night than the one I have. I wish I remembered telling my parents about Jimmy Mack's jokes and Fred Hampton's blood; about the bullets and the sorrow; about the clamor of the L—but that is not the memory I have.

I enter the flat to find them fierce with worry over my whereabouts and beside themselves with fury over my refusal to pledge allegiance and pray that morning in homeroom. The belt and the yardstick lay on the dining room table like a courtroom exhibit. The rituals of preliminary words begin: the words needed to anoint the moment with enough resolve to commence flogging. Then they set upon me with their

implements. I would like to say that I took the beating in my revolutionary stride: my back straight, my eyes dry, the searing pain on my thighs
and buttocks melting into water and rolling off.

One thing I can say in my defense, however, is that I walked into everyone of those beatings with my eyes open. It could even be said that I
provoked them: I knew that acts of political defiance at school presaged
such evening rituals at the gulags, what some people call "home." And I
was not a passive victim, for I could always find a way to get my licks in.
That evening was no exception.

At last they have finished. They are spent and exhausted, though still
very much upon me. With the belt and the splintered yardstick, they
stalk me to my bedroom. They chant their tired dreary chants. Better
not do this! Better not do that! Better be the first to pledge and the loudest to pray! Better straighten up and fly right!

I stumble before them crying my eyes out, snotty at the beak. My
siblings peek through their cracked doors: political lackeys cowered by
kickbacks of candy, chump change, and Saturday morning cartoons. I
give them the evil eye: state collaborators.

Richard Daley's two goons follow me into my bedroom. My teeth
are chattering. As I sit on the bed I suddenly know how I'm going to get
my licks in. It's been tacked to the wall for weeks, just waiting for me to
wield it as a weapon. As I look at the wall so does my dad.

"What are you signifying?"

It's a photograph from *Life* magazine. A middle-aged Chinese man
about the same age as my father; beside him is a Chinese girl, maybe
three or four years older than me. The man is kneeling. The girl is standing. The *Life* photographer has synchronized the opening and closing of
his shutter with the pull of a trigger, with the plume of flint from the
pistol she holds. She is blowing the man's brains out.

"Play with me if you want to, uh huh, that's right play with me if you
want to," he says.

I am lucid. I look him right in the eye.

"It's a picture from the Cultural Revolution. The man owns a lot of
land. An avaricious businessman. The girl is a member of the Red Guard.

He refused to divide his land with all the people who are poor and need to eat."

My parents are perplexed. They look at the picture and look back at me. They still don't get it. How am I going to get my licks in if the lesson is over their heads? I break it to them gently: "The man is a counterrevolutionary. He's also her father."

Now they get it. They get it big time. Dad's eyes go wild.

"Haven't you had enough?"

I guess not, Slick.

"Do I have to beat the living daylights out of you?"

Go for what you know, Homer.

I stare back at him. Only one of two things can happen here. I will break this stare down. Or I will get more of his rage.

"He's stone crazy," mom intervenes with a clinical observation. "I'm tired, let's go to bed." They make their way to the wardens' quarters. They are no longer upon me.

—⁂—

It was early May in Berkeley. I was in gym class thinking, *Why can't I just lose ten pounds and be normal? I'll never climb that rope to the ceiling.* White T-shirt, dark shorts, and ashy legs. The gym teacher blew his whistle. Three lanky boys raced up the rope to the ceiling. Each of the three columns of eighth grade boys edged closer to the ropes. *And my hands are all sweaty.* In Minneapolis I stayed in shape by playing park board football and little league baseball, but during my father's sabbatical years I'd not been in one place long enough to play sports. The lines were dwindling. My turn was approaching. I was one boy away from triumph or humiliation when I was saved by Richard Milhous Nixon.

A leathery sound was thumping the air outside the gym. All the boys looked up at Garland who had scuttled up the rope like a Marine. What is it? we yelled. He looked out the uppermost windows and yelled, "It's the man! It's the army!" We broke formation and ran out of the gym into the field by the swimming pool. In vain, the gym teacher blew his whistle for us to come back. It's not the army, a boy was yelling, it's the Guard, it's the goddamn National Guard! The sky above was littered with large green crickets; crickets that did not chirp but pounded and lacerated the air—more choppers than I had ever seen, even on the riots on TV. We shouted up at them the way we yelled at the Alameda County sheriffs or the Berkeley police, those Blue Meanies in our daily midst. "Hey, pigs! Fucking pigs! Fly somewhere else, pig!" But they couldn't hear us. The roar of their engines and the thunder of their propellers drowned out our epithets. We looked like patients in a nut house trying to shout at god. Some of them seemed to be laughing at us.

The more ingenious, or experienced, boys among us comprehended our folly and quickly herded us up into a chain of human signifiers. I watched with awe and stunned admiration as these boys pushed and pulled us into two clusters of words written on the field. One read "Fuck you!" and the other read "Off the pigs!" Then one of the boys yelled at me with sharp irritation for not playing my part. He shoved me into place: I was now the dot on the second exclamation mark. Now the Guardsmen in the choppers read us loud and clear.

Ropes unfurled from their large open bellies. The Guardsmen repelled down and took up position. They were no more than twenty feet away. We all got very quiet. "Like Vietnam," I whispered to Garland.

"No," he said. "Like Oakland."

Their commanding officer approached our gym teacher who listened carefully to the terms of surrender. "There's trouble up at Cal," our teacher told us. "The Guard is," he looked at the officer, "commandeering our gym for their base of operations." The boys in the back shouted obscenities. The Guardsmen came toward us with their bayoneted rifles; I am sure I am not the only one who almost fell victim to potty training amnesia as they approached. But they were not coming for us; they were simply pushing past us. They went into the gym and unpacked their gear.

—⁘—

Bells were clanging in the corridors of Willard Junior High. Garland and I could not find Rebecca Jones. Kids ran to and fro like folks evacuating a disaster area. We caught Harold Milton on the fly.

"What's going down," I asked.

"It's Cambodia, Tricky Dick's bombing Cambodia."

Later in the day there'd be a rumor that the Guard had actually killed students in Ohio. Some of the kids would say that fifty had been mowed down with machine guns. Some said it was sniper fire from soldiers on rooftops. The stories were wild and erratic and wrong. The bells stopped ringing and we heard our principal's voice over the loudspeakers telling everyone to go to homeroom and await further instructions. *Shit, forget homeroom.*

"It's on," Garland said, "the shit is on." He and Harold broke into a flat out run. I followed them as the principal's voice persisted. We reached the lockers and they spun their combinations.

"What are you just standing there for?" Harold said. "Open your locker, man."

"What for?"

"The gloves those SDS cats passed out at the teach-in."

Why, I wondered, do we need gloves in May? But later in the day, as I stood on the blood-speckled and debris-strewn cobblestones of Sproul Plaza with the teargas canisters landing all around me, I would understand. I'd see Harold move through the mêlée like a jackrabbit. I'd watch him grab the sizzling canisters with his gloved hand and throw them back at the National Guard.

We left Willard in a mad dash up Telegraph Avenue. I knew what kind of trouble awaited me at home. Stay away from the Black Panther office! Go to class not to teach-ins! And stay away from UC Berkeley! And time after time, day after day, I had ignored their commands and managed to lie my way out of a beating, or at least out of a serious one. But I had a sense that today would be different. If, as Garland said, the shit was really on, then who could say when or if and in what condition I would get home tonight? The students at Cal were really throwing down that day; and the Guard had come to shore up the Berkeley police and the Alameda County sheriffs. And just as the Guard had the pigs' back, we had the students' back.

When we got up to Cal, it was groovy. So groovy we couldn't hardly move. For a moment all we could do was stand at the edge of the fray and watch the technicolor dust-up between the university students and the pigs. But when Harold threw that first teargas canister back, the Blue Meanies spotted us and charged.

We ran up Bancroft toward the ROTC building. Garland had run the other way. Now it was just Harold and I. We cheered as some Cal students set an army truck parked next to the ROTC building on fire. After a while the taste of teargas mixed with the fumes from the burning vehicle felt worse in my lungs than that awful air that blew up to Chicago from the factories of Gary, Indiana. We ran in a wide circle behind Barrows Hall, stopping for a moment to try and break a few windows (but we were too puny or our projectiles were too small—the windows survived our assault) and came out on the north side of Sproul Plaza, by Sather Gate and Strawberry Creek. We were now at the rear guard of the students who were fighting the pigs in pitched battles between Sather Gate and the corner of Telegraph and Bancroft.

And once again, it was groovy; it was like watching the same movie from a different camera angle. Everybody was mixing it up except Harold and me. We just stood there and watched. A cluster of students would catch a Blue Meanie who'd wandered too far from his formation and pelt his ass with rocks, bottles—whatever was at hand. Then his formation would get it together and come to his rescue and the students would scatter. But such scenes of students dominating cops were the exception. For the most part the students were either holding their own or on the run. One of the many things I could not figure out that day was this: How had the National Guard beat Harold, Garland, and me up to Berkeley's campus? When we left them they were still setting up camp in our gym. We had not seen them leave the school nor had we seen them pass and overtake us on Telegraph Avenue. But somehow they were already there.

The Guardsmen were not much older than the students at Cal. In fact, since there were so many graduate students in the fracas, the Guardsmen may have been younger on average. And unlike the Blue Meanies, who swore and shouted and grunted and punched and dragged folks by the hair in their hysterical attempt at crowd control and cultural commentary, the attitude of the National Guard was impossible for me to read. They fought with cold precision. In single file they ran through the demonstrators as though they were going nowhere in particular; their bayonets raised slightly above their helmets. Suddenly, the soldier on point would cut left or cut right and the whole formation would coil behind him. They coiled first into a human snake. Then the snake came full circle as if to bite its tail. When the demonstrators got hip to what had happened it was too late: they were trapped inside a circle of bayonets pointing at them. Three or four Guardsmen would step back a few paces, opening the enclosure like the door of a corral. Through this opening the Blue Meanies entered—their nightsticks raised, their dispositions starved for revenge. When every student was beaten to the ground, the Guardsmen's point man broke formation and the human snake slithered through the Plaza in search of another unsuspecting cluster, while the Blue Meanies dragged those who'd been subdued over the cobblestones to paddy wagons in wait.

Harold and I saw how one or two kids from Willard got trapped inside one of these tail-biting snakes. We also saw how the Guardsmen were standing far enough apart for the kids to slip through their legs and escape before the Blue Meanies entered. That was all we needed.

"Let's go!" said Harold.

We reentered the fray on the assumption that our size made us asswhupping-proof. Two bigger fools had never been born. Once or twice we found ourselves in the Guard's circle and with glee and irreverence we slipped through their legs, leaving the university students to their fate. The Guard didn't block us and the pigs didn't chase us. We were superheroes. No more of that sideline shit for us. We dashed about with gloved hands hurling teargas canisters at the enemy. We soon got tired of being the two stars of the movie, so we went back to the embankment of Strawberry Creek by Sather Gate and gave all the extras some face time in "our" film.

The combat between the students and the pigs was right in front of us. I held up my hand and slapped Harold five.

"'Dare to struggle, dare to win! And if you don't dare to struggle then goddamnit you don't deserve to win!'" I said. "Quotations from chairman Fred Hampton and Rebecca Jones!" I let out a howl.

He gave me back some skin, but coolly.

Then he said: "I've been meaning to talk to you about your subjective deification of Fred Hampton and other Black leaders. Now you even deifying Rebecca Jones. This morning when we were playing chess, you jumped out of a really subjective bag."

"What are you talking about?"

"These people aren't gods, Frank, they're people, okay? Just people. Yes, I think the Panthers are the vanguard—like Huey P. Newton says, it's historically correct. But my mom's a sociologist and one time after a Panther rally, she said that the problem with Black movements is the emotionalism. Mom says it's not objective." He shook his blonde locks.

"Well, I've read the same books you have—maybe more. My dad's a psychologist and my mom's a grad student. So, I know all that."

"You don't act like you know it."

"I do, too! *You* don't act like you know it."

"Can we speak rationally? How can I be guilty of Black political emotionalism? And, Rebecca Jones? In the same sentence with Fred Hampton? It's bad enough hero-worshipping Hampton but—"

"What's wrong with her, she's a Black leader."

"And I'm a White leader—though I prefer another word, a 'people's leader.' That's not the point."

"You're just jealous of her."

"Of *Rebecca Jones?* Please. I'm the one who turned her on to Mao."

"I'm not listening to you."

"Ask her. Go and ask her. I've known her since first grade. Ask her if she knew who Mao was last year in seventh grade. Ask her, When was she elected president of the BSU—*just this year!* And who turned her on to Mao? Who gave her Mao's *Little Red Book* and told her 'You need to read this if you're going to be a Black leader, this is what the Panthers are reading?' It was me, okay?"

I turned away from him. I was hurt and speechless, but I didn't know why. I watched the students getting their heads beat in and tried to ignore him.

"We can't communicate if you're going to be defensive," he said. "I'm trying to offer what my mom calls constructive criticism and—"

"And my ass. Okay? And my ass."

"This isn't working."

"You worship Tom Hayden *and* Rennie Davis."

"That's absurd. I recognize them as—"

"Tom Hayden spent all night in the fucking park at the Chicago Convention wondering whether you people should take it to the pigs or wait for the pigs to take it to you. What was he waiting for, a sign from god? The pigs had just beat Rennie Davis unconscious—un-fucking-conscious and Hayden's just—"

"We discussed this last week: I told you, Hayden found himself in coalition with David Dellinger who my mom says is a pacifist. Hayden had agreed to Dellinger's terms. *Before the shit went down in the park.* At least get your facts right. Eventually, Hayden and his people *did* take it to the pigs; it just took him a while to—"

"You all take a while, don't you."

"That's racist."

"So."

The smell of tear gas and the sound and pageantry of boots in hot pursuit of sandals and sneakers seemed to move in slow motion. The only thing in real time was my rage and my mounting sense of inadequacy.

I wish I'd had the presence of mind to say, How dare you and your mother comment on what a Black person feels about Black leaders or anything else. Where was your mama when Medgar Evers died? Your mama made you, but Medgar Evers and Fannie Lou Hamer made your mama. The only time in history when you people can get it together and form your little People's Student Union or your little People's Park is when this country spills the blood of the Fannie's and the Medgar's, when Black folks are on the move. Without us you would crumble in the face of anything more taxing than a primary. And sometimes you can't even handle that. But I said none of this. It was only a feeling then.

From Sproul Plaza to California Hall all the way out to Bancroft and Telegraph, the fight unfolded before us. What more was said that day between Harold and me is not clear to me. What I do recall is one minute feeling criticized and inadequate and then the next minute losing touch with my surroundings.

A sharp pain bites into my ribs. My vision turns to vapor. A world of sound rushes into my head and I am once again aware of the teargas and the din of the mêlée

I am falling backwards. As I tumble, I see above me the hulking silhouette of the National Guardsman who has hit me—with what, I do not know. But he hits me again, or perhaps it was just a shove with the butt of his rifle. My heels can no longer hold me. I roll down the embankment, thrashing through the thickets, and land at the edge of Strawberry Creek.

The misty air at the bottom of the hill was soothing on my face. It was dark down there, cool and quiet. I had fallen into another realm where there was no turmoil, no Blue Meanies, no National Guard. The pain in my ribs and in my gut was subsiding, as were my sense of shock and the feeling of humiliation. Scratched and grass stained from the fall, I crawled on all fours and whined, not for Mao but for mommy. A few feet away from me was a young woman wearing a peasant dress and a tie-died T-shirt. Her arms were all scratched up and her face and eyes were puffy from teargas. She was bending down to the creek, dabbing her bandana into the cool water, raising it to her eyes for relief. I recognized her as an agitator, one of the SDSers who came to our school and conducted anti-imperialist teach-ins. I remember thinking, *Oh shit, I better get away before she sees me.* I was close to her but she was damn near blind from the gas. I didn't think she'd seen me. I stood up and looked around for a link of stones dry enough to hop across the creek on. On the other side I would scale the northern embankment of Strawberry

Creek that ascended to Wheeler Hall. I would rise on the far side of the fight and run north and east to the science and technology buildings, where nothing was going down, and run home in a gratuitously wide arc from Hearst Street to Shattuck Avenue to Adeline where we lived. I'd had enough of the Revolution for one day. As I started to cross, I felt her firm grip on my shoulder.

"Hey kid," she said, turning me to face her, "don't you go to Willard?"

"Yeah," I said, wondering why I didn't just plead the Fifth.

"Ever heard the saying, 'You can't fight city hall?'"

Wow, teargas must give you brain damage.

"Well, speak up: you ever heard that expression?"

Man, we got to boogie; this chick is stone crazy.

"Well, yeah, I guess. Everybody's heard it."

"That's right kid, everybody's heard it! All our lives we've heard, *you can't fight fucking city hall!*"

I looked up the south slope of Strawberry Creek and saw rocks flying and feet running. I could not decide which was worse, to be up there with the violence or to be down here, alone with Ms. Loony Tunes. She wiped her eyes and face one last time. She wrung out all the excess water. She tied the bandana around her hair.

"All our lives, kid!" She was on the verge of tears.

Yeah, well, this is my bus stop, lady. I started to leave. She grabbed me again.

"I can't dig it, kid. And you can't dig it either, can you?"

"No," I politely shook my shoulder from her fist. "I can't dig it."

She leaned her face, pink and puffy from the gas, into mine. She looked around. "And you know who put that shit out on the street, kid?"

"I never really thought about—"

"City Hall!" she screamed, "City Hall! That's who put it out on the street." She grabbed me by the hand, "And I can't dig it," she pulled me behind her up the south slope, "and you can't dig it either, kid." She was older than me and her fit of temporary insanity made her stronger than me. I bounced uphill behind her like a rag doll. "Now's let's you and me get back up there and kick some ass!"

As soon as we broached the crest of the hill, however, and she relaxed her grip and plunged into battle, I slid back down the embankment, with my ass as a sled. I scurried across the creek—to hell with dry stones, I ran through the water—and up the other side.

When I got home dad, mom, Fawn, little sister Amy, and baby brother Wayne were seated in the living room/dining room area. The entire attention of the room was focused on my mother. Her face was as puffy from teargas as Ms. Loony Tunes's. Wayne kept trying to find a spot on mom's lap but she was too consumed with her misery to cradle him. The smell of fried onions and pork chops wafted from the kitchen. Dad had all but forgotten his culinary creation. He held a cold damp cloth to mom's eyes while Fawn and Amy stood beside her like failed bodyguards. Everyone stared at me like I was the murderer at the end of a long whodunit.

Dad said, "Where have you been?"

I couldn't remember how the lie I'd planned to tell went. Then I realized I hadn't planned a lie. It had all happened so fast: the helicopters, the Guard, the news of Nixon and Cambodia, the mad dash to the locker and then to Cal, the spat with Harold, then the encounter with Loony Tunes. *I don't have a line for him.*

"I asked you a question."

"I...I was playing basketball."

"On a wet court made of dirt and grass?"

Damn, man, I thought psychologists were the trusting and forgiving types.

We oscillated between his interrogation and my half-ass lies. He told me he'd better not hear I was up at Cal, he'd better not, he'd better not!

Right, Slick, I heard you the first time.

Mom takes a hit off her nebulizer. She says she almost died up there. "What with my asthma and the teargas and those crazy hippies." *They're not hippies, mom, why can't you get it straight?* "I was trying to leave my French class in Dwinelle Hall. I was going to Telegraph for fish and chips—can't stand that dirty old street, why I went that way I don't even know." Mom is talking through her tears.

As she spoke it was steadily and terrifyingly setting in on me how close she and I had come to each other that day. When she stopped crying I asked her, with as much caution and feigned disinterest as my pounding heart could fake, "So, ah, you were on Bancroft and Telegraph, mom?"

She looked at me curiously, "I didn't say anything about Bancroft."

"Yeah," dad echoed, "she didn't say anything about Bancroft."

"Well, uh, she said Sproul Plaza, and Sproul Plaza comes out where Telegraph meets Bancroft."

"You sure know a lot about a place you don't go to," he said.

Mom went on to describe the beginning of the demonstration-turned-mêlée from her side of the terrain. The students stockpiling rocks and projectiles as they gathered like storm clouds; the football helmets and hard hats that they passed around; the impromptu speeches damning Nixon and his war, telling ROTC to get off campus; how she pushed through the crowd only to find herself face to face with the police and the National Guard; how she tried to move east along Bancroft, moving uphill from Telegraph, hoping to circle round the combat zone and get home safely. But there she was, stuck at the corner of Bowditch and Bancroft.

You stand there staring at her with your mouth open. What shocks you is the realization that, through the smoke of burning army vehicles, through the mass of the crowds, amid the militarized crunch of concrete beneath the shoes of the sheriffs and the boots of the Guard, you and your mother had approached—almost met—each other. Your outstretched hands had nearly touched hers in the haze of tear gas, the bark of bullhorns, the din of breaking glass. At Bancroft and Telegraph you had passed each other. And you stood in the same crowd on Bancroft and Bowditch. And when a bomb went off in the building above, the same downpour of crushed glass had showered you both. We are there, my mother and I, a most unlikely pair, in the same spot, at the same time, beneath the same windows of the same building when...

"...a bomb exploded," you and she say, simultaneously.

"What did you say?" Dad breaks my trance.

"Nothing. I mean, I was asking: Did a bomb explode? It just doesn't sound right."

"Are you contradicting me?" mom asks. *That was close, better to call her a liar than to tell her I was there too.*

"No, I'm just asking."

"Look at this! Just look at this." She puts her nebulizer down on the table next to crystals of crushed glass. "All that came from my hair. A wonder it didn't get into my eyes. A wonder I'm not blind."

Instinctively, you run your fingers through your naps in search of broken glass. They think you've lost your mind.

—⁂—

Ten days after Harold lost me to the boot and rifle butt of a National Guardsman, Black students were murdered at Jackson State in Mississippi, when police shot into the windows of a coed dormitory. I remember thinking, How could they shoot at girls? The day after the shooting, I found Harold Milton where we'd met every morning since I came from Chicago and spoke in social studies about the murder of Fred Hampton. He was seated at a table on the cool stone tiles in the shade of the outdoor corridor. Our chessboard was just the way we'd left it the day before. He was studying it.

"You're late," he said, "We only have ten minutes before the bell."

I sat down in disbelief.

"Last night they shot some more college kids," I said, "this time it was in Mississippi. Rebecca's gone to the auditorium; she's mobilizing the Black kids." He kept studying the board. "I was looking for you," I said, "that's why I'm late."

"Why were you looking for me, this is where we meet."

"Why aren't you mobilizing the People's Student Union? Rebecca's calling on the BSU to strike. She wants to get down like we did for Cambodia. She's got a list of demands."

"Cambodia was different."

I asked him what he meant by that; as far as I could see the pigs had killed people in Cambodia, they had killed people at Kent State, and now they had killed people in Jackson, Mississippi. It's all the same: the People vs. the Pigs.

"Cambodia was like, well, like a universal thing, man. My mom says people got down all over the world behind it. But what went down at Jackson State...well, that's like a special interests happening."

"Well, fine." I sat down, feeling completely defeated. He knew so much more about the world than I did. His mother was a radical and she talked to him, explained things to him, and encouraged him politically. I couldn't compete with that. Then I stood up and said that I was going to the auditorium to listen to Rebecca speak and that after that the Black Student Union, the Brown Student Union, and the Yellow Student Union were going up to Cal and we were going to say, Stick 'em up muthafucka, this is a hold up, we come for what's ours. But he was holding all the pins, and he used one to take the last bit of air out of my balloon.

"You'll be wasting your time; they're not on strike at Cal."

I was stunned. I was shaken. But above all I felt betrayed. I didn't dare call him a liar, because the one thing he always had straight were his facts.

The auditorium was desperately free of the masses of kids from the People's Student Union. I had never had such a visceral understanding of the term "minority" as I had on that day in a large room with so few of Harold's flock about. Rebecca was on stage giving a speech. We cheered her on. We raised our fists. We left school and went out into the streets. We chanted and cursed as we marched up Telegraph Avenue. I would like to remember us as two hundred strong, but we may have been less than forty. We arrived at the campus on the edge of Sproul Plaza hoping to find the campus in the throes of hand-to-hand combat as it had been ten days ago. But the air was so calm we could hear the fountain gurgling and no teargas clouded our eyes. We dispersed under the weight of our embarrassment.

"Where are they?" I remember saying to myself. Rebecca heard me. But she was too livid too speak.

"Are we just a special interest?" I asked her.

"Who said that?"

"Harold."

She let out a short sharp laugh. She was silent a moment. "C'mon," she said.

We walked to the top of Bancroft Avenue, where it ends at Piedmont; where one can see the bridges and the sparkling water as the sun pours crushed glass into the bay. She brought me to UC Berkeley's Greek Amphitheater. No one manned the gates or the ticket windows. We walked right in. As we entered we heard the high-pitched trilling of a woman singing folk songs. There they were, university students who just ten days ago had fought the pigs and dragged me up the hill to fight "City Hall." They were holding hands and singing songs.

"How did you know?" I asked her.

She surveyed them with contempt.

"One day it's armed struggle, the next day it's folk songs," she said. "Then it's summer break and home to mommy and daddy. 'Special interests.' When it's them, it's 'war;' when it's us it's 'special interests.'"

We walked down the hill to the Berkeley/Oakland flats. Somewhere near Shattuck and Ashby we parted. We hadn't held hands. There was no Martha Reeves music to send us on our way. Gone were the hungry, grown-ass kisses that I'd tasted in December. And when I got home, no one asked me where I'd been.

—⁂—

It would be a lie to say that Jocelyn Brown and I planned the next day's civil disobedience against Batman (Sister O'Meara) and Mussolini (the Reverend Mother). We hadn't even dreamt of it. I was too sad and morose from last night's beating to have planned anything.

Outside in the schoolyard I stood alone, pushing small mounds of snow along a ledge. When Jocelyn came she told me how she had gone home to her mother's hot cocoa and a long evening chat about Jimmy Mack's teasing and Fred Hampton's crib. Then she'd gone upstairs and written a letter to Olivia before she went to bed.

"What happened when you got home?" she asked.

I turned away from her and kept to my industry of snowballs. The bell for homeroom rang. She kissed me. Right there on the playground, she kissed me.

Batman held her rosary in one hand and with her other hand she fondly patted her chocolate drops as they entered. Both she and the flag seemed weary from yesterday's fracas. She greeted us by our surnames, as was her custom. "Good morning, Miss Grant. Brisk day isn't it, Mr. Jackson? Mr. Jefferson. Miss Cooper and Miss Washington." Our names were not names at all, but fungible clusters of hand-worn bills and forgotten occupations. She prattled on as she might on any sunny day crossing the bridges of Dublin, as though nothing had happened in yesterday's homeroom. "Aha! Miss Wilderson, good morning to you. And where is Young Wilderson this morning?" *Take off your mask, Batman, you see me at the end of the line.* "There you are! With the unsinkable Molly Brown." "My name is Jocelyn." "Just an expression, dear girl. Like the bridges of Dublin, just an expression. We missed you this morning, the flowers and me." We are all inside; seated and accounted for. She closes the door. She stands in front of us.

"Let us stand, children, for the pledge and a prayer." We might have all stood that day—even me, for I had no desire to have my hand crushed in the door and my thighs lashed again at home. But she had greeted us with such smug amnesia: as though nothing had happened yesterday, as though we had not even the power to disturb her sleep. "First, the pledge of allegiance." *I am not standing. Am I alone? No, to my right, Jocelyn is not standing either. And to my left, down the row a bit, Wolfman is seated and folding his arms.* So it begins.

"Three Cretins, have we? Same three as yesterday. It's the pledge of allegiance or it's the Reverend Mother. That goes for you too, Jocelyn." Everyone is standing but the three of us.

Sister O'Meara faces the flag and places her hand over her heart.

"I had better hear three chairs scraping the floor or I'm out that door again." She begins: "I pledge allegiance to the flag of the United States..." but the chorus of voices normally in lockstep with her is faltering. Now chairs *can* be heard scraping the floor but they are not the chairs of the three Cretins under review. Batman spins around and to her horror my sister Fawn is sitting down. Then Jackson sits down. And Washington and Jefferson take their seats, as do both the Grants. The founding fathers have lost their patriotism. Soon the whole class is seated.

"So be it," Batman declares. She leaves the room. The sea of black faces rolls from Wolfman to Jocelyn to me, each wave asking what now... what now? Presently, through the frosted pane of the classroom door, we see Batman and Mussolini conferring. As soon as they enter Mussolini gives us the coup de grace while Batman looks on. She reminds us that god and country are the pillars of a Roman Catholic education; that if we wanted to protest we should have gone to the University of Chicago high school or to Kenwood, the public school where disruption is part of the esprit de corps. But here we start the day with the pledge of allegiance and with a prayer to all-mighty god. Now, stand up this instant!

No one rises. No one speaks. The stillness and the silence are so tremendous that we can hear things we've never heard before: the vibrations of old, loose windows in the wind; the clanking of radiators gathering steam, their slow, malevolent hiss.

"Who speaks for this mutiny?" says Mussolini.

The class tries not to look at Jocelyn, Wolfman, or me. They are not trying hard enough.

"Mr. Reilly," she says to Wolfman, "do you really wish to sully your mother's name?"

Wolfman has neither the tools nor the temperament to tell her to stop driving a wedge between him and the rest of us. He looks at her the way he looked at that eleventh grader in October, right before he laid him out. Her gaze now turns to Jocelyn.

"One would think our conversation yesterday about limited financial resources—remember?—and deserving pupils would have given you pause." She glances around the room, "It should give many of us pause."

Jocelyn doesn't flinch.

Now Mussolini looks at me. She smiles.

"I spoke with Dr. Wilderson and your mother this morning. Apparently, the three of you had a—how shall I put it—a *session* last night. Am I correct? Not the kind of session one wants to repeat, now is it?"

I hate you! I fucking hate you! I am choking and trying not to cry.

She tells us to stand. "Let's try this again."

From my dry quivering mouth come words limp and pathetic—like the creaking of a door or the squeak of a rodent. "How come we never get to talk about anything important in homeroom?" *Don't cry, you idiot, don't be a fucking namby-pamby.*

"I beg your pardon."

"We always have to do what *she* wants to do," I thrust my finger at Batman.

"She is Sister O'Meara. *She* is the teacher."

"Yeah, but—"

"No buts, Young Wilderson."

I feel like I could cry any minute. I'm so embarrassed that the class knows I was beaten last night.

"Fred Hampton was shot and killed right here in Chicago and people are dying every day in Vietnam and *she* says we can't talk about it in homeroom, but we have to pledge and pray and, and, and it's not fair! We have rights too, you know." The tears are starting to spill. I don't know what I just said but I wish I could have said it better, the way Wolfman would've said it—with force and authority; or the way Jocelyn would have said it—with Olivia's anecdotes to back her up. The Reverend Mother rejoins, but I am too deaf to hear her.

Jocelyn says, "Stop talking down to him. Mark Clark and chairman Fred Hampton were murdered by," she takes a deep breath, then she crosses the Rubicon, "by the pigs!" Mussolini recoils and Batman stares with disbelief at her little flower protégé. "The ruthless, Gestapo pigs!" The kids are howling and cheering. Now Jocelyn points to me, "And you call him 'Young Wilderson' just to put him down. *His* name ain't 'Young Wilderson,' his name is Frank. And what you did yesterday to their hands, that was torture, that's what my sister calls it, torture—

like they torture the Freedom Riders down South. You're torturing us and we're just kids. How'd you like it if we tortured you?"

"That's quite enough young lady."

"You're not my mother."

"I can call your mother."

"Then call her. And that flag up there—that flag made us slaves, you don't even care 'cause you don't care about us."

We're all nodding at Jocelyn. Somebody says, "amen." Batman and Mussolini are on the ropes. Batman wants Mussolini to do something, fix this thing, quick. But they're out of ammo. The Reverend Mother exits the room. Sister O'Meara follows her.

Wolfman yells, "Long live Il Duce!" Our laughter shakes the walls.

THE MOTH

From the outside
       looking in
           a frantic moth
               seeks entry
before the wind
       chills
          what's left of its life.
In lieu of raising the sill
          I pick up this pen
             and write this poem.
The moth dies.

9

On Sunday I'll be thirty-seven. Sunday is also Easter. Christ will rise and I'll be thirty-seven. There's a parable there...somewhere. I can't write today...

Khanya was calling me to breakfast. I closed my diary and went to the kitchen. Reba, Doreen, and Khanya were seated at the breakfast table. Reba was in her school uniform. She looked like a poster child for private education. Doreen was a young woman who'd had as many jobs as a woman twice her age. Her eyes didn't shine. I felt that she took our offers to pay for her to take secretarial courses as some sort of trick to lay her off. It had taken her a long time to respond with any sort of interest.

Khanya's face was radiant and alive. Gone were the days of that haggard and tense look which she'd worn all through law school. I sat down and kissed her passionately.

Reba patted Doreen on the side of her arm as though trying to revive her from sleep. "See what they're doing, *ous* Doreen?"

Doreen ignored her. She had a habit of ignoring Khanya and me, as well, which made being her employer somewhat unnerving. But things were good now. Now that Khanya and I both had steady work the night belonged to us again, as it had when we lived in New York. We had money to go out dining, dancing, or to the rare film worth seeing. Our love life was almost as magical as it was when we lived in New York: nights of jazz in the Village; an evening at the art deco Angelica cinema where they served pastries and espresso and screened foreign films and the classics; that little Jamaican supper club where they served the best jerk chicken, just a hop and a skip from where we lived. We called it "our secret kitchen." Though we couldn't re-create New York in Jo'burg, we now, at least, had the money to make the Jo'burg nights our own.

Reba pointed to a rose that sat in a glass of water on the breakfast table. "Where did that come from?" she asked, like an SS interrogator in a late-night movie. Unlike Christmas or Easter, the renewal of our romance was no holiday for Reba. That morning's breakfast was the first time she'd seen us in the last twenty-four hours.

The night before, Khanya had called me from the office of one of the clients of her NGO, and said, "I'd like to start celebrating your birthday early." Her voice was inviting.

"How early is early?" I said.

"I'm finished here. What's it like on your end?"

I was sitting in my office at Vista University in Soweto with a stack of essays that I'd promised to grade by Monday. There's always tomorrow, I thought, and opened the bottom drawer.

"What did you have in mind?" I asked.

"I'll tell you in person." she said, and I could feel her warm embrace reaching through the wires.

I laughed and closed the papers into the drawer. "I should have a birthday every day."

"I'm at a client's office near Hillbrow," she said, "should we meet somewhere there?"

"The Café Zurich?" I kidded.

"No," she said, flatly. We hadn't been back to the Café Zurich since the catastrophe of our first date four years ago. Then she said, "What about the place where we first met, when you told me you were a big shot from New York."

"Very funny."

"I'll meet you at Kippies."

Within an hour I was standing in the square at the Market Theatre, the square where I'd first seen her four years ago at the crafts fair.
There'd been a brief thunderstorm in Jo'burg, and the cobblestones
were wet and glistened in the afternoon sun as though they'd been polished by hand. Bree Street ran along one side of the square. Along the
left side of the square was the Market Theatre itself and the Museum of
Africa, both under one roof that once was a large warehouse. Directly
across from the Theatre and Museum was a restaurant that catered to
late night patrons of the arts and occasional stockbrokers who stayed too
long in their offices near the Stock Exchange, four blocks over, on Diagonal Street. At the far end of the square, straight on from Bree Street,
was Kippies, a jazz nightclub Khanya and I used to frequent in the early
months of our romance when I was a researcher flush with American
dollars. We used to boast that we were the only two people in the world
who could say they'd seen Hugh Masekela at the Village Vanguard in
New York on Thursday and caught the same show at Kippies in Johannesburg the following Friday. It's a wonder our friends could stand us.

She was waiting at a corner table, on which a candle and two White
Russians rested.

"It's happy hour," she explained with an unabashed grin, when I eyed
her two glasses.

"I see."

"And it ends in twenty minutes," she warned.

"Then I'd better order *two* rum and cokes."

"Sounds like a plan, professor."

The bandstand was empty, save a drum set with no drummer, a few
speakers hunkered down like rocks in a quarry, and three lonely micro-
phones rising up like reeds. I got two rums and one coke—I could only
manage three glasses in two hands as I walked back across the club—
and returned. She handed me a red rose and said happy birthday and
kissed me. Reba would eye that same rose warily the next morning at the
breakfast table.

"I thought we'd see a play," she said, "but there's a film festival at the Market Theatre."

"Even better."

We finished our drinks and left. We laced our arms around each other's waist as we walked, or stumbled, across the square to the Market Theatre.

"Have you had one too many miss?" I said in the tone of a highway patrolman.

"These roads are worse than in the location, officer." *Location* being a common word for township.

"They're cobblestones," I said, through a hiccup.

"What's a cobble-stone?"

"It's a stone of cobble!"

"No wonder you're in higher education."

For some inebriated reason we hadn't seen the poster by the front door announcing that evening's film. When the queue had finally pulled us up to the ticket counter I hiccupped again and asked the bored sales clerk for the name of the film. She looked at me the way one normally looks at a drunk.

"I have a right to know what I'm paying my money for, don't I?" I said, as she drew back from my rummy breath. There was no plate glass between her and me, only bars like the old-fashioned ticket windows of country train stations.

"Husbands and Wives," she said, "by Woody—"

But Khanya and I were already laughing, deep in the throes of our own private joke. Woody Allen had been one of the staples of our late night cinema sojourns to Tribeca when we lived in Harlem.

"I take it you want tickets?" she asked, vacantly. She was a young African woman, a little younger than Khanya, with a noticeable amount of eye makeup. Probably an actress trying to make some extra money, I thought. She looked at me as though she'd seen me before, as though she'd smelled my breath before; some director, perhaps, who wouldn't cast her but wanted to play, nonetheless.

"You did this on purpose," I said, to Khanya, and tickled her on the side of her waist for we were still coiled around each other. Khanya writhed and pulled away from me. She held up a scout's honor hand.

"No, I promise you."

"This must be a really big decision for the two of you," the ticket clerk said. "But there are people behind you who have settled the issue." I was too drunk to be insulted.

"Can our marriage survive an evening with Woody Allen?" I asked Khanya.

The woman in the booth sucked her teeth and looked heavenward. I fished about for some bills.

"The management doesn't cater to patrons under the influence," she said.

"Ha!" I replied with another blast of rum breath. "She's calling us drunkards."

"I'm stating the policy and you're taking up a lot of time."

Khanya took the money from my hand and counted it out.

"You're five bob short," the woman snorted.

"I'm sorry, sisi," said Khanya, and forked over the proper change. "He's nervous," Khanya confided, "It's our first date."

"Thought you were married," the woman said counting out the change.

"Don't be ridiculous," said Khanya.

Luckily for us *Husbands and Wives* was a comedy, for we were in a laughing mood. But the people seated near us weren't so lucky. Our giddy mood held on, even through the serious parts. After the film we crossed the cobblestones and shared a roast duck, a baked potato, broccoli, a Caesar's salad, and a bottle of merlot. One plate. One fork. One glass. We took turns feeding each other. Finally, the waiter asked us to settle the bill, "But take your time—no rush." Then, having taken our time, as invited, the manager informed us of the waiter's long journey home. We weren't too tipsy to take a hint.

It was late, but not too late for a kombi. And although we had to wait a long time for it to fill with people and go, we didn't mind. We disembarked on Rocky Street in Yeoville, a good ten blocks from where we lived. It was a perfect night for walking and we wanted to savor it. The street was so quiet one could hear water rippling in the municipal pool on the other side of the wall. We stopped in front of a jewelry store. Shop windows have a warmth about them when they are dark and empty, free of the vulgarity of commerce. It's as though a black velvet curtain was dropped just behind the display window; there's only you and the one you love reflected in the glass and the gems on display smiling up at you. Then we passed a jazz club as it was closing and the last patrons trickled out into the street.

At the corner of Rocky Street and De La Rey we turned and started the uphill climb to our house. De La Rey is a strange little border street that runs along a ridge where several incongruities converge. West of De La Rey is Yeoville, with its tidy bungalows and modest apartments. North and east of it are the brazen mansions of Bellevue East and Observatory, with their hardwood floors imported at the turn of the century from the forests of California, Oregon, and Washington; the first homes of founding industrialists, mining magnates, and colonial lawyers. Later, in the twentieth century, there were notable, but rarely mentioned aberrations to this pristine pattern: for example, after handing the command of MK to Chris Hani, Joe Slovo retired and quietly passed away in Observatory; and Gandhi lived there when he practiced law.

Halfway up the hill we paused. The sky was thick with stars.

"We never saw this many stars when we lived in New York," said Khanya. "Not even in summer, when we'd sit and talk all night beside Grant's tomb."

"There's no sky like the African sky."

She took my hand. "It's too early to go inside," she said, "I'm enjoying being out here with you."

So we turned onto Gill Street. Crickets hummed in the night. Behind us, to the west, the faint sounds of Rocky Street were dying. Ahead of us, darkness settled in the walnut trees and the slumbering English estates. We wandered to the old Union Observatory. Its front door was locked, and its doomed eye above was closed to the heavens.

We walked around to the back of the observatory and settled on stairs of concrete and moss. "Are you happy here?" she asked. She was still looking up at the stars.

"I'm hopeful here," I said.

"Those aren't all stars, you know," she said, still looking up. "Some are satellites. American. French. British. Soviet. What do we call them now, Russians?"

"It'll be a while before the dust settles. Post-Soviets, I guess." I surveyed the sky. The lattice of light looked like sugar spilled on a dark counter. "I imagine everyone has satellites up there."

"Except Africans," she said.

"Yes, except Africans."

"The West could have prevented the genocide in Rwanda."

"How so?"

"Think of all those countries looking down as the genocide was beginning. Taking pictures. Watching. Pretending not to know. Why don't they care about us?"

"I don't know," I said.

"What was the name of that song by War you used to sing?"

"'The World Is a Ghetto.'"

"Yes, the world is a ghetto."

"I was just singing."

She tapped my forehead playfully with her forefinger. "You were being honest." Then she sighed. "I'm hopeful too but we've lost so much ground. When I read all the euphemisms in the press about the 'New' South Africa..." her voice trailed off. "When you first came here—I mean came here to stay—you said everyday was worse than the day before."

"I was joking."

"You weren't joking. It's alright. You've lasted two years here. I only lasted seven months in New York." She put her arm around me and drew herself closer to me. "I'm glad you're hopeful now."

"One day we'll move down the street into one of those mansions."

She laughed at this.

"Why not?" I said. "And I'll be the only Black American to vote for Mandela in the first election of the 'New' Republic. But we'll ride out a few drab years of neoliberal compromise in our Observatory mansion."

"*Our* neo-liberal compromise," she laughed.

"Let me finish the story my dear. Ride out his neo-liberal compromise in our Observatory mansion until his term is over and it's time to elect Chris Hani."

She laughed even more.

"Sounds like a perfectly good plan to me," I protested.

"Chris Hani will subdivide these mansions and move poor people into them. We'll be lucky to keep our corner of the fourplex."

"It's a huge corner, honey."

"They won't let Hani become state president. It's like a dream I used to have when I was a little girl in Attridgeville. I'd seen some Afrikaners with a movie camera taking home movies of their children and I wanted a movie camera. All I could dream of was a camera that would take home movies of me. I never told my parents. I thought if I said anything I'd put a curse on the dream; that speaking my dream would kill it. I know it doesn't make sense but I was a little girl."

"They know that we want Hani. Mandela knows. Mbeki knows. De Klerk knows. Tony Leon knows. Eugene Terre Blanche, Bill Clinton, and the CIA know. It's no secret. But they can't stop it. He could win tomorrow if he ran against Mandela." I hugged her. "You'll get that movie camera."

When we got home, I was still a little unfocused from happy hour at Kippies and the wine at dinner. I kept trying to open the door with the key to my office. Khanya hardly noticed. She was in her own little world, laughing about a scene she'd suddenly remembered from *Husbands and Wives*, in which Liam Neeson is performing cunnilingus on Judy Davis who—not aroused in the least—is musing on the names of her friends and imagining that they are not people at all but hedgehogs and foxes.

I was creating such a racket rattling the door with the wrong key and Khanya was chuckling so openly at her memory of the film that we woke Doreen. She let us in. Only when she switched on the porch light did I see that the key I was holding was the key to my office at the university. Doreen looked at us reproachfully and reminded us that Reba was not only sleeping but had school in the morning. Then, with the ornate grace of a martyr, she informed us that we hadn't called to say we weren't coming home and that she'd had to fix rice and beans while we had no doubt gone out to eat. I left a message on the machine, Khanya snapped, and there's plenty of meat in the freezer. But Doreen was a consummate Luddite who didn't trifle with answering machines. We escaped into our bedroom.

"God," I sighed, with my back pressed to the door, as the sandpaper scorn of Doreen's slippers scraped down the hall, "who works for whom around here? And why does she slide everywhere she goes? Don't they lift their feet in her village?"

Khanya pinned me gently to the door.

"Doreen has skipped the few drab years of Mandela's neoliberal compromise," she said. "As far as she's concerned, Chris Hani is already state president."

"But we haven't even voted for Mandela yet." I was kissing her neck. "One must go through a capitalist reformation before one—"

"Darling, Doreen doesn't seem to care," she said, with her lips on mine.

"Maybe we should rethink the revolution."

"Tomorrow," she said, "we'll rethink it tomorrow."

The next morning, I didn't know if kissing Khanya as passionately at the breakfast table as I had kissed her last night was an act of love toward her or an act of defiance in the face of all the attitude I was getting from Reba. I busied myself with the pouring of orange juice and the buttering of toast. Reba stared at me, that infernal, unblinking stare of hers, as unfathomable as water, in which nothing can be read.

Pay her no mind. We're going to have a pleasant morning. Yes, a pleasant morning. We won't let the little people hurt us.

Now she was tap-tap-tapping her oatmeal with the back of her spoon as though beating an insect to death.

I looked at her. "We are married, you know. We can kiss at the table and behave ambiguously if it suits us." *Don't explain yourself to her. Who's in charge here?*

"What time did you get home last night?" Reba said.

"Excuse me?" I asked.

"Ous Doreen said you came home late and woke her up."

"Well," I turned to Doreen, "I apologize, Doreen."

If Reba's forte was staring, Doreen's was not looking at you at all. She nodded, without looking at me, as if to say, apology accepted, just don't let it happen again. *Of all the cheek*, I thought. *Who pays the bills around here?*

"Ous Doreen said you were both drunk."

I shot Doreen a sharp look.

"I doubt very seriously if Doreen said anything of the kind."

Doreen got up from the table and cleared her dishes and a few other things and brought them to the sink. Khanya shot a few short bursts of Setswana in Doreen's direction, but Doreen kept her back to us as she washed the dishes.

"Reba, stop playing with your food," said Khanya. *She's not playing with her food, she's beating our brains out.* "You'll miss your bus," she said. Then she rose, grabbed her briefcase and kissed everyone except Doreen. In a more modulated but no less authoritative Setswana than a moment ago, Khanya gave Doreen instructions for the day. Then, in English, she gave me a thumbnail translation of what she'd said, seeing as how I would be the noncommissioned officer in her absence. She reminded me that it was Friday; Doreen was washing rugs and linen today and needed to get started because she was going home for Easter. It was my day to walk Reba to the bus stop. Reba and I considered each other warily as Khanya disappeared through the swinging door.

She was back all of a sudden. "Frank, we said eight tonight. It's late for dinner. But your Black expats—what's their name?"

"The Coopers," I said, "from Northwestern—or is it the University of Chicago?" I'd written it in a file I'd begun on them for Stimela and had forgotten it instantly.

"Well, they want to make it for eight. They're going on a tour bus through Soweto," she said, rolling her eyes.

"You're not going out again tonight are you!" Reba said in a high plaintive voice. *The children of lovers are orphans.*

Khanya told Reba that the Coopers of Chicago were coming for dinner, along with Naledi, who was bringing her new boyfriend for us to "look over."

"It's for daddy's birthday," she added, apologetically.

"His birthday's on Sunday," said Reba.

Some delicate words of appeasement were offered...and refused.

"Easter's on Sunday," Reba said, "what are we doing on Easter?"

We agreed to think of something nice, but not now; the hour of the bus was drawing nigh and Khanya was late for work. As Khanya left I told her I'd be home for most of the day but I'd have to go to Soweto at some point to get the papers that I forgot at the office. They're to be graded by Monday, I explained. She frowned and blew me a kiss. As Doreen tidied up, I counted out change for Reba's milk money and money for peanuts.

"No sweets," I said, "Is that clear?"

She said she wanted to buy potato chips today instead of peanuts.

"Too high in cholesterol," I objected.

She said that Khanya had said she could. There was no foolproof test for perjury as far as this statement was concerned. Khanya was down the hill by now and Doreen has never been a witness for the prosecution. I said "alright" for lack of evidence.

While Reba went to get her jacket and books I made her lunch and packed her lunchbox. She came back ready to go.

"Where are your books? Reba, this is the third day in a row."

"I left them at the office," she said

From over by the sink I could hear Doreen laughing under her breath.

Reba was testy and irritable as we walked to the bus. School wasn't her favorite pastime. Her teacher complained about her short attention span and the way her behavior interfered with other kids. As we walked

I tried to explain the importance of bringing one's books home and of minding one's teacher. She kept straggling behind me and threatened to report me to Khanya if I didn't slow down.

"What's a Black expat?" she asked as she hopped on one leg then two, now one again, over an imaginary hopscotch.

"A what?"

"Mommy said your 'Black expats' are coming to dinner."

"Oh. Yes. People who got lost twice." I laughed alone at my private joke.

"What happened the first time they got lost?"

"They were slaves. That was hundreds of years ago"

"I know what a slave is!"

"Really," I said, perking up, "are you learning that in school? They never taught me about it until—"

"Not in school."

"Where?"

"Ous Doreen says she's a slave."

"Did she, now."

"Yep. 'I may as well be their slave!'"

"You and Doreen sure find a lot to talk about."

"Uh-huh."

"When you should be sleeping."

She looked at me wide-eyed and guiltily—as though she'd been framed.

"Bet you don't know the name of this tree," she said, changing the subject.

"It's a slave tree. Didn't Doreen tell you?"

"Seriously."

"It's a pepper tree. You would know that too," I said, swooping down for the coup de grace, "if you brought your books home."

She turned up her nose and walked on ahead of me. I was going to make a comment on her newfound capacity to hasten, but thought it better to stick to the subject of books and reading. After all, I was winning.

"I know these things, not because I'm smarter than you, Reba. I'm not. But because I read. I'm always reading." I showed her the book that I'd taken from the shelf before we left home. "See this? *Das Kapital.* I first read this book when I was twelve years old. Know how much of it I understood back then?" She kept walking ahead with her back to me, not responding. "Not one word. But year after year I kept at it. Then, a Black Panther gave me Frantz Fanon's *The Wretched of the Earth* when I was almost fourteen. And I read that too. I still didn't understand much. But I kept reading it, year after year. And now I can even teach these books. See, I'm always reading, Reba. You should always have a book nearby. That's what my parents used to say to me. I've told you this before."

"Over and over and over."

"Well...it hasn't sunk in. Now, you asked about trees."

She started half-singing, half-humming to drown me out.

"Quiet please. I'm going to tell you. Johannesburg stands on high-veld grassland, where there're no naturally occurring trees."

"Ha!" she said, spinning round and walking backwards, "There's trees everywhere in Jo'burg."

"Very observant," I said, holding up my finger. "But they weren't always here. Do you know how they got here?" She didn't respond. She was walking ahead, again, with her back to me. "Do you know how I know how they got here?" Still no answer. "Fair enough, I won't hold you in suspense: I know because I *read.* That's how I know. My knowledge is attained vicariously, through the written word. The English and the Afrikaners planted over a million trees: acorn, oak and walnut from the Cape; fruit trees from...from..."

"Thought you knew everything."

"The point is there were no trees here. They planted one million trees. Now, there are six million trees in Jo'burg. I'm not an apologist for colonial expansion, mind you. That's not the point of this little exercise. In fact, I'm against it. What I'm saying is that *reading* is essential. And you can't read if you don't bring your books home. And if you don't read you won't become an intellectual."

We'd reached the bus shelter with its sloping roof and its three wood-paneled sides protecting the little bench from the elements in all but one direction.

"I don't wanna be an intellectual."

I was startled by the finality of her assertion. It was as though she'd said she had no more use for air and would breathe water from now on.

"Don't want to be an intellectual? Then what on earth do you want to be?"

"Rich."

"Rich! That's not a vocation, it's an affliction."

"Well, it's what I wanna be."

"I'm going to pretend you didn't say that. No, better yet—I'm going to address it. Dialectically—with this book here. Marx. Someone you should read, given your aspirations. Ah, here's just the passage we need: 'It remains in his mind as something more than a particular use-value.' That is to say, the chump change the worker earns is believed (by the worker) to be something other than chump change. Marx is going to elaborate the ruse of this debilitating fantasy. For 'it is the worker himself who converts the money into whatever use-values he desires; it is he who buys commodities as he wishes and, as the *owner of money*, as the buyer of goods, *he stands in precisely the same relationship to the sellers of goods as any other buyer.*' So, he—or in your case, she—thinks. Emphasis mine, by the way. But Marx is saying that this is all an illusion: there's still the daily intensification of work and the parasitical extraction of surplus value—blood sucked right from the worker's veins. Marx is saying that money, even lots of money, a decent wage, only acclimatizes the worker to the problem—makes him a fool of the capitalist."

She responded with stony silence. I replied to her silence with silence of my own. The silence of reading. She placed her lunch box on her lap. She looked straight ahead at the street. After a minute or two she turned and stared at me. I tried to concentrate on *Das Kapital*, but it was impossible. I found myself reading first the same paragraph over again, then the same sentence, then I was backtracking over words. But I was determined not to give her the satisfaction of disturbing me; determined not to turn and look at her.

Finally, she spoke. It was her dulcet voice. Her please, will you buy me some chips voice. Her please, may I go out to play voice. Her daddy I love you voice.

"Fuck you son of a bitch," she said, sweetly.

"Say what!" I almost leapt off the bench. I looked at her large unblinking almond eyes; eyes that had charmed her grandparents' dos and don'ts into dust when she lived with them. "What did you say to me?!"

"Fuck—you—son of a bitch."

"Have you lost your mind?"

The orange school bus pulled up to the curb and sighed to a stop.

"I'm doing what you told me."

"Doing what I told you?"

"Being an intellectual."

The doors opened and the little demons inside called to her like she was a rock star.

I suddenly realized that when Khanya and I got married it had been my idea to put a moratorium on corporeal punishment. *What was I thinking?*

"Don't mess with me, little girl."

"You said, 'Reba, you must always be reading, or you won't be an intellectual.'" She grabbed her lunch box and put one foot on the stairs.

"I know what I said!" I grabbed her arm. "Explain yourself!"

"I was reading."

"Reading what!"

She pointed to the wooden panel of the bus shelter. Years of illicit communiqués were carved into it. Jim is a puff. Henrietta loves Jules. Mpo's number is four double two nine five. The name of a school mascot or a pet. And there, next to where my profile must have run parallel with the panel, was scrawled "Fuck you son of a bitch." I was stumped and discombobulated. She shook free of me and got on the bus.

"When I don't read, you say, 'Reba, you must read,'" she said, looking down on me from her perch beside the driver. "When I do read, you say, 'Reba, you mustn't read.'" The door creaked closed. I could have sworn she was laughing.

—◊◊—

Khanya had wanted to make a curry dish with paper-thin leaves of silver, like they served at Elaine's on Rocky Street. But I had insisted on demonstrating the culinary talents I'd acquired by watching the legion of Zulu sous-chefs at work in Luigi's kitchen. I'd been gone from Luigi's a year and a half. A year and a half since a White man slapped me into next week. It seemed like a lifetime ago.

It was an odd sort of gathering. Reba and Doreen sat at the table in the center of our coliseum-sized kitchen. The rose from our night out was still there. Doreen, having already eaten, drudged through her task of seeing to it that Reba finished eating without a million distractions and got off to bed. This was a task no one would envy. Like the Great Houdini, Reba knew a thousand ways to slip the noose of bedtime. In the corner, by the pantry we'd converted into an office, sat Naledi and her new boyfriend, Tembisa, who she'd brought for Khanya and I to "look over," a young man who'd played professional soccer for one of the township teams like Moroka Swallows. He'd been involved in an accident (that he was reticent to talk about). It had kept him in hospital long enough for him to lose his spot in the line up. Now he was looking for work. Naledi was looking smart and prosperous, having come directly from court in her business jacket and skirt. Her leather satchel, common to solicitors marching through the halls of the Supreme Court on Prichard and Van Brandis Streets, lay on the floor beside her. Naledi and Tembisa were both twenty-six years old; the same age as Khanya. I wondered how long a love affair between a Wits-educated solicitor and a washed out footballer could last.

Harold and Gloria Cooper were standing by the window overlooking the fire escape. They said they were more comfortable standing. They weren't really expatriates, but researchers over on a spring break visit. They were in their late forties and had children in their late teens, one who'd started college last September.

And there was Khanya, whose NGO still worked with Naledi on a case they'd first encountered when they were in law school. The clients consisted of an entire Motswana village that had refused incorporation into the homeland of Bophuthatswana in July of 1989, a day or two after Khanya and I first met at the Market Theater square. With their bare hands, the villagers had killed two policemen who'd tried to break up their rally. More than three years later, the case was still in the courts.

And there was me: trying desperately to direct the conversation while trying to remember how to make Luigi's famous Italian (Zulu) sauce at the same time. I'll be thirty-seven years old on Easter Sunday, I thought; is this where I was meant to end up, teaching at university in Soweto, working in the shadows with Stimela's people, making pasta for two lawyers, a jock, and two expats at the edge of Johannesburg?

Such a range of professions might have been common at any time in Black South African social circles, but such a range of ages was not. When I first arrived, Black South Africans tended to socialize horizontally along age lines. But the revolution, the joy of upending the world and making it anew, had drawn zigzag lines across many long established patterns. The pattern of horizontal association may have also applied to Indians and Coloureds, but I did not know any of them outside of ANC political settings. The curious thing about being a Black American in South Africa in the 1980s and early 1990s was this: one could be "adopted," so to speak, and with great ease, by any one of the Black communities, Zulu, Xhosa, Tswana, Sotho, Pedi, Venda, Tsonga, or even Coloured, simply by falling in love with someone of those communities. One could not, however, fall in love with a White or an Indian and be adopted by either of those communities. But the others were porous enough to enter and be made to feel (reasonably) welcome. (There would always be grumbling from in-laws, however—"he's not a real African.") The catch, however, was that once the Black American "landed" somewhere, he would have to stay there—no sliding from Tswana to Tsonga, for example, and certainly no sliding back and forth between Zulu and Xhosa. If one married a Coloured woman, then one's network of relations would forevermore be Coloured. If, as in my case, one married a Setswana woman, then one's network of relations would remain among the Setswana, with extensions to the other Sotho language derivative groups. But it would take conscious strokes against one's set pattern to develop a sphere of, say, Zulu or Coloured intimates. Some things in South Africa still hadn't changed, even with the revolution.

But the revolution had elaborated a new nomenclature, epitomized in the word "comrade," one that intervened in age relations. This little word had smoothed some of the rough spots on the generational playing field. The word could inoculate a gathering, such as ours that evening, against the awkward scrambling for prefixes: Mrs., Mr., sir, bra (brother), sisi (sister), ous, or uncle, when Tembisa, Khanya, or Naledi—all in their twenties—addressed the Coopers, who were in their forties. And, if the wine flowed generously, even "comrade" could be dropped, for everyone knew it was implied.

I watched Reba as she played with her food, playing her wait-out-the-bedtime game, and with burning irritation I recalled our tête-à-tête that morning. *She* didn't need a word like "comrade" to level the playing field. But the revolution had yet to usher in any such nomenclature that would level the playing field between a six-year-old child and her thirty-seven-year-old stepfather.

Harold Cooper was a tall man who'd played forward on a Big Ten basketball team, "Before all this slam dunkin' and showboatin'," he said, "we played as a team; not five hotshots trying to look pretty."

Like my parents, Harold and Gloria taught psychology at a university and worked as psychologists for a holdover organization from Johnson's Great Society—like the Job Corps or the Urban League. They'd met in grad school. They were in South Africa to "find a project" and go back and write up "a great proposal" which would allow them to return with a grant for an extended stay. *That's how I ended up here.*

We'd relaxed our no smoking in the house policy with Harold (an offer I would never have extended to Zach) if he'd agreed to hold his

Sherlock Holmes pipe out the window with one hand and blow his smoke out the window as well. Gloria kept him company by "this big lonely window," as she put it. She said she liked the aroma. I thought she was lying only because I seemed to recognize both of them. They were who I was when I first arrived: anxious. Scared. Jet lagged. Desperately bonding over idiosyncrasies they would have quarreled over at home, for no other reason than to feel grounded and secure.

Harold pointed out the window with the stem of his pipe. "There's a woman washing clothes outside your garage. And will ya look at that! There're people living—there're people coming out of....Which one of those garages are yours?"

"None of them," I said, as I diced chilies and sprinkled them into the skillet.

"Not too many," Khanya said to me. She turned to Harold and Gloria. "We eat a lot of Indian food here, so we're used to spicy food. But I've been to your Midwest—not much in the way of spicy food there. You have a lot of cheese if I remember."

"That's Wisconsin," said Gloria. "Next door to Illinois. But make it as spicy as you want. We're here to experience life as it's lived," she said boldly.

"What's going on down *there?*" Harold said, still looking out the window.

"Yes," said Gloria, "what are those people doing?"

It must have seemed like we were trying to evade the subject, for I kept tending to arrabiata sauce and Khanya continued to wash vegetables in the sink. Between us we only had one good ear for the conversation and Naledi couldn't answer, for this was the first time she'd come for dinner since we moved from our tiny flat in Braamfontein.

Naledi and Tembisa went over to the window. "They live there," said Naledi, hesitantly, "isn't that right Khanya?"

"What? Oh...yes, they live there."

Gloria shook her head, sadly. "How can people live in a garage?"

"They're Zulus," said Naledi, with a cavalier wave of her hand.

"Natal cockroaches," said Tembisa, as though he'd provided not an ethnic slur, but a scientific explanation.

"Isn't that derogatory?" said Gloria. It wasn't a question.

Harold puffed on his pipe and observed us all, as though we were anthropological subjects who'd just performed a rare tribal custom that he would now ask for permission to record. "Interesting. Very interesting. That's what we're here for, the nitty and the gritty."

There was a certain dissonance in the room that no one seemed able to interpret. Khanya, Naledi, and Tembisa had no idea that these two Black Americans were, in a manner of speaking, treating them—and not just the Zulu squatters below—as research specimens; it wasn't the kind of thing the three of them could get grant money for and go to the US and do. Harold and Gloria would probably never be *their* specimens. But they seemed to have a disconcerting awareness of being observed without knowing to what end. I was wondering how the hell I would write any kind of report on Harold and Gloria—a report that Oupa would not needle me about—if this conversation derailed onto what was and was not politically correct speech. To make matters even worse, Tembisa's "Natal cockroach" had tickled Reba's funny bone and Gloria was looking at me with that, don't-you-teach-your-child-right-from-wrong look.

Gloria, this morning this little girl looked me in the eye and called me a son-of-a-bitch and told me to fuck off. Then, an all-child jury acquitted her. No jail time. No community service. And I received no victim's compensation. Nothing. The law's on her side.

Doreen, who was not a trained meteorologist but who could always predict foul weather, got up and left the kitchen.

"Well," said Gloria to Tembisa, "isn't what you said derogatory?"

Revolution or no revolution, Tembisa didn't take kindly to being corrected by a woman. He may have been a beneficiary of the revolution, but he was still a jock at heart.

"You know what a cockroach is, don't you?" he said.

"Interesting," Harold puffed intently, "very interesting."

"I grew up with cockroaches on the South Side of Chicago," Gloria announced, almost proudly.

Reba had chimed in. "Not with these cockroaches you didn't. They'll kill you if you wear an ANC T-shirt."

Where the hell is Doreen!

My anxiety level went off the radar screen. Anything could happen between Tembisa and Gloria. And we didn't need Reba thrown in as a wild card. The sooner she got to bed the sooner I'd be able to manage the conversation.

"Finish your food and eat, Reba," I said.

But Reba had already been inducted as Tembisa's lecture associate. "If you wear a T-shirt," she jabbed the air with her fork, "they will kill you with pangas. Zulus don't have good listening skills."

"Now, why is that?" Harold asked her, delighted to have found another uninhibited specimen for his research.

"Don't encourage her, Harold," I told him, "she has a penchant for exaggeration. Finish and eat."

"How can I finish *and* eat?"

"The child does have a point," said Naledi.

"I always have a point," said Reba.

A conspiracy was brewing all around me. I could feel it.

"Reba, you know what I mean."

"I'm still not satisfied with your explanation," said Gloria to Tembisa, like a deaconess of the AME Baptist Church admonishing a deacon on the misappropriation of funds. "Why do you call them cockroaches?"

Woman, will you puh-leez quit! Can't you see he doesn't give a rat's ass how he sounds? He's not political. He's not even rational.

"Go ahead, Tembisa, give it to us straight," said Harold, "the nitty and the gritty."

"They leave KwaZulu-Natal. They travel to Jo'burg. Live twenty in a room. First it was Hillbrow. Then it was Yeoville. Now they're here in Bellevue East. They're like roaches."

"Twenty in a room, aren't you exaggerating?" asked Gloria.

"Let the man talk, honey," Harold nibbled on his pipe stem, "let the man talk."

"He is exaggerating," I chuckled, but the panic in my voice made me a far less credible witness than Tembisa. *I've lost track of the timing for the pasta. How long has the water been boiling? How long has the sauce been simmering?*

Reba tapped her glass with her fork in an attempt to quiet the room. "Didn't anybody hear me when I said they kill you for wearing a T-shirt?" She was pouting. A bad sign indeed. Her *pap* stood like a mound of cold white clay on her plate. She had hardly touched her chicken leg.

"I heard you, baby," Naledi cooed, "You're absolutely right."

I peered angrily around the stove and snapped at Naledi. "You're a solicitor, for crying out loud. There's no chain of causality in that! The rules of evidence don't allow you to say, 'Your honor, my client was wearing an ANC T-shirt and the Zulus don't like these T-shirts.' You know as well as I that there are complex political dynamics at play here."

"I'm not in court," Naledi responded.

"Yeah," said Reba, "can't you see she's in the kitchen?"

Everyone was amused, everyone but me.

"This death for wearing a T-shirt logic is the kind of sensationalism the Western media thrives on," I said. "We can't send two Americans home thinking comrades like us really believe that—that that marks causality for us."

"I don't care what they think," said Tembisa. "I know what I know."

"Yeah," said Reba, "we know what we know."

Harold stroked his beard and clenched his unlit pipe between his teeth. Interesting, I could hear that brain of his, very interesting.

As Naledi, Tembisa, and the Coopers carried on the conversation among themselves, I whispered to Khanya.

"Can't you do something with her? Call Doreen."

"Doreen's listening to her soap operas on the radio."

"I don't give a—"

"Shhh," she whispered.

Tembisa offered the Coopers another trinket of fideism, at which Harold yelled over to the stove and sink where Khanya and I were.

"This is what we came here for," he roared. "You don't hear this on NPR—or even on Pacifica."

"Ethnic tensions," Gloria nodded. "You haven't been away so long, have you, Frank, to have forgotten that we even have them back home? Mama never forgave me for marrying a man as black as Harold." Harold fidgeted uncomfortably, as his skin tone was projected on to the wall for all to look at, but then he eased back into his open-minded anthropological self. "Every time I gave birth, here's mama at the hospital with a brown paper bag. Puttin' it right next to the child's face—can't even see yet, let alone walk or speak. Damn near had to admit *her* to the hospital when Harold Jr. was born and came out two shades darker than the bag. Blamed Li'l Harold's color on Big Harold."

"Still does," her husband mused. He tapped the tobacco from his pipe on the outer ledge of the window. He started to fill it again, but stopped. Something in his wife's story had made him not feel like smoking anymore. He looked straight at us. "I gather you and Khanya think Naledi and Tembisa are selling us a bill of goods? Lot of anti-Zulu propaganda. But if what li'l Reba here says about the T-shirts is even half-way true?"

"It's all true!" Reba cried.

"And a little child shall lead you!" Gloria cried, like she'd just been sanctified. She winked at Reba. *Don't do that, please, don't do that; don't encourage her.*

"Now, Frank," said Harold, sitting down for the first time all evening, turning a chair back to front and straddling it. "If they're coming all the way from Natal to the Transvaal for jobs, equal opportunity, or to avoid persecution in their own province, that's one thing. I doubt even ole Tembisa here would have a problem with that." Tembisa gave him neither a yea nor a nay. "But if they comin' here for devilment, well that's something else entirely."

"It's complicated, Harold," I said. *Dinner must be ruined. The penne looks like night crawlers.*

Harold beckoned toward the window. "Ya'll got four garages down there. All strung out under one roof. Now, I've seen a helluva lot of folks coming and going since that woman started washing clothes. Helluva lot for a four-car garage."

"For any garage, honey," said Gloria, "no one should live in a garage.

"Let me ask you this," said Harold, "How many folks actually live down there?"

Khanya stopped tossing the salad and looked to me for an answer. But I was looking to her for one. We didn't know how many people lived down there. We didn't even know their names.

"Sixty-five!" Reba chimed in.

"*Sixty-five?*" said Gloria, as though she would faint.

"Sixty-five," repeated Harold, shaking his head, "hmm, hmm, hmm."

"And a little child shall lead you." Gloria looked lovingly at Reba, then reproachfully at Khanya and me.

"Or maybe fifty-five," said Reba, beginning to doubt her credentials as demographer.

"This is preposterous!" I crossed to the kitchen door. "There are not sixty-five, or even fifty-five people down there." I pushed it open and yelled down the hall: "Doreen!"

"We don't know exactly how many people are there," Khanya told the Coopers apologetically, "they're a transient population."

"Like I said," Tembisa sipped his drink like a man who'd just won a bet, "Natal cockroaches."

"Frank," Khanya said, "Doreen's listening to her soaps."

"Doreeeen!" *Soap or no soap, she better come get this tokoloshe.*

"Reba," said Khanya, "it's well past your bedtime."

"Why?" said Reba. "There's no school tomorrow."

"But there *are* ethnic tensions here?" ask Gloria Cooper. "You would admit that wouldn't you—and it has become violent, hasn't it? Perhaps we should make a study of *this,*" she said to Harold, who nodded enthusiastically.

"Tembisa," said Harold, "think we could interview you—on tape I mean?" My heart sank.

"There are always ethnic tensions," Khanya interjected, before Tembisa could answer, "but this violence is not caused by ethnic tensions. It's state-sponsored violence."

"But doesn't each individual have to take responsibility for his or her own actions?" Gloria asked.

"A long history of collective struggle," said Khanya, growing testy, "has helped us mature, politically. We're not seduced by the cult of individualism that runs rampant in the US. I lived in New York."

Gloria raised an eyebrow.

"Interesting," said Harold, his gaze roamed the room from Khanya to Tembisa to Naledi to me, "very interesting."

"If you want to know where the violence is coming from, Gloria," said Khanya tapping on the counter with a tossing utensil, "I suggest you dig a little deeper than individual responsibility, or 'ethnic' rivalry or T-shirt murders. I wouldn't go to Compton and come home with a report that people shoot each other over the colors red and blue. If you want to interview someone, interview F. W. de Klerk. He's the most violent person in the country. I'd start with him if I were you."

"*Uh-uhhhh,*" Reba was shaking her head. "My teacher says president de Klerk is a man of peace. She said he got a gold star by his name for being good. That's what Miss Draper said."

"It was the Nobel award," I said, hustling over to the table where she sat, "not a gold star by his name."

"Miss Draper said it was a gold star for being good."

"Miss Draper's a fool," I said.

Reba gasped. Her mouth hung open in disbelief. "You called my teacher a fool?"

"Ah...no...that's not what I meant."

"I'm telling her when we get back from Easter."

"Reba," said Khanya, "what's said in the house, stays in the house. Understood?"

Reba didn't answer her.

Where the hell is Doreen?

"I wouldn't be able to sleep one night with those people living behind my house," said Tembisa.

Tembisa, please, shut up!

"Alright, Tembisa," I said, "what's your solution?"

"Run them out," he said, wildly. Harold and Gloria looked at each other as though they'd just put the finishing touches on a winning grant proposal. Yep, their gluttonous eyes flashed, we've got a live one here.

"Run them out, where?" I said.

"Anywhere."

"Back where they came," Reba offered.

"Reba, hush!" I said. "I mean it."

Khanya tried to reason with Tembisa. "The Zulus down there don't carry pangas or knobkieries. They don't fly IFP flags or wear its colors. They're just ordinary people who happen to be Zulu and have nowhere to go."

"You *like* Zulus?" Naledi asked her.

"I didn't say I like them. I didn't say I dislike them. Sure, they can be chauvinistic. And they want a federated New South Africa; I want a unified state. They're patriarchal—okay. And they can be—"

"Homicidal," said Tembisa

"They're not genetically predisposed to murder," said Khanya.

"They are." Tembisa was furious. He was shaking with anger.

"No they're not," said Khanya, "no more so than anyone else."

Tembisa rose to his feet. He was in such a state of agitation that I wondered how long he could remain standing—or what he intended to do.

"There's no such thing as a homicidal chromosome," laughed Khanya. She walked over to the window. "Look at them. They're *ordinary* people."

"They looked like ordinary people when my train reached Nancefield Station," said Tembisa, "but when we got off, they were killers."

"What are you talking about?" I asked.

He pushed his sleeve all the way up to his shoulder. There was a long gauze bandage that stretched from just below his shoulder to just above his elbow.

"Tembisa," Naledi said, softly. She wanted him to stop now. But he ripped the bandage off. Someone gasped. Then, all was silent and still. One could tell that it had been a deep gash and that it had sliced his muscle open and possibly severed a tendon. It may have cut clear to the bone.

"They're more on his back," Naledi said. "His football career is over. For a long time he wasn't able to sit up straight or lie on his back." She tried not to look at his arm. She didn't want to be reminded how close he came to death. Finally, she made an attempt to put the bandage back on, but he gently pushed her hand away.

Khanya and I were at a complete loss for words, as were the Coopers. Finally, Harold ventured forth. "How did it happen, son?"

Tembisa told us how he'd taken the train from Johannesburg Station at Noord Street to Nancefield Station in Soweto. How there had been no incidents in the shunting yards where the trains often slowed down and became more vulnerable to attack. By the time the train reached Nancefield Station everyone was relaxed. "We weren't even thinking about Zulus," he said, cutting me a look, as if to say, I've earned the right to say "Zulu" instead of "IFP," or "cockroach" instead of "human being," if I damn well please. They disembarked and from out of nowhere, from behind the kiosks, from under the benches, from inside the station waiting room, who knows, he said, they sprang up out of thin air, and bludgeoned us with knobkierries and hacked at us with their pangas.

"How did you escape?" Harold asked.

"I outran them. Others weren't so lucky."

So transfixed was I on Tembisa and his wound that I hadn't seen Reba climb down from her chair. She nudged her way into our cluster. She looked up at me and said, "Told you. He was probably wearing a T-shirt."

"Come with me." I turned her around by the shoulders. "Now." I marched her to the door.

"I haven't finished eating," she protested.

"Doreen'll come get your food, you'll finish in your room."

She stonewalled at the door. "I haven't said goodnight to everyone."

I turned her around. "Say goodnight."

"From way over here?"

"From way over here."

"Goodnight," she surrendered. They all waved goodnight to her and turned back to Tembisa.

I knocked on the bedroom door while keeping one hand on Reba's shoulder, lest she try to bolt. There was no answer. The radio was chattering away but it wasn't so loud that my knock couldn't be heard. "Doreen," I said. Still nothing. Gingerly, I pushed open the door. Doreen lay on the bottom bunk, her head on the pillow, a tiny transistor radio propped up against the wall beside her. Someone in radio land had probably just received a much-deserved comeuppance for Doreen broke out into laughter. It was strange, I'd never seen her laugh before. I wasn't charmed by the fact that her laughter coincided with my arrival.

"Can you turn that down for a moment, please?" She eyed me but did not turn it down. I told her to see that Reba brushed her teeth, put her pajamas on, and went to bed. If she *really* wanted to eat, then Doreen was to come into the kitchen and get the rest of her food. Under no circumstances was she to allow Reba to—I almost said "invade"—return to our dinner party. Khanya would be in shortly to kiss her goodnight. Doreen nodded without lifting her head from the pillow.

Whatever transpired in my absence from the kitchen was enough to nullify once and for all any political explanation for the violence that Khanya and I were trying to assert. I told Tembisa how sorry I was for his having been assaulted. *The arrabiata sauce looks like death warmed over.* With one hand I reached for the colander and with my other grabbed the pot of hot water and penne from the stove.

"Careful," said Khanya, as the hot steam rose up from the pot.

At that instant, Reba reappeared through the swinging door in her lions-and-tigers pajamas, dangling a teddy bear in one hand. "I'm back."

I was livid. "Reba!"

"What darling pj's," said Gloria, as though she'd just looked up the word 'darling' in the dictionary and found Reba's photograph there, "come here cutie-pie, give your auntie Gloria some sugar."

"Gloria," I said, "please, don't encourage her. This could go on all night. Reba, it's past your bedtime."

"But I have a question," she pleaded.

"Then ask Doreen."

"Ous Doreen said I must ask you."

I began straining hot water through the colander. "Be quick."

"What were you doing this morning?"

"This morning?" I balanced the pot of hot water and penne on the edge of the sink. "This morning? It's Friday, I walked you to the bus. And don't think I've forgotten what you said."

"Nooo. *Before* that."

"Before that I made your lunch. Before that I ate breakfast. Before that I was writing in my journal. (Trying to write in my journal.) Before that you were sleeping. Which is what you should be doing right now."

I hoisted the pot and resumed pouring the hot water and pasta into a colander.

"I mean before *that*, when I peeped in your bedroom—"

"Peeped in my room?"

"—and you had your head between mommy's legs and she—"

"Reba!" Khanya shrieked, as the pot fell onto the counter and scalding water and penne splashed everywhere including my hand. I yelped in pain. Khanya lunged at Reba, trying to cover her mouth—

"—wasn't sleeping—"

—but sound kept escaping from it as she pushed through the door—

"—so don't say she was *sleeping*," she yelled, her voice disappearing down the hall.

I held my hand under the faucet and ran cold water over it. I could feel Tembisa, Naledi, and the Coopers shifting behind me, trying not to laugh.

Then, Harold said: "That's what we came here for. The nitty," now, the others joined his refrain, *"and the gritty!"*

I turned on them, sharply. "Perhaps," I said, coolly, "we should reconnoiter in the living room. Take the wine. I'll join you presently." They all cooed their offers to help clean up the mess.

"Thank you, no, it's all under control. There's a collection of jazz recordings in the living room. I'll salvage dinner and join you shortly."

As they left, I turned back to the sink and ran more cold water over my hand.

"Let me see it," said Khanya when she returned. "You'll live." Then an uncontrollable grin stretched across her face. "The guests think she's funny."

"Oh! Well! 'The guests think she's funny'! Richard Pryor jump back. Li'l Reba's in da house!"

"Keep your voice down, honey."

"Dinner's ruined," I sighed. She helped me pick bits of penne off the floor. Then I mopped the floor while she cleaned the counter. "What are we going to do?"

"Organize something else," she said.

"Like what, it's almost nine?"

"Let's go out. Your homeboy wants *da* nitty *and da gritty.*" She laughed until it hurt.

I sucked my teeth "He's right off the Chicken-Bone Express."

"Let's walk down the hill to Elaine's. Treat them to a curry."

"You win," I said, grateful for the miracle of her solution.

"What do you make of the Coopers?" she asked.

"Like I said, just up from Tupelo."

"So, they're not here to ruin the revolution."

"They couldn't ruin a bowl of grits."

"That means you won't be up all night writing a brief on them?"

"No...why?" And then I knew why.

"Tonight," she smiled, "we're locking the door."

APRIL 10, 1993

Despite our late night with Tembisa, Naledi, and the Coopers, we were both up early. We ate a light breakfast and went to work out at the Yeoville Health Club (which had recently "gone multiracial"). It was a beautiful morning. A cool, soothing, breeze sifted through the walnut and

jacaranda trees. As we walked we laughed and joked abou. ... ...
asco and we prided ourselves on salvaging the evening wit.
to Elaine's—for they had given us the large table by the win.
and Tembisa had gotten on like a house on fire and so had N
Gloria. Khanya and I had somehow relaxed and not found it n
to impose the "correct picture" of political strife on two people who, for
all we knew, were never coming back.

For the first time in my life, I felt as though I belonged somewhere.
It was a strange, inexplicable feeling that I kept to myself as we walked
to the gym, a good feeling, but a frightening one as well. Much like Khanya's wish for a home movie camera when she was a child. A voice inside of me was saying, *Don't ever go back; this is your home.* I'd never lived
anywhere that I thought of as home. Not even Kenwood—*especially* not
Kenwood. I recalled a story my father once told me about our "ances-
tors" on the White Castle Plantation near New Orleans. When the Civil
War ended most of the slaves whom the master had named "Wilderson"
wanted to stay on the plantation rather than go out into the world and
find a home. They knew how diabolically crafty the Whites were and believed that this sudden announcement that the war was over and that the
Union had won was a hoax to lure them into the swamps and slaughter
them. Go, the master told them, shoo! Make your new homes elsewhere.
But they'd rather cling to the familiar terror of the plantation than risk
the unfamiliar terror of the world beyond. Well, I thought, maybe they
were wrong. Maybe there is a Black home. Maybe this is it.

By the time we got to the gym, I felt so alive and so confident that I
rushed to the bench press in the free-weights area and asked Khanya to
calculate 225 pounds into kilos, that I might load the bar and have her
spot me as I bench pressed.

"You'll get a hernia," she said.

"I benched a hundred ninety-eight pounds last week."

"And you had a sore back."

I began loading plates on the bar and calculating the conversion
without her help. "When I played ball, two twenty-five was my warm up
weight."

Jh-huh."

"Outside linebacker, jack! When I knocked 'em down, they stayed down, ya dig."

"That was a hundred years ago, Frank. You're almost forty now."

I spun around to see who else might have heard her reveal my age. But the gym was relatively empty. Two young toughs were hee-hawing it up at the other end of the free weights area. But they seemed not to have heard. I was grateful for this, for though I tried not to show it, they had always intimidated me. They brawled in the evenings and bragged about it as they lifted weights the next day. And they were the two who circulated a petition demanding that the owner not let the gym "go multiracial" two years ago. They never spoke to us. We never spoke to them.

She leaned close to me and whispered, "It's okay to age. I'm not going to spot you and be party to an injury. Let's warm up on the bicycles."

She read a magazine and pedaled sensibly. I hunched over the handlebars and tried to win the Tour de France. On the wall above us the television droned on with some inane morning show on cooking or gardening. The same program droned on another television at the other end of gym where the two toughs pumped iron.

"I've gone a mile already. How far have you gone? Let's race," I said, trying to look at her odometer.

She covered her odometer with her magazine. "We're not competing, Frank."

A strange voice was coming from the television above. A voice that had not been there before. A male voice. Official and informative. Disembodied yet ubiquitous. First my ears, then my eyes followed the voice upward to a White man in a suit and tie.

"We interrupt this broadcast..."

Why is he interrupting? What is he saying?

Then, all I heard was Khanya saying, "No...no...no." But the man kept speaking, ignoring her pleading that he stop.

"I repeat: Chris Hani, the commander of the ANC's armed wing, Umkhonto we Sizwe, and general secretary of the South African Communist Party, was gunned down less than an hour ago. Hani, perhaps the most popular Black politician in South Africa after ANC president Nelson Mandela, was assassinated in the driveway of his home in Hakea Crescent, Dawn Park, Boksburg, within—we believe—the last thirty minutes. This, according to a neighbor, an as of yet unidentified witness who called the police between 10:15 and 10:30..."

We sat on the bicycles and stared blindly at the screen. *It's a hoax! An elaborate hoax!*

"This would put the time of death..." *Death? What does he mean death?*

My arms felt like jelly. *We've been betrayed, horribly, horribly betrayed. Please, not another Fred Hampton. Please, please. I'll do anything you ask.*

"...a red Ford Laser driven by a White male pulled up behind Mr. Hani in the driveway, as Mr. Hani returned from the grocer. The assailant shot Mr. Hani twice in the body and then stepped forward and shot him another three times in the head."

Good and dead, they said in Chicago, as they lorded over his body. Now, he's good and dead.

"...these reports are unconfirmed and the name of the witness has not yet been released to the SABC."

I thought I heard someone laughing, but that couldn't be right.

"...the vehicle's license plate number and there are reports—again, unconfirmed—that a suspect is already in custody..."

Someone was laughing...one of the body builders at the other end of the gym. I got off the bicycle and stood facing them. *I'm just as much of a body builder as they are. But what kind of fighter am I?*

They looked at me and stopped laughing. But something told them that not only could they take me, but they had already won. There was no need to fight. The news flash had taken the fight away. One of them turned away from me. But the other one stared me down across a forest of free weights and machines. Then he turned to his friend.

"You live by the sword," he said, loading two iron slabs onto the bar and slid beneath it, "you die by the sword."

Khanya and I left the gym without changing into our street clothes—determined not to let them see us biting back our tears. When we turned the corner we cried.

—ɯ—

I woke up to find Khanya lying beside me staring up at the ceiling. Dry tears laced her temples. I turned and faced her. We folded into each other's arms.

But we knew we couldn't stay in bed all day. It was Easter and Doreen had gone home. There was Reba's breakfast to think of. Yes, someone had to think of breakfast and Easter...and my birthday. *God almighty, how can we go on. What did we promise Reba? A trip to the zoo? A movie at the mall?* It was hard to believe that those things were still there. *What right do they have to survive?*

On the morning news, an anchorman seated behind the desk pressed the Cuban cultural affairs attaché (the closest thing to an ambassador de Klerk had permitted Fidel Castro) for a post-mortem sound byte. When they killed Chris Hani, he said, they murdered the future of this country. Then there was a clip of a mass meeting in Port Elizabeth, where an orgasmic Eugene Terre Blanche, leader of the Afrikaner Resistance Movement (AWB), thrust his chin out to a cheering crowd and said, If Hani had *not* been shot, I would have done it myself!

Night came, but not soon enough. We put Reba to bed at half past eight and then went to bed ourselves. We curled into each other and prayed...for what?

"This is the end of Winnie," said Khanya, "The end of power for women in the ANC."

The sun rose and the week pressed on. At one point during the week, an all-night vigil was held at the First National Bank Stadium outside Soweto. When it ended, Black youth attacked passing cars and set fire to the nearby homes of Whites. At least two people were killed before the riot police arrived. One of the White men who was burnt to death in his home turned out to be a musician in the Terre Blanche AWB Orchestra.

In the townships young men and women waylaid ANC officials, demanding the mass distribution of guns and calling for a complete overthrow of the state. At the universities, SASCO blazoned the walls with hammer and sickles, and blood-mad calls: "To war comrades to war!" "No peace without Hani!" and "Kill the Farmer, Kill the Boer!"

Everywhere, the streets were clogged with people toyi toying, stoning the cars of Whites, hijacking them, and setting them alight. Rumors of the occupants' fate circulated for days to follow.

On any given day from Easter Sunday to Monday, April 19, the day of Chris Hani's funeral, as many as three million people stayed away from work and wreaked what havoc they could, stoned whomever they could, broke whatever they could, set fire to whatever they could, and cursed what would neither break nor burn. It was nothing in the midst of all this mayhem to hear someone laughing, to hear someone crying, or to see someone standing on a corner screaming at the sky. Some simply stood in the street, stunned and in disbelief. Was he dead? Was he *really* dead? Somebody say it isn't so.

A crowd of disciplined mourners would be marching down the street only to turn the corner and surrender to paralysis. Then the same mass of bodies would rock back and forth, like a large, sloshing wave, followed by the sound of breaking glass. From out of the same crowd, a throng of angry teenage boys carrying dried ears of corn would emerge. *What on earth are they doing?* One of the boys breaks a storefront window with a huge lead pipe while the other boys set the ears of corn alight; a poor person's Molotov. They throw the flaming ears of corn inside and set the building ablaze.

Then the paralysis would set in again and the crowd did what seemed to be nothing. A mass catharsis in the street as cars and shops burned all around: each man and woman clinging to the autonomy of their grief. Each man and woman demanding that their grief be admitted to the sea of grief.

Then someone said, "Chris Hani, where are you? Chris Ha-*ni* where are you?"

Nelson Mandela went on television and demanded, with "all the authority at my command," that people remain calm. "Honor the memory of Chris Hani by remaining a disciplined force for peace." A young man standing near me in the crowd sneered, "Hani's death is the best thing that ever happened to you." No one reproached him. No one raised a hand when he picked up a stone and smashed the window and climbed over the jagged glass and, one by one, smashed the television sets with their flickering images of Madiba. The people set fire to the store.

Mandela sent his protégé, Thabo Mbeki, to Chris Hani's home in Boksburg, only to have Mbeki jeered and cursed by more than ten thousand people, the way they had once jeered and cursed the South African Police. Nelson Mandela retreated to his home in Soweto. When he arrived, he was booed.

Trevor and Stimela's faces were dry and taut, as though they'd been crying for days. I walked with them, east, up the steady slope of Jorissen Street in Braamfontein. We hadn't spoken since we left the rally at Wits. The sun reflecting off the sidewalk warmed the cool autumn air. We were on our way to Hillbrow. Three days had passed since Chris Hani died.

A Twilight Child approached us. His nose was dry with snot. His hair hadn't been combed in ages. His clothes were sooty and so was his skin. He held his hand out to Trevor.

"Baas, please, two bob for some chips."

Trevor pulled his gun out from under his shirt. The boy froze. He was too paralyzed to run. Trevor snapped the clip from the butt of the gun and handed the boy a bullet. Then he handed him a large note, perhaps it was twenty rand. "Here," he said, "buy a gun and kill a White politician." The terror in the boy's eyes melted away. He was still holding the bullet and the money and we'd only walked a few feet when Stimela turned back. He ejected a bullet from *his* gun and gave it to the boy with another bill. "Then wait five years," he said, "and kill a Black politician."

In Hillbrow Stimela told me that I wasn't invited up to the safe house with them. Whatever was about to go down, I was not going to be part of it. Trevor gave me the keys to the other safe house several blocks away, the one with all the tokoloshe manuscripts and photographs and darts. There were no weapons clustered on its floor, no collections of telecommunications equipment that Stimela had either stolen from Special Branch or acquired during his training when the Soviet Union was still the Soviet Union. It was a passionless flat that I knew all too well, in a building that history would no doubt forget when the ANC came to power. It had been one of the first buildings to go "multiracial" in 1991 when the Separate Amenities Act was repealed; in the wake of little old English ladies who used to retire in such buildings had come domestic workers and gardeners with calloused hands who could now live closer to the northern suburbs where they worked.

—〰—

I turned the key. I opened the door. There was so little furniture in the flat I could hear the echo of my presence. The living room was not the least bit legendary. The papers on the table could only be called contraband if the use to which they were put could be decoded and then connected to other, more 'decisive,' operations. There were no pictures on the walls. Not even the clowns or wild horses or Jesus hands in prayer painted on black velvet, purchased by the poor and the parvenu in second-hand shops and the lobbies of cheap hotels. Only a bulletin board to which was tacked an essay by June Sinclair on the contradictions between tribal law and Greco-Roman jurisprudence; an abstract from Nico Cloete's missive warning "level headed" moderates of the vice grip of Leftist extremism and Rightist extremism which could upset the delicate balance of a new democracy; and photographs of Etienne Mureinik, Charles van Onselen, and other assorted tokoloshes.

It was all the same as before. The same two IBM clones. The same dot matrix printer. The same eight-foot folding table where propaganda was produced and psychological warfare was strategized. I was struck by an urge to turn on all the lights but that would be undisciplined. Instead, I checked each room for signs of disturbance other than our own from the last time we were there. I turned the computer on. Then I turned it off. I turned off the light. I opened the blinds and then the window. But even with its astonishing view of Johannesburg's skyline, the flat could not be redeemed. Not tonight. The city danced and sparkled beneath a grimy moon as it always had—as though no one had died. There were nights when I worked in that room and found it difficult to bridge the gap between what transpired there and the struggle on the ground. Tonight it was impossible.

After a while Precious Jabulani arrived. She busied herself with preparations for another all-night session—the sifting through files, the booting of the computer, the jotting of notes, the laying out of manila folders on the table. I tried to make myself useful but it was no use. I sat down on a folding chair at the far end of the table. *No, not tonight. Not another useless strategy session. Hani's dead, what's the use.* She was seated at the computer with her back to me, but she could hear the silence; she could feel the stillness. She turned around.

"I don't want to do this," I said. "Not tonight."

"What do you want to do?"

"I want to kill somebody."

"Yes," she nodded, "yes." Then she came to the end of the table where I sat paralyzed. She reached across the table and put her hand on mine. "We must move on from this. That's all I know."

"The whole world is against us. The whole world wanted him dead."

"Then the odds are even," she smiled.

"Be serious, Precious. Look at this room. It's surreal. A funny house of the Negro." I could feel my throat quivering and my voice quaking. "What goes on here? It's absurd."

"What's absurd?"

"All of it." I swept my hand around the room. "This secret flat—*safe house!* Files and photographs you can get in any library or newspaper archive; pages and pages of our scribbling, to be read by whom, and for what, now that Hani's dead. Mandela wouldn't even use it for kindling. Before, we could say why we did what we did, the only question was how to measure the effects of what we did. Now, I can't even answer the first question."

"The answer is the same as it was when Hani was alive. Even more so."

"I'm sorry reverend, but the church is empty."

Precious pulled my wrist, gently. "Come. Let's go to the kitchen. We could both use some tea."

I wouldn't move. I couldn't move. "Chris Hani's *dead.*"

"It's going to be a long night, Frank. Come."

"A comrade told me it was the Heritage Foundation in Washington DC."

"Comrades are saying all sorts of things."

"Fifty-thousand dollars from the Heritage Foundation. Thirty-thousand dollars from a West German minister of parliament. And someone from the ANC, someone high up enough to sell a vital piece of information—the timetable of Hani's bodyguards. All that money from all over the world converging on us. And we're gathered here tonight, brothers and sisters, to write yet another pamphlet?"

"Tea, comrade, now."

She was right. It was better in the kitchen. The kitchen was small and comforting: the sink, the counter; the cabinets with sugar, cups, and boxes of tea; the stove and the ancient refrigerator huddled around us like steadfast guardians keeping the vast unknown at bay. My voice neither quaked nor echoed as it had in the outer room. The kettle sang its arrival and the world seemed safe again.

The room was too tiny for a table or chairs, so Precious hoisted herself onto the counter and I leaned against the fridge. We sipped our tea in silence. She placed her cup and saucer on the counter and chose her words carefully.

"Don't romanticize all this," she said.

"It's the way I can deal with my sense of powerlessness."

"You'll become a victim of your own game. You won't pull through the lows. And you'll crack too soon under torture. Romanticism puts us all at risk."

"Doesn't everyone crack under torture?"

"I said too soon."

"What's too soon?"

"Anything less than seventy-two hours. The time it takes for us to break a room like this down. The time it takes to disappear."

"No one ever tells me anything—not in advance anyway. I never know what's going to be asked of me."

"Anything."

"Anything," I repeated. I let out a deep breath. "Oupa knows I'm a fraud. Oupa's the fraud police. He can see my fear."

"He's more afraid than any of us."

"He doesn't show it."

"That's how afraid he is."

"I can't imagine him feeling powerless."

"The power isn't inside us—it wasn't even inside Chris Hani. The power is in the question not in the person. The power to *pose* the question is the greatest power of all. That's what makes these dingy little rooms, as you called them, very real—not surreal."

"So, now it's back to the dingy little room?"

She jumped off the counter and complimented me on my astonishing clairvoyance. She gave me the names of two leading organizers in aboveground structures, SASCO and NEHAWU. Stimela had authorized her to provide them with the address of this particular safe house. They would be along in one to one and a half hours. We were to discuss the work she, Jabu, Trevor, and I had been doing here, and explain how it had augmented aboveground action in the past. We were to brainstorm a more calculated and intentional coordination between our clandestine activity and their organizing efforts. There had always been such coordination—and it was never stronger than those moments when it was most strongly denied—but now, Precious emphasized, with Hani's death, now it needed to be expanded and intensified. With Hani dead, the power to pose the question was at risk as never before.

"The masses want the Boer's blood, because a Boer, or his surrogate, may have pulled the trigger. We may have to avenge them with the Boer's blood, because that's where they're directing their rage. But we have to direct that rage elsewhere as well."

I followed her out of the kitchen. "How does one say, 'tokoloshe, I see you'?"

She fetched her jacket from the chair by the computer. "That's what we've been asking ourselves in these dingy rooms all along."

"You're not staying?"

"I'm needed elsewhere."

Years later, when they all—except Oupa—felt they could fill in the gaps, the "something interesting" about the "elsewhere" where Precious was needed, Stimela recalled the encounter that night in the safe house from which he and Trevor had turned me away. How Jabu Mosando, who spoke the least and was always last to laugh, took Chris Hani's death the hardest. Pangs of resentment and confusion rushed through every fiber in his being, making it impossible to concentrate on the instructions Stimela was giving him. Why, he must have thought as he listened to Stimela, did you lead me down this path? He had abandoned Steven Biko's Black Consciousness for the Freedom Charter and its wretched nonracialism. He'd swallowed his pride and let any White man or woman who outranked him in the organization pontificate. He'd even taken orders from them. He'd done more than simply tuck Biko's dog-eared copy of *I Write What I Like* into his bottom drawer. He'd followed his cousin and converted in good faith. Found a new religion. Look what happens when we trust ourselves to Whites, he must have thought as he looked around the table, as his cold gaze fell upon Trevor Garden. There was Stimela Mosando, pointing to their respective positions on a street map; his cousin, urging them on. And Precious listening intently; Oupa, nodding vacantly. And Trevor Garden, once again. He'd come full circle to Trevor. He's still here! Jabu must have bit his lip and tried not to burst with rage. What the hell is this White man doing here! He had an urge to take an empty bottle from the middle of the table and open Trevor's skull with it. They'd trained together, he and Trevor, at a secret base in the Transkei. That's where they first met. Some APLA comrades were on that bus with them, on their way to be trained as well. A soccer team—that was their cover. A Black soccer team with one White player? Right. His presence had jeopardized us from the beginning. When they'd left the city and were sailing down the open road, the APLA comrades started singing, "One settler, one bullet," as they looked to where Trevor and Jabu were seated. Jabu had stood up and told them to stop. Now he wondered why he'd bothered. He'd been in shootouts with the cops with Trevor. They'd even fought the PAC together in the internecine wars of the 1980s. What shame he felt now for having shot at another Black man with this piece of shit by his side. Africa for the Africans, he must have thought. Who the hell is this Boer who can't even shake his ass?

Trevor was handling one of the pistols, checking the chamber and the safety. When he laid it down on the table, Jabu picked it up and re-checked. One settler, one bullet.

Stimela finished the briefing and asked Jabu if what he had said was clear. Yeah, Jabu said. Stimela went to the door and checked the hallway. He motioned to Jabu.

"Good luck, comrade."

"Brother," Jabu corrected him.

"Jabu, I know how you feel."

"Do you?"

"I feel the same way."

"What way is that?"

"Go, Jabu, quickly."

Stimela tried not to make extended eye contact with the others as he sat back down. He could take only so much of their rage and mourning into his body if he was to do what had to be done tonight. He needed room for his own.

But despite his best efforts, his gaze lingered on Oupa. What was he to do with Oupa? Unlike Jabu, Oupa never worried about being on the right side of history, as long as he was on the strong side of power. Frankly, Stimela was a bit surprised that Oupa had even showed up tonight. Mandela had sent an order throughout the entire network: all MK units are to stand down, it said, repeat stand down. Why was Oupa even here? His allegiance was to Madiba first and to the revolution second—if at all. Stimela had always known this. But one can't submit every comrade to an ideological litmus test. It may have been why Stimela never pressed Oupa into the clandestine intellectual work I did with Precious, Trevor, and sometimes Jabu, work that subtended SASCO's campaigns. Oupa had come up through the ANC Youth League, not through the student movement. He had gone to a technikon, not a university; he had once said he didn't know why these varsity brats, as he called them, didn't settle down and study, instead of ruining their chances for a better life. A better life, that's what Oupa wanted. If the revolution brought it, fine. If Mandela's people and the tokoloshes brought it, well, that was alright too.

Stimela asked if the boot of Trevor's car was loaded with the RPG, the grenades, the long-range rifle and scope. Trevor and Oupa nodded. Stimela led them to the door and, when all was clear, he sent them on their way. Now he and Precious were alone.

Precious went into the bedroom to change. She emerged wearing traditional African fabric wrapped around the lower half of her body and an ordinary shirt beneath an ordinary sweater. Stimela was still at the table rubbing his face with his hands. He looked up and smiled at her.

"Do you need to talk?" she asked.

"I've been talking all night."

"You know what I mean."

"What would I say?"

"Whatever comes to your mind."

"That's not how we operate."

He handed her a small assault rifle wrapped in swaddling like an infant. "Your missus kept you late."

"Why didn't I sleep in the back room where I always sleep?"

He thought for a moment. It was too complex, a simple little cover story, still too complex for his bursting brain.

"The child is ill and you've tried the White doctor. You need to take her to your sangoma."

"Him," she said, "I need to take him to his sangoma."

He didn't mind her allegory; in fact, he was thankful for it. He wanted her to care for him. But he needed her to go.

"This isn't just for Chris Hani," she said, at the door. "You know it's more than that."

"Yes, yes." He would have said yes to anything to avoid her eyes, to send her on her way. "But I'll have to answer to Mandela's people for it."

"Not if all the others hit their targets." When Hani had lived, a set of targets had been drawn up: people, buildings, installations to be hit in retaliation for the assassination of a leading ANC or SACP official. The target Stimela's people had been assigned was a Broederbond meeting place on the West Rand. It was a standing order, I was told, which Hani had given himself. Little did he know that one night it would be carried out in response to his own assassination. Or would it? This is what Precious was asking. "There'll be too many of us to be disciplined. It won't be—" and then she stopped, rather than say the word *insubordination*. "Will the others hit their targets?" she asked. When he didn't answer she said, "It's what we must do, regardless of the others."

"I know." He cracked the door and checked the hall.

"We have a mandate from the people."

"I know." He heard the elevator bell and closed the door.

"A mandate doesn't come from one person," she said. She stood next to him at the threshold and rushed through her words for fear the coast would clear before she could finish. "And one person can't counterman it—not even Mandela."

"You know I know." He cracked the door again and peered down the hall.

She pressed him again: "Will the others hit their targets?"

"The others are the others." He opened the door.

I am told that Oupa said hardly a word to Trevor as they headed west along the wide expanse of Empire Road. At one point Oupa asked if he could smoke, without the slightest hint of a request in his voice. Trevor was always amenable to smokers, as long as he could roll down his window. Tonight would have been no different. That and the logistics of their rendezvous was the extent of their conversation. An albino terrorist and an African apparatchik, what could they have to discuss?

Trevor and Oupa turned west off the N1, the Western Bypass, onto the 18, or Main Perth Highway that soon became the Voortrekker Highway. The wind blew sternly through his window and cleared the car of Oupa's cigarette smoke. Many months later, Trevor told me how his thoughts strayed to his father and mother. For the first time in his life they were ugly. Disfigured in his mind's eye. Beyond repair and redemption. Had they been this unredeemable all his life and he'd simply kept the image at bay through mental gymnastics, those clever mind games that always got him firsts in school? Now he wondered just how long ago it was, how many years exactly, was the first moment of the first day when he got his first real glimpse of them, not as his parents but as strange, misshapen monstrosities? Those shoulder bars, the shreds of cloth and bits of thread he'd torn off his Voortrekker uniform at graduation—were they bits of his uniform or tufts of hair he'd ripped from his mother's scalp? He'd always thought his parents bullheaded. Racist, yes. But whose weren't where he came from? But he'd never thought of them as murderers. Now, he could think of them as nothing else. He shuddered and gripped the wheel. It's nothing, he told Oupa, just a chill from the wind.

—⁋—

To my knowledge, Precious Jabulani had never given birth. Nor had she ever been responsible for a child. Still, she sat at the bus stop and cradled the small bundle the way she'd seen mothers, aunts, or nannies in the park cradle a child. My madam kept me late, cleaning after her party. I missed the last kombi. She would tell the officer that she must wait without promise for a rare kombi, one that mopped up the late night workers and brought them home for twice the price. It's that, meneer, or sleep in your park. Don't sound cheeky, she thought. But no officer came and no one had asked. Few cars had even passed. She sat at a bus stop two blocks west of the target. She was still wearing the sweater, the bright print of fabric wrapped around her into a skirt, and a *doek* wound around her head, its final fold tucked invisibly behind her ear. She hummed, quietly. She rocked, gently. She waited, patiently.

On the corner diagonal to the target, a municipal worker used his garbage spike to pluck bits of refuse from the ground by the trunks of plane trees lining the avenue. The features of his dark face were all but dissolved by the night. At the side of a nearby building he stumbled upon a drunk, a dismal little heap of a man who'd taken up residency on the pavement. The drunk's knees were drawn up. His forearm rested on one knee; on the other, his hand dangled a bottle sheathed in a brown paper bag.

"Hey, m'china," rasped the street cleaner, "take your carcass home."

Jabu looked up at his cousin. "They're in there," he said, then lowered his head back down.

At the opposite end of the street, a block further west of where Precious waited, Oupa stood watch on the roof of an apartment building. Beside him was the arsenal he and Trevor had transported: a rocket-propelled grenade launcher which, if he was lucky, could take down a helicopter (all he'd get was one shot) and a long-range rifle that could crush a rhinoceros at one hundred yards. Strapped to the shank of one of his short, stocky legs was that garter which held up his sock and kept his knife in place. Of this I am certain for I can still see him cleaning his fingernails with the tip of that blade without taking his eyes off me. He doesn't like me, I used to think, he's probably killed ten people and he doesn't like me. To Oupa I was just a mascot, a tiresome little terrier yapping at the heels of the team.

With his binoculars he studied the streets. To the east he could see the pearls of Jo'burg's skyline. Was he looking at me? Was I looking at him from my window in Hillbrow? We were more than fifty kilometers apart; the same distance between us when we sat at the table. To the west he saw the black expanse of open veld, sliced down the middle by a luminous highway leading to Botswana. But he marveled no more at the dark endless night to the west or at the skyline to the east, than he had marveled at my files. Without passion or preconception, he reexamined the intersection where a municipal worker was clearing the sidewalk of a drunk and the target building across from them, with its two lit windows on the second floor. No sign of police in any direction. With his flashlight, Oupa signaled to the little red car on the street just below him, parked a block to the left of where Precious waited.

Trevor flipped his high beams, two swift torrents of light hurled down the boulevard. For an instant, the light caught a nanny and her child in profile. It kissed the cheek of a drunk as he raised his head from his knees. Then it twinkled and died in Stimela's eyes.

Precious had already freed herself from the fabric wrapped around her legs when Trevor's car came barreling down the street. She could run freely now in slacks and running shoes. She unbundled her "baby" from its swaddling, an AK-74, the stunted, flash muzzled grandchild of the AK-47. She ran along the plane trees as Trevor's car sped past. She took position behind a tree opposite to where Trevor's car had stopped. Quickly, she surveyed the terrain, looking up and down the block as Jabu and Stimela crossed the intersection diagonally and ran to the car. Precious braced herself against the tree and, on bended knee as though genuflecting in the house of the Lord, she aimed up at the two lighted windows.

She kept her gun trained on the windows, but she watched the three men out of one eye as they faced the façade and pulled the pins of their grenades.

From his perch high above them, Oupa watched as the first volley of grenades smashed through the windows and exploded. Not the huge shock explosions of fire and destruction from war movies but brief bursts of light, then cream puffs of smoke billowing out from the broken glass like a firecracker going off in someone's mouth.

In the fractional interlude between the first explosion and the next volley, Precious leapt from behind the plane tree to give them covering fire. But she didn't pull the trigger for she didn't like her angle. It gave her a straight-on shot of the windows, but it would also mean firing directly over her comrades' head. She ran into the street and, standing several yards from them, blasted the windows at an angle. Still, her angle to the building was inadequate. Some of the rounds sailed through the window while others only grazed the wall. But it was good enough for covering fire. She stopped as the next volley of grenades sailed through the broken glass. Then she covered them again, with steady bursts from her gun.

But one grenade missed its mark.

Months later, it would still be a mystery to Trevor. He hadn't seen it bounce off a sill or ricochet off the façade. And Precious, though standing a good distance from them, would have seen, or even heard, it had it dribbled down the steps. Jabu would have surely seen it hop, hop, hopping toward him. They would have known what to do. They knew the "immediate action drill" by heart. In the camps, they'd drilled it till they couldn't drill it any more. "The chance of being hit by shrapnel varies directly with the surface area you present to the explosion—it obeys the inverse square law with respect to the distance," their commanding officers had said. Like poetry, they learned it by heart. But no training in the world could prepare them for a blast that comes without warning.

They threw up their hands like useless prayers.

Precious had been standing far enough away from them. She was the only one who wasn't hit. But searing fragments tore into Trevor's armpit and the skin along his side. Hot shrapnel slashed a map of Peru up Stimela's thigh; etched a burning Galapagos on Jabu. Precious saw Stimela double over and fall to the ground. She wanted to scream. She wanted to run to his side but she held her position and kept shelling the windows. Trevor will handle it when he comes to. But Trevor stood dazed, touching his face with his fingers. He came to life when he realized his face was free of wounds. Jabu seemed to be wounded the least. Together they reached down and pulled Stimela up. He was alive. Breathing. His eyes were still open. They tried to put him in the car but he propped himself against the car and shook his head.

"Finish it," Stimela told Jabu. Then he let Trevor ease him into the back seat.

Oupa couldn't believe what he was seeing. He picked up the high-powered rifle and made ready.

Precious drew up beside Jabu as he lobbed the last grenade.

As they drove away, Oupa lowered his rifle. From the smoldering windows there were no signs of life; even the lights had gone out. Sirens were approaching but Oupa saw nothing in the street, save Precious Jabulani's shells, glistening like gold teeth.

He rolled up the arsenal in a duffle bag and went through the door in the middle of the flat roof. He made his way to the room of the woman who cleaned the building. She lay in her bed as though she'd been holding her breath for hours. He put the duffle bag under her bed and told her the password that the people who would come for it would use. She gave him a blanket to go with the pallet she'd built for him on the cement floor. She turned down the wick of her lamp. I don't believe he told her what happened in the street. He wasn't one to peddle needless information.

THE NAMES WE GO BY
   for Alice

In a time too poor for names uncles aunts your
parents and a brother more angelic than
the stars called you sister

I see that past before me as night always
night with flocks of sheep bundling a sky
of red dust and ruin

You are there in the deep incomprehension of your kin
beyond broadcasts of depression or war
knowing how the tails of comets
to be seen
must not be looked upon

From my coast I practice cartography
I trace your voice for trees twisted by wind
I listen to your eyes for a reason
I grope back the way I came through other loves
for a place pulled away by sand and sea that place
our hearts went down for air *sister* I

am here
amid the useless prayers the names
we go by

10

MENDOCINO, CALIFORNIA: DECEMBER 31, 2001

10:42 P.M.

From the window of our cottage I gazed upon a dark blue path unfolding in a dark blue realm. It stretched out to where thousands of years ago rock and soil caved and fell, leaving only a jagged precipice to pay homage to the sea. A crescent moon slung its empty hammock high above, offering its slender light to fog and mist rising up from the cliffs. Alice and I were alone in the cottage. It had rained all day, depriving us of all diversions other than ourselves. Torrents of rain pounding the quaint town of Mendocino to which artists, bohemians, organic gardeners, and potheads fled when Haight-Ashbury was no longer Haight-Ashbury: a town of retirees who had thrown in with Henry Wallace when Truman could no longer be trusted; a town of middle-aged couples who prospered but showed no signs of being tethered to any activity that could have enabled prosperity; a town with a main road that kept a faithful distance of eight tenth's of a mile from the cliffs to which it ran parallel. All along the road, the building façades had also been faithful, whether by consensus or decree, to their nineteenth-century architecture: the old hotel with its sturdy captains' chairs in the parlor and rockers on its long veranda; the trinkets, stationary, and postcard shops; the alternative bookstore, the artists' boutiques, the ladies boutiques; the organic, fair-trade coffee and pastry café; the organic juice bar; and the seafood restaurants where no fish that had ever been farmed was ever served, where one lunched lazily from noon until three along the railings of extended balconies and searched the sea with binoculars provided by the maître d', gazed far out to where the horizon yawned and curved toward Asia, and waited and watched for the sighting of a whale whose only reason for living, if one's fellow diners were to be believed, was to surface, snort, blow geysers of water from its back, and submerge again, that a metonymic chain of *aahs* and *oohs* might lace total strangers together in a kinship they had heretofore not considered.

A town for tourists who would chafe if someone called them tourists.

Normally our Day-After-Christmas trips up the rugged coast above San Francisco were our moments of reprieve. That is, if we held our breath. Alice was in her element as we drove beneath the towering redwood trees and the sharp cry of a hawk soaring high above. We played a cassette of birdcalls as we drove along the winding highway and tried to match names to the calls. She liked to teach me about nature. Her lessons on nature were what she could offer. And much of my writing had benefited from her tutelage, her sharp eye for color and detail. Her poetry was tactful, consistent, and sure. I had learned a great deal from her use and creation of imagery, the impact of her lines. This bond enhanced my love of her. But I was uneasy about the ethical foundation of those beautiful and compelling images. So much of her poetry was about the "natural" world. In that she was like other White poets I'd encountered on the poetry circuit from Santa Cruz to Monterey, from Marin to Mendocino: beautiful imagery with unnerving implications, as though they shared a secret code or religion that allowed them to talk to bobcats, birds, and flora and transpose those intimate conversations into verse—as though they spoke more often to plants and pets than to people. They failed to muse on questions of who they were and how they came to be; questions that would interrupt the loop of desire from their love of nature to their love of themselves. Their art was the gaze of their own conception.

Zipping along the highway, Alice would spot what to me was a blur of green stubby things and name it as a field of artichokes. She even knew the history of barren, unmarked land, and could paint a watercolor portrait of luxuriant wheat fields that had once grown there from the edge of the highway to the edge of the sea. Along the shoulder, where I saw only "Next Gas 45 miles," she witnessed the brilliant yellow and orange of poppies and the tender blue and white of the lupine that line the roads and covered the fields in broad masses. Even I could see the eucalyptus trees, for their blue green foliage was strewn everywhere. But she knew the names of the tree's entire family line and could mark the dates and places its kith and kin had first been planted. And where the land was treeless, she recollected the cruel industry of loggers and was silent, as though saying a prayer.

I was appreciative of her wealth of knowledge of the natural world for I was passionate about learning, whatever the subject. I was also tense and unnerved as she spoke and hoped she wouldn't talk too long. Her rapture, her capacity to name her entitlements freely and without embarrassment, alarmed me. It was as though she thought she belonged not to a race but to "nature." I kept my eye on the road.

"That's nice," I said, not knowing to what, "tell me more." *We're on vacation. We're in love.*

It wasn't true that I saw absolutely nothing as we drove. I saw the highway signs announcing the towns—like Aptos, where the college that we worked was; or Marin, where'd we stop for gas and coffee and where she'd tell me stories of her days there with Harry, her husband before Herby; or Mendocino, the coastal town two hundred miles north of Santa Cruz, our Christmas hideaway. White towns with Indian and Spanish names. White orchards irrigated with Red blood, as though genocide were a nutrient of pleasure.

In 1873, Charles Nordhoff wrote one of the first tourist guides for California. *California for Travellers and Settlers* was an instant success. In the same year that Nordhoff's seminal guidebook was published,

Captain Ben Wright and his men killed one thousand Indians who'd laid down their weapons and come forward to sign a treaty. So many were murdered that day that, in the end, he was able to boast of having made a "permanent" treaty with them.

There's a stunning mutuality between the prose in *California for Travelers and Settlers* (the celebration of the steam baths, the astonishment at the sight of the redwoods and oak, the adventures on steamers from Santa Cruz to San Francisco, the accounts of harrowing stagecoach rides through the Sacramento Valley) and the poetry of Nordhoff's modern day heirs.

We finally came upon the sign that read "Mendocino County." Now the highway plunged along an intaglio of narrow coves, river valleys, and pocket beaches. *Little River. Albion. Elk.* The villages on rocky heights above the sea pushed forth to meet us, then slowly vanished in the rearview mirror. Sea fog drooped from the stubby fir and cedar trees bowed by wind in eternal genuflection. It hung in the branches of redwood, cypress, and pine like the beards of the dead.

Isn't it beautiful, she had commented, the way the fog glides in from the sea? Yes, I had replied, absently. The way the sun makes the fog glisten, she said. Yes, I repeated, not knowing to what. In summer the fog is the redwoods' only source of water, she said. Yes, I said, then, No, I didn't know that.

We drove on, with the villages on our left dotting the cliffs and the forests on our right. *The cliffs' erosion creeps this way. One day it will claim where we are.* The sun's chin was already shining on Vladivostok, its eyebrow bidding us adieu. It was early evening on the day after Christmas when we reach the village of Mendocino. This town reminds me of Hanover, New Hampshire, I told her, of my college days at Dartmouth. It's as though Hanover or Norwich, Vermont, were plucked out of New England and dropped on these cliffs by mistake. New England incarnate on the California coast. Later, I learned that, indeed, Mendocino had been "settled" by itinerant Yankees; these Cape Cod cottages and Maine-like salt boxes perched boldly on this fog-shrouded promontory, this lost coast that seems too hazardous for human habitation, these gingerbread

Victorian homes with their wooden towers, their cast iron weathervanes, and their white picket fences, the Masonic Hall with its rooftop statue of hand-carved redwood, and the unrepentant white steeple of the Gothic Revival Presbyterian Church high up on the hill, were no accidents of nomadism, but a desperate bid to sustain filiation in the "wild."

That was five days ago. Now it is the last night of those five timeless days and nights that hang suspended between Christmas and New Years, the 31st of December. No lectures to prepare. No papers to grade. No dreaded faculty meetings to attend. For this we both are thankful. But today the rain droned down on Mendocino so unmercifully that we scurried about with our heads lowered like bulls. The tarred streets were deep with eddies and the untarred streets were deep with mud. The outdoor attractions—the whales, the shoreline below the cliffs, or the lighthouse beyond—were too far apart to walk to, and the indoor attractions were too close together to drive to. The wise ones either went one place and then returned to their lodgings to change and warm away the chill, or stayed by the fire and cuddled. Now it is night and the rain has stopped but the lighthouse, the bookstores, the cafés, and the restaurants have closed. Now it is night and the redwoods of the state park are impenetrable, and though whales may surface, they surface in darkness and for their own ends, their own communal needs. We are alone together in the throes of intimacy, however uncertain.

10:45 P.M.

I close the curtains and turn to find her standing with her back to me at a small writing table she's covered with newspaper. She is slicing an apple into crescents and cutting soft havarti cheese into squares. There is a bottle of merlot we'd opened yesterday and beside it two small glasses from the bathroom in lieu of proper wine glasses. She arranges medallions of cheese and apple slices around the perimeter of a paper plate and places a cluster of rice crackers in the middle. *Will I spend my life with you?* The question sweeps over me so swiftly that it leaves neither the trace of where it came from nor a hint of why. I think it is the streak where her hair parts and the roots of gray push the brunette coloring away from her scalp. She worries about it, but I think the streak of gray adds to her beauty and enhances the allure of her cheekbones and dramatic eyes. If anything, her age is a stabilizing force of my love for her.

She must feel me staring at her, for she stops pouring the wine. Without turning around she says, "You're quiet tonight," adding, "you've been quiet all day."

"I think the fire needs more wood."

"I'm not saying you should speak. Not unless you want to."

"Are we staying up till midnight?" I ask.

"We could. We don't have to."

"It's what most people do, I guess."

"We're many things," she says, "but we're not 'most' people."

She goes to the bookshelf on the far wall opposite the fireplace. I stoke the fire with the poker. She calls out the names of the dead as she fingers their spines.

"Mark Twain? Virginia Woolf? Melville?" And with each name she looks over to me standing by the fire shaking my head. "Ayn Rand!" she laughs, vigorously. I say I'd rather have a root canal. "I guess the proprietor doesn't know you," she says, and stoops to the bottom shelf where the board games are kept. "Monopoly? No, the proprietor has no idea his lodger is a communist. Aha! Scrabble."

"You cheat," I scoff.

"I improvise; that's why I have tenure." Then she must have recalled the day a year ago when we worked all day and half of the next clearing twenty-five years of books and lost lectures from her office; the letter that came in the mail informing her that she could only teach on an ad hoc, as needed basis—that was the policy once one has retired. She must have recalled how she'd joined me as an adjunct instructor down the road at the University of California, Santa Cruz. Until that too fell through, when my politics, her politics, our politics, got us fired. "That is," she says, "I used to have tenure."

"Bring the board," I say, forcing cheer through the eye of a needle, "two can *improvise*."

I push the sofa closer to the fire and bring the cheese and sliced, apples, rice crackers, and wine to the table in front of it where she is unpacking the Scrabble board. I sit next to her on the sofa.

"Well," she says, ruefully, "you and I seem to have made it through another year."

We both look at the clock on the mantel and realize how premature her pronouncement is.

"Well...almost," she says.

We laugh. What else can we do?

Long ago, before I even met Alice, Jim Harris had foretold all of this; said it all in South Africa. But I would not cathedralize his wisdom. I'd gone to his house to hear the familiar cadence of a voice from back home, to listen to him play—or try to play—the trombone between sips of brandy and tokes of herb. Jim Harris was at least fifteen years older than me, another Black expat in Jo'burg who'd been living abroad ("on the run" as he put it) for a very long time. When I arrived in South Africa in 1989 he was one of the seventy-five to one hundred Black folks who'd immigrated before me. He hailed from Kentucky which I, with my Midwestern snobbery, always thought was kind of funny. I couldn't imagine anyone actually living in Kentucky. To my mind, Kentucky was so backwards it was mythical: a state that was on the map but didn't really exist, or perhaps a place dreamt up by a Hollywood producer that Daniel Boone might have a place to live. But Kentucky must be real because Jim Harris was real and Jim Harris was from Kentucky. He was an irascible old man who liked to pretend he had little patience for my incessant questions, when in point of fact he recognized something of himself in me. This did not, however, temper his mood if I held onto to his joint for too long.

"Whoa, greedy bastard. I said toke not *tokes*. Pass that shit on."

I struggled up from the La-Z-Boy in his living room and stumbled over to the where he sat on a folding chair in front of a music stand that held the jazz musician's *Blue Book* and a book of classical scales. I didn't bother to tell him that he couldn't practice his scales and smoke a joint at the same time. Logic wasn't Jim's strong point.

"How long have you been in Southern Africa, Jim?" I asked as I sat back down.

"Harare. Lesotho. Jo'burg. Damn, near fifteen years."

"You were married to a Black woman from the States and then to an African woman?"

"White woman too."

"Which do you prefer?"

"The one I got right here," he said, indicating the joint in his hand. He hit it hard and passed it back to me.

"Be serious," I said.

"I'm serious as a heart attack on a hospital holiday," he said. "Can't be with a Black woman from back home."

"Why not?"

"It's like looking in the mirror. Ever look in the mirror?"

"What's so hard about looking in the mirror?"

"Don't play like you don't know. One minute she wants to fight the power. Next minute she wants you to curb all that rage. Then vice versa."

"What if you both want to fight the power together?"

"You do, but you can't never synchronize your watches."

"Well, I married an African woman."

"That won't last."

"Why, because yours didn't?"

"Okay, you're special. So, let me play my horn in peace."

He went back to practicing scales and I looked around for a magazine.

Finding none, I said: "Why won't it last?"

"Too complicated."

"Explain it to me anyway."

"Not it, Negro. *You.* Your ass is too damn complicated. African woman ain't used to all that complication; all that mental anguish and shit. She thought she loved you 'cause you don't come home drunk at night like these here Soweto niggas. But after a while even that don't make up for all your complications. These Black women over here got history and language. How long you think an African chick's gonna put up with all your complications? My advice: leave her before she up and leaves you."

"That's so reactionary."

"That don't make it any less true."

"It's painful," I said, "the way you put it."

"Yeah," his eyes softened and he laid the trombone across his lap, "That's why I don't think about it. Ain't no percentage in it."

"Percentage?"

"Never mind. Say," he blew a few notes on his trombone, "whatchu think of my tone?"

Jim was a labor union organizer for South African musicians. He'd finally landed a gig that interested him and that would make allowances for his...lifestyle. One of the musicians, or, in the parlance of South Africa, cultural workers, told him that he could become a great jazz trombonist. There was something inspiring in Jim's capacity to launch headfirst into art as a rank amateur and at sixty-plus. But there was nothing inspiring in the fruits of the launch thus far. He continued trying to improvise, raising his eyebrows and nodding at me all the while.

I smiled, weakly. "Sounds great, Jim."

"Don't lie, now."

"I'm not lying."

"Don't lie, Negro."

"I'm not lying. It sounds great."

He beamed. "Recognize the melody?"

Yeah, a moose breaking wind. "Well...um..."

"Man, you don't recognize the *melody?*"

"Maybe I'm too high."

"You ain't too high, you just don't know your music. That's Coltrane's *Naima.*"

"Oh, yeah, now that you mention it."

"Wanna hear *Equinox?*"

"Well—"

But he was already blaring away. When he finished I told him Coltrane would have been speechless.

"You know it too!" he said. "The cats down at the jazz union said I got great tone. All I need to do is keep on keeping on."

"Jim, what are these complications?"

"I told you, I don't wanna talk about that. Bring up all kinds of memories. That's why I got this horn and Mary Jane here." He took another hit. "'Cause I don't want to think about all that."

"You gonna leave me hangin'?"

He peered around his music stand. "I'm not trying to leave you hangin'." Now he studied me as though he was trying to make up his mind about something. He must have decided against whatever it was, for he shook his head and said, "Come back when you and Khanya are divorced. I'll explain it to you then." He picked up his horn and started to play.

"What makes you think we're getting divorced?" I asked indignantly, which made him laugh into his horn and blare out a fierce sound that had surely never come from a trombone before.

He was beside himself with laughter. "You got married didn't you?"

I waited, plaintively.

"It's like this," he said. "The Black African woman meets the Black American man, you dig, and she says to herself, I got me something like nobody else. He's romantic, he can sing—don't tell me you didn't sing to her—aha, you blushing green and purple, nigga, I know you tried to sing. 'Cause she got all those Motown and Stax records from the States and she *expects* you to sing. And she's the only Black woman on the planet you can sing to and not get laughed out of bed behind it. I know you never sang to no Black woman back home. First melody out of your mouth and she says, 'Your trifling ass can't sing.' She knows what singing's all about. But you can come over here and fool these PYTs, can't you? Yeah, she thinks she's got something special, something different than that ole South African who only wants to hang with his friends 24/7 and stay out all night at the shebeen. Then a year goes by, maybe two, three if you lucky." He began playing his trombone.

"Will you stop with that insufferable horn and finish the story!"

"Insufferable." He let the horn rest, and reflected: "Now there's a word you don't hear everyday from a Negro."

"Jim, please."

"She likes all your fancy talk, all your romance, all your Marvin Gaye, but no one warned her 'bout all your *complications.* That's what my African wife told me when she left. 'You too complicated. Sit around and brood all day. Mad at the White man. Mad at the world. Somebody serve you a stale hamburger, you got a ready-made conspiracy theory. The government been trying to poison you, or sterilize you, since 1965 when you had your first stale hamburger, and you told me it was arsenic—that J. Edgar Hoover had gone undercover as Ronald McDonald just to get you. I can't take it anymore, Jim.' Yep, that's just what she said to me. Heartless. When that African woman comes to finally understanding you, understanding how your mind works—oooee! Watch out."

"Why didn't it work with the Black woman from Kentucky? She's just like us."

"You right. She got the same complications. I saw that movie *Waiting to Exhale.* I said go ahead on, girl, exxxx-*hale!* Just don't exhale on me."

"So, you married a White woman."

"You know it."

"That's no solution."

"Who said anything 'bout solutions? This reefer ain't no solution but we smokin' it."

"But I couldn't do that."

"Sure, you're different."

"What's that supposed to mean?"

He went back to playing his trombone.

"I just don't see how I could talk to a White woman," I yelled over his "music."

Another guffaw blared through his horn.

"*Talk to her?* Who said anything 'bout talk to her? Worse thing you can do is talk to her."

"Why?"

"'Cause she ain't got no sense. All that whoody-whoody-who White broads be talkin'. Sound like pigeons on Quaaludes. Don't get me started, now."

"That's a gross generalization."

"It's gross alright, I don't know about the other thing. You best not talk to her. Not if you want her to stay. She won't wait no two, three years to split like these African women."

"Why?"

"'Cause she already knows you're complicated. And she knows where in the complications she fits in. So when you first get with her, y'all sign a little prenuptial agreement."

"That says what? And who would witness such a document?"

"Look, Negro, I'm speaking metaphorically. The agreement's in your mind, you dig. You don't even tell her about it; that only would raise more complications. It goes like this: you agree not to *ever* tell her what's on your mind—especially don't tell her about herself— and in return she won't never leave you." He looked around the mantle for a roach clip, then sat back down and said, *"Talk* to her? She got her face and her body all over the TV and the billboards. She don't need to hear what you got to say. She don't need you. She got a family. She ain't no cosmic hobo, like you, Negro. If her people in Cincinnati don't want her no more 'cause she done contaminated herself with you, she can pick up and start all over again in Santa Fe, find herself some new relations...some new billboards...you dig." The reefer was slowing him down, but it didn't affect his concentration. "You start talking to her, you go from being her sweet, Sweetback...to being her complication...to being all by yourself...better not *talk* to her."

"So, who can we be with, Jim, I mean, really be with?"

He cast that hangdog look of his across the room at me. He cracked the seal on another bottle of brandy. He rolled another joint.

"Come on, Frank...let's get tore down."

10:49 P.M.

Alice shuffles the faceless alphabet that we will turn into words. She choses her seven letters carefully, as though she has X-ray vision and can see through the smooth, blank ivory of the tiny tiles, as though the words have already revealed themselves to her. I grab mine swiftly and at random, as though it makes no difference, as though it made all the difference in the world, as though words are a trap.

"It's your turn," she says.

"What...oh."

"Is something wrong?"

I love you, what could be more wrong? I love you because...why? Because we share the same rhythms? We love the same music? We respond to the same poetry? Because you're mature and exquisite—and I've always loved older women? Because you cheat at Scrabble? Because you're good in bed? Because you're idea of a hideaway such as this cottage by the cliffs and the unrelenting sea is my idea of a hideaway by the cliffs and the unrelenting sea? Is that it? Is there more? Would more matter? Is it even true? And if it's true is it essential? Don't I really love you because when I rub against you there's always a chance that the color of ivory will subdue the color of coal, because only you can validate my most prized possession, my hard earned erudition? When I say I am erudite, I doubt it; when you say it, I am sure. Is it love or is it...

"Envy."

"Envy? I don't see how you're going to get 'envy' on the board," she says, "There's nothing remotely suggestive of it."

"What..."

"Envy. You said, envy.

"Did I?"

"We don't have to play, you know."

I love you because you are not a cosmic hobo. You have the one thing I want: a place and time in the universe, something to salvage as opposed to nothing to lose.

I placed the letter "L" to the left of her "O."

She says: "I wish you would talk to me."

She places a "V" to the right of the "O" and we laugh...it eases the tension.

"A cliché," she says. "Go ahead, say it. It's what you're thinking."

"You're projecting," I smile.

"Am I?" She leans to my side of the sofa and kisses me. "Who put the "L" there?"

It has been like this for a long time. A clichéd and melodramatic tension between what we want of and from each other, *love*, and where and how the implacable fault lines divide us. And I have pushed the envelope even further. Pushed it further and harder than I pushed it when I pushed Etienne Mureinik from the balcony of his hotel—if indeed it was I who pushed him—if indeed, he was pushed.

Just two years ago, in December of 1999, I'd written a letter and stuffed it, late one night, in the faculty mailboxes. It began with what must have appeared to the faculty's confused eyes as a red herring. It spoke not about my excruciating encounters with them, but began, instead, out of left field by discussing the plight of two students whose troubles with the College had been the topic of recent debate.

Reading of Sonia Rodriguez's and Selma Thornton's troubles with the Student Senate and its White liberal adviser Tim Harold reawakened my disdain for Cabrillo as an institution and for the English Division as one of its flagship entities.

I then went on to explain how Selma and Sonia had resigned their posts in the Student Senate in protest over Harold's decision not to allow thirty students of color to have funds to travel to a conference on race at Hartnell College. Instead, Harold spent the money on T-shirts. He had also put the sign-up sheet for the conference not in the Student Center, but in some obscure location where it would never be found thus sabotaging the excursion further. This seemed like a trivial enough matter, but it compounded the hurt and sense of isolation and rebuke which so many Black and Latino students felt at Cabrillo but could not name. I felt a piqued kinship with their unspeakable pain and used the rare moment of it having turned into a tangible event as a way into what I wanted to say to the faculty and administration...and to Alice.

In defense of his actions, and as a way of indicating the absurdity of Selma and Sonia's objections, Harold issued a public statement in which he did not comment (or at least the newspaper did not report his comments) on his funding priorities; rather, he simply said "The sign-up sheet was posted for a week, the same way we treat any workshop." To this, I wrote:

Whereas Selma Thornton attempts an institutional *analysis* of the Student Senate by way of a critique of Tim Harold and his practices, Harold responds with a ready made institutional *defense* and, later in the article, a defense of his integrity (a *personalized* response to an institutional analysis). He brings the scale of abstraction back down to the level most comfortable for White people: the individual and the uncontextualized realm of fair play. It's the White person's safety zone. *I'm a good person, I'm a fair person, I treat everyone equally, the rules apply to everyone.* Thornton and Rodriguez's comments don't indict Harold for being a "good" person, they indict him for being White: a way of being in the world which legitimates institutional practices (practices which Thornton and Rodriguez object to) accepts, and promotes, them as timeless—without origin, consequence, interest, or allegiance—natural and inevitable.

  "The sign-up sheet was posted for a week, the same way we treat any workshop." The whole idea that we treat everyone equally is only slightly more odious than the discussion of how we *can* treat everyone equally; because the problem is neither the practice nor the debates surrounding it, but the fact that White people can come together and wield enough institutional power to constitute a "We." "We" in the Student Senate, "We" in Aptos, "We" in Santa Cruz, "We" in the English department, "We" in the boardrooms. "We" are fair and balanced is as odious as "We" are in control—they are derivations of the same expression: "We" are the police.

  The claim of "balance and fair play" forecloses upon, not only the modest argument that the practices of the Cabrillo Student Senate are racist and illegitimate, but it also forecloses upon the more extended, comprehensive, and *antagonistic* argument that Cabrillo *itself* is racist and illegitimate. And what do we mean by Cabrillo? The White people who constitute its fantasies of pleasure and its discourse of legitimacy. The generous "We."

So, let's bust "We" wide open and start at the end: *White people are guilty until proven innocent.* Fuck the compositional moves of substantiation and supporting evidence: I was at a conference in West Oakland last week where a thousand Black folks substantiated it a thousand different ways. You're free to go to West Oakland, find them, talk to them, get all the proof you need. You can drive three hours to the mountains, so you sure as hell can cut the time in half and drive to the inner city. Knock on any door. Anyone who knows 20 to 30 Black folks, intimately—and if you don't know 12 then you're not living in America, you're living in White America—knows the statement to be true. *White people are guilty until proven innocent.* Whites are guilty of being friends with each other, of standing up for their rights, of pledging allegiance to the flag, of reproducing concepts like fairness, meritocracy, balance, standards, norms, harmony between the races. Most of all, Whites are guilty of wanting stability and reform.

White people, like Mr. Harold and those in the English Division, are guilty of asking themselves the question, How can we maintain the maximum amount of order (liberals at Cabrillo use euphemisms like *peace, harmony, stability*), with the minimum amount of change, while presenting ourselves—if but only to ourselves—as having the best of all possible intentions. Good people. Good intentions. White people are the only species, human or otherwise, capable of transforming the dross of good intentions into the gold of grand intentions, and naming it "change."

...These passive revolutions, fire and brimstone conflicts over which institutional reform is better than the other one, provide a smoke screen—a diversionary play of interlocutions—that keep real and necessary antagonisms at bay. White people are thus able to go home each night, perhaps a little wounded, but feeling better for having made Cabrillo a better place...for everyone...

Before such hubris at high places makes us all a little too giddy, let me offer a cautionary note: it's scientifically impossible to manufacture shinola out of shit. But White liberals keep on trying and end up spending a lifetime not knowing shit from shinola. Because White people love their jobs, they love their institutions, they love their country, most of all they love each other. And every Black or Brown body that doesn't love the things you love is a threat to your love for each other. A threat to your fantasy space, your terrain of shared pleasures.

Passive revolutions have a way of incorporating Black and Brown bodies to either term of the debate. What choice does one have? The *third* (possible, but always unspoken) term of the debate, *White people are guilty of structuring debates which reproduce the institution and the institution reproduces America and America is always and everywhere a bad thing*—this term is never on the table, because the level of abstraction is too high for White liberals. They've got too much at stake: their friends, their family, their way of life. Let's keep it all at eye level, where Whites can keep an eye on everything. So the Black body is incorporated. Because to be *un*incorporated is to say that what White liberals find valuable I have no use for. This, of course, is anti-institutional and shows a lack of breeding, not to mention a lack of gratitude for all the noblesse oblige which has been extended to the person of color to begin with. "We will incorporate color-ed folks into our fold, whenever possible and at our own pace, provided they're team players, speak highly of us, pretend to care what we're thinking, are highly qualified, blah, blah, blah…*but,* and this is key, we won't entertain the rancor which shits on our fantasy space. We've killed too many Indians, worked too many Chinese and Chicano fingers to the bone, set in motion the incarcerated genocide of too many Black folks, and we've spent too much time at the beach, or in our gardens, or hiking in the woods, or patting each other on the literary back, or teaching Shakespeare and the Greeks, or drinking together to honor our dead at retirement parties ("Hell, Jerry White let's throw a party for Joe White and Jane White who gave Cabrillo the best White years of their silly White lives, that we might all continue to do the same White thing." "Sounds good to me, Jack White. Say, you're a genius! Did you think of this party idea all on your own?" "No, Jerry White, we've been doing it for years, makes us feel important. Without these parties we might actually be confronted by our political impotence, our collective spinelessness, our insatiable appetite for gossip and administrative minutia, our fear of a Black Nation, our lack of will." "Whew! Jack White, we sound pathetic. We'd better throw that party pronto!" "White you are, Jerry." "Jack White, you old fart, you, you're still a genius, heh, heh, heh.") too much time White-bonding in an effort to forget how hard we killed and to forget how many bones we walk across each day just to get from our bedrooms to Cabrillo...too, too much for one of you coloreds to come in here and be so ungrateful as to tell us the very *terms* of our precious debates are specious."

But specious they are, as evidenced by recent uproar in the Adjunct vs. Minority Hire debates, or whether or not English 100 students should be "normed." The very *terms* of the debates suture discussions around White entitlement, when White entitlement is an odious idea. Whites are entitled to betray other Whites, nothing else... Beyond that you're not entitled to anything. So how could you possibly be entitled to a job? How could you possibly be entitled to decide who should pass and who should fail? How could you possibly be entitled to determining where the sign-up sheet for Diversity Day buses will or will not be placed, and how funds should be allocated?

Okay...so some of you want to hire a "minority" as long as s/he's "well mannered and won't stab us in the back after s/he's in our sacred house;" and some of you want to hire an adjunct (Jill or Jeffery White) because, "What the hell—they've been around as long as Jack, Joe, Jerry, and Jane White, and shucks fair is fair, especially if you're entitled." And entitlement is a synonym for Whiteness. But there's only one job, because for years you've complained about the gate, while breathing collective (meaning White) sighs of relief that it was there to protect you from the hordes. (Somewhere down the street in Watsonville an immigrant is deciding whether to give his daughter or his wife up for the boss to fuck that he might have a job picking your fruit. Somewhere up the road in Oakland a teen is going to San Quentin for writing graffiti on a wall. And you're in here trying to be "fair" to each other, while promoting diversity—whatever that means. By the time you've arrived at a compromise over norming or faculty hires—your efforts to "enlighten" whoever doesn't die in the fields or fall from the earth into prison—the sista has been raped and the brotha busted. But then you've had a difficult day as well.) So, do what you always do. Hire the most qualified candidate. Here are some questions and guidelines to speed the search committee on its way and make everyone feel *entitled*.

Question: Do you promise to ignore any administrative decrees which norm students, especially students of color, and thereby contribute to making them acceptable candidates for White Supremacy's scrutiny?
Answer: No (disregard candidate)
Answer: Yes (continue with the interview)

Question: Do you

a. spend your time chitchatting with White liberals about gardening, sea turtles, writing-composition exercises, the last departmental party, and/or how much light you brought to your students' eyes when you found for them that epiphany in the Great Books haystack?

b. spend your time chitchatting with White liberals about how wonderful it is when White women can take the place of White men, to carry on the institutional mandate of White men—even in the absence of White men—and call that "women's liberation"?

c. spend your time chitchatting with White liberals about how best to add a Black or a Brown to the chitchat of a. and b. above, so that Cabrillo can pass "incorporation" off as "integration"?

d. find the thought of a, b, and c nauseating and incomprehensible, in your most generous moments, and/or strategies for the reproduction of White pleasure at the expense of paradigmatic change (i.e. revolution) at those moments when you're free to be yourself—find them to be strategies which fortify and extend the interlocutory life of White supremacy?

Answer: a, b, or c (disregard candidate—s/he's already on your hiring committee)

Answer: *d (continue with the interview)*

Question: *Do you wake up in the middle of the night screaming "I hate White people and how they waste their lives as well as ours!" and then realize it was not a dream?*

Answer: *No (disregard candidate)*

Answer: *Yes (continue with the interview)*

Question: *Do you think the debate over a White adjunct or "minority" hire, functions as a ruse to keep our minds off of more structural change? In other words, does the debate represent a dialogue between liberal White adjuncts who feel some erosion at their sense of entitlement and liberal White tenured folks who want their White friends to be happy?*

Answer: *These are important issues. Besides, I've known these folks a long time. They're my friends. They're good people. We're all good people. We say so at our parties. (Disregard candidate.)*

Answer: *Yes, White folks have a knack for talking about power at the lowest level of abstraction possible — when they talk about it at all. This is why they love to get together with each other so often over bullshit, to either talk about bullshit, celebrate bullshit, or honor and congratulate each other for all the bullshit they've done (euphemistically referred to as careers). The bullshit keeps their minds off the real shit. (Continue with the interview.)*

Alternative answer: *Yes: In countries like South Africa when Whites in the English department where I worked (Vista University, Soweto Campus, 1993–1996) managed to continuously flit about over questions of What's the best way to run the institution?, rather than How can we undo ourselves and become Black?, the students would burn one or two of their cars in the parking lot and we were able to get back, rather quickly, to the questions at hand — questions of power. (This would be my answer, but it's based on my personal experience. Others might not have been fortunate enough to live through such ideal times. Unlike memos and debate, fire is a most asignifying method of communication. Funny enough, all the White folks in our English department got the message. Banter and books ain't everything.)*

Question: *Are you structurally/organizationally involved in, and committed to, the liberation of Black, Red, and Brown people in America?*

Answer: *No (disregard the candidate and write an angry letter to Human Resources for sending the committee someone who doesn't even meet the minimum requirements—give HR your standard line about "standards")*

Answer: *Yes (put candidate in pool of finalists)*

Question: *Have you ever committed an act of violence and/or rage against the United States Government or institutions that legitimate it, like Cabrillo?*

Answer: *No (disregard candidate)*

Answer: *Yes (start salary negotiations)*

I hope this helps you solve some of the problems foundational to your passive revolution(s).

Merry Christmas,
Frank B. Wilderson, III

—⁂—

Christmas came with no response. Alice thought there would be an immediate response, for *she* had responded...to me...in the kitchen. It is not the kind of thing that I can easily characterize. She loved me. Or at least she thought she did. Although she had experienced my hatred and everything that was in that letter firsthand, I do not believe that she ever considered that I might make such pronouncements publicly. As she read the letter at her kitchen table that evening before I set out to Kinko's and then on to the one hundred mail slots, she oscillated between joy and horror. Sometimes she laughed out loud, sometimes her eyes narrowed and she winced. She was smart enough to know precisely what was at stake. That this was not simply a letter about *them*, it was a letter about *us*. She knew that what the letter demanded could never be granted, not if the world was to go on being the world. It was demanding their death, her death, and it wasn't too particular as to how that death came about. It was such a clear, uncomplicated demand. Of course, at the time I had no idea that I was making a demand. I only knew I couldn't breathe.

I'll never go against my family. This she had said long before the letter was even written, when it was just daily grunts and groans, symptoms of despair and resentment. I'll never go against my family...as though she had always known that with me she risked solidarity with the dead with no guarantee of acceptance from the dead. Her words seemed to have come out of the blue, like please pass the salt, or, are we ready for coffee?

You hadn't said a word about her family—had you? You didn't even know that Lisa's story and Virginia's racism were waiting in the wings. Suddenly you felt your breath seeping from your body without returning. You reached for her hand across the kitchen table, as though reaching up from water. No, I'll never ask you to go against your family. You may have even said that in reply. You know you thought it. You'd become her "complication." Go part of the way with me and I'll be content, you thought, but whatever you do, don't leave me. You ridiculous Tom. You drooling impediment. You impossible Negro.

11:20 P.M.

I don't recall if she placed the letter "E" beside the "V" or if I did. Perhaps neither one of us did. I do remember her winning, though. She always won at Scrabble.

11:22 P.M.

Though the rain has long ceased, the wind still clicks cantankerously around the north face of the cottage making the rocky chairs creak, or sending an empty watering can scuttling over the stone veranda. The proprietor keeps the porch well stocked with firewood beneath a tarp. We listen as the tarp implores the wind to untie it, that it might drift over the cliffs.

We are waiting for the New Year to strike. Quietly. Imperceptibly. Trying to make it through another year. We are grateful not to be submerged beneath the din of a crowd in waiting for the one bell and a tinny band to play, that perfect strangers might tilt toward each other like falling manikins and kiss.

The wind is silent. I zip up the thick fleece jersey she gave me six days ago for Christmas. She dons her indestructible blue jacket that she wears for outdoor work in inclement weather. We venture out onto the porch. The rocking chairs and the railing are still wet from the rain, so we stand side by side, looking out over the terrain of stubby grass and gravel that stretches out to were the precipice gives way to the sea. We can hear the water lapping the rocks, but we can see no clear line where the land ends and the cliffs begin. She puts her arm around my waist. I put mine around her shoulder.

"The moon's disappeared," she says.

"It's just behind those clouds."

"What should we do tomorrow?"

"I don't know. It's New Year's. It depends on the weather. It depends on what's open."

"We should come here in summer."

"Think of the people who come here in summer."

"Yes," she says, "there's that."

"The fire's getting low."

"Let's stay here a while."

She goes inside and returns with a towel and some old newspapers. She pats down the rocking chairs and makes a newspaper pad for each one. We rock silently, listening to the sea, waiting for the moon to return. She asks if she said something to offend me on our drive up the coast. I tell her, I don't remember saying anything on the drive. That's why I asked, she says, you didn't say anything...not really. I rock back and forth uneasily, as though riding the chair to my escape.

She isn't always the obliging liberal that she is when she's with her family and friends, I tell myself. We're alright when we're alone together. Really, we are. I wonder if she had these same arguments with that Black militant of her Black affair in the 60s? It was probably different then. He was part and parcel of her striving for autonomy from the White men in her life; much the way Shelleen was for Ginny, Belinda, Edna, Helen, and the others. She could flaunt him, the way she used to flaunt her body: see, look at me, she could say to them, I have the power to be you and to betray you. But she needs no such cachet now. A Black lover can't give her the same cachet today, as he could back then. I was necessary then. I am all but expendable now. Whoever he was, he was smart: he had courted her while letting her keep her illusions. He loved her, or at least said he loved her, while letting her keep her illusions. He was a man of Jim's generation. They had more sense back then.

She places her hand on the arm of my chair to stop my rocking.

"You may as well say it," she tells me, "whatever it is—whatever it was."

I surrender. I bite the bullet and tell her of my silent anger at all the road signs, town and park names of massacred Indians. But I don't tell her of my thoughts about her impromptu homily on "nature," because I had enjoyed it as much as I had resented her for it, because I did not know where enjoyment ended and resentment began, because I didn't want to argue. So, I left it with the Indians, instead of complicating it with the Blacks.

She says she shares my indignation. I say, yes, I know she does. Safe, I think; we've dodged a bullet.

"You must really hate me. It's not just something you said in a fit of anger."

"I try not to hate you."

"That's not an answer."

"Okay...I hate you, just as you hate me."

"You're wrong. I love you."

"You're not in touch with yourself."

"You're so condescending."

"That doesn't change anything."

"How do you know what I think?"

"I know what you can't afford to lose—your relations, your world. You might not feel toward me what I can't help but feel toward you—what seizes me when I least expect it—but that's no indication of your love for me. It's a sign of how stable things are, of how many cops are within ear shot."

"I feel crushed by your explanations."

"You invert the world when you say that."

"I didn't say *you* crush me. I said I *feel* crushed. You can't tell me you don't feel crushed as well."

"No…you're right."

"I don't see how Ginny, Belinda, Helen, Edna, Darcy, or the men for that matter…how are they going to change, if it's so hard for me, and I'm sleeping with you?"

A few weeks after I wrote my open letter to the faculty, a delegation of women comprised, I am told, of the very people Alice mentioned, went to see Shelleen Johnson, their newly elected chair—the woman they'd elected, presumably, to lead them. They placed a copy of the letter on her desk like a subpoena. They'd spent half of December and half of January mulling over it, stewing in the soup of its venom. It had spoiled their Christmas. It had sullied their Seder. It had flattened their New Year's champagne.

Well? Well, what? Shelleen responded. But her response did not have the bite of sarcasm that it might have had had large numbers of Black folks been within striking distance. Still, I believed her when she told me that her voice was firm, for she was born and raised in Mississippi and she knew how to quash a flutter from her voice. Firm as her tone was, however, the words would have been uttered cautiously, for Mississippi had also taught her the latent power of a gathering such as this.

Have you seen this letter, Shelleen? Shelleen might have nodded and laced her fingers and clasped her palms across her stomach and leaned back in her chair, lengthening the distance between her and the inevitable. Or, she might have simply said, Yes; or been coy and said, He put one in everyone's box. We want to know what you're going to do about it. Do about it? Yes, do about it. He's a member of the faculty who had something to communicate; he communicated it; I don't see what's to be done about it. You don't see what's to be done? No, do you? We want to know what you think of it? Well, it's provocative. *Provocative?* Yes. It's racist; he says we're all guilty until proven innocent. Not all of us. The silence that fell upon Shelleen's words was deafening. So this is where you stand, their expressions suggested, after all we've done for you. It may have been Belinda Ritz who broke the silence and said, So, you agree with him, you're in support of this screed? Shelleen sighed deeply and thought, now is my nigger moment. Lord have mercy. I'd almost made it through the day without my nigger moment. But there it was laying in the cut, hiding in the bushes, crouched in ambush by the side of the road. They just won't let me be. Finally, she said, I might have written it differently. How differently? Nigger moment let go my toe. How differently, they asked again. Frank's language is a little crisp, to be sure, and there are several expletive deletions that I would have omitted. But which I'm three seconds off of, if you heifers don't get out my office. But the content, Ginny asked, do you agree with his argument? I would have no argument with it, Shelleen told them. Well, they said, rising in subdued indignation, It would seem that we're done here.

Not long after Shelleen's interrogation, I got a call from another instructor, who was also a woman of color. She was nervous as she spoke and took a long time to say why it was she had called, as though she was trying to make up her mind as to whether or not she was going to tell me the "something disturbing" she had called about. Apparently she had recently moved into the office of someone who'd just gone on maternity leave and was shocked to find the computer had simply gone into sleep mode but had not be shut off or logged out. The in-box of the emails appeared. It was there that she found an extended dialogue between a select group of faculty. There was a consensus of indignation and self-righteous condemnation regarding the letter. None of this surprised me nor was any of it conclusive enough to be of significance. But then she said that toward the bottom of these exchanges, one of them had written "someone needs to spank Shelleen." And, she added, to this there was general agreement. We need hard copies! I exclaimed. She quickly hung up the phone.

Shelleen Johnson resigned her post as chair shortly after the parlay with her "sisters." She left as much as $20,000 above her salary on the table. She put in for an office in another building—one where she would not run into them. She returned to full-time teaching. She parked in a lot far away from them. She went for her mail at night. She did whatever photocopying she needed to do at night as well. But her "sisters'" visit wasn't the actual last straw; her early "retirement" had been building for months. If anything, the last straw came *after* their visit; when they "spanked" her. They had given her sisterly winks and nods and even bold assurances that they would support her in her efforts to hire more women of color and another Black woman in particular. But when, in March of 2000, a Black woman made the short list, they pulled the rug from under and threw their weight behind a White man. (No doubt they would say that she had pulled the rug from underneath them in the months leading up to the hire.)

Belinda Ritz, "the last White man in the department," confided the details of the "secret" job search proceedings to Alice. That was Friday. At first, Alice refused to tell me what they'd talked about—only that it was the behind the scenes scenario. "It was told to me in confidence," she said. But there was an assumption behind her refusal that we both knew too well: *I can never go against my family.* She knew I could not be trusted. She knew that I was not simply *for* Shelleen, but I was against her and her relations. She also knew that she was choosing sides. And she experienced pain and displeasure from the thought of *being* on a side, and more pain and displeasure from the thought of *choosing* a side. She hated me for this as much as she feared what I might do with the content of her talk with Belinda Ritz. Promise me you won't divulge this, if I tell you. How dare you ask me to promise to protect that piece of shit? I replied, you should have been on the phone to Shelleen the moment she left. So she told me; whether because she'd been persuaded by the argument or guilt tripped by the attack, I don't know. That was Saturday. But the story of "sisterly" betrayal during the vote was underwhelming. I had

without even knowing the details. And there was nothing
\n didn't already know. It wasn't nearly as potent as the email
, "Someone needs to spank Shelleen." On Monday Shelleen
d her post as chair. She penned her own open letter to them, one
i. .ich she called the college a bastion of "social apartheid."

11:39 P.M.

A metronome of light pulses slowly on a distant headland. We make
plans to go to the lighthouse if the rain is still ceased by morning. We go
inside and rekindle the fire. It feels good to work at this small task side
by side with her. I twist newspaper into paper logs. She lays down kindling in haphazard plaids. I stack the logs. She lights a match. She tells
me stories of the fires she built for her father to keep him warm during
the Depression. I tell her of the fires I'd built for mine, that he might
stare into them during a depression of another kind.

She tries to find soft music on the radio but there is none to be found
so we settle for news from the BBC. We sit on the sofa in front of the fire,
cover our legs with a blanket, and put our feet on the low coffee table,
long cleared of Scrabble tiles. In London it is already the first day of the
year 2002.

*With middle-class protestors threatening more demonstrations and the
leadership of his party in open rebellion against him, Argentina's interim
president Adolfo Rodriguez Saá resigned yesterday after only one week in
office, plunging the country into a new round of uncertainty and turmoil. The
US State Department added several Islamic organizations to its list of terrorist organizations and the Pakistani government promptly arrested their
leaders. The arrests were also a last-ditch effort by Pakistan to forestall war
with India. In science: experts in the structural engineering community attempted to reconstruct the unprecedented stresses that destroyed the World
Trade Center—from changing methods of internal bracing to innovative escape systems…*

We listen aimlessly until we realize that president Bush has discovered
a flat-faced, 3.5-million-years-old fossil in Kenya named Kenyanthropus

platyops, and that a team of anthropologists had angered Democrats in Congress by blocking federal funds for stem cell research...until we realize that we haven't been listening at all.

"We're not really listening, are we?" she chuckles.

"I thought you were."

"Let's turn it off," she says, "there'll be music again at midnight."

She pours two more glasses of merlot and we watch the fire and drink the wine.

"Do you think we'll get our jobs back at UCSC?"

"Not after what you wrote," I laugh.

"What *I* wrote? We both wrote it. Besides, no one really believes a White woman could have written that letter. And if they know anything about your letter at Cabrillo, they'd see your hand in it, not mine."

"Still, your signature's on this one."

"I was surprised they even hired us; with Cabrillo being right down the road. Don't they talk to each other?"

Mocking an upper-crust British accent, I proclaim: "The University of California at Santa Cruz does not loiter in the lower frequencies."

"I'm retired, officially. I can go on like this until I—" but she doesn't finish the sentence. "I can teach my one class a semester, at night, at Cabrillo. They're happy to have me in that capacity. Teaching the writing course at night. Out of their hair, so they don't have to see me, or risk seeing—"

"Me."

"Yes, you. Helen almost broke down and cried while taking notes in the faculty meeting. She literally begged me to warn all the women—White women, of course—a day in advance of any visit you might make to the campus, whether as a guest lecturer in my or Shelleen's classes, or simply to pick me up. She said she feared for her safety when you're around. You should have seen them all nodding. I've never seen such a sight. Shelleen said she'd seen it before, in Mississippi, but never thought she'd see it in Santa Cruz."

"They're not so teary at a research university. Helen's behavior would embarrass them."

"That's what I'm afraid of, that they'll fire us without tears—without even blinking an eye. All this comes at a bad time for you."

"And for you."

"I'm not facing three years in prison."

"Eighteen months."

"There's no difference to me."

"I guess not."

"Cabrillo, prison, and now even your PhD advisor may have black-listed you."

I bristled. "Whitelisted."

"I'm sorry. This Manichean language is hard to shake. What if Ivanna *white*listed you?"

"Ivanna thinks she's my Svengali. Her letters of recommendation won't get me extra rations in San Quentin."

"How can you joke about this?"

"I'm not going to prison. They'd have to send the White people who were arrested with me to prison as well. They won't do that—we counted on that when we planned the action."

"I wish I had your confidence."

—⁂—

I had been organizing with the third world Liberation Front in Berkeley since May of 1999. Several months later, six members of twLF were charged with assaulting police officers during a building occupation. I went to work clandestinely with an inner circle of the twLF on a plan to take over the Alameda County courtroom during one of our comrades' court appearances. It was not designed as a move to rescue them, as Jonathan Jackson had attempted across the Bay in Marin twenty-nine years before. It was to be an unarmed occupation of the court, one that would allow us to appropriate the space for our own ends.

On the day of the trial three hundred twLF cadres held a demonstration outside the building. Twenty-four cadres had been handpicked to masquerade as ordinary courtroom spectators. Once inside, we would wait for the bailiff to call "All rise," then storm the inner sanctum of the court and force the judge, the prosecutor, and their staff from the room. We had no idea how we were going to handle the two policemen inside the courtroom. They would be Alameda Country sheriffs. We hoped that the Berkeley city police would be reluctant to enter the courtroom itself, preferring to let the sheriffs clean up the sheriffs' terrain (as they had done once in the past); and that it would be at least thirty minutes before a strike force of county sheriffs could get all the way from Santa Rita to Berkeley. There'd be just enough time to let the press in to witness the takeover; to announce our demands (that the twLF Six must be released and all charges must be dropped); to accuse the university and the county of racism (for the twLF Six were made up of two high-profile Black activists, two high-profile Latino activists, and two White activists—when the original arrest "haul" had included more than 100 people, who'd been freed after these six were picked from the crowd); and to levee our own list of charges against the state, the county, and the University of California. As it turned out, it took hours, not minutes, for the sheriffs to arrive. We had time enough not only to lay out our press statement and issue our demands, but to commandeer the court for the purposes of putting our adversaries on trial—in absentia, of course. The University of California executives' rap sheet included the gentrification of Black people in Oakland; the research, development, and manufacture of nuclear arms in Livermore; and oppressive labor practices, especially toward the staff whose paychecks were 35 percent lower than any other staff pay at comparable institutions in the state. Ranking university administrators, and their lackeys in state government, received sentences ranging from three months of community service to working for the third world Liberation Front to up to 20 years in prison. They might have faired better had they not had such a shoddy lawyer—me. The prison sentences posed an ethical dilemma for us since we were committed to prison abolition. The dilemma was resolved by re-sentencing the high-end offenders (like chancellor Berdahl) to 20 years of service to the third world Liberation Front. The occupation and the mock trial made front-page news and Alameda County ended up dropping the charges against the twLF Six. *We* went on trial instead. And each count against us was a felony. Alice was right, the difference between three years and eighteen months hardly mattered.

As if that wasn't enough, I had had a watershed row with my esteemed advisor, Ivanna Delvers, a premier intellectual of psychoanalysis, cinema studies, and feminism. A woman who could, she wasted no time telling me at the start of this dust-up, make (or break) my future; an academic for whom four hundred people would assemble at the Louvre just to hear her speak. She told me that if I wanted to go on being a member of her stable—my word, not hers, but the whole affair had an equestrian quality about it, as though I were an untamed show horse—then I must abandon my "paralyzing and tautological" research on antagonistic identity formations. She reminded me that she had turned away from such radical political research long ago, and had turned to postmodernism, phenomenology, and "love." And she could not countenance my theory that there was a structural antagonism, a structural breach, between Black people and the world. It made for bad theory, she said, with which, she added, I was disrupting her seminars. I've been tolerant with you, hoping you would evolve; from the tautology that you were so full of when you arrived from South Africa. My patience has run out.

What scared and angered me about her dressing down of me was how aware I was of it as an encounter between two asymmetrical powers. My hands were sweating in their familiar way and I hated myself for that. She wasn't interested in debating my research, nor was I being asked to explain. She was handing me an ultimatum.

I don't need this shit. A lot of good knowing her will do me if I go to jail.

I decided not to fight by her rules but to pour gasoline on myself and light a match...then hold her in my arms.

"It's arrogant for you to presume to speak for all Black people," she continued. "There are Blacks in my neighborhood. You can't possibly tell me that they want the same thing you want."

"You're right, Ivanna, we don't all want the same thing. Some of us want your house. Some of us want your car keys. Some of us want your bank account. Some of us want to have sex with you. Then we want you to die and shrivel up and blow away."

She stared at me. For a moment she couldn't blink. I held my hands on my lap beneath the table so she could not see them shaking. Her cup clinked apprehensively against the saucer as she tried, and then aborted her attempt, to lift it to her lips.

"What does this mean," she asked—a tear rolled down her cheek, "for you and Alice?"

11:49 P.M.

Alice watches as I stir the fire. She is trying to come up with the names of professors whom I can ask to work with me, after the row with Ivanna, but she is drawing blanks. She wants me to get in the spirit of this brainstorming with her. I top off our glasses and offer a toast.

"Here's to a sensible judge in the Alameda court and a new advisor... in heaven."

"You're not being serious," she says. Then raises her glass: "To an *inebriated* judge and a new advisor on earth, one with a Teflon skin. And here's to getting our jobs back at the university. They fired Sam and Winston as well. I can't believe they're that stupid: you, a Black man; Sam, a Native American; Winston, a Filipino; and me, a White woman. You'd think the bad press alone would give them pause."

"They'll say we were contract workers in a pool of contract workers; and that we're still *in* the pool, but we're just not needed in the classroom. Melvin did try to warn me."

"Whatever happened to Melvin?" she asked.

"Who knows? Landed on his feet, I'm sure. Folks like him always do. Besides, he didn't laugh that day. And even if he had, he's got tenure."

I can still see Melvin's face when he told me my laughter was a crime. When you laugh, he said, you laugh alone, like a comic in a basement. What possessed me to let Melvin take me to lunch just to chastise me? Who was he anyway? One of those church-going brothers. Those nice, respectable brothers who get early tenure and bleeding ulcers in the same year. A let-me-pull-you-by-the-button-and-give-you-some-advice-fore-you-hurt-yourself-and-the-rest-of-us brother. A passin' it on, passin' it up, eyes on the prize brother. Oh brother, my brother.

"Are you listening to me, Frank?"

I'm adjunct. He's tenured. And lunch is on him. So, yeah, "I'm listening."

"This is California. Not South Africa. *Santa Cruz County*. Not Berkeley. There was no call for your performance this morning in the diversity workshop. And what they say you did last week when the Twin Towers went down! Do you ever think about your career? Do you think about *anything?*"

"Melvin, I'm confused. By 'diversity' do you mean a political movement or a bowl of Fruit Loops?"

"There're a lot of funny Negroes in prison, they always got room for one more. We're in a national security crisis and even the progressive White folks won't tolerate Blacks like you who take up all the air in the room. They've changed the tune since you been gone. They got tired of that ain't-got-no-life-worth-living blues Blacks used to sing. They're singing a mellow, sedate kind of blues, one everybody can sing."

"Ain't-got-no-Spanish-in-my-schools blues. Ain't-got-no-driver's-license blues. Ain't-got-no-free-press blues. Ain't-got-no-sibba-lubbaties blues. Like that?"

"Laugh on, Negro; they'll run you out the afternoon session like it was Little Rock in sixty-five. The way folks feel about us right now—the Asians, the Latinos, sometimes even the Indians—all these folks get together with the White women...Yeah, they're all against the Bush administration. But not *one* of them is anti-American. We can't jump out of a bag like we used to."

"So, how do you feel?"

"Remember last week on TV when all the newscasters asked, Why do they hate us? And all the Black folks kept quiet? I plan to ride this thing out and survive. But you! This morning was bad enough but that stunt you pulled last week, slapping five with those baggy-pants, bald-head, dread-lock, hoop-earring, and I-don't-know-what little riff raff.

Slapping five, talkin' 'bout 'we did that shit;' and the Twin Towers are *still* burning? Frank, the Towers were still burning!"

"Come on now, Melvin, these White—excuse me, these multicultural professors are exaggerating. I didn't say, 'we did that shit.'"

"You didn't?"

"No, it was one of the students."

"Don't trifle with me."

"Look, let's imagine there's a smidgen of truth in it."

"Did it or did it not go down?"

"I'm standing in the hallway, right? Just finished lecturing, okay? I'm minding my own business, Melvin."

"Spare me."

"The Black students ambushed me with their enthusiasm. I didn't know what all the excitement was about. I thought the Raiders had won a road game."

"You're a mess."

"What do you do? The brothers and sisters roll up on you. The brother holds his hand out for some skin. You just leave him hangin'?"

"You damn skippy you leave him hanging! He is a *young* Black man. You are a role model. You leave him hanging or you string him up and dress him down."

"Sounds like a lynching."

"Sounds like a grown man who knows what time it is."

"Speaking of which, shouldn't we be getting back to the Fruit Loops Convention? Don't want Little Rock in sixty-five again, do we?"

"People in high places are angry with you—and with Alice; but mainly with you."

"What if she had written it, by herself?"

"No White woman could've written that letter. Besides, they know all about the letter you wrote two years ago at Cabrillo. Doesn't matter if she wrote this one. As far as they're concerned you wrote it. And they want to know if you intend to be a role model."

"I'm a cross-eyed manic-depressive, they'd never have me in the Role Models."

At the door of the afternoon session I ask Melvin if he had any West Indian in him.

"All that 'role model stuff' and how Blacks need to stop breathing so other people can breathe—all that immigrant integrity."

He drew his face to mine and hissed.

"If I make it through one—just one!—of these workshops and the Koreans don't signify on me about all what they lost in the LA riots, or the Latinos don't signify on me about how it ain't a Black/White binary no more, or some fool don't—christ-almighty, Frank. Here I am trying to help you."

Just then a thirty-something Latina opens the doors to the conference room and beckons us in. She is a facilitator for the team of diversity consultants who have organized the day. She smiles at Melvin as she holds the door open. I don't get a smile. Melvin and I take our places in the last two chairs of the Circle of Diversity in the middle of the gym.

"Behave!" he whispers.

One hour down, one hour to go. I'd like to behave but I'm bored to tears. *Will he make it, folks, or will he die of caffeine deprivation? We'll find out right after this message from Geritol. Do you have iron-poor blood?...*

The facilitators want to end the workshop with a session called "Celebrating Our Diversity in a Time of Terror." *This should be good.*

But it's not good. One droning monologue after another. The Hawaiian gets up and says something in his language then asks us what it means. *I give up, Bubba, what does it mean?* Now the Latina, who wouldn't smile at me, talks about all the people getting turned away at the border and the unfair labor practices, and how her people were here long before 1848. *You go, girl. Christ, I need caffeine.* Finally, the last one stands. A Black man who is also one of the organizers. A soft, respectful, hush settles over the room. Can't nothing hush a room like a pensive Black man about to speak. Yes, indeed, we got church right here on campus. *Show us whatchu got, Reverend.* He puts his clipboard on the floor as he rises slowly. He sighs deeply. Ohhh, how deeply he sighs. He rubs his hands over his face. *That's right, Reverend, take your time; we right here with you.* He moves slowly, ponderously, to the center of the Circle of Diversity. He looks around the Circle of Diversity, peering into each and every face. You're beautiful, he tells us, you're all so beautiful. Did we hear him, he says, you're beautiful. *We hear you, Rev, let the church say amen.* He says, If we didn't know it before we came, we should know it now. Beautiful! All the colors of the rainbow, he says. Beautiful. *Preach, Rev! Bowl of Fruit Loops ain't got nuthin' on this here congregation.* And we should know it when we leave. And each and every one of us, he proclaims, has their own immigration story. Let me tell you mine, he says: I emigrated from Alabama to Los Angeles...

I can't hold it any longer. I bust out laughing. And as I'm laughing, I'm looking at him, thinking, good one, Rev, we got these Fruit Loops, got 'em good, couldn't've done it better myself! And I'm laughing and waiting for him to laugh, but he's not laughing with me. He's waiting for me to stop. So is everyone else.

If he could, Melvin would be wearing a sandwich board disclaiming any and all affiliation with me; but he can't, so he just leans away from me and shakes his head. The immigrant from Alabama just stands there. He looks at me. He looks at me hard. Ghetto hard. Beat-the-black-off-you hard. Toe-to-toe hard. Larceny: his eyes are accusing me of grand theft oxygen.

"Are you finished?" he says in his most dignified voice, that voice Negroes keep next to the telephone for bill collectors, "Or do you have something to share?"

—⁂—

I was in Berkeley when the Twin Towers fell. Alice was in Santa Cruz. What shook me most was not the event itself but its aftermath: the way it catalyzed aphasia in the voices of White and Latino radicals with whom I was associated in Berkeley. The prison abolition movement, the coalition to free US political prisoners (including incarcerated Panthers, members of the Black Liberation Army, and American Indian Movement leader Leonard Peltier), the few cadres who were left in the third world Liberation Front—they all started to lose their nerve. They no longer freely espoused their anti-American sentiment or analysis (at any scale, be it the scale of the university-industrial-complex, the scale of the local police, the scale of the state, and certainly not at the scale of the nation). They feared, as ironic as it sounds, being labeled traitors, a label that they had worn brazenly as late as September 10th; or worse, being lumped with Islamic fundamentalists, which was even more absurd given the rabidly secular orientation of them all. To be sure, there were fault lines among them, between anarchists, marxists, and post-colonialists, but none were of a transcendental nature. After 9/11, the meetings collapsed into anxious lethargy. No one wanted to fight the state anymore. Now the concern was how to distinguish ourselves from "the terrorists" and how to "reach out to middle America" as though "middle America" and the state were somehow separate entities. I realized that I was once again in Kenwood, yes, even here among the sworn enemies of capital and the state I was back in Kenwood. They were the children I'd gone to school with, all grown up now. In times of crisis their true concerns emerge: their troubled meditation on filiation, White filiation, which was now shot through a prism, its dispersed light reaching out to embrace immigrants of color—but not me, not the Indian or the Black; we were not the children of immigration, but dry bones and chattel. The questions now had less to do with revolution than they did with the loss of a parent.

Because the school year always started in late September at UC Santa Cruz, and in late August in Berkeley, and because I was an adjunct lecturer at both schools, I'd spent the last week of August and the first few weeks of September in the North Bay. As always, Alice and I spoke several times a day on the phone. But in the wake of 9/11, I had tried to keep our calls as short as possible, feigning work, or fatigue, or a call coming in on the other line. I did not want to experience the quality of the hurt that I was experiencing in discussions with my "comrades," to hear in her tone what I heard in theirs: their fear of falling afoul of their "family." Nor did I want to explain the exhilaration of many Black people when they watched the Towers fall; to rationalize an emotional response and thus cripple its emotional truth in the face of a "moral" consensus.

She called to see if I'd received the email from a university administrator telling us to attend a mandatory we-are-the-world-diversity workshop facilitated by some people the university was bringing from out
of town. Mandatory? I asked, not having read the email. That's what it
says, even for adjuncts, she replied, in light of 9/11 we're told. I groaned,
silently. People are coming from other campuses, she added. I groaned,
again, silently. Your friend Melvin's coming as well. Now I groaned out
loud. I can see you're not looking forward to this. Are you? I said. *Just
tell me, so we can have it out once and for all.* A thousand betrayals flashed
through my mind. I remembered the scene when, after months of agitating together with Naima, Shelleen, and me against her "sisters," Alice ran into Helen in the parking lot after a night class and cried and
apologized to Helen for the havoc our agitation had supposedly wrought
upon the scene. Alice told me of this episode, later; how much later, I
had wondered. And I still wondered as I held the phone and held my
breath. I had accepted her apology to us as, I presume, had Naima. And
I had cursed myself for my acceptance. Now, as I waited for her answer,
I cursed myself all over again. I held my breath and recalled her quiet
tantrums, her spontaneous betrayal when I let her know that I had been
introduced to a woman named Lisa and that I'd learned about the years
of abuse Lisa endured at the hands of Virginia. At that moment Alice
had been faced with leaving the Coalition Against Institutional Racism,
the organization she'd been a founding member of, and siding with Virginia or staying with us or fighting against Virginia just as she'd fought
against Ginny, Helen, Belinda, Edna, Darcy, and the rest in months after Shelleen and my open letters. No one in CAIR ever heard the in-
vectives toward Lisa that came out of Alice's mouth that day. We were
alone at the café. No one in CAIR heard her defensive rationalizations
of, and her embarrassing apologies for, Virginia's actions. No one heard
her say, She's my daughter (as though Lisa wasn't someone's daughter
and had no children of her own). Instead of saying—in fact omitting,
She's my racist daughter. No one saw the spittle froth in the corners of
her mouth. No one but me. And no one bore witness to my waffling, my
assurances one minute (you won't have to fight her, not directly) and my

condemnation the next (you should be out in front of this). My drooling impediment, my impossible Negro trying to comfort and kill her in the same conversation. They all saw her the day after. They witnessed only the dénouement of solidarity, not the climax of betrayal.

Well, I repeated, without so much as exhaling, Do *you* want to go? You know I don't want to go anymore than you do, she replied. Why do you always test me? she said. Because you can always take your place, I said, there's always a place for you...you can be...or not be. There's more, she said...Frank...are you still there? Yes, I'm still here. She read me another email from another university administrator. It was a directive for the faculty to use a Walt Whitman poem celebrating New York and America to help "the healing process" on our first day of class. I didn't want to accuse her of being in sync with this order and thus start the argument that we had just avoided, so I simply asked her what she thought we should do. And I held my breath. We can't let ourselves be sutured by this national pageantry of mourning, she said. I exhaled, deeply. I wrote a letter, she added, that is I started a rough draft of something I thought we might work on together. Of course, you don't have to, if you don't want to, she continued, I can send it off myself. No, no, please, I said, let me see it, I'd love to work on it with you. It's just a draft and—. Send it to me, Alice, send it as an attachment, and we'll work on it together. It was a good draft, and through our phone calls back and forth that day and our email exchanges we worked on it some more.

September 17, 2001

Dear Oakes Core Faculty Members

Our response to the Whitman poem takes two avenues, a desire not to be incorporated into the national pageantry of mourning, and a critique of the poem itself. It was not clear to us why the poem was sent out to the faculty with the notation that "It's most appropriate for use next week." Were we to assume—since it came from an administrator—that we are being directed to use the poem; and if so, to what end are we to use it?

Since poems are widely open to interpretation, what interpretation was being given to the poem that it would be sent out to us? Is the poem and its circulation, at this point, a literary gesture which unveils the contradictions, antagonisms, and inherent conflict that could have precipitated last week's bombings—i.e. the US as a settler society at home and as a ruthless empire abroad—or does it work to valorize the kind of common-sense assumptions which make America a legitimate entity in the eyes of its inhabitants?

On Whitman and "Crossing Brooklyn Ferry"

As humanities instructors we appreciate the material power of words in times like these but we ask ourselves, why reach back 150 years to translate these events through Whitman, when one could more easily reach back 30 years and translate the events through Malcolm X? Whitman wrote poems celebrating Manifest Destiny in which the redwoods would fall, the Indians would die, the fish would be taken from the stream, but in their death they would all be happy to participate in the westward progress.

We confess that individually, and later collectively, our first response to the poem was one of horror; because Walt Whitman is speaking of Manhattan as a White possession without any acknowledgement of the fact that it was stolen from the Indians. And to underscore the absence of the acknowledgement he dares to use the Indian name for the island. Whitman is speaking as a White settler in possession of the new land— "our" Manhattan. Who is he speaking for and what is the bond?

The current media manipulation of national emotions urges people to join in a national-circling-of-the-wagons hysteria. Whitman celebrates our coming together as one people, but what are we coming together for? Conflict and antagonisms are erased in the celebration. Who is Whitman not speaking for and what would be their take on this moment of viewing "mast-hemm'd Manhattan," if you consider, for instance, that ships carried slaves, carried products generated by slavery and stolen for the benefit of White Americans. And what do we make of the "splendor" he wants himself and "the men and women generations after" him to be "drenched" by? What generations is he speaking of? The generations lost through the genocide of Indians or the generations lost through the institution of slavery, or perhaps generations of Mexican Americans lynched in the southwest, or generations descendent of Japanese Americans interned in the camps, or generations of Chinese slaughtered by miners? What, besides blood, in the American legacy drenched these generations? The question is, who is Walt Whitman talking to and about? This is also the question begged by this national pageantry of mourning. As to the question of why this poem was sent out to us, if the intended interpretation was that it represents the arrogance of White America at work in the world, an arrogance that might have motivated the recent events, then perhaps our labor over this letter was not necessary.

On a national pageantry of mourning

This national pageantry of mourning to which we are all being called is no more than an alibi for a patriotism that will consolidate the forces necessary to further militarize society. The national pageantry of mourning is now the new cultural accompaniment for the entrenchment of a security state that will spread its tentacles and probe into every facet of our lives. It calls upon the same structures of patriotic feeling present in Italy, Spain, and Germany which incubated fascism.

Therefore, for the record, we need to make what is probably the most difficult assertion possible in this time of mindless patriotic fervor: We are not in opposition to American policies, but to that which makes "America" possible. We are against settlerism (nostalgically present in Whitman's poems) and empire, whether it is manifest in the genocidal gunboats off the Philippines, the F16s of Israel and weapons stamped "made in USA," or in Whitman's poetry.

Those of us who've dedicated our lives to the end of America as an entity (not to the end of its "rogue" practices) are in mourning every day. We mourn over the homeless that we step over as they die each day, also in the thousands, also in the streets. We mourn over the American Indians over whose dry bones we build our churches, our mourning convergence centers. We mourn over the real and social death of a people who once were Africans and now are slaves. We mourn for Palestinians who have seen their desire for the end of the Israeli state beaten down to squatter camps on two strips of desert. We mourn for every blade of grass that has ever been touched by America, and now that it is getting stronger in its "Resolve" we mourn even more. And we often mourn alone, or in small numbers, because institutions (for instance the media, universities, and houses of worship) give no symbolic value to those whom America kills in the name of "democracy." The voices of these dead have been excruciatingly absent this past week.

The first thing which is demanded of every "citizen," Left or Right, Black or White, demanded through gestures like the flag atop cars, the vigils of mourning, the poems of nostalgia, is that s/he put his/her sorrow on display. This collective strip-tease of emotions is then the act which binds people, people who might otherwise be able to see, and act upon, the historical and material antagonisms between them—such as the antagonisms between settlers and Indians, masters and slaves. And we do not mean Indians of the past or slaves of the antebellum. To paraphrase Native American writer Leslie Marmon Silko, *if time is an ocean, rather than linear (as White cultural imperialism defines it), then 500 years ago is simultaneous with this minute.* The past is past only for the sake of Whites' comfort and safety.

After we are bound by the common sorrow over this "uniquely American tragedy," then (in some "progressive" circles like the academy) we can entertain whatever questions might arise from this event. This is ass backwards as far as we're concerned. Because, as a form of cultural accompaniment to a political project, it (re)inscribes the legitimacy of the American nation *before* any politics can be done around the oppression of the American nation. Such are the cultural gestures of liberal reformers, among whom the two of us cannot be counted. For we don't look for solutions *within* the national project, because we are well aware of the words of Malcolm X: "Uncle Sam created the problem. He's the criminal. You don't take your case to the criminal. You take your criminal to court!"

In lieu of a national pageantry of mourning
The morning after the recent events our solution is the same as it was the year before, the month before, the day before: Refrain from the use of nostalgic poetry to valorize the country, take down the flags, stop the public vigils and refuse public demands of national allegiance, issue an apology from the US government to the *entire* world, stop funding Israel, stop Plan Columbia, dismantle NAFTA and NAFTA for Africa, dismantle the US government, and give the land and surplus value back to Indians and Blacks, respectively, (in the hopes that they will draw no borders and accumulate no wealth but institute a world whose pledge of allegiance is "Everything for everybody and nothing for ourselves") and then walk away from "America," the most deadly act of terrorism the world has ever known. To the relative success or failure of *these* desires we celebrate or mourn.

Sincerely,
Alice Wilson
Frank B. Wilderson, III

At last, it was ready to send. I phoned her and told her how much I loved it. The timbre of her voice told me she was smiling. It doesn't have your rage, she said, I'm a poet not a prose artist like you—and how does a White person transpose Black rage anyway. I doubt anyone reading it would agree with you, I said, they'd see my hand in it, even if you'd written it when I was in a coma. Yes, she chuckled, if there's credit to be had, they'll give it to the White woman, if there's blame to be had they'll give it to you. The world, I laughed, is a ghetto.

She was right about the distribution of blame. Virginia called Sam, another lecturer, proclaiming, "My mother's being brainwashed." But he was the Native American instructor who would soon be fired with Alice and I. "No," Sam told her, "she's not being brainwashed, she's being politicized." Maybe the letter gave Virginia and the others something solid to hold on to, a concrete justification for their growing distrust of Alice and a way of disavowing its converse, the rising trust of Black people. Alice has been "brainwashed" would stop the ground from slipping from under their feet.

Another delegation of Shelleen's "sisters" assembled one day at noon in the room where the photocopier, the reams of paper, the boxes of pencils and pens, the large two-volume Oxford English Dictionary, the surplus chalk, and the new erasers were; the room behind the reception area where Helen sat, the room beside the mailboxes, the room a little to the left of the room where Shelleen had sat for less than a heartbeat on her porcelain throne. From what I was told, it wasn't an entirely new delegation from the one that had subpoenaed Shelleen; in fact, it was an ensemble of simple addition. I'd like to say they all held hands in a circle, sang "Kumbaya, My Lord," and made benedictions to Mother Earth and Sister Moon as they swayed back and forth, flinging their hair. But I wasn't there, so I don't know what song they sang. From what I was told, the meeting wasn't even planned; unlike their sojourn to Shelleen's office they had not intended to meet. One had come to photocopy her syllabus. Another had come to sip her chamomile tea in peace. Helen would have been there because that's where Helen worked (when she wasn't managing Shelleen). Some had simply come to check their mailboxes and, seeing the others in the inner room, stayed.

He's a brute! He was a terrorist in South Africa, that's what *I* heard. It was right there, in that awful screed he wrote to us: *terrorism.* A homegrown Osama. Poor Alice. Yes, poor Alice. What does she see in him? The myth, I hate to say it, but it must be the myth. She's not *that* stupid...is she? It's nothing to do with intelligence, dear; her brains aren't between her legs. But at her age? What's age got to do with it? Well, I thought she was a practicing Buddhist, they're not supposed to crave. Virginia's the Buddhist no one really knows what Alice is...not anymore. We used to know. Now, I won't let you all run her down! No one's running *her* down; it's him. Yes, him, let's not lose sight of that. He doesn't know how things are done here. He knows but he doesn't care. Still, we can't abandon her just to spite him. Agreed? Agreed. Why *not* abandon her, she abandoned us. That's right, you can't rescue someone who doesn't know they're lost. He'll dump her, now that he's turned her against us. Come on, it's not like she didn't have a hand in it. You're both right; he'll dump her, and yes, she had a hand in it; but he coerced her, she's a victim of domestic abuse. And when he dumps her that's when we'll be able to show her how wrong she was. How? By our openness and our willingness to forgive. By our love. We'll be there for her, she's family.

12:09 A.M.

"I'm trying," Alice says, "but you treat my effort like a seduction, it deepens your resentment."

"I never said that."

"You don't want your shame on the historical record. You fear that, don't you?"

"Perhaps."

"So, what do we have, lust? Your hallucinatory whitening and my Negrophilia, colliding in bed?"

"What do you want me to say?" I ask her.

"If only we were both a little less educated, hadn't read so many books. We could fall in love without incident. Even Lenin had it easier when he asked, what is to be done? I've asked myself that everyday since the day I met you."

"No, you haven't. You think you have but you haven't."

"Fine."

"You met me when you were a child, twenty-one years before I even was born; but you waited until you were in your sixties to ask yourself—"

"You like to hurt."

"I don't like to be hurt."

"I'm sorry...it was a stupid thing to say."

"It wasn't stupid. You're never stupid. If you were stupid it would be easier. It was spontaneous. You shouldn't feel so at ease when you speak. It's not fair to the rest of us."

"What I wanted to say was how I feel about you—how I feel about us. I want to believe that we...you and I..."

"Yes, me too. It's just..."

"I know...I know. My goodness! Look at the time."

THE CONVOCATION OF CONQUEST

my chair was missing from the table
an oversight I'm sure
standing there I considered the distance
we'd walked just to arrive and the
horses apathetic to the prey of their riders
gaining in spite of themselves with heads
so enormous cold mist from their nostrils
fell upon the moon upon you and
me and the men and women
we took with us from the corners of sleep
one dream one table one people with one
unnamable loss and no place set
even aside

11

JOHANNESBURG: APRIL 19, 1993

I waited all night for a knock on the door of the safe house. First by the open window high above the streets of Hillbrow, where I watched the traffic mice move below. Waited until the space between laughing, shouting, and the tap of horns was eternal, until the neon winked no more, and the burnished belt of light, the highway that girdled Jo'burg, grew dim. Later I would hear how Trevor, Jabu, Precious, and Stimela fled on that highway, how Trevor and Jabu and Stimela had been hit, how Stimela bled and Precious pressed his wound and how Jabu told Trevor to slow down.

I drifted from the window to the computer. I tried to write a scenario. We'll need a scenario tonight when the comrades from the union and the student movement arrive, I thought, yes, we'd need a scenario. Who are we going to back now that Chris Hani is dead? Cyril Rhamaphosa? One of the Mayekiso brothers? Winnie Mandela? Every name I came up with, every scenario of aboveground and underground maneuver to support that scenario, every impossible image of an impossible future had no currency. *Will we ever recover from the death of Chris Hani? Have Mandela and his people won by default? Is there no resistance to the new world order?* I felt as though my life efforts had been for naught. I had staked everything on this revolution. *The arrogance of your narcissistic navel gazing!* But there it is, I thought, there it is. I could see no reason to hold yet another secret meeting on Lenin's question, What is to be done? From the computer I drifted back to the window and then to the long table in the middle of the room. I lowered my head onto my hands.

I dreamt that it was not the autumn of 1993 but April as I'd always known it; a Minnesota April of belated winter and fragile spring. I was at my parents' lake house, a white cottage with a red chimney of bricks that spread like thick wisteria up to the roof. Clumps of snow still choked the trunks of trees that encircled the house. Elsewhere the ground was cold and moist or cold and hard, awaiting the return of grass. Here's where I'll plant my roses, my mother was saying, and over there, that's for your father's vegetable garden. She was as striking as she had been when we were children: poised and elegant in her slender blue mackintosh, her bright blue Wellingtons, and a blue scarf tied under her chin as though she'd been chosen not to garden but to model gardening apparel. I am beside her now, gathering wet leaves and winter ice. Let's make a castle of leaves and ice. But she shakes her head at this and says, No, we need compost. She pushes the leaves this way and that way. And I do the same. We love you, she says, without looking at me. Now dad and I are standing out on the lake. This is my icehouse, he says. He pats the side of the hut with his hand. The walls are made of wood, he says, but the floor is the frozen lake. I drill a hole, I plop my line, I sit all day till something bites. As he speaks, I look down and see ripples of water under the ice. It's going to crack. Dad, I say. But he won't answer. *Dad.* He gives me a stern look. Then: what is it? My arms are cold. If you're sick, he says, go to sickbay.

As I woke, I could feel my forehead resting on my forearm. I could feel my forearm resting on the table. One eye opened to a sliver of drool drying on the surface. The cool morning air chilled my arms. Why doesn't Khanya close the window, I thought. Then I heard the fits and starts of early morning delivery trucks in the streets below, the sounds of those who work before work begins, and I knew that I was not at home...nor at my parents' lake house. I went to the bathroom and washed the cat butter from my eyes and the dry spittle from my chin. I went to the kitchen and washed my teacup. I emptied the kettle in the sink. I turned the computer and printer off. I took one last look at the city's towers, their gray walls and glass tinged with the morning's orange light. I closed the window and went down into the street.

There was not enough time to go home to Bellevue East and then trace back through Hillbrow on my way to Vista University in Soweto, not if I was to give my first lecture on time. I sat on the upper deck of a city bus and wrote the best notes I could on Coetzee's *Waiting for the Barbarians*. Enough to bluff my way through forty minutes unless some earnest, eagle-eyed student in the front row said, Mr. Wilderson, would you like to borrow my book? At the Bree Street taxi rank I scrunched into a kombi for Black people that was headed for the Old Potchestrom Road. In my office I took time I couldn't spare to call Khanya. I had to let her hear my voice. I had to hear hers. Desperation. Followed by relief. That was her voice. But her words were simply, You forgot your books and the papers you marked and you didn't take your lunch, she said, not for me, but for whoever may have been listening. For this I was thankful. I bluffed my way through my lectures, feeling first glee and then disappointment, for no student was the wiser. The day ended and I went home and awaited word from Stimela.

Between the night of the bombing and that night, two weeks later, when Red Beard's agents crept up to Trevor Garden's dorm room and tapped softly on his door, leaving him with the terror of a small dress rehearsal of what they'd stage in the morning—the helicopter swooping down on his car, one yellow casspir chasing him up the hill, and one bouncing down the hill, now spinning sideways to block his escape—in this brief intermezzo of freedom, Trevor Garden wore a rain poncho wherever he went, whether it was hot or cold, rainy or clear. One day he and I were alone in the safe house, the propaganda safe house to which no one came when I waited. I was to find out later that Mandela's people had summoned key Leftists whom they thought (and rightly so) would retaliate for Hani's death. They had paid "friendly" visits to those who would not be called in: You must not want a position in the New South Africa, because you're certainly not behaving as though you do? Oh, you *do* want a job in the New South Africa. Then stand down. No retaliation.

No propaganda offensive. No exploitation of the riots and the mourning in the streets. Above all, no elaboration of intransigent demands. We're that close, just *that* close, to coming to power; we won't stand by and watch Hani's people fuck it up!

But the elaboration of intransigent demands was the very purpose of our meeting.

Stimela Mosando had spirited Precious Jabulani to Tanzania, for reasons which I would only comprehend in bits and pieces, through half-spoken scraps of speech delivered to me over the next few months, and then finally, fully explained to me in the last year of my time in South Africa. It was April of 1993; Precious would not return until that September. Jabu was in hiding. Oupa...where was Oupa? I would never see Oupa again, not in person. He would come to me in a photograph, however, one month after the first elections of the "new" republic. It was a large newspaper photograph, in May of 1994; accompanied by a celebratory article proclaiming a New Day for Democracy in a New South Africa. A jubilant crowd, having just applauded Mandela's speech calling this the hour of Peace and Reconciliation, having held their ears against blue jets breaking the sound barrier, having cheered and pushed skyward through streamers and confetti, now poured through the street. African women wore bright green head wraps and bright green dresses patterned endlessly with the portrait of Mandela. They danced around the dignitaries who led the procession. Sprinkled randomly throughout were men wearing dark suits and sunglasses, men who were neither leading nor celebrating. As I looked closer, I realized they were not randomly sprinkled, but wedged in strategic proximity to the dignitaries—at their elbows, as it were. The granite slates of their sunglasses looked not at the camera but off to the sides; not at the dancing women but up to unseen windows and balconies. One of them was Oupa. So that's where he disappeared to, I would think when I saw the photograph. He's a government agent now. I thought we'd said we'd never let that happen; never work for a government that reneges on its mandate; never work for the state, but work, always work, for the revolution. But at that moment, I would remember that it was what Stimela had said; we had all nodded our assent. But Oupa hadn't nodded. He listened quietly and cleaned his nails with his knife.

In the immediate aftermath of Chris Hani's assassination, no one could see the future; we who mourned him most wondered if there would be a future. Chris Hani was dead and the moderates were filling the void with their easy acquiescence to the new world like the ocean filling a void. Neither Trevor, as he sat at the computer, reading with rising irritation the words I had spent hours writing, nor I, as I sat behind him at the long table and tried to keep my ego in check—neither of us could have imagined that the first non-racial elections were just a year away.

Trevor made another coarse comment about my compound sentences and grammatical structure, a morass, he griped, from which the subject of speech stands no chance of emerging. We're writing for the masses, he said. Comrades must pick this up on a train to the mines or in a kombi to their job and not have to go home for a dictionary and a grammar book. This reads like a self-absorbed White prick from Parktown.

I absorbed his tirade in bemused silence. But I wondered why his shoulders shook as he spoke. His voice reached high tones and octaves that I was sure he'd not reached since puberty and at one moment I even thought he would break down and cry. I'd never seen him like that.

I needed to ease the tension, so I started horsing around—telling jokes about the ridiculous poncho he was wearing. It was the worst thing I could have done. I just wanted him to be Trevor again, the old Trevor: the sure-eyed witty literary student, the albino terrorist with a smile and always something pithy to say.

"What kind of idiot wears a rain poncho indoors?" I said, and tugged at that gray nylon tent. "Take this bloody thing off," I said, mimicking the polished English accent he used when he needed an acoustic disguise. As I pulled the poncho he cried out in genuine pain. I had caused the gun and the holster hidden underneath to scrape against skin torn just days ago by flying shrapnel. He stood up. I took a step back. He gave me a sharp look and went to the bathroom.

"Seventy-two hours." His words floated out through the open door. Then the water ran again, drowning them out. I crept over to the bathroom. Through the cracked door I saw him. The poncho was on the toilet. He still had not removed his shirt. He was hunched over the sink, his head turned down, not looking in the mirror. He held onto the sink as though trying to keep from falling overboard. "Time enough to get Precious across the border." I returned to the computer and began looking at what he'd done to my words. Did he say dismantle the network? I wondered.

He emerged from the bathroom, draped his poncho over a chair, placed his gun then his holster on the table, and clapped his hands. "How 'bout some tea, comrade." His voice was false. "Rooibos! Best tea in the world. I'll make it. None of your *decaf* coffee," he said in a mock American accent. "Tea worth coming to South Africa for, am I right?" He ducked into the kitchen without counting my vote. Soon he returned with two steaming cups.

I sipped the tea and watched him. He put his gun back in the holster, slung the holster over his neck and shoulder, and positioned it all very carefully so as to avoid further abrasion of his wound. Then he poked his towhead through the neck hole of the poncho as it fell like a shroud from his shoulders to his legs.

"Something on your mind?" he said.

"What were you talking about?"

He simply said, Pardon me, com, which meant please stand so I can take my place at the computer. I let him have his place back. I sat at the long table and watched his back as he tapped the scroll key, moving my missive up the screen.

"You've been here how many years?" he said. I didn't answer. "You simply refuse to write for the masses. It's a bloody handbill, not a conference paper."

"Seventy-two hours. Dismantle the network. Get Precious to Tanzania? What's going on, Trevor?" But what I really meant was, What's going to happen to me?

He spun around in the chair. He looked at me the way he'd looked at me when I'd pulled the holster against his wound. Then a broad smile spread across his face.

"Something interesting," he said, and turned back to the computer.

I was livid. "Am I in or am I out? Or am I just in limbo?"

"You're a clerk. You're a scribe. You hold elected office in the ANC. So do hundreds of other people. You give the odd speech above ground. You deliver the odd weapon here, help strategize the odd move that the ANC can't own up to. So do a lot of other people. Don't romanticize your role. You'll end up telling your story in pubs for a pint."

"I don't drink beer."

"You will," he said, tapping at the scroll key.

I would see Trevor Garden once more before he was captured. It was a chance encounter. I came upon his car as I crossed Yale Road and cut through the carpark between the Law School, where I was to meet Khanya, and the dormitory where he lived when the rent in Auckland Park became too steep for him. Though the sun gleamed on his newly washed car, I was rushing and would have surely missed it, tucked as it was discreetly between a maintenance truck and a four-wheeled oddity, an American station wagon, had he not called out to me.

"What's you're hurry, professor?"

I turned and saw him getting out of his car. He rested his right arm, the good arm, the one saved from the blast, along the top of the open car door. He was still wearing that poncho.

"Hi," I said, a little coolly, remembering his crack about pubs and pints. Still, there was no hiding the fact that I was extremely happy to see him. He was happy to see me as well.

"You're a long way from Soweto," he said.

Yes, I know, we're out in the open and it doesn't matter that it seems as though the carpark is empty. Make it look like what it should be: a chance encounter between a former Wits lecturer and his former student. Make it look like what it is.

"Vista's on strike. The students and the workers. I'm surprised you haven't heard."

Of course, you've heard. You had a hand it, as did Jabu and Precious. Where is Precious?

"No lectures today. Khanya and I have a date. She's working at the legal clinic."

"Where're you two going?"

"Café Zurich," and then I laughed, "to see if it's multiracial."

"I don't get it."

"It's an old joke."

"I'd give you a lift but I'm—"

"Going in the opposite direction."

"Another direction," and he almost added 'com,' but he said, "my friend," instead.

"I'll see you to the pond," he said. When we'd put a few yards between his car and us, he said, "It's not been swept." I let him talk. He needed to talk. "I shouldn't be armed. That could give them an excuse." I knew better than to ask him to explain. We stopped beside the pond by the Law School. The breeze felt redemptive. A willow by the bank swayed gently, the tips of its branches touched the water.

"Sometimes I think it's better to die quickly, in a hail of bullets," he said. "No lingering pain." Then he said, "I'm sorry. All this gibberish. Look, com, give Khanya my best." He started back to his car. He turned around.

"And I'm sorry for the other thing."

"For what?"

"I know you don't drink beer."

SOMETIME IN JUNE 1993

I got off the bus in Hillbrow and decided to walk the rest of the way—not because the bus wouldn't take me from a SASCO rally at Wits in Braamfontein to our home in Bellevue East, but because I had reached my third year of marriage and my second year in exile and an anxious finality had begun to dawn on me: that I was married and far away from "home."

Only by walking could I put some time and distance between me and the love of one woman; me and a shameless desire to leave.

Through the bog of my dilemmas he came upon me. You'd think a Black man could spot a White man coming from miles away, especially in a street like Hillbrow's Pretoria Street, chock-full of Black people on their way to the kombis or bundling in and out of shops before closing. But he had an uncanny way of blending in with blackness; not through the mimicry of gait or attire but by the simple fact that he had abandoned his people—their needs, their compulsions, their points of attention. In their presence he fidgeted uncomfortably, as though he had a train to catch. He was one of those odd accomplishments (as much Nana's as his own) who relish deeds of treachery against their kith and kin; his wrists, scarred and swollen from the bite of electric cables, were proof of this treachery as much as they were of the relish his kith and kin took in his return.

We stood on Pretoria Street and talked about, of all things, the lectures he'd missed. He was drugged with pills that would steady his nerves and keep his hands from shaking, but he was coherent, at least he was coherent. What does one say to one's friend, one's student, one's comrade, one's commander when meeting him for the first time after six weeks of torture?

The lit-crit faculty and graduate students were throwing a party for him that night. Christ-almighty, I thought, after six weeks of torture, we're talking about *school*. The thought of going to the suburbs to "honor" one of suburbia's wayward sons who'd waged war against the very scaffolding of suburbia seemed surreal. Trevor found it mildly amusing. But after six weeks of isolation and torture he was grateful to be wanted by someone, even the people he held in contempt.

Finally, I mustered the nerve to ask him how and where they'd tortured him.

"Here," he said, drawing my attention once again to his wrists.

I looked at them the way one looks at the razor marks of a botched suicide asleep in a recovery room. The sun was setting behind the tall apartment buildings of Hillbrow. Soon the streets would empty out the workers, and the Twilight Children would cross the pavement in their rags and torn shoes, with their faces perpetually snotty from sleeping on warm sidewalk grates in damp air, and from sniffing glue to stay high long enough to last the homeless night.

We could have been any two people trafficking in whatever's forbidden in stores; me a thirty-something educator in need of illicit release, he, my twilight-trick for the night. Except for one thing: he was White and I was Black. Somehow the roles needed to be reversed, for in all the possible play of codes elaborated each night in Hillbrow's web of vice, there was still no place for a Black john and a young White trick. I was Black and he was White; therefore, to give any coherence whatsoever to this mise-en-scène it would have to be translated by the occasional on-looker as a drug deal transacted foolishly out in the open. I could then be a Nigerian, a Zairian, or a refugee from one of the Frontline States holding the wrists of a young White junkie, collecting my debt, staking my claim, testing South Africa's blue-eyed veins. I couldn't stop looking at the teeth marks on his wrists where the cables had pinched him and set his skin on fire.

"Did they—" My eyes fell from his wrists to his groin.

"No," he said. Then he told me his interrogator said he never went for the testicles; they didn't want it to be "personal." I was unable to find any solace in the fact that his balls had been spared if, indeed, they had been spared. Torture is worse than death, I thought. Death lays the body to rest. Torture defiles it and returns it to the living without its shadow.

The night before his arrest there had been what might be called a "dress rehearsal." Special Branch came to Barnato Hall, the student residence where he lived in a room the size of two or three closets. He could hear them whispering outside the door. They knocked softly, like elves rather than members of the Special Branch. He didn't answer. As quietly as he could he drew his Glock-9 to his side. He sat up in bed and scrunched his knees against his chest and waited. Quietly, they knocked again. He flicked the safety off. The moon was high and soft through the blinds of his window. Lines of light cut across his feet, the sheet, across his knees, and face. So still was the air he could smell dust on the windowsill beside his head. Nothing stirred. Not even the stars. They had gone as quietly as they came.

He stayed that way (weapon at the ready, knees drawn tight to his body) all night. No bowel movement, no food; twice he got up to piss in a tin can meant for pencils and pennies. On the morning of the second day he rose long before the breakfast bell, threw together a few essentials, holstered his gun, draped himself in his poncho, and slithered down the fire escape. He made his way across the green to the student parking lot. The flat light rising over the Faculty of Arts and Social Science buildings of east campus was not yet high enough to dry the grass and check the slow cold seepage of dew into his tennis shoes.

There's no silent way to start a car so he turned the key, revved the engine, spun out of the lot, and took his chances. From the parking lot one turns left into a tunnel, fifty yards or so of underground road which separates the Law School and Barnato, west campus, from Yale Road and east campus.

Once inside the tunnel he knew he was trapped. He heard the leathery thud of helicopter blades thumping the air. He floored the accelerator, dashed out from the tunnel, and turned right on Yale Road. He climbed the hill at breakneck speed. But already a yellow casspir was rambling up the hill behind him. He couldn't see the chopper in front of him nor in his rearview mirror but the sounds of its blades were as present as the upholstery of his car, which meant it was right on top of him. Clear the hill, he thought, if I can only clear the hill. It was then that a northbound casspir bounced over the hill in front of him and spun sideways in the middle of his lane. He slammed on the brakes only to be rammed from behind.

Several hours later they strapped him to a wooden chair on the tenth or eleventh floor of Sun City. He wasn't sure of the floor: he had tried to count the number of stairs and landings as they marched him up with a hood over his head, but they had suspected this, and marched him down again—four flights, he thought—then up three, and down five, and up six. That made ten, yes, he said, the tenth floor, if his math was right. He and his interrogators were operating under the rule of 72. Trevor had 72 hours to keep from talking. Long enough to let the rest of the unit cover its tracks, dismantle current safe houses, and find new DLBs. Long enough for Stimela to get out of the country, cross the border into Tanzania. Heinus Bezeuidenhout had 72 hours in which to make him talk. After that the information would be useless. It was a dance to which both partners knew the steps all too well.

The din of Hillbrow's traffic grew soft. Soon the Twilight Children would come out for the tourists, for the johns, for the night and its shadows beyond the grasp of the police.

"For years I've been in this struggle as a White person. An albino terrorist, as you once said. Detention and torture was a kind of favor de Klerk did for me. For six short weeks I experienced what it must be like to be Black one's whole life. Think of me as a lucky one."

No, I thought, the lucky ones keep their shadows, yours they peeled away.

I'd been holding his wrist so tightly he had to wrest it free. I felt my lip trembling.

"Don't weep for me." He disappeared his wrist into his pocket. "Weep for Jabu. What they did to Jabu," he said, shaking his head.

Like Trevor, Jabu had been arrested near his dorm at Wits. They showed him no warrant. Take your toothbrush, was all they said. They covered his head with a sack and drove him not to Sun City (John Vorster Square), where Trevor was, but to a park. They placed him on a park bench. We know your cousin Stimela is behind this, they said as they beat him. Tell us where he lives. He didn't know, he kept repeating, he didn't know. Finally, he could take no more, so he told them Stimela stayed in Yeoville, but he didn't know the address. He'd managed to sound believable—so they stopped. If one moves one's finger west to east on a map of Jo'burg's northern edge, one comes to Braamfontein, Hillbrow-Berea, and then Yeoville. Both of Stimela's safe houses were in Hillbrow. By saying Yeoville, Jabu had, in fact, told a lie, but had also made a cartographic association that gave his demeanor a quality of truth. They left the park and took him to John Vorster Square. In the booking area Jenny van der Stel brought him tea. She was young and White and pretty. And her uniform was tight fitting around the firmness of her curves. She asked him, politely and even invitingly, where he had been on the night of April 19, 1992. He sipped his tea and stared at her. She told him he could talk with her and go to sleep in his cell or the officers in the next room, the men from the park, could take him upstairs. Still he was silent. They took him upstairs and suffocated him with a wet towel. They rubbed and boxed his ears. Then they poured cold water into his eardrums. The next day they brought him to the Krugersdorp police station where they tied his hands and feet together and suffocated him some more. Then they put him on the cold cement floor and jumped up and down on his stomach. The following day they brought him to Brits, just east of Rustenburg, where the grassland is flat and the trees are scattered, just shy of the mountains hollowed out by platinum mines; Brits, where citrus groves sweeten the air along the highway (unless one's head is covered with a sack). They took him to Brits because he was "being uncooperative." They placed a hand grenade in his palm and pulled the pin. Hold on tight, they said, as they placed another grenade on his groin. They left the room. After some time they returned. The pin was reinserted. Well? they asked. He still wasn't talking. We didn't find your cousin in Yeoville, they said. I think he's been lying to us. No, he's a good kaffir, a university student, they don't lie; he's tired that's all. You're right, he's just tired and confused. He needs a holiday is what he needs. They dragged him to his feet, threw him into a windowless kombi, and took him to a farm. They tied him to a stake in the barn and began to beat him again. He begged them for mercy. They asked him what he thought of the idea of their framing him on drug charges in lieu of a confession for the bombing.

Trevor was quiet. Then he said, "Jabu fucked with them on that farm."

"How could Jabu fuck with *them?*"

"He told them an elaborate story about arms caches buried in the suburbs of Parktown, Rosebank, Sandton. Then he signed a confession to that effect and actually led them to the houses where the DLBs were. He stood in front of the houses, pointing at each one while the police took his picture for evidence."

"Whose houses were they?"

"Who knows. Jabu sure as hell didn't know. Special Branch went back, detained the residents, and tore the plaster from the walls in search of our DLBs."

"And found no guns!" I laughed.

"And found no guns. But they made a few enemies. These were loyal South Africans; some of them were members of the Nationalist Party."

"They must have really moered Jabu after that."

Trevor looked as his feet. He didn't want to go on, but I had to know. "Two days ago, at the obligatory braai—"

"You had barbecue with your torturers!?"

"Their way of saying 'no hard feelings mate.' My interrogation had been winding down but they kept beating Jabu right up to the braai. They brought us to the place where the braai pit was and they beat him some more while they made me turn the meat and tend the fire. Then they bound his hands and ankles behind him and together and they looped a rope around a branch of the tree under which I stood and they strung him up—suspended him in a bow pose just above my head. Four of them went back to the table a good distance from the tree while another one climbed up a step ladder, pulled the pin from a small grenade, and stuck it in Jabu's mouth. He hung there until I cooked the meat and it was ready to serve. He never relaxed his jaw."

There. He'd said it all. Or he'd said all that he could possibly say without falling apart. Now and then the silence was pierced by the sounds of braking cars on pavement still wet from the rain and the spinning sounds they made as the light changed and they drove off. Tears welled in my eyes.

"I'm being followed," he said. "I'm sure of it. What do you see behind me?"

Lamplight, dusk, and the last flecks of sunlight settled in to welcome the night. Behind him and across the street a queue of Africans stood along the yellow wall of Checkers grocery store, hoping the security guard would search their bags fast enough to let each one of them into the store before closing. A middle-aged White woman walked past them to the front of the line. The guard, who was Black, and knew his place, asked politely *if madam wouldn't please stand in line with all the others.* She turned her beak and demurred in the direction of the throng, "I'll not queue with kaffirs. Nor will I let one search my bag." She was inside before he had time to be insulted. He turned to the queue of "kaffirs," to the only people his gun and uniform was big enough to stall, and continued searching bags.

But I saw nothing untoward. Only Checkers, the queue, a prism of primary colors running in rainwater along the curb, and the wet hiss of evening traffic. He's losing it, I thought. He's been burned all up and down his body and walked all this way succumbing to hallucinations and the haze.

"Try again," he said, "this time *see* without looking, as though there is nothing to find."

"Checkers, the queue, a White woman who just won't wait, that's all I see."

"That's all you've *selected.*"

"Blocks and blocks of parked cars."

He nodded, "Continue."

"That's it," I said with sympathy and exasperation, "they go on and on for—Jesus Christ! How could you have known?" He didn't answer. His body stiffened. "They're at least a block away," I said.

His face tightened. "Give me as much detail as you can. Pat me on the shoulder first, and break out laughing."

"It would help," I said, slapping his shoulder and bustin' up at the sides, "if you could actually tell a joke." I let the fake laugh shake and ripple through my body and then tried to relocate the parked car. "A small Opel. Blue. Or a Toyota. I can't tell from here."

"That's okay." Now it was he who grabbed my wrist.

"The contour of a woman and behind the wheel the figure of a man."

"Yes." It was the yes of desperation, impatience, or both.

"She's sitting on the driver's side with her hands on the wheel. She's wearing a garden on her wrist. One of those Longines-Wittnauer wrist corsages—with a watch buried somewhere inside."

"Jenny van der Stel," he whispered into his neck. "The booking sergeant at Sun City."

Checkers was closing, having only let in half the queue for evening shopping. I didn't see the White woman whose allergies to Africans were given special consideration. No doubt she'd fetched her milk, her bread, her morning eggs and sausage, and had gone.

"What's the man doing?"

"He's lighting a cigarette and pretending to talk to her the same way I'm pretending to talk to you."

"And his belly is big?"

"I can't tell from here."

"Has he bratwursts for hands?"

"Perhaps—I'm not sure."

"His spectacles pinch his nose and his beard is red."

"Yes."

"We're old friends, Red Beard and I."

I can still remember the party later that night. At last, his true identity had been revealed to them, a living room full of young, White, increasingly tipsy lit-crit students who began the evening feeling ashamed of their own willful abstention from the anti-apartheid struggle, whether armed or unarmed. They were in awe of and, it should be added, cowed by and resentful of Trevor. As the evening wore on, they fell prey to a profound sense of betrayal; a sense of betrayal that Trevor's family—who were not liberals—had no qualms in expressing. But the students and faculty at Wits considered themselves to be more enlightened than the ordinary red dirt Boer. Trevor's "betrayal" coupled with his embarrassing presence (never mind the fact that this party was their idea, not his) frayed their equanimity and eroded their compassion. As their speech, loosened by liquor, grew thick and slurred and uninhibited, they lit into him. You're a fool. You're pathetic. You're a dupe of a retro-Marxist dream. Haven't you learned anything from what we've studied? We're in a new postmodern era, capitalism is either going to devour us or burn itself out—you can't *struggle* against it. I felt sorry for Trevor, but more than anything, I felt rage toward *them*, some of them my former students;

a rage I could not express without risking a dressing down later in the week from Stimela.

The wounds on his wrists where they hooked him up to a battery were still fresh and weepy. Trevor excused himself, went to the bathroom, and took the pills he and Jabu had been given by the ANC. Then he returned and sat cross-legged on the floor with his post-interrogation interrogators, as though he was joining them in a game of spin the bottle. If only he'd had a pill to stop the spread of Cretin-itous. You sanctimonious little shits, I wanted to yell, living up here in Sandton with your Black gardeners and Black maids who taught you how to wipe your ass. He wasn't fighting capitalism. He was fighting the you in him.

I tried to imagine what these White students would have said to Jabu, had the party been for him: We're in a postmodern moment; just let capitalism burn itself out and go with the flow till it does? Would Jabu's suffering even register with them, the way Trevor's suffering did? No, I realized, they would resent Jabu's intrusion; they would think his wounds had nothing to do with them. What is it like to take your suffering by proxy?

September 3, 1993

Dear Professor [Edward] Said,

I heard rumours that you had leukemia. I do hope you're doing everything you can to take care of yourself. You have meant and continue to mean so much to me. My time as your student has left its stamp on me in ways that I'm just now beginning to realize.

The struggle here looks more hopeful on the campuses than it does on the factory floor but the students have not had any form of intellectual or logistical support from academics in this country. They want a revolution that's well behaved. Their anxiety over SASCO's "tactics" stunts their capacity for solidarity. The other day I went to Wits and had coffee on the Concourse with two lecturers I knew from when I taught there last year. They were infuriated with SASCO and with Nelson Mandela's "inability to bring them to heel."

"We're bloody well fed up with SASCO and its tactics," one of them said. "Sabotage and the targeting of professors who, you know as well as I do, Frank, are the only ones who wanted them admitted in the first place. They only isolate themselves." I said that the reasons for SASCO's "isolation" had nothing to do with its tactics—and that it may be "isolated" here in Braamfontein but it wasn't isolated in Soweto. "Who invited you to South Africa, anyway?" he snapped, and toddled off to lectures. The other lecturer at the table was a woman whose father was Greek and whose mother was Irish. She'd come from Greece when she was ten. When her colleague left she said, "I'm going back to Greece." And then she waited, as though she was waiting for me to condemn her for having said it; or as though she'd already condemned herself. Then, apologetically, she added "on holiday. But I don't know if I'll be back. There's a civil war brewing."

I don't know whether I felt empathy for her or betrayed by her.

Last night Reba dreamt of the Coloured boy and girl she plays with downstairs. They were hugging each other when some White people came out of a building and stared at them. They stopped hugging. Then she woke up. Khanya dreamt that she was riding in a kombi when Inkatha impimpis opened fire with automatic weapons. She was shot in the stomach but no blood came out. She walked through the township going house-to-house knocking on doors, crying for assistance. The people all closed their curtains in fear. Finally, she came to a house where two children were alone. They opened the door for her and she entered. Then she woke up. If I dream any more, I don't remember.

Yours Truly,
Frank

—⚬—

By the end of September, Trevor and Jabu had physically healed and, like all good soldiers, they tucked whatever psychic scars there were inside.

And Precious Jabulani returned from Tanzania. Trevor and Jabu had managed to keep her name, and the names of a handful of people who provided logistical support for the operation, out of their interrogation sessions. But Stimela was further underground, even more of a fugitive, than he was when I first met him. I rarely saw him during this time.

It was in this period that we stumbled onto a gold mine of intelligence. I would like to say that it was a vein of high-grade intelligence that we mined through sophisticated sleuthing rife with risk. In point of fact it was the lowest of low-grade intelligence: an appendix in a book about the Broederbond, a book that we had never heard of and which forces within and/or loyal to the government had managed to keep out of print since 1977. It was *The Super Afrikaner,* a book about the Broederbond. Trevor and I simply came across it at a used bookstall at the Market Theatre Square flea market and crafts fair, the place where I first met Khanya in 1989. I was thumbing through the book when the Indian merchant who ran the stall came from behind his counter and gently took it from my hand. It's not a good book for a nice American like you, he said, it could get you killed. I bought it immediately. Trevor and I turned to the back and there it was, the index: a list of something like 8,000 of the original 12,000 names from the top secret Broederbond membership list. Just before the book went to press, in the 1970s, state agents broke into the computer room of the newspaper where the two authors worked and erased four thousand names from the hard drive before fleeing with the building security on their heels. But the 8,000 names that were still left provided our clandestine propaganda efforts with an opportunity we could not have imagined in our wildest dreams: the revelation that a good number of senior lecturers, professors, and administrators at Vista University (where I taught) were members of the Broederbond.

We were ecstatic! In that flat, with its long uninviting folding table surrounded by a menagerie of hopeless chairs that didn't match and two lonely computers hooked up to a dot matrix printer, Jabu, Trevor, Precious, and I set to work like children whose wages were candy. With the help of SASCO comrades on Vista's campus we developed files and case histories on the Broeders at Vista, much the way we had done on the foreigners inquiring about the ANC, and the tokoloshes of laissez-faire at Wits. The student population at Vista was nearly 30,000 strong, whereas it was 18,000 at Wits. And the percentage of Black students at Vista was 99 percent, compared to not quite 20 percent at Wits. Still, we were not convinced that our efforts were wisely spent on Broeders. We saw them as the waning personas of power. But a series of unexpected events evolved after Chris Hani's death in April that justified our dividing our attention between British liberals and hard-line Afrikaners.

There had been a series of strikes in the wake of Hani's assassination that were put down brutally by the police and after which the tinny taste of teargas hung in the air. It was not uncommon to see students crossing campus on crutches or in a neck brace or with a swollen eye. The proliferation of teach-ins, rallies, civil disobedience, and strikes at Vista University's Soweto campus, alone, had brought the entire university (a constellation of seven campuses in seven Black townships) closer to the brink of a wholesale takeover than the same such activities had at Wits.

I was a bona fide member of the faculty at Vista, not an adjunct as I'd been at Wits, which meant that my public pronouncements could be made in the name of my "stake" as a "stakeholder" and it would be difficult for someone to paint me as an agent provocateur, as Wits vice-chancellor Robert Charlton did when he spoke to the press.

After a few weeks we had a document, or the text for a document, but we did not know what form that document should take or how the propaganda should be distributed. Should we feed it out parsimoniously over a series of leaflets? Should it be one multi-page broadside that we would give to the Trots to publish as a manifesto of some kind? The problem with the first idea was that we had too much information and contextualization to be fed to the public piecemeal. And the problem with the second idea was that the Trots were White, with a sprinkling of Indians and Coloureds—which is to say they had no presence whatsoever on any of the Vista campuses; we could not feed them the propaganda and then have them distribute it to the masses because it would not have anything remotely approaching an organic endeavor.

We decided that the only way to solve this problem was to have the bourgeois media solve it for us: get the press to publish it. So we hammered and anviled long into another night until we had a proper magazine article.

But this presented us with another problem: someone's name was going to have to go in the by-line. Their eyes settled on me. I already had a public profile as an ANC member and elected official, which gave me legitimacy in the eyes of "progressives." I had the sort of legitimacy a bourgeois editor would respect, in that I was a lecturer at Vista and could claim I wrote this in an effort to vouchsafe the "integrity" in higher education. Since the bombing, I said, both Trevor and Jabu have been outed as MK, they're aboveground power brokers and influence peddlers in SASCO. (What do you mean by influence peddlers? Jabu, smiled. Sorry, com, I said, you know what I mean.) The point is, I continued, they could just as well put their name to this as I could.

"There's no assurance that this thing will get published," Precious said, "and furthermore the longer it takes the more risk there is of the Broederbond taking decisive action to stop its publication and to, well, neutralize, the author. We're at a delicate conjuncture, with elections being talked about for next year or 1995. But it's not *that* delicate. They won't think twice about killing an MK 'terrorist' who had the cheek to write an article like this *after* he got out of detention. They'll think twice about Trevor—he's White. And they'll think twice about you—you're an American. Now, Trevor's also a 'terrorist,' which means his White skin won't give his by-line the legitimacy it would normally have. Comrade, you should transpose this into the first person, using an episode from your own experience at Vista and set about finding a home for this piece."

She was right. There was no way to argue with her. And I really did not want to argue. There was something disingenuous about my prior protest, for I was excited by the prospect of taking on the Broederbond with my name. Fighting British liberalism was dreary and uneventful for they rarely offered themselves as targets the way the Afrikaner did. But there was also a decidedly sincere quality to my protest. I was genuinely afraid. The Broederbond struck fear in the hearts of nearly everyone who knew anything about them.

Precious predicted that it would take time for the article to be accepted. That was an understatement. By the end of November it still did not have a home; two months of editors being thrilled with, excited by, and committed to the piece, only to be called after their somber meetings with their legal departments or with their wives (who claimed that their children needed a father). I'm sorry, Frank, really I am. Good luck with this piece...and...take care of yourself, by all means take care. Or: Why don't we wait a year or two—until we're sure there are going to be elections...come back after the elections, we'll run it then. The longer this went on, the more at risk I was; with each editor's goodbye handshake and parting words, "Are you going to be alright?" my anxiety and paranoia swelled.

I told Khanya about the article but not its entire genesis. That little bit alone was enough for her to imbibe my anxiety. We bundled Reba and ourselves into a sleeping compartment on the Blue Train headed for Cape Town. From Cape Town we went to False Bay on the Indian Ocean (a place I'd heard Trevor speak of), where high on a promontory we rented a cottage of hand-packed stone and dormer windows looking out onto the sea. The view was stunning from every angle. Reba looked through the binoculars and asked if we could see the penguins of Boulders Beach from there. No, I thought, but we can see the shoreline and the road that rises from it.

As fretful as the delay was, it was also a blessing in disguise. I was able to polish the article while we were on vacation and when we returned in January, Jon Qwelane, an African and the publisher of the national magazine *Tribute*, contracted to publish it. He effectively waved his legal staff and their "ifs, ands, and buts" out of his office and set me to work with his editor and art director. Now it was done; the article was slated as the lead article for the April issue. On April 1, 1994, twenty-three days before the elections, the article hit the newsstands.

Within days, the cars of Vista's Broederbond members (and those of their campus lackeys) were burning in the parking lot, their offices either ransacked or under siege. Some left with armed escorts. Others left under their own steam, but did not return. The head office, in Pretoria, home to 220 administrators and staff, of which over 200 were Afrikaners, became an armed fortress. And those who remained on the seven campuses (especially the Soweto campus) found themselves in the throes of a new authority, led by SASCO and *its fellow travelers*. Without planning it, without knowing it was happening, we had created a vacuum of power and authority that waited for us to fill it. The campuses were soon under the control of the People's Action Committee. And the Action Committee set about transforming the new space, the new soviets, that they had commandeered. Our article had something to do with that. It was like a dream come true; something we always agitated for, but never *really* dreamed possible—not in the wake of Hani's murder.

In fact, the article and its possible effects were the last thing on my mind the night before it hit the newsstands. On March 30 or 31, 1994, I had a disturbing encounter with Nelson Mandela himself, one that dropped a pall, once more, over my marriage. By the time Khanya and I left the Parktonian Hotel, I was thinking not about revolution, but about us, about how right she was when she said I brought her there under false pretenses.

I can still recall the saris of the Indian women and the smart brown suit of the patriarch of that Indian family (perhaps they were the grandparents and one of the other couple was their son or daughter and perhaps the children were their grandchildren—perhaps they'd returned from exile just in time to vote in the all-race elections). I don't recall their family name, though I should; Mandela hissed it, almost spat it at me. I can see them now, how they arranged themselves around Mandela for a photograph by the buffet table at the far end of the hotel ballroom.

Mandela had already rebuked me once, in the auditorium, not more than ten minutes ago. Now, he looked startled and cross as I came up to him, as though he was astounded that I should elect to sign up for even more abuse.

Now is the time for compromise, he had said to me in the auditorium. Give and take on both sides. Peace and reconciliation. Applause crescendoed like a flock of birds rising from cathedral stairs. It was the big soiree thrown at the end of each month by *Tribute* magazine the night before their current issue hit the newsstands. In the front matter of each issue one could always find photographs of the attending glitterati brandishing cocktails like trophies. Khanya and I were not of the ilk normally invited, but my article on Vista and the Broederbond had been given top billing as an investigative exposé. And the magazine always invited the freelance author of the lead story for the month. The soirees were always the same. First, a speech from the distinguished guest of honor, followed by a thirsty pilgrimage from the auditorium to the bar and buffet in the reception room, where an evening of networking ensued. Normally, they gave the speaker only half an ear, for in the main, the galas were opportunities for aspiring Black entrepreneurs to collect coveted business cards from White industrialists. But tonight they had before them someone to whom they gave their full attention. The next state president was on display.

The applause for compromise, peace, and reconciliation died down, but I remained standing. "Comrade Mandela," I said. The people seated around me looked at me as if to say, Didn't he just put you in your place? What will it take for you to sit down? "Comrade Mandela." Again, comrade Mandela. Not Mr. Mandela. Not sir, like the fawning advertising mogul who asked the first question. Comrade Mandela. It stitched him back into the militant garb he'd shed since the day he left prison. He'd already sat down again. He bristled at the sight of me still standing, speaking to him free of the gilded tones that were mandated by the gilded invitations.

"If I might be allowed a follow-up question." He's an old man, a voice inside me was saying, you're disrespecting an old man. But another voice was there as well, Stimela's voice—we feel so disempowered in his presence, we know he's not god, and yet... And Mandela's own voice: his voice of appeasement when he traveled abroad and thought no one at home would see the news, such as when he made it clear to a throng of European journalists that, should COSATU use its arsenal of labor strikes to move the country toward socialism, he would use

he same arsenal of force on the workers that the ANC had used on the
Boers.

It's one thing to challenge him in a room full of comrades, I had said
o Precious, Jabu, and Trevor (relieved that Oupa wasn't with us, but
Oupa wouldn't have been there, I realized, not for this effort. Where
was Oupa, I wondered). In a room full of ANC cadres, only the *affect* of
he crowd would be against me. That is to say, the comrades would be
on Mandela's side emotionally, but their intellectual consent would rest
with our critique because it is their own critique. But to out him at the
Parktonian Hotel? That was another matter. I can't imagine myself find-
ng my voice, I had said to Precious, nor can I imagine the emcee allow-
ng me to finish a sentence at the Parkonian Hotel.

Precious, who loved Mandela in the same way that Khanya loved
him, but who'd been trained that the things she loved most were the
very things that could destroy her, said, "In the past three years, forty
thousand exiles have returned from under the stones of Western capi-
tals like London, New York, Toronto, and Washington DC, with their
ideology of free enterprise and meritocracy. We have only this window
of time before we lose the power to pose the question—and the power to
pose the question is the greatest power of all. Don't worry," she assured
me, "he'll show his hand."

"How do you know?" I asked her.

"Your impudence works wonders on people," she smiled.

I pressed on. "Comrade Mandela, as you know there are two issues
at stake despite what the—" and to my horror I almost said, despite
what the tokoloshes say. "Despite what businessmen and university
principals might say. First, there's the question of Black access *to* the
university—in a Black country, I might add." As I spoke he abandoned
all pretense of etiquette and leaned toward his aide. They partook in
a whispering dialogue. "Then, there's the issue of the ANC's Reconstruction and Development Program, which many comrades are saying was developed by European and American consultants, and not
the masses. A Reconstruction and Development Program that bears no
resemblance to the demands that came down from ANC branch and

regional structures. SASCO has called for *the power to pose the question*, and the power to govern universities, to be devolved to the people. But the Reconstruction and Development Program mentions no such devolution of power. How do you calibrate the gap between the will of the people and the RDP?"

He was on his feet. Furious. As though he could kick me to death. White people in this country have worked hard, he said, struggled for decades, centuries, to build their institutions. He was trembling with anger as he spoke. We in the African National Congress will not fill them with anxiety and fear by suggesting that we are going to seize control of what they have worked so hard to build.

Another round of thunderous applause. We were still looking at each other. We were both wounded. It was as though Muhammad Ali had just pulverized an amateur, backed him into the ropes, and turned his face to mush, while a crowd of blood-speckled spectators cheered. But who was Ali and who was the amateur?

Then, as though something or someone had pinched him from a dream, he changed his tone but not his tune. He was less strident. He said that he was in favor of establishing transformation committees at each university. But he knew as well as I did that SASCO had not called for "transformation committees." He was using his prestige to corrupt and hollow out SASCO's demands. SASCO demanded transformation *forums* (like those that would soon be established—rise from the fires of student/worker revolt—at Vista), not committees. Forums, so went the demand, to be placed over and above the university councils.

These committees, Mandela continued, are what all the stakeholders want. More lies, I thought, there are only comrades and tokoloshes; "stakeholders" is a word that mystifies the antagonism. Over the next two or three years, these committees will study the concerns of all the stakeholders, he said, and then submit their findings and recommendations to my cabinet and...blah, blah, blah...until the struggle has hemorrhaged and died.

Now, as I headed for the buffet table where he and the family of exiles were being arranged for a photograph, I decide to tell him that the answer he'd given to my question during the preceding Q & A needed clarification. As I sliced through the room of his admirers, Khanya was in hot pursuit of me.

"Don't make a scene, Frank."

But I pressed forward across the ballroom.

"Didn't you do enough back there?" she said, referring to the repartee in the question and answer period.

I turned to her in the middle of the crowd.

"You mean, 'too much' don't you? 'Frank, didn't you do too much back there?'"

"Yes," she said, "too much."

"A month away from the elections and suddenly it's too much to hold him accountable to the Freedom Charter. The mind boggles. You know what just happened back there—in a room full of White businessmen? Blood suckers. We asked him a question and—"

"*You* asked him a question. A rhetorical question meant to embarrass, not to engage."

"He should be speaking to us when he speaks, not to the mandarins of surplus value."

"When are you going to start living in the real world? I work for an NGO. When he comes to power *my people* will have to beg for money from *his people*. Not Winnie's people, you don't raise money in squatter camps, and not Chris Hani's people, they need Mandela more than I do now that he's dead."

"You've always been a survivor." But no sooner had I mailed that callous letter than I wished for the keys to the letterbox: *P.S. I'm sorry, Khanya, I know that's not true.*

"And you've always been a fool," she said.

We were drawing attention to ourselves.

"Now who's making a scene?" I said. I wanted to retain my dignity and my sense of being right. But I wanted her to love me, too. I tried to hold her hand. "It needs to be a public encounter, in front of witnesses," I whispered.

Her eyes widened.

"You're working for Stimela! Our night out and...You're using me as cover."

I asked her to keep her voice down.

The Indian family and Nelson Mandela were moving away from the buffet table. Mandela's bodyguards were a pace or two behind them, which was good. If I was going to make contact I had to make it now and I had to slow down before I reached him, lest his guards think my approach had malevolent intentions (and take the necessary counter-measures). This meant turning my back on Khanya in the middle of our argument. We were not divorced as we are today. Nor were we sepa-rated, as we would be that rainy night the following year when Stefaans Brümmer called. Still, I knew that after I did what I had set out to do, we would go home sharing no more conversation between us than was necessary to count out the fare for the kombi; that all night long I would lie awake counting the ceiling's dim stars of stucco and know she was doing the same.

In a way, Khanya was right in what she was saying as she tried to check my advance on the floor of the ballroom. What happened back in the auditorium should have been enough. But I wanted something more from him, something for me, a surplus—not for Stimela, not for Pre-cious, not for people on the ground, but for me. I wanted him to return to me my dream of him, the dream Khanya spoke of when she called him her "father" after Richard's braai. *Please tell me you didn't mean what you said. So many people have died. So many more have been scarred for life. All that carnage for a few committees? Say it isn't so.*

I'd broken through the levee of people who were keeping a respectful distance from him and his friends. I rehearsed my lines: *Mr. Mandela, sir*—no "comrade" this time—*I want to struggle with you over your response to my question regarding the RDP and the devolution of power; part of your answer was unclear.* You're lying, I thought, his answer could not have been clearer.

"Mr. Mandela," I was upon him and his friends. "Sir," a note of hu-mility. "I'd like to struggle with you over your answer to my ques—."

With unbridled brusqueness he said, "These are the—," and he told me their family name and spat out the years they'd been in exile; he thrust his palm into my solar plexus. "We want to take a picture—in peace!"

It wasn't the stiff-arm of a rugby winger warding off a tackler, but a thrust of frustration from an old man who was tired and vexed, who'd been goaded into saying what he knew in his heart he should not have said. I let the blow knock me back in order to memorialize his aggression for the onlookers.

As his bodyguards ushered me away, I caught a glimpse of Khanya, still embedded in the onlookers. For a split second I saw myself through her eyes: a man: a man whom she loved: he made her laugh and took her seriously: a man she'd held close on late-night subways in Manhattan: she'd made love and plans with this man and had once been proud to show him off: a man who'd gamble all of that on one, maybe two, simple truths. Her father had warned her, Why hadn't she listened?

Mandela stalked us all the way home. He sat between us in the rickety kombi as it climbed the Braamfontein slope to Hillbrow. He made any conversation more complex than short phrases and grunts impossible. He bid us to be silent as we hastened from the neon anarchy of Hillbrow to the tree-calmed boulevards of Berea. His displeasure cottoned our ears and dampened our taste buds against the soft sounds of jazz and the scent of sage-roasted chicken wafting in the Yeoville air. When we finally reached our apartment in Bellevue East, he had the nerve to let himself in. The couch wasn't good enough for him; he insisted on sharing our bed. All night he sat there, daring us to reach through him and love again.

Were Chris Hani alive in 1995 when Stefaans Brümmer called the Orrs' house to interview me, it would have been impossible to imagine an amalgamated spy agency comprised of MK *and* the Boer's Special Branch, one run jointly by F. W. de Klerk, the head of the Nationalist Party, and Thabo Mbeki, the most conservative member of the ANC. But that was the state of things a year after the incident in the Parktonian Hotel.

Whenever I think of Stefaans Brümmer's telephone call I wonder whether he was baiting me or just being a good reporter when he implied that I knew what he meant by "your subversive activities." Then, he added, deliberately, "Nelson Mandela thinks you're a threat to national security. Would you care to comment?"

For the first time in the interview I felt as though I would stammer. I remembered how I felt when Mandela jabbed his palm into my solar plexus and the look in Khanya's eyes as his bodyguards pushed me past her. I felt that jab again, in Stefaans Brümmer's voice *(would you care to comment)*. I saw that look again in her eyes as she warmed herself by the gas fire in the parlor and spoke quietly with the Orrs, pretending not to listen. Her eyes were not angry, not like they'd been last year, on the last night of March. But they were worried, for us.

She could have lived with Joe Nhlanhla saying I was a threat to national security, or Thabo Mbeki; certainly F. W. de Klerk's censure would have had either no effect on her or the opposite of what she felt now. But the idea that Nelson Mandela *himself* considered me a threat to national security was too much for her to bear. I even touched my stomach as though I still felt the press of his hand. *A threat to national security?* It was too much for me as well.

"If active dissent is a threat to national security," I told Brümmer, "then yes, it's true. But to my mind the real threat is the state president himself and his cabinet of 'National Unity.'"

"May I quote you?"

I looked into the parlor. They were all looking at me; they could no longer pretend to be talking about the days of rain we'd been having or Khanya's work at the NGO. Mr. and Mrs. Orr, Khanya—they had all heard it, there was no use pretending. They watched. They waited.

"I don't know," I said. "I need to think about it."

We said goodnight to the Orrs and retired to the yard, to the carriage house I'd been renting from them for the last few months of our separation.

From the moment I arrived in South Africa, and pushed and shoved and punched my way into an inn that wasn't "multiracial" to the night

Stefaans Brümmer called, there had been a kind of reprieve from the untenable fact of Blackness I'd known since Mrs. Proudwell commended my mother for bearing two Negro children who did not smell like Negro children. Struggle in South Africa had done that for me in a way that had happened in only one other period of my life: Detroit, when Smooth bought me bean pies, recounted the Algiers Motel Incident, and told his posses I wasn't no gumpy; Chicago, when Jocelyn and I slow danced for her laughing uncle and shared grown-ass kisses in the snow on our way to the murder of Fred Hampton, on our way to the revolution; and in Berkeley, on the barricades when Nixon invaded Cambodia and Ms. Loony Tunes dragged me up the hill.

Struggle...the South African revolution...Our coming within a hair's breadth of ridding the country of capitalism...this, I had thought, dedicated Marxist that I was, this is the struggle that will also rid the world of Negrophobia. It was a blind faith I never threatened with scrutiny. I simply incorporated my dream to no longer be the slave of my appearance (the slave of thick lips and guilty eyes; my dream to free my mirror of all compensatory gestures—you're Black but you're intelligent, Black but fairly handsome, Black but you come from good...*good Black stock?*), incorporated it into the dream of a proletarian dictatorship. For five years I kept the faith. But now the world was rushing in again.

Khanya and I told ourselves that our divorce was about many things, but not about the world rushing back in. Who *in* the world would have believed us? And is it truth if it has no place in the world? So we found, for ourselves and for others, recognizable stories to make sense of it. Her not wanting to leave South Africa. My fear of raising Reba and the other child she wanted us to bring into the world. "Lifestyle" issues. Her tight-shouldered miserliness. My profligate spending. Her prompt fidelity to creditors. My middle finger installment plan. Her desire to find *one* profession, yes, Frank, I mean it, one job, in one place, that we'll call home once and for all. My urgent sense that I had to keep moving. It was all true enough. It was false as well. Part real. Part ruse. And it was the part that was ruse that saved us from having to face what had faced us in New York when she sat up in bed one morning and wondered aloud why she

should trade one South Africa for another. The ruse of stable domesticity gave her the faith she needed to keep the dereliction of Blackness
outside the door. Just as the ruse of movement, my movement, or The
Movement, *any* movement had done for me. The Movement was no longer and I would not pray at her shrine of domesticity.

Conflict set in, in the guise of "issues." Whoever heard of two slaves with
"issues"? How simpler to have said without artifice what we really wanted:
the adulation of White womanhood, the freedom of White manhood. White
skin: the one true phallus. We might have avoided three years on a switch-
back trail of separations and reunions, which is not to say we'd be together
but merely to say we'd have cut through our symptoms to the chase.

When we went inside the carriage house, she asked me what Brümmer wanted. I told her; I set about feeding Ginger, the tiger-striped cat I
had taken with my books and my clothes when we separated, as I did so.

"How do we explain to our friends that the *anti*-apartheid government says you're a traitor?"

I was still stooped over Ginger. She ate her food and looked up at me
like a grateful supplicant. The eyes of one's pet never judge. "Perhaps
they're not our friends," I told Khanya, "if they can't understand."

"I went to a government official for funding for one of my dispute
resolution projects in the township. 'Why do you want funding from
us sell-outs, why don't you get it from your husband's liberated zone at
Vista University?' He knows Pretoria won't pay the academics that took
part in the takeover. My husband hasn't been paid in months, I told
him. And then we were in a row. I didn't go there for a row. I went for
money for badly needed projects. That phone call tonight, from the *Mail
& Guardian*—don't toss your hand like it's nothing! They're tired of you!
They're not *comrades* anymore! They're the government and they're getting tired of you! When I came to New York and refused to believe what
a racist society it was, what a dangerous place it was, when I wanted to
hold on to my dreams you said, 'Wake up and smell coffee.'" (*The* coffee. I had a mind to take issue with the absence of a definite article, if
that would stop her from talking.) "Now I'm telling you to wake up and
smell coffee."

I did not want to wake up and smell the coffee but nor did I want her to leave. So I said what needed to be said and I said it as though I meant it; there and then, I did. It wasn't long before we found ourselves where we'd intended to be an hour ago when we stood in the rain and waited for a kombi with no more than the frayed poster of Mandela to keep us dry—not on opposite sides of this miniature living room, but in the miniature bedroom, in bed, kissing and caressing. I said I'd move back in with her and Reba, and yes, Doreen. She promised to move to Amsterdam or even back to the States and go for that filmmaking degree she'd always wanted instead of the law degree. With that ensemble of vows and caresses, we made love and fell asleep.

"Stop!" she screamed. "Frank!"

I bolted up and turned on the light.

"They grabbed my feet." She was breathing hard. She was trembling. She placed her face in her hands. "They were going to get you too. I felt their hands."

Ginger sat at the foot of the bed, licking her fur.

"There's your NIA agent," I said. "Ginger's paws, not Mandela's hands."

Khanya didn't find this amusing. She yanked hard at the blanket, extracting an agonizing cry from Ginger and tossing her to the floor.

"Only White people keep pets in the bedroom."

"I beg your pardon."

The unintended force of her own words startled her. But it was too late. She had crossed the Rubicon.

"Animals belong outside, is what I'm saying."

I should have let it go, but I too had crossed the line.

"You're saying I'm White. What your father said. What your mother may as well have said. You married a White man. Don't turn away from me."

"I have to actually work in the morning. You're not due on the barricades till noon."

I remained seated beside her in bed. She kept her back to me and pulled the cover over her shoulder.

"Would you please turn off the light?"

I did not turn off the light.

"I'm White. Fine. I'm White cargo. White property. They made me out of you. What's your excuse?"

"Frank, please, the light."

"What's your excuse?"

"My excuse for *what?*"

"Were there curling irons and spandex on the Great Bantu Migration? Did you criss-cross Africa in Gucci shoes?"

"I don't straighten my hair anymore." She pulled the covers over her head, "Then leave the light on. It's you who won't get any sleep."

I promptly turned it off.

We lay in the dark for a long time; not touching; not speaking; not sleeping.

Finally, I made my voice say, "I have an aunt..." But I couldn't bring myself to speak.

"Did you say something?"

"No...it's nothing."

"Please," she turned toward me, "say what it was. I'll listen."

"I have an aunt...she says, you should never go to bed angry with each other. It's bad for the soul. At least that's what she says."

"What does she say we should do?"

"I never asked her. I didn't know I'd need to know one day."

"I want to say I'm sorry, but I feel...defensive."

"My mouth runs ahead of my brain," I said. "And you're right. How could you not be right? I grew up in Kenwood. I hate them. I crave them. I'm toxic."

"You know that commercial for the Sales House department store."

Yes, I knew it.

"They show five African couples from five different countries across the continent, dressed in their traditional African attire. Then we hear classical music and the scene cuts to a man in a tuxedo and a woman in an evening gown, and the announcer says, 'South Africa.' I cringe when I see that. It's like they see right through me."

I reached out my hand and she took it. We moved toward each other and embraced in the middle of the bed, where we started.

—⁂—

In August 1996, Stimela got word that I was leaving and came to say goodbye. The early spring sun was hot, but not as hot as it would be when October would bleed into summer. Still, we kept to the shade of Observatory's sycamores.

In his short life Stimela Mosando had already witnessed the Children's Revolution of June 1976, the fall of the Soviet Union on Christmas Day 1991, and the triumph of neo-liberalism on April 24, 1994, but no one knew his story; he had always fought on the losing side, not the side of the historical record. Now he was an ANC representative on the city council of a heretofore all-White city council of a heretofore-White city that bordered the West Rand township where he and Jabu were born and raised. As we walked past the mansions that had once belonged to British mining magnates in the nineteenth century, then Gandhi in the early twentieth century, and even Joe Slovo until his death, mansions that Khanya and I had joked, quite soberly, about living in one day, a sleek BMW crept behind us at a distance of half a block.

"My driver," Stimela explained, beckoning back to the car. "is supposed to be my bodyguard. He's NIA. Isn't that nice? MK and the Communist Party are now the state police. They work for the moderates now. Imagine Lenin working for the Mensheviks. The party and the former insurgents are now the tail being wagged by the ANC dog.

"They suspect me. They think I'm a whistleblower. There's nothing worse than a whistleblower. Which is why they'll ask me to stand for a seat on the Communist Party's Central Committee. They want to see if they can contain or co-opt me. It won't be so messy. I've been given a very nice job at an NGO—counting semiconductors—one of the NGOs we used to siphon money from to buy arms and pay the rent of safe houses. I stop talking about ANC government corruption and I get to keep my new job, my new car, my *lovely* driver, my seat on the city council, and maybe I'll even get a seat on the Central Committee. It's the carrot...for now. What do you think, comrade Frank, should I take the carrot?"

I was going to answer him not because I knew the answer, but because he asked me. But he didn't wait for my answer.

"I have a going away present for you, to, well, to compensate you for being put at risk so often without telling you why."

"A BMW?" I asked, looking back at the shiny car and the government driver.

"A story."

"About what?"

"Something interesting." And he laughed. Then he said, "Comrades needed to emerge." That was how he started. "People who could not be *whitemailed,*" he smiled, in genuflection to the way I always cringed at words like *blackmailed, blackballed,* or *blacklisted,* "by Mandela's people. We needed such people to emerge in the wake of Hani's death and we needed them to emerge quickly."

He explained how, a long time ago, a year or two before Jabu first met me at Richard's braai in Soweto, Red Beard and his agents were hot on the trail of both Trevor and Jabu for political "crimes" committed in the township wars between the ANC and the PAC; not that Red Beard cared who became hegemonic, but now that the dust was settling, now that it was clear that the ANC had won, it was ANC "culprits" who needed to be apprehended. He knew that he was looking for two trained operatives, one Black and one White. He knew that they were probably students. And as time progressed Red Beard knew more and more. He was closing in on Trevor and Jabu. The only way Stimela could save them from torture, a capital treason trial, and certain death was to offer the police a more valuable quarry. So he sent Jabu and Trevor on vacation. They were to hole up in a bungalow near Fishhoek in False Bay (where I'd gone with Khanya and Reba during my Broederbond scare). They ate conch from the shell and swam in the Indian Ocean and awaited his orders. When Stimela was sure they were safely out of Johannesburg, he stepped from the shadows and placed his own head between the lion's jaw.

I must have stopped. I must have looked as shocked as I was—sensing where it was leading but not believing for one moment the path we were on. He placed his hand beneath my elbow and nudged me on.

"No one should be tortured," he said, "but nor should we have to live in this world."

I asked him if Trevor and Jabu had given him and Precious enough time to flee before they "emerged," the MK regulation-time for enduring torture so that networks might be dissolved.

At first he took it as a joke. "They were both great! Especially Jabu. The stories my cousin told them. When they released him I asked him for some of whatever he'd been smoking. It must have been some good dagga." Seeing that I wasn't laughing, he became testy.

"I held out for two weeks. Two weeks of complete fabrications like the arms caches hidden in homes of the northern suburbs that Jabu led them to when he was tortured. Enough time for *everyone* to realize that I'd been arrested, for them to disappear and salvage as many DLBs as they could."

And then?

"And then I gave them the world; but they kept at me for five months. 'It's not information we want, kaffir, it's lost time.' I begged them to kill me. They laughed." He didn't explain his release to me; how it was that two years later, in 1989, I came to meet his cousin at a braai, and a little more than a year after that, I met him as well. Instead he returned, without segue, to Trevor and Jabu and their capture after the bombing. "Comrades needed to emerge," he said. "And we needed a foolproof way for them to emerge as two people who could move in aboveground structures and speak with authority, be *listened* to," he emphasized, "when speaking out against the neo-liberal 'consensus.' To emerge without *credentials* would have been to not emerge at all—not in that short space of time."

In the beginning he had no idea that so many units were not going to hit the targets Hani had set out for them in the event of a major figure's assassination. He had no idea how tightly Mandela's people would put the screws on; how much nerve so many people would lose in the wake of Chris Hani's death; how many trained insurgents were willing to let the masses take it to the streets and not back them up; that instead of the leadership mobilizing its energies to intensify the mass uprisings, they would wait on the sidelines to see which ANC faction would prevail. This is when it must have hit Stimela: *new comrades need to emerge.*

"Who better to give comrades their credentials," he said, as we stopped and his "gift," the shiny BMW, pulled up beside us, "than the police."

The little man with dark glasses behind the wheel held his gaze on us. Stimela's voice was neither cold blooded nor remorseful. It was informative. It was interpretive. It was the voice of necessity. The so-called "moral" questions no longer occurred to me. But I felt weak, nauseous. I remembered the things that had been done to Jabu's body—and to Trevor's; what they told me and what they left to my imagination. And I felt ashamed, believing that I could not have made such a sacrifice. But I remembered something Trevor had said to me: Stimela will never require you to do anything he knows you're not ready for, he said, though he may test your willingness.

Stimela placed his hand on the door.

"Wait..." I said. He turned and waited. I wanted to ask him to fill in the details. Did you or Trevor or Jabu drive back to the bombsite and throw Trevor's identity document into the rubble; or was it someone else, some untrained subaltern, like me? Did Trevor think the document was going to *be* thrown into the rubble on the day I pulled his poncho and tore his wound or had it already been done? But I asked him none of those questions.

Instead, I asked: "Did we kill professor Mureinik or did he die by his own hand alone?"

This made him roar with laughter and the little man at the wheel, who could hear nothing of what was being said but could hear Stimela's laugh and feel the vibration of the car, smiled at us.

"You're a greedy capitalist," Stimela chuckled. "You want a little something for yourself. You must remember," he admonished me with his finger, "you can't kill a tokoloshe. One thing's for sure. Mureinik killed Chris Hani."

The *Sunday Times/Extra* did a feature on me and two other Black American expatriates. "Coming Home To Mama Africa" read the bold headline. The subheading read: "Fed up with racism back home, African-Americans are flocking to SA in search of a better life in the new land of liberty." Above the article was my photograph, four columns wide. Then there was the caption. "Frank Wilderson, who has been living in South Africa for four years, was tired of the political oppression black people faced in the US." "Here to stay," it read.

Shortly thereafter, I left...went home, whatever that means. First, to Los Angeles, where I slept on my brother's couch and taught in the Compton Unified School District, a district so under-funded and short-staffed as to make many schools in Soweto look like prep schools; then to Northern California where I worked as an adjunct lecturer at colleges and universities from Santa Cruz to San Francisco while earning a doctorate in film studies and political theory. Three and a half years slipped away and the twentieth century ended.

Having weathered the Y2K scare of a midnight meltdown (vanishing bank balances, febrile clock hands spinning counter clockwise, the collapse of sea and air navigation systems, the implosion of medical life-support technology, nuclear warheads firing of their own free will, riots at food distribution centers, and the earth spinning backwards on its axis), Alice and I woke up on the morning of the new millennium, thankful that we had not fled to a bunker for the winter break and that the electric locks on the car still worked.

After our vacation I returned to Berkeley. Amid the bills and junk mail were two letters from South Africa; neither one had a return address. One was a large oversized official envelope. The other was a personal letter. The two envelopes' pastiche of stamps (leaping Springboks characteristic of the era of the Nationalist Party regime and multicolored arrow stamps that looked like a traffic sign but, in point of fact, was the flag of the "New" South Africa) reminded me of a sobering line from Antonio Gramsci's *Prison Notebooks:* the old is dying, but the new cannot be born. I thought I knew what the large envelope contained and was in no hurry to face its accusations, so I opened the letter.

1ˢᵗ of January 2000

Dear Frank

I trust you are still standing at the brink of the wounds of this age. Political or psychological.

As for me, I am still "dissembling," watching, learning, occasionally fucking someone up who knows not from whence his deserved but inconsistent misfortune has come. Mostly, however, I am wrapped up in a sense of myself which sees value in (a small collective) putting ideas out there that sometimes link up to counter-discourses and suddenly people are moved to think and believe extraordinary things.

In all of these displays, I remain utterly obscure.

This is my lot in life. What has become of yours? I miss you.

Love,
Trevor

So, I thought, we'd been friends after all. But I could think of nothing pithy or purposeful to describe what had become of my life since I left, nothing that would translate into the political language that once gave us sustenance.

I took the icy plunge and opened the second one. It was a long, two-hole-punched document, common to the British Commonwealth, with a green ribbon looped through the holes as fasteners so as to make it appear more like a gift or an invitation than a writ.

IN THE HIGH COURT OF SOUTH AFRICA
(TRANSVAAL PROVINCIAL DIVISION)
CASE NO. 4865/2000

In the matter between: KHANYA VICTORIA DOROTHY WILDERSON (born PHENYO) (Plaintiff) and FRANK BENJAMIN WILDERSON III WHEREAS in this matter the above Honourable Court on the 9th day of JANUARY 2000 made an order giving KHANYA VICTORIA DOROTHY WILDERSON (born PHENYO) leave to institute action against FRANK BENJAMIN WILDERSON III an adult male student of the University of California, Berkeley (hereinafter referred to as "The Defendant")

PARTICULARS OF CLAIM

1. On 20 August 1990, and at New York, USA, the parties married in community of property and the said marriage still subsists.

2. There has been an irretrievable breakdown of the marriage between the parties and the marriage relationship between them has reached such a state of disintegration that there is no reasonable prospect of the restoration of a normal marriage relationship between the parties, by reason of the following facts:

2.1 The parties have been living apart since 1996 as the Defendant refused to live in the same place and house as the Plaintiff.

2.2 Since June 1998, the Defendant has, on countless occasions, telephonically stated his desire to terminate the marriage relationship between the parties.

2.3 In June 1998 the Defendant told Plaintiff that he was intimately involved with another woman...

It went on for fourteen pages, but I did not go on. Like Trevor's letter, I put the writ away. There was no disputing the "particulars of the claim," no picking over this one or that one that could rescue the ego, or salvage the picture I had painted of myself. To protect myself...to see myself as something other than a philandering cheat. I told myself that I took so long to tell her about Alice because I was trying to let her down gently. That's why I agreed to a "trial separation" when I left South Africa; why I said she could join me at some point and we'd make things right again. That's why it wasn't cheating. Over the next two years, I would bring it out and read a page or two, or a line or two, whatever dose of embarrassment I could bear that day—and then put it away.

—๛—

One night I came home from school and my mother's voice was calling me from the bedroom. I dropped my books and raced into the bedroom. But I stopped as my hand reached for the phone when the word "cancer" came through the speaker. I sat on the bed and waited for her to finish. Then I re-played her message. I tried not to listen to it but the pertinent phrases cut through. Dad has cancer…can you come home…we'll pay… if it's a question of money.

No, I thought, there's so much that's unresolved between us. As though the gravitas lay in our unresolved issues rather than his illness. I picked up the phone and held it until the dial tone ceased and the needle-voice told me if I wished to make a call to hang up and try again. *It's almost midnight in Minnesota, too late to call. Maybe in the morning it won't be true.* I went to bed.

Several days later I sat beside his hospital bed. Mom was seated in the chair she'd slept in. The room was choked with flowers and cards from well-wishers. People he'd known over the forty-two years of his ascent from assistant professor to vice president for student affairs; people he'd met through mom in her thirty years as a principal and school administrator; and people whom they'd counseled separately and together in their psychotherapy practice in their private office downtown.

Dad was lean and weary from days on a liquid diet, from the interminable waiting, from the surgeon's knife, and from the painkillers pulling him down into sleep. Before the operation a priest had stood by the bed, murmuring piously, waving forgiveness and salvation, up, down, left, and right. For the first time in thirty-six years (since the Sunday morning I walked into their bedroom and informed them that their children were all Maoists and would remain home from Mass to conduct anti-imperialist teach-ins) I prayed with them. When the priest left, dad thanked me for it.

It was all over now. The surgeon entered like a Western Union page with a message that a dear aunt or uncle would soon be home for the holidays. There'll be no radiation and no chemo. He was all smiles and reassurance: you can go home soon. When can I have a steak? dad asked.

We left University Hospital and returned to Kenwood, but only to collect the things they would need to convalesce at their lake home. In response to some news on the car radio about Colin Powell, I said what a fool he'd been several years ago when Baby Bush forbade him to go to the conference in Durban where reparations for slavery was debated. I was wearing a "Reparations Now!" T-shirt that I'd bought at a rally. It had raised a critical and disapproving eye from mom at the hospital, though dad had chosen to ignore it. Once he told me that, at some point when I was growing up, he decided it was bad psychology to tell me to do something; the best way to secure my compliance was to tell me to do the opposite of what he wanted and watch me hop to his true demand. Now mom was saying, The White people who are alive today had nothing to do with slavery, why should they have to pay? And dad, now that he had had his steak and the certainty of death, the one true certainty, had receded, weighed in as well. Sharing neither the gestalt of my T-shirt nor the logic of mom's rejoinder, he proclaimed, Well, of course they've benefited Ida-Lorraine, so they do owe us something; but Frank isn't wearing this T-shirt to promote dialogue and seek a solution, he wears it cynically—to arouse, to provoke, to incite. It's purely political…irresponsible…iconoclastic. I doubt you'd ever be satisfied, he said, leaning forward from the backseat where he was supposed to be resting, no matter how much they paid us. And all these years, I said, as I turned onto to the freeway, I thought you weren't listening. The exchange between dad and me only fed mom's frustration, for now she had an adversary in me, but no more than a qualified ally in her husband. You are your father's child, she said, and looked out her window. Driving out to the lake I was struck by how acutely I longed for them to acknowledge my isolation. But that would have meant that they had found some way to acknowledge theirs.

In the evening we went out to the dock to watch the water and the boats and the houses on the opposite shore fold into evening. A loon was cooing, calling forth the night.

Mom sipped her ice tea and then set it gently on the small round metal table between her chair and mine. To my right sat dad, indulging in the Scotch whiskey the surgeon said he could imbibe only by watching someone else drink. But I had only merlot in my glass and he couldn't possibly watch someone drink wine in lieu of whiskey. From out on the lake, or deep in the reeds along the shoreline, the loon kept cooing, a soft throaty murmur, coaxing our memories from us.

"They wanted to skip you up at Kenwood. Do you remember?" mom asked. "From second grade to fourth grade. Always asking if they could skip you up."

"You were never really interested in my life in South Africa." I replied with my memories as though they were the answer to hers.

"It's going to rain," dad said. "You can always tell by how the water moves; like the Mississippi when I was coming up. Yes, we might have a thunderstorm tonight."

Like figures in a fragile tableau gathering we sit and sip our drinks and look out at the lake. On the hill behind us the cabin stands, gleaming with a fresh coat of white paint and its roof speckled with new shingles that sparkle between the old. All around, birch trees and oak play their shadow fingers on the walls of the house and the hillside clearing where it stands. As the hill slopes toward the lake, the clearing narrows and spindly tamaracs with their roots soaking loam press tightly to a footpath that is rescued from the bog by the gray wooden planks of the dock. The dock thrusts out over the water, the reeds, and the obstinate mire beneath: muck and mud hidden from view by clouds and trees reflected on the plane of water. Like the crossbar of a capital "T" it fans out to the left where we sit and sip our drinks and look for the loon, and to the right, where a small boat is tethered with its engine sticking out of the water like the stiff tail of a hunting hound, its oars tucked to its torso like a bird's clipped wings, and a tackle box and fishing pole patiently awaiting my father's return.

"That's not true," mom says. "When you came back your father had you speak at the Skylight Club."

"The sanitized version."

"No one censored you," dad says. "You might have censored yourself."

"Do you want to know now?" I ask.

"If it's positive," she says. "We're always interested in your positive contributions."

"In other words, 'no.'"

"We saw this all the time when we practiced," mom informs me. "Young Black men blaming the world for their being adrift. But you're not young anymore. In two years you'll be fifty. I can pinpoint the *moment* this complex took hold of you. You were twelve years old, so puffed up with your exhortations about the war in Vietnam and your slogans. We drove to St. Paul. I was having business cards made. You insisted on having some made for you as well. My nerves were shot that day and you weren't giving me any peace. The printer, however, thought you were the 'cutest thing' who said the 'darnedest things.' 'Where'd he get all those four dollar words from, lady?' As though Black kids don't know how to speak. And you, just performing for him and wearing out my patience. White folks can't raise their own children and don't want to let you raise yours. They just reach right inside. I said I didn't have money for an extra set of business cards. 'That's alright, lady, it's on the house.' That's alright—pay no attention to the mother. 'What's your name, sonny—how do you want it spelled? Roman numeral three at the end, eh? This kid, I swear, this kid! Now give us a business address, sonny. And oh, what's your occupation?' To which you replied, 'Know-It-All. I'm Mr. Know-It-All.'"

"Mom, are we going to need a Ouija board to find the moral of this story?"

"Don't speak like that to your mother."

"I didn't know we came from a plantation. I still don't know what happened in the hold of that ship. So, I didn't know it all."

"May I finish my story?"

"Let your mother finish her story."

"And there I am, late and tired; and you're instructing this man, *'Know*, hyphen, *It*, hyphen, *All*. So it rolls off the tongue, Mister, like Niagara Falls.' Never even been to Niagara Falls. A week later I find one of your business cards clipped to a university memo. It's lying on my pillow. 'Dear Mrs. Ida-Lorraine Wilderson. I would like to schedule a meeting with you.' You remember this?" she asks dad. He nods, and knocks back his Scotch. Oh yes, I remember, he says, whether he does or not. "'Please RSVP with your memo and your card on my pillow. I have twelve years of grievances to discuss. Sincerely, Master, (in six months, Mr.) Frank B. Wilderson, III.' *Twelve years of grievances?* You were only twelve years old!"

"Mom, I don't remember any of this."

"Classic persecution complex." (Dad sips his drink and nods as she speaks.) "The patient recalls only the episodic kernel of what *others* did to him. From there he embellishes. I did go out to lunch with you. On a yellow legal pad you'd written two pages of 'grievances.'"

"What were they?"

"I don't remember. Yes! I remember one. Your weight problem. You attributed it to me; accusing me of transmitting an overabundance of 'fat cells' to you at birth. The Jules have never been fat. And the Wildersons are big boned, but nobody's fat. But rather than take responsibility for your weight, you charged *me* with the transmission of fat cells."

Why do I come back here? The moat between us only widens. I remember something different about that year. I remember her excitement at the fact that the next sabbatical we were about to embark on would give her the chance to do primary research for her dissertation in the public schools of Detroit, Chicago, and Berkeley. I remember her telling her news to a woman who lived several doors down, who didn't have money but who married a poor man whose rich aunt died and left them a house in Kenwood; a woman Kenwood neither claimed nor wanted. Someone they would have called "poor White trash" if they spoke like that. When mom told her the news, the woman said, You poor thing, all that work, I'm glad I'm free, White, and twenty-one. I remember mom's face as we walked back home and how I wondered what it was about our condition that even "White trash" wouldn't touch. Somewhere out there, the loon calls back, *you knooow...you know.*

"You can't make positive contributions," mom says, "unless you learn to take responsibility. Blaming everything on race is like conjuring fat cells out of thin air. Persecution...that's not the way, son." Then, more to the loon than to me, she says, "We fought, too. You didn't appreciate our methods; you didn't try to understand them; but we fought, too. You can't fight all your life. You have to breathe sometimes. I can't breathe."

"It's your asthma," dad says. He doesn't want her to speak to me in the uninhibited way she speaks to him when no one is around. "Frank, run up to the house and get your mother's inhaler."

But the wine won't let me move.

"Yes," mom says. Then, finding it in her pocket, "No...that's okay, it's here." She takes two immense hits, holds them in, and exhales. I start to say something but she holds up her hand. "Listen," she says. She sits up straight.

"It's just the loon," I say.

"No, there's music coming from one of those houses across the lake. Listen."

"Yes, I hear it."

"Someone's playing the piano. What's the name of that piece?"

"I don't know, mom."

"You *do.* Of course you do. It sounds like something Fawn used to play. What's it called?"

I strain my ears to comprehend but the notes weave a tapestry of sound with the waves rolling gently to shore, with the soft knocking of the boat against strips of tire fastened to the dock, with reeds, rustling, and the loon, cooing. The distance and the gathering dusk are such that I can see no movement in or around the wristlet of homes across the water, much less discern the place from which this faint music comes. It seems to float up from the lake itself and move toward us so imperceptibly that I can neither chart its progress nor gauge its nearness until the moment it is here.

She asks me again. I let recognition shine in my eyes.

"It's a Brahms intermezzo," I tell her. "It must be a Brahms intermezzo." She smiles and sits back.

"I would have been a lot closer to you," dad says, after some time has passed, "if I hadn't watched you squander your remarkable talents over the years."

My back is up. "Now we can own the docks we were sold from, so let's forget all about the voyage; to say nothing of the sale—is that it? Is amnesia a 'remarkable talent?'"

"What," says mom, "do you want from them?"

I close my eyes.

"It may not be a persecution complex," dad says to her, "I've always thought it was approach avoidance. We saw that all the time too. One displaces one's inability to reach one's goals onto—"

"Shhh!" I take a long gulp of merlot. "This is unprofessional: the retard is still in the room."

Dad removes his eyeglasses, presses the hand that holds them to his lips, and observes me. Putting them back on he continues. "The Pentagon's against you. Foreign policy is against you. How can *foreign policy* be against you, you were born here? The university—Yes, there are problems! Yes, there's still work to be done! There will always be problems. But we now have what we didn't have when I was coming up, the vote and access to the plebiscite. One can lobby, one can caucus."

Or one can stand on the Nicollet Mall with a tin cup and a cardboard sign: Ninja Turtles killed my parents need money for...

"...kung fu lessons."

"Kung fu lessons!? What the devil are you talking about? Do you still smoke marijuana?"

"I was daydreaming."

"More like not listening."

"The caucus, the plebiscite, the lobby," *at the Biltmore.* "I heard you."

"Approach avoidance is the diagnosis of someone who won't, or feels he can't, act in an imperfect world. Have you ever considered that your political theory, your critique, is an excuse for your not reaching your goals?"

"I've been writing for years."

He upends the dregs of watery Scotch and melted ice into the lake. "Writing what?" He pours himself another. "You never finish."

"I don't know how a Black story should end."

"Then don't write a 'Black' story," mom offers. "Write a story. But get the writing done. All that money on a Dartmouth education; not that we minded."

"Time was, I could have asked Mondale to run you for office; maybe even Humphrey. Don't look at me that way."

"What way?"

"That smirk."

"I'm not smirking."

"I never smirked at my father."

"I'm not smirking."

"Compromise and acquiescence," he says. "We know what you think of us. But if we let our minds meander through that loopy Alice in Wonderland logic of yours, we'd have no choice but to buy guns and drive all the way to Washington, DC, and shoot every White person in sight."

"That's pure hyperbole."

"How is it hyperbole?"

"You wouldn't have to drive all the way to Washington."

He shakes his head. "You have a warped sense of humor."

Mom slaps her leg. "Where did we fail you?"

"You didn't fail me. You never had the power to fail me."

"Never had the power?"

"Something *happened* to us in the hold of that ship."

"Well, I wasn't there." She is on her feet now. "What do you want from them?"

"A proper account."

"What would that look like?" she asks.

"An execution."

"Whose?" dad insists.

"Everything. You should want that too."

"Don't try and guilt trip us," she says.

"How can I guilt trip you? You're a victim too."

"I—am—*not!*—a victim. Look at that house. Turn around and look at it."

"I don't need to look at it."

"And our farm on the other side of the lake. Look at it." she says. "Nearly two hundred acres. No victims here. If you've learned nothing from the Civil Rights Movement, I'm sorry for you. But check your bags before you get on board, 'cause all that excess luggage is yours, not mine. Keep on," she says, as she brushes past dad and me, "and they'll give you that execution."

She turned up the dock. Dad rose as well.

"She lights candles for you. Each year you survive your rash enterprise she lights a candle. Bring her glass and come up."

"I'm going to stay here for a while."

"Turn the chairs over or bring the cushions in. It might rain."

"I'm going to stay out here." I looked up at him and said, "Do you remember, we had no compass or clock?"

"Well, now you know what time it is." He followed her. I did not turn to watch them go.

"Supine in our sustenance and *shit!*"

"Watch your mouth!" The dock rocked with the weight of their frustration.

"The living stretched out with the dead."

There was no reply.

I sat tideless and still, my back pressed to their departure. There was still no reply.

I cannot say when the music ended, only that it had ended. The setting sun was so low it silhouetted the bungalows on the opposite shore; and it mattered not whether the loon was far beyond my depth of field or in the reeds nearby, for its voice was inside me, admonishing me. *Leave them alooone...leave them alone.*

Turning around, I said, "We are worthy of our suffering."

A light wind gathered on the water and chilled my arms.

In the clearing on the hill the cabin stood mute. No smoke plumed from its chimney. Shadows climbed up its walls, but they were the shadows of birch and oak, not the shadows of my parents' approach. And below, the path through the spindly tamarac above the marshland surrendered to the last seeds of daylight. Fold upon fold of quiet wave pushed forth, knocking the boat gently about, as though from their footsteps on gray wood.

Glossary

5 Recce—Part of South African Special Forces, the 5 Reconnaissance Commando was established in Northern Natal.

32 Battalion Affair—"32 Battalion" was a highly secretive and unconventional elite force inside the South African Defence Force. It was formed in the 1970s to lend support to anti-Marxist forces fighting in Angola. In April 1992, 32 Battalion raided the Phola Park squatter camp (a pro-ANC area) in the East Rand, killing two women, raping three, and injuring more than 100. The raid lasted twelve hours. In May 1992, police officers and members of 32 Battalion carried out another series of raids on the Phola Park squatter camp. Only after the Boipatong Massacre and the ensuing international outcry in June 1992 did the government announce that 32 Battalion would be disbanded; though its members would be absorbed into other army units rather than being dismissed. (Human Rights Watch)

ABSA—the Amalgamated Banks of South Africa, a banking conglomerate created by the Broederbond when the Nationalist Party came to office

Afrikaner Volkstaat—Afrikaans for the "people's state," it refers to a proposal for the establishment of self-determination for the Afrikaner minority in South Africa.

amandla—a Xhosa and Zulu word meaning "power" used as a rallying cry against apartheid

APLA—Azanian People's Liberation Army; the armed wing of the PAC

ANC—African National Congress

assegai—a short, stabbing spear possibly invented by Shaka

Attridgeville—township west of Pretoria

AWB—The Afrikaner Weerstandsbeweging, or Afrikaner Resistance Movement, is a right-wing paramilitary organization.

baba—father, man

bakkie—pickup

baas—"boss"

bang worsie—scared kitten

bantustan—area designated by Apartheid government as African homeland

Battle of Cuito Canavale—For 137 days in 1987–1988, the internationalist forces of Cuba, fighting alongside the MPLA and ANC Umkhonto we Sizwe insurgents, engaged the South African Defence Force in the Cuito Canavale region in southern Angola, which borders what is now Namibia (but was then South West Africa—under South African occupation) and drove the SADF back into Namibia. Some analysts have argued that the Battle of Cuito Canavale hastened the end of apartheid in nearby South Africa by at least twenty years. (Martin Henry, "Cuba and the End of Apartheid," *Jamaican Gleaner*, 15 April 2004)

Boers—descendants of the early Dutch, German, or Huguenot colonists of southern Africa; often used interchangeably with "Afrikaners"

braai—barbecue

Broederbond—The Afrikaner Brotherhood was a secret, exclusively male, Protestant organization for the advancement of Afrikaner interests.

CAIR—Coalition Against Institutional Racism

casspir—personnel carrier

CIA—Central Intelligence Agency

CIVICS—the Civic Movement. Organs of alternative government in South African townships during the apartheid era which galvanized millions of South Africans into a potent force that often superseded the ANC, the Communist Party, and trade unions. "Organizing through their common identities as squatters, as women, as church goers, as youths, or simply as neighbours, they succeeded in building a social movement capable of mobilizing the people to wage a successful boycott against rent and service charges, to organize alternatives to the services they were deprived of, to resist evictions and to plan for land invasions." (Mohamed Halfani. "Inside Apartheid: Memories of a Tanzanian Visitor." *South Africa Report* 8:3-4 [January–February 1993])

CODESA—The Congress for a Democratic South Africa, a negotiating forum, began in December 1991, and hammered out the terms and conditions of the transformation and the first all-race elections.

COINTELPRO—The Counter Intelligence Program was an operation of the United States Federal Bureau of Investigation aimed at investigating and disrupting domestic dissident political organizations and individuals.

COSAS—Congress of South African Students

COSATU—Congress of South African Trade Unions

DLBs—dead letter boxes; secret caches for arms

doek—a scarf that covers the head, once a standard item of clothing for many African women

dorp—small town

dumela—Sotho word for hello

Egoli—colloquial name for Johannesburg; Zulu for "City of Gold"

fana—boy

Front Line States (FLS)—states that border South Africa and formed an anti-apartheid alliance. They provided aid to South African refugees, as well as land and material support to ANC and PAC training camps. Though the alliance ended after apartheid, the member states still bear deep scars from the backlash of the former South African regime. It is estimated that 2 million people died in the FLS as a result of South Africa's systematic destabilisation. ("Mzansi Afrika" http://mzansiafrika.blogspot.com/2004/03/frontline-states.html; Wikipedia)

heyta!—"What's happening!" or "Howzit going!"

hey batong!—"Wow!" or "Oh boy!"

Hippo—large armored personnel carrier

Inkatha Freedom Party—The IFP was founded in 1975 by Gatsha Mangosuthu Buthelezi in what is now KwaZulu-Natal. Bloodshed frequently occurred between the IFP and the ANC, with many of the attacks carried out by Inkatha supported by the South African police force.

IMF—International Monetary Fund

impimpi—police informer, sellout (Africanized from "pimp") *induna*—captain, headman (Zulu; also used condescendingly for the foreman of a work crew)

Internal Stability Unit (ISU)—now called Internal Stability Division. It is one of six divisions of the South African police, responsible for preventing and quelling internal unrest, and for assisting other divisions in combating crime.

kaak up—foul or mess up

kaffir—derogatory term for Black people

knobkierie—a short round club with a heavy knobbed head

koeksister—syrup-coated deep fried doughnut in a twisted or braided shape

kombi—minivan (e.g., VW van)

kraal—African homestead, animal enclosure

lekker—great, delicious, excellent

lobola—dowry; a set amount paid by a prospective husband to the bride's family

location—alternate word for Black township

Madiba—Nelson Mandela

MDM—Mass Democratic Movement

m'china—dude, man

meneer—mister; sir

MK—abbreviation for Umkhonto we Sizwe

moer—"to beat" in Afrikaans, or "to hit or beat someone up"

MPLA—Popular Movement for the Liberation of Angola

muti—African medicines and herbs (in Zulu, *umuthi*)

my *broer*—my brother (often a self-mocking or camp expression)

NIA—National Intelligence Agency

NPA—National Peace Accord

NP—Nationalist Party

NEHAWU—the National Education Health & Allied Workers Union; affiliated with COSATU

Operation Breadbasket—founded in 1962 as a department of the Southern Christian Leadership Conference (SCLC). It stemmed from what King called the "second phase" of the civil rights movement, an expansion to northern cities where thousands of African Americans confronted economic exploitation in urban slums. In 1966, King selected Jesse Jackson to head the

Chicago chapter. A key goal was to foster "selective buying" (boycotts) as a means to pressure White businesses to hire Black workers and purchase goods and services from black contractors. (*King Encyclopedia;* Wikipedia)

ou—guy, chap, bloke

ous or *ousie*— aunt, or auntie. Also a term used by White people for an African woman (supposedly polite, but perceived by Black South Africans as condescending and racist)

PAC—Pan Africanist Congress

panga—machete

pap—Pronounced "pup," it is Afrikaans for a boiled cornmeal porridge.

RDP—Reconstruction and Development Program

ROTC—The Reserve Officers' Training Corps is a college-based, officer commissioning program.

RPG—rocket-propelled grenade launcher

SABC—South African Broadcasting Corporation

SACP—South African Communist Party

SADF—South African Defence Force

sangoma—African healers who use a variety of roots, bark, herbs, and flowers

SASCO—South African Students Congress

Separate Amenities Act—The Reservation of Separate Amenities Act (No. 49) of 1953 stated that all races should have separate amenities that need not be of an equivalent quality. Under the provisions of this act, apartheid signs were erected throughout South Africa.

SNCC—Student Nonviolent Coordinating Committee

Students for a Democratic Society (SDS)—a US student activist movement

shebeen—unlicensed drinking establishment (in township)

sisi—sister (can be polite or condescending depending on context)

sjambok—rhino-hide whip; to whip

Stompie affair—James Seipei (aka "Stompie Moeketsi") was a young Soweto activist-cum-police informant who was kidnapped and killed by members of the "Winnie Mandela's football club" on December 29, 1988. In 1991, Winnie Mandela was convicted of kidnapping and being an accessory to assault, but her six-year jail sentence was reduced to a fine and two years probation on appeal. Consequentally, she was forced to resign all posts in the ANC and the Women's League. But in December 1993, she was elected to the Women's League presidency. After the all-race elections of April 1994, she was elected to the post of Deputy Minister of Arts, Culture, Science, and Technology. (Wikipedia; Hugh Pope and the London *Independent,* February 14, 1995)

SRC—Student Representative Council (student governments)

stand-down—a temporary stop of offensive military action

swart gevaar—the Black Threat, or the perceived security threat to the apartheid South African Government from the Black African population

tata—father

technikons—similar to vocational schools and/or community colleges in the US

tokoloshe—troll

toyi toyi—a Southern African dance originally from Zimbabwe used in political protests in apartheid-era South Africa

tsotsi—gangster, thief (from the habit of wearing zoot suits)

Twilight Children—A direct outcome of apartheid, the vast majority of South Africa's estimated 9,000 street children are Black; virtually none of them are White. (Johann Le Roux, "Street Children in South Africa: Findings from Interviews on the Background of Street Children in Pretoria, South Africa," *Adolescence,* Summer 1996)

twLF—third world Liberation Front

ubuntu—loosely translated: good will or spiritual well-being

Umkhonto we Sizwe—The "Spear of the Nation" was the active military wing of the African National Congress.

UNITA—the União Nacional para a Independência Total de Angola

veld—southern African grasslands

voetsek—"Bugger off, fuck off, go away," and/or "I'm through with this/you!"

Voortrekker Monument—a monument in Pretoria built to honor the Voortrekkers (pioneers) who left the Cape Colony between 1835 and 1854

wena—you

yebo—yeah; yes; right; got it; I hear you

Acknowledgments

This book would never have been published without the inaugural efforts of several stalwart enthusiasts who put their individual and collective energies behind it when it was a mere one hundred pages and a proposal. They include: Ishmael Reed, who has supported my work since the summer of 1980 and asked key people to take note of it. Gabriella Pearce, an editor at Palgrave who fought valiantly to have it published at her house, though that was not to be. Beacon Press's Gayatri Patnaik, Executive Editor, Tom Hallock, Director of Sales & Marketing, Pamela MacColl, Director of Publicity, and Helene Atwan, Director of Beacon Press who bought the book as soon as the Palgrave deal fell through. The book owes its very life to them, for it was written and nourished at Beacon.

Special thanks to the Jerome Foundation for the grant that financed my first trip to South Africa; and to the Artists and Writers colonies of Blue Mountain, Yaddo, and Ragdale for their wonderful residencies that allowed me to live for concentrated periods of time as though nothing in the world mattered more than writing.

Many people provided aid and inspiration, often without knowing that they were doing so—some while the book was germinating, others while it was being written. In lieu of individualized narratives (which could be a book on its own) I must opt for clustering them together by the region of the world from where their inspiration and aid originated.

From the USA: Randemar Hernandez Abreu, Marie Dutton Brown, Jacqueline Hackett, Janet Neary, Sigrid Radulovic, Matt Richardson, Omar Ricks, Wanda Sabir, Charles Sugnet, Alexis Vaubel, Alan Vaughan, Lois Vossen and Gary Whitmer. From South Africa: Amanda Alexander, Franco Barchiesi, Teresa Barnes, Ashwin Desai, Nigel Gibson, Allan Horowitz, Tefu Kelebonye, Ulrike Kistner, Kamogelo Lekubu, John Pape, Andile Mngxitama, Prishani Naidoo, John Shai, and S'bu Zulu.

Adrian Bankhead and Saidiya Hartman read the manuscript and made many helpful suggestions for revisions; but this does not begin to explain my gratitude to them for how they read: as two Black people who looked unflinchingly at the void of our subjectivity and thus helped the manuscript stay in the hold of the ship despite my fantasies of flight.

Jocelyn Burrell, Asha Tall, and Alexander Dwinell, the publishing collective of South End Press, made the impossible happen! They read more than 500 pages over what was probably no more than a weekend and interpreted the political stakes in ways that I had only begun to glimpse. They guided me through the final edits while engaging me in eye-opening conversations about the ideological and aesthetic work memoirs in general and this memoir in particular perform. And they brought it from manuscript to bound galleys in record time. I did not think it was possible for an institution imbricated in market forces to be so ideologically savvy and so nimble in the realm of production.

The embarrassment of riches of Heinrich Böhmke, Joy James, and Jared Sexton! What I have said of everyone above I could say of these three and still not have said enough. Heinrich taught me how, in struggle, to embody strategic rigidity but remain flexible tactically. Joy showed me how to maintain one's credentials as an academic without sacrificing one's principles as a revolutionary. Jared taught me that the truth of the paradigm (though not the totality) is not capital and not Oedipus, but anti-Blackness. Three treasures of wisdom that they saw fit to pass on to me—any shortcomings in my inculcation are my own.

This journey has been fraught and torturous and would have been impossible without the intellectual companionship and support, the solidarity without the promise of acceptance, the constantly evolving pedagogy we have shared, and the love of my partner Anita Wilkins.